Islamic Perspectives on Wealth Creation

Edited by

MUNAWAR IQBAL
and RODNEY WILSON

EDINBURGH UNIVERSITY PRESS

Edinburgh University Press Ltd
22 George Square, Edinburgh

Typeset in Baskerville
by Koinonia, Bury, and
printed and bound in Great Britain by
The Cromwell Press, Trowbridge, Wilts

A CIP record for this book is available
from the British Library

ISBN 0 7486 2100 8 (hardback)

Contents

Tables

Figures

Contributors

Abdel-Rahman Yousri Ahmad: University of Alexandria
Idries Al-Jarrah: University of Wales, Bangor
Abdel-Hameed M. Bashir: Gambling State University
Humayon A. Dar: Loughborough University
Seif I. Tag El-Din: Markfield Institute of Higher Education, Leicester
Karim Eslamloueyan: Shiraz University, Iran
Sudin Haron: Universiti Utara Malaysia
Zubair Hasan: International Islamic University, Malaysia
M. Kabir Hassan: University of New Orleans
Munawar Iqbal: Islamic Development Bank, Jeddah
Badrul Hisham Kamaruddin: Universiti Utara Malaysia
Mervyn K. Lewis: University of South Australia
Nezamaddin Makiyan: Yazd University, Iran
Philip Molyneux: University of Wales, Bangor
Mohamed Nasr: Advanced Management Institute, Cairo
Abdulqawi Radman Mohammed Othman: Tadhamon Islamic Bank, Yemen
H. Lynn Owen: University of Wales, Lampeter
Saqib Rashid: Cairo University Fulbright Scholar
Abd Elrhman Elzahi Saaid: International Islamic University, Malaysia
Rodney Wilson: University of Durham

Acknowledgements

The editors would like to thank the Islamic Research and Training Institute of the Islamic Development Bank for sponsoring the International Seminar on Islamic Perspectives on Wealth Creation in July 2003, and the University of Durham for acting as hosts. Mrs Barbara Farnworth of the Institute of Middle Eastern and Islamic Studies helped with the administration of the seminar, and Gaffar Ahmed, a Ph.D. student in Durham, provided invaluable assistance during the seminar by co-ordinating the work of the Durham postgraduates who ensured the smooth running of the event. We are grateful to the Arab Banking Corporation for sponsoring one of the dinners during the seminar. Thanks are also given to those who chaired the seminar sessions, including Professor John Presley of Loughborough University, Dr M. Shahid Ebrahim of the University of Nottingham, Ramli Muktisjah of the Erasmus University, Rotterdam, Sheikh Abdusalam Mreish, the respected Shariah scholar and advisor and Rumman Faruqi of the Institute of Islamic Banking and Insurance in London. Over sixty abstracts were received for the seminar, and thirty papers presented. Unfortunately only selected papers could be edited for this volume, but the editors would like to thank all those who participated in the seminar for their helpful contributions to the discussions.

Munawar Iqbal
Rodney Wilson

Introduction

Munawar Iqbal and Rodney Wilson

In the global economy wealth determines power and influence, but much of the capital accumulation on which this wealth is based results from debt finance involving interest payments. Such a system brings widely acknowledged injustices, notably problems of developing country debt, and corporate insolvency resulting in unemployment and social hardship when family financial obligations cannot be met. For Muslims such economic injustices can never be acceptable, hence the need to develop systems of managing finance that are compatible with Qur'ānic teachings and the Sharī'ah.

Wealth creation and value preservation are among the greatest challenges facing Muslims and the Islamic World as a whole. In this regard there is a need to focus on the longer-term issues of Islamic capital accumulation and its contribution to the development of Muslim societies, including those in the West. Many of these societies remain poor, yet there is much positive experience to learn from. Wealth creation results from savings and investment, but this is most likely to be successful only if the institutions created to harness and deploy funds share the values of the societies they serve. The growing Islamic banking movement has become a global financial force, and it has the proven ability to harness funds that might otherwise be underutilised. There is a wealth of successful practice that demonstrates how adherence to religious values brings social development, and that moral financing makes good business sense.

COVERAGE

The approach of this volume is thematic, whereby key issues relating to Islamic wealth creation are examined. To attract deposits Islamic banks have to satisfy potential customers that their operations conform to Sharī'ah law, while at the same time providing financial products that compete with those available from conventional banks. Efficiency in harnessing and allocating funding is also crucial, not least because both shareholders and investment depositors have a stake in an Islamic bank's profitability. Wealth of course includes real assets, and not just bank deposits. As their family home represents a major part of their wealth for most Muslims there is much scope for Islamic mortgages, while

Islamic insurance is needed to protect wealth. The remit of the book includes business as well as personal wealth. Large- and medium-scale Muslim-run businesses require equity finance and new businesses may need venture capital.

The topics covered in this work, such as product development, retail banking, banking efficiency, mortgages, *takāful* (Islamic cooperative insurance), risk management, equity finance and venture capital, have hitherto received little attention in the Islamic finance literature. The contributions draw on a wide range of country experiences, from Malaysia to Iran, Egypt and Sudan, as well as that of Islamic finance in the West. Many are the result of original research involving fieldwork surveys or the analysis of primary banking and financial market data. In many of the cases the work was undertaken for successful PhD theses for universities throughout the United Kingdom, the results of which have not hitherto been published.

WHITHER ISLAMIC BANKING?

Islamic finance has become a major industry worldwide, yet many questions remain about its future. Should its aim be to provide distinctive financial products, or simply to mimic conventional banking while making all the adjustments necessary so as to ensure that financing operations comply with Islamic Sharīʿah?

Zubair Ḥasan questions the direction in which Islamic banking is heading by highlighting the gap between the ideals of the founders of the modern movement and Islamic financial practice. The former stressed social and developmental goals, whereas most Islamic banks focus on short-term commercial financing through deferred-sale contracts.

Abdel-Rahman Yousri Ahmad sees the way forward as being through greater involvement by Islamic banks in participatory finance and innovation in financing contracts. For example, *muḍārabah*-based profit-sharing finance could be provided for longer periods, *muzārʿah*-based agricultural finance revived and *istiṣnāʿ*-based project finance modified so that the bank plays only an intermediary role. Yousri Ahmad is critical of *murābaḥah* (mark-up) finance as currently practised, and suggests that the trading and financial aspects of this contract need to be separated, with the Islamic bank handling the financing while an affiliated company is established for the actual trading. A similar division of labour and specialist structure is proposed for *salam* (advance purchase) contracts. These ideas are likely to provoke much further debate.

ISLAMIC RETAIL BANKING ISSUES

It is at the retail level that Islamic banking has its greatest impact by attracting deposits from those who might otherwise have avoided using financial institutions because of concerns over *ribā*. As Islamic banks cannot pay interest there is arguably a greater need for them to focus on the quality of service, clients being rewarded qualitatively rather than in quantitative terms. In Malaysia and Kuwait, Islamic banks have been successful in providing a wide range of retail services from debit and credit cards to vehicle finance and a range of savings and investment products. In Iran the experience requires much improvement, despite a genuine desire to transform the whole banking system to comply with Islamic Sharīʿah.

Nezamaddin Makiyan uses an econometric model to show that government direction largely determined how Iran's state-owned banks allocated funding, and that the returns of different economic sectors had little impact. In other words the banks themselves had little autonomy, and with inflation averaging over 20.0 per cent, borrowers were being subsidised by the banks in a manner that was not viable in the longer term without government support. Macro-economic conditions had the greatest impact on funding allocation, and the Islamic characteristics of the banking system appeared to make little difference.

An especially encouraging picture emerges for Malaysia as Sudin Haron and Badrul Hisham Kamaruddin demonstrate. Bank Islam Malaysia was the pioneer in developing Islamic finance, but to encourage both its spread and greater competition the government in 1993 introduced an Islamic banking scheme allowing conventional banks to provide Islamic counters. This was followed by the establishment of an inter-bank Islamic money market in 1994 to provide liquidity for Islamic operations and in 1996 financial reporting guidelines specifically for Islamic banks. In addition a Sharīʿah Advisory Council was established at national level. Sudin Haron and Badrul Hisham Kamaruddin outline these developments, but the main objective of their contribution is to compare and contrast the development of Bank Rakyat, originally a rural cooperative institution established in 1954 to aid Malay farmers, with that of Bank Islam Malaysia. Although Bank Rakyat was not primarily motivated by the need to avoid *ribā* it does serve a predominately Muslim client base. In 1996, however, it started operating according to Islamic principles. This first account of its experiences in the aftermath of conversion has lessons for other banks converting throughout the Muslim World.

The contribution of Abdulqawi Radman Mohammed Othman and H. Lynn Owen on the Kuwait Finance House, the second-largest Islamic retail bank internationally, is also interesting from a methodological perspective given the nature of the empirical investigation. They focus on how customer service quality is managed and measured by building up their own framework for assessment based on compliance, assurance, reliability, tangibles, empathy and responsiveness. A questionnaire was drawn up to cover these issues to which 360 customers of the Kuwait Finance House responded. Most customer dissatisfaction appeared to relate to the amount of time they were required to wait before being served in branches, but most were satisfied that the operations of the Kuwait Finance House complied with Islamic law, and there was much goodwill shown towards the institution.

MEASURING ISLAMIC BANKING EFFICIENCY

From a methodological point of view the empirical contribution by Idries Al-Jarrah and Philip Molyneux is especially interesting. They assess the efficiency of banks in four Arab countries – Bahrain, Egypt, Jordan and Saudi Arabia – in terms of their operating expenses, price of funds, wages bill and cost of capital. The sample covered 82 banks over the period 1992–2000, the majority of which were commercial banks, although there were also a number of Islamic and investment banks included. Interestingly, the Islamic banks were found to be the most cost and profit efficient and investment banks the least efficient. Banks in Bahrain and Saudi Arabia were found to be more efficient than those in the other countries, and larger banks more efficient than smaller institutions, a finding consistent with most other studies.

M. Kabir Hassan and Abdel-Hameed M. Bashir use data compiled from the annual income statements and balance sheets of 43 Islamic banks in 21 countries over the period 1994–2001. High capital and loans to asset ratios result in greater profits for Islamic banks, a finding that is consistent with that for conventional banks. A greater tax burden has a negative impact on profitability and sound macroeconomic management a positive impact. Overheads appear to be positively correlated with profits, suggesting that active management, despite being more costly, is nevertheless worthwhile.

Abd Elrhman Elzahi Saaid provides a country study of Islamic banking efficiency in Sudan, where all banks have been operating in compliance with Sharīʿah law since 1989. In Sudan, Islamic banks play a major role in the collection and distribution of *zakāh* and as such perform an important social function by helping the poor and needy. In addition, unlike in most Muslim countries, *mushārakah* (equity participation) contracts are the dominant method of financing. A standard econometric technique, the stochastic frontier approach, is used to estimate the allocative and technical efficiency of the six Sudanese Islamic banks between 1992 and 2001. The banks were found to be inefficient in terms of the allocation of capital, labour and deposits, as well as technically inefficient in terms of the productive use of these factors. Saaid believes that such inefficiency may reflect a failure by management to contain costs, a complicating factor being the sanctions imposed on Sudan that hindered the introduction of new technology.

ISLAMIC MORTGAGES, INSURANCE AND RISK MANAGEMENT

Many Muslims needing finance for house purchases have been forced to use conventional interest-bearing mortgages in the absence of Sharīʿah-compliant alternatives. Islamic mortgages were offered to a few clients on a very selective basis from the late 1980s in the United Kingdom and Malaysia, but these mortgages now seem poised for a significant expansion as major financial institutions are becoming involved. In the United Kingdom the discriminatory double stamp duty on Islamic mortgages has been removed, which should help make such mortgages competitive. Humayon A. Dar in his contribution examines Islamic mortgage products, and demonstrates how these can be designed to have different risk characteristics to conventional mortgages. This work will undoubtedly prompt debate both among Sharīʿah advisors and those providing Islamic mortgages.

Insurance products are a major means of harnessing savings in many Western countries, but in Muslim countries religious objections to conventional insurance have resulted in it being relatively underdeveloped. *Takāful* or Islamic cooperative insurance is of course acceptable in Muslim countries, but there is some misunderstanding of how it operates, and of the differences with conventional insurance. Mervyn K. Lewis attempts to clarify the exact nature of these differences and their financial implications. He shows how *takāful* insurance has expanded since the early 1980s and discusses what is and is not permissible. The treatment of family *takāful* insurance is especially clear, and parallels are drawn between it and the unit-linked policies offered increasingly in the West.

Insurance is necessary to deal with unavoidable risks, but many financial risks can of course be managed. Seif I. Tag El-Din examines how risk aversion limits the use of profit sharing in Islamic finance, as with *muḍārabah*, and encourages Islamic banks to rely on fixed-return financing methods such as *murābaḥah*, *bayʿ bi thaman al-ājil*, *ijārah*, *istiṣnāʿ* and *salam*. This approach explains the financing preferences of Islamic banks of which Zubair Hasan is so critical. Tag El-Din's solution is to restructure *muḍārabah* contracts so that risk is more optimally shared between the *rabb al-māl* and the *muḍārib*, both of which are risk averse. Two tools for reallocating risks are forward contracts and put options, the latter involving the right to sell at a fixed price. Tag El-Din sees the former as a natural extension of the *istiṣnāʿ* contract, but admits Sharīʿah scholars have reservations about put options. He suggests that the position on put options should be reconsidered, as these can be used to protect sellers against the risk of falling prices. He believes indemnity against such risks is entirely justified.

EQUITY FINANCE AND VENTURE CAPITAL

Stock markets are relatively underdeveloped in the Muslim world, but their potential is considerable, especially in countries such as Iran that have substantial industrial sectors. Such markets are often viewed as highly speculative, which results in Islamic scholars regarding them with suspicion, and condemning those who trade in volatile stocks for short-term gains.

Karim Eslamloueyan examines how equity prices have been determined in the Islamic Republic of Iran after the relaunch of the stock market in 1989. As interest-based transactions are prohibited in Iran and capital movements are controlled, interest rates and international interest rate differentials have little impact on stock prices. Developments in the real economy however affect stock prices, notably the level of industrial production that negatively affects stock prices in the short run, perhaps because over-supply damages profitability. The exchange rate has no impact on stock prices in the long run, perhaps because of the insulation of the domestic economy, but the goods' price level is inversely related to stock prices in the long run, and positively related in the short run. The latter could be explained by higher prices bringing higher profits, but that these are unsustainable in the longer run as output expands and new entrants to the market appear. The significance of Eslamloueyan's findings is, however, that in a country where interest transactions are prohibited, the stock market is less speculative.

Both Mohamed Nasr and Saqib Rashid are concerned with the financing of businesses that are too small to seek equity capital through a market listing. Their focus is on *mushārakah* contracts that in practice represent a form of venture capital financing. Mohamed Nasr tests the pecking order hypothesis that owners of small enterprises prefer internal to external financing, and debt rather than equity financing, largely because they fear losing control of their businesses. The hypothesis was tested through a survey in the Shubra area of Cairo of 95 small enterprises. Almost all the enterprises were sole proprietorships or family businesses. Only one-third of respondents were prepared to accept a partner, and of those who were prepared to dilute their ownership stake, most wanted to retain a majority holding and felt that the role of any partners should be confined to providing finance. Given this ownership preference, there was a reluctance to accept Islamic participatory finance, the preference being for *murābaḥah* and *ijārah* agreements rather than *muḍārabah* or *mushārakah* contracts.

Saqib Rashid in his contribution is more optimistic about the potential role for venture capital, and in particular *mushārakah* contracts. He examines its role in terms of the company life cycle, with the venture capitalist involved at the seed or idea stage and immediately after, but playing a rather minor role subsequently as the successful enterprise expands and matures. In the West, venture capitalists usually hold preferred stock, often of a convertible nature. The legitimacy of such stockholdings is clearly a concern for Sharīʿah scholars but, as Saqib Rashid asserts, the devil is in the detail. The morality of so-called vulture capitalists can also be questioned, given their premise of heads I win, tails you lose. Venture capital it seems is much more ethically ambiguous than some advocates of *mushārakah* might care to admit.

VALUE OF THE STUDY

It is hoped that this work will provide much food for thought, not only in terms of empirical methodologies, but also in some of the ideas generated by reviewing potential Islamic financing solutions in the light of the moral contradictions and ethical uncertainties that an Islamic critique of conventional financing highlights. The contributors provide a distinctive yet comprehensive perspective, as the development of Islamic banking and financial instruments is linked to the process of wealth creation.

As many of the authors are drawing on empirical work involving the use of econometric techniques, the studies are interesting from a methodological perspective, and should appeal to economists and finance specialists as well as those working in Islamic studies. There are many Muslim economists and finance specialists who have doubts about the applicability of techniques with which they are familiar to Islamic finance. This work should help dispel these doubts, especially the rigorous contributions by Idries Al-Jarrah and Philip Molyneux and M. Kabir Hassan and Abdel-Hameed M. Bashir.

Wealth creation is both a complex and long-term process. Those with faith are concerned not merely with the earthly riches that man manages on behalf of the Almighty, but more importantly with spiritual fulfilment. Honest adherence to Sharīʿah in wealth management will bring its own reward, as through this the faithful can realise the goals of Islam, *maqāṣid al* Sharīʿah. Wealth creation is about much more than increasing personal material satisfaction; rather it is about serving the wider community, and through this pleasing the Almighty. Social concerns permeate the contributions to this work, as Islamic finance concerns a fair system for wealth creation.

The distinctive characteristic of Islamic capital accumulation should be justice, compared to the injustices and inequalities associated with secular capitalism. All too often the present societies of the Muslim World are characterised by inequalities and lack of access to economic opportunities. One mission of Islamic economics is the development of a more inclusive financial system that the faithful can respect. This study provides some indications of how this noble goal can be achieved.

PART I

Whither Islamic Banking?

1

Islamic Banking at the Crossroads: Theory versus Practice

Zubair Hasan

This chapter examines the reasons behind a widening gap between the conventional theory and current practice of Islamic banks. 'No risk, no gain' may not be sufficient as a general principle for organising Islamic finance. It is also not always valid to say that Islam is averse to granting a time value for money. The overuse of deferred payment contracts in Islamic finance threatens to violate the juristic principle of *sadd al-dhara'*, that is, controlling the potential avenues for circumvention of the law. Some structural changes in Islamic financial arrangements are suggested to create a balance in the use of profit and loss sharing (PLS) contracts and deferred payment contracts in Islamic banking.

INTRODUCTION

The ideas relating to Islamic banking and finance were among the first to appear in the writings intended at formalising Islamic economics. They were perhaps put into operation even before theoretical developments on the subject achieved any degree of sophistication. The literature on banking and finance has of late been growing so fast that discussions on other topics in Islamic economics have become few and far between. This may seem understandable as financial factors are becoming increasingly decisive in the processes of creating wealth in modern societies.

A distinctive feature of the recent discussions on Islamic banking has been the growing wedge between its conventional theory and current practice. Interestingly, while the evolution of the theoretical position and its continual support come from what one may call for convenience the Jeddah School, the structural design, instruments and practices of Islamic banking are of late being forged mostly away from the Red Sea, particularly in Malaysia. According to the School, the theoretical foundation of Islamic banking essentially rests, or should rest, on participatory risk-sharing finance – *muḍārabah* and *mushārakah*.[1] By contrast, practitioners in the area worldwide find these instruments inadequate, and prefer to make deferred contracts with assured fixed incomes the fulcrum of Islamic banking.

A fairly old paper by Abdul Halim on Islamic banking and finance recently published (2001) by the Institute of Islamic Understanding of Malaysia (IKIM) puts this divergence into sharp focus. The issue attracted attention at some seminars on Islamic economics and finance held in 2002 in Indonesia and Malaysia,[2] and in this chapter the implications of the divergence between theory and practice are explored further.

THEORETICAL FOUNDATIONS

The theoretical edifice for Islamic economics including money and banking started taking shape in undivided India after the 1930s depression. It was an important part of juridical writings aimed at evaluating modern knowledge from an Islamic perspective. The literature, produced mostly in Urdu, was simple with a modern outlook. It reached and became popular with the lower rungs of Muslim society. After the partition of British India in 1947, the dominant part of this endeavour understandably found itself located in Pakistan. The process of Islamising knowledge in economics, as in other areas, expanded and thrived in that country even though contributions from India continued.

As one of the major consequences of the recommendations of the First International Conference on Islamic Economics held at Makkah in 1976, Jeddah eventually emerged as one of the leading centres promoting research in Islamic economics. Many scholars, including some of the pioneers in the discipline, moved from the subcontinent to the two main institutions established in the metropolis: the (International) Centre for Research in Islamic Economics of King Abdulaziz University and the Islamic Research and Training Institute – popularly known as the IRTI – of the Islamic Development Bank. In due course, three of the main journals in Islamic economics were almost exclusively devoted to the conducting, promoting and disseminating of research in different areas of Islamic economics.[3] Their contribution to the growth of literature on the subject is immense and well recognised. No less has been their influence on related writings emanating from other parts of the world.

Initially, these institutions projected an integrated view of Islamic economics in the sense that areas in mainstream economics were not demarcated. Soon, however, the process of category identification began. One major such separation was that of money, banking and finance from the rest of the discipline. This division received recognition in the bifurcation of the Islamic Development Bank's annual prize for contributions to the promotion of Islamic economics into Islamic Economics for one year and Islamic Banking and Finance the next. There may have been reasons for the dichotomy but presumably it did hinder in some measure the balanced growth of the much wider field of Islamic economics. Banking and finance, however important, are no more than subdivisions of the major discipline of economics, secular or Islamic.[4]

More important is the fact that the research work stemming from these centres of excellence reveals a common position ascribable to the majority of writers on a number of important issues. There are of course some differences among them, but these often relate to detail, emphasis or form. To illustrate, the School, unlike mainstream economics, shuns in general the idea of scarcity of resources for Islamic dispensation, is not generally receptive to the concept of minimum wages, does not approve of any trade union activity, sees the distribution of income governed by marginal productivity as equitable, usually considers mainstream economics value-free, is opposed to a maximising behaviour on the part of an economic agent, especially the entrepreneur, and is averse to a share for labour in profits of business as a matter of principle.[5] The situation is no different with respect to the theoretical foundations of Islamic banking. As such then, one may talk loosely of a Jeddah School of Islamic Economics.

Modelling for Islamic banking and finance drew its inspiration for the School, as for others, primarily from the almost unanimous view of the Islamic jurists that there is no difference between the prevalent institution of interest and *ribā* that Islam prohibits. Even though there are many – perhaps more powerful – reasons for the prohibition, the School highlighted one in particular: interest is not allowable because it confers a gain on the capital owners free of any risk-bearing. This constituted an apparent difference between *ribā* and the profit from trade that Islam allows. 'No risk, no gain' was, indeed, paraded as an inviolable precept in the area of banking and finance.[6] The precept implied that it was predetermination of interest without regard to the outcome of the business that kept it free of risk and thus constituted the main reason for its Islamic prohibition. There was little realisation that the implication could conflict, as we shall see, with some other Islamic norms the School upheld.

The precept was suggestive of an answer to the question: if interest were abolished, what must replace it in the financial sector of the economy to induce saving and investment so crucial for creating wealth? The School unequivocally declared that in the absence of interest any reorganisation of banking 'will have to be done' on the basis of partnership, that is, *mushārakah* or *muḍārabah* contracts. It was also claimed that modern writers on Islamic economics were unanimous on this.[7]

Mushārakah was akin to equity financing of the modern era and could hardly raise a vivid sceptre of Islamic import, nor was it an instrument deriving much glory from the past. In contrast, *muḍārabah* was one pre-Islamic institution that expanded fast in Muslim lands over time and became the most thriving form of business financing by the dawn of the thirteenth century. Naturally, in the modern era of Islamic resurgence, the School saw the theoretical foundations of Islamic banking and finance more in the instrument of *muḍārabah*-based participatory finance, though *mushārakah* was never ignored.

The preference for *mudārabah* provided much food for thought and opened numerous possibilities for the modelling of Islamic banking. The historical model was the first to attract attention. In this puritan model, the owner of capital provided the entire funding to the entrepreneur-operator and had nothing to do with the management of the business. The contract between the parties stipulated a share for the financier in the profits of business while he alone would bear the loss, if any. Usually the contract was for the execution of a specific project. The model suited and worked well in a community where trade was the dominant occupation.[8]

The modern business scenario is radically different. With the rise of the modern corporation working on the principle of limited liability as the dominant form of business organisation, the puritan model of *muḍārabah* lost much of its significance. There were two major points of departure. First, today businesses contributing the bulk of the output in modern economies are founded on a large scale, not for executing short-run piecemeal ventures, but for running an ongoing manufacturing or service activity. Second, financiers usually provide only a part of the total capital. It is in this light that the efficacy of the financing modes for Islamic institutions has to be evaluated. These institutions act as outside financiers providing for a specified period just a fraction of the needed investment. They may also not be willing to eschew a supervisory role to safeguard their interest.

Interestingly, the problems that the puritan design poses under the changed circumstances were anticipated quite early on and discussions on the *modus operandi* of the mixed sort of *muḍārabah* structures did make their appearance in some of the pioneering works on the subject. In the course of time, they gained currency in the literature as the profit and loss sharing (PLS) models, though investigations into their nature and ramifications were not common or always clear.

In fact, the bank was envisaged as providing money to a firm, the entrepreneur, in participatory contracts on a PLS basis. The loss, as and when it arose, was to be apportioned between the firm and the financier in the same proportion as their respective contributions to the total capital employed in the firm's business. However, the position was a little more complicated in a mixed case on the sharing of profit. A brief explanation may be refreshing.

In a mixed *muḍārabah* model, the bank advances money to a firm on the condition that a pre-agreed proportion, σ^*, of the profit accruing to the money advanced will go to the bank. To illustrate, assume that the outside financier contributes a proportion, λ, of total capital K, and the firm in an accounting period earns a profit P, giving the rate of return $r = P/K$. In this case the profit earned on the money advanced by the bank will be λP. Of this amount the bank would get $\sigma^* \lambda P$, that is, a rate of return $r^* = \sigma^* r$ on its investment, if transaction costs were ignored. The firm will retain $(1 - \sigma^*)\lambda P$ for providing entrepreneurial services to the bank. This much is clear and undisputed in the literature. The difficulty arises in establishing what guides parties to negotiate for σ^*, that is, what precisely are its determinants, and how will its equilibrium value be arrived at in an economy? A further question is its efficacy for use as an instrument of credit control by a country's central bank. Some scholars have deliberated on these questions and offered solutions, but a consensus has yet to evolve.

The sharing of profit between the bank and the firm is only one half of the story. The other half relates to profit-sharing between the bank and its depositors. To simplify matters, let us assume that the bank has no funds for advancing to business other than those it receives from its customers in deposits (D), that the bank is able to invest D in full, and that there are no transaction costs as before. In this scenario λK would equal D and $\sigma^*\lambda P$ would be the profit the bank would share with the depositors in a pre-agreed ratio. If the sharing ratio for the bank were Φ, it would retain $\Phi\sigma^*\lambda P$ of the receipt for entrepreneurial services and distribute the remaining $(1 - \Phi)\ \sigma^*\lambda P$ as profit among the depositors.

Thus Islamic banks would operate on the pattern of what is called in the literature a two-tier *muḍārabah* model. It is sometimes suggested that depositors would receive the same rate of return on their money as the bank would earn on investing it. This equality of ratios proposition is patently untenable even in the absence of transaction costs at both ends.[9] We have taken above r^* as the rate of return the bank earns on λK. Let R be the rate of return depositors earn on their money with the bank. At the macro level, the banks would receive a mean rate of return on deposit investments as under:

$$r^* = \sigma^*\lambda P \,/\, (\lambda K = D) \qquad (1)$$

On the other hand, the rate of return R for depositors would be:

$$R = (1 - \Phi)\ \sigma^*\lambda P \,/\, (\lambda K = D) \qquad (2)$$

Since $(1 - \Phi)$ is less then one, the rate of return R would obviously be lower than r^* the banks get on their investment. And the banks would eventually earn a net profit equal to $\Phi\sigma^*\lambda P$ for their entrepreneurial services. Who will have a higher rate of return on D in the two-tier *muḍārabah* – banks or depositors – will depend on the value of Φ. The higher Φ is, the greater will be the rate for the banks as compared with depositors and vice versa.

The literature contains ample demonstration that in a macro frame participatory finance has the potential to give a higher rate of return to both the firms and the banks compared to interest finance, if only because profit rates in the economy tend to be much higher than the rates of interest. In addition, business firms would continue to enjoy the benefits of 'trading on equity' in *muḍārabah* profit-sharing the same way as under interest-bearing finance.[10]

THE CHALLENGE

Despite the higher profit potential of *muḍārabah* financing in principle, the mode could not make much headway in modern Muslim societies. It did nevertheless emerge as a significant deposit-collecting mechanism with some Islamic financial institutions. For example, *muḍārabah* companies multiplied fast, especially in Pakistan. But these companies could not find business investment opportunities sufficient to absorb the bulk of the deposits they received. They were thus tempted to make money in the speculative buying and selling of shares traded on the stock markets. The surplus funds accumulating with the Islamic institutions, including banks, led some of the School to believe that the malady could hardly be escaped unless competition from interest-based financing was totally banished: in this respect, Islamic banks could only flourish in a puritan setting![11]

The proposition was neither logical nor practicable. It was tantamount to admitting that the Islamic interest-free system inherently lacked the ability to compete with its mainstream counterpart. What was needed was not despair, but rather the search for the causes behind *muḍārabah* non-performance and a remodelling of the system to meet the changing requirements of the market. It was primarily the failure in this regard that caused Islamic banking and finance to follow the course of least resistance: that is, to take refuge in the indiscreet use of Islamic deferred obligation contracts.[12]

And it is at this juncture that Abdul Halim's paper, alluded to above, challenges the School for its theory of Islamic banking and finance, and defends the almost exclusive reliance of the system at present on assured income contracts. It is a rather lengthy paper with extensive documentation. Broadly, it raises two issues relevant to the context.

First, Halim stresses the undisputed point that the juristic permissibility or otherwise of any basis for financing or a financial contract is determined through the feasibility of its derivation from the sources of Sharī'ah. But he sees no such juristic feasibility for the 'no risk, no gain' precept. To him, the adherents of the School embrace rather naively the concept of business 'risk' central to capitalism and seek to inject it with an Islamic import through using the Sharī'ah's all-pervading notion of *al-'adl* or justice.

A pre-fixed return like interest in the face of uncertainty about the future outcome of business does not meet the norm, the School argued: justice demands that the provider of capital funds must share the risk with the entrepreneur if he wishes to earn profit.[13] Arguably, this could be accepted as one justification for PLS contracts but in no way constitutes an exclusive principle. One would indeed find the School all at sea in defending other fixed rewards like wages or rent should one choose to stretch the argument to its logical extremes.

However, Halim offers a different reply emanating from Islamic injunctions. He argues that profit or loss arising from any contract is to be explained from a juristic viewpoint. Relevant to the issue are such Sharīʿah norms as effort to earn (*al-kasb*), placing one's trust in Allah (*al-tawakkul*), provision of the means for living is derived from Him (*al-rizq*), and whatever He has ordained – profit or loss – must eventually come to pass (*al-qaḍā wal-qadr*). None of these basic elements of faith has ever featured, says Halim, in an explanation of the 'no risk, no gain' axiom of the School. One may add that not every gain is the result of risk-taking or is commensurate with it: profit and risk need not have a one-on-one correspondence even in Islamic economics. Profit can rarely be defended as a just reward on the risk-bearing criterion.

Interestingly, one does not come across any valid response in the literature to the points Halim raises.[14] One must record that his observations do not question *per se* the permissibility of *muḍārabah* or *mushārakah* as instruments of Islamic banking and finance. They challenge the School for the principle it regards as underlying the two modes. For Halim, all PLS contracts are equitable from an Islamic viewpoint not because they encompass the capitalist concept of risk but because their legitimacy has been, in the first place, derived from the sources of the Sharīʿah – in particular the Sunnah.[15]

The rejection of the risk principle leads Halim to his second point – the search for all-embracing norms governing business transactions in Islam. This he finds in what provides the Sharīʿah basis for an important transaction category: contracts of exchange or *ʿuqūd al-muawadāt*. Quoting extensively from the Qur'ān, learned commentaries and jurists, he explains the difference between interest (*al-ribā*), and sale (*al-bayʿ*) in order to establish why Islam rejects the former and upholds the latter. Of the relevant verses discussed, the focus of his attention has been verse 275 from Sūrah Al-Baqarah, especially the portion which is translated as: 'But Allah has permitted (that is, pronounced as *ḥalāl*) *al-bayʿ* and forbidden (that is, pronounced as *ḥarām*) *al-ribā*'.

Quoting from three of the leading commentaries on the Qur'ān – Ibn Al Arabi, Al Qurtubi and Al Jassas – the author discusses at length the meaning of *al-bayʿ* and *al-ribā*, and as also the question of their permissibility or otherwise in light of the above verse. The term *al-bayʿ* in its generic meaning encompasses all types of contracts of exchange unless forbidden by the Sharīʿah. *Al-bayʿ* means any contract of exchange whereby a given quantity of a commodity or service is exchanged for a given quantity of another commodity – including money – or service.[16] The delivery of the commodity or service on the part of each party to the contract may be simultaneous or one of them – not both – may defer the discharge of his obligation to a future date. Hence the term *al-bayʿ* encompasses many types of deferred contracts of exchange, including *salam* sale (*bayʿ-al salam*), sale on order (*bayʿ-al istiṣnāʿ*) and leasing (*al-ijārah*).

The term *al-ribā* as used in the verse in question means what has come to be known in *fiqh* as *ribā al duyūn*, that is, additional consideration imposed by the creditor on the debtor as an inducement for the former to extend the deferred liability period. This is not allowed due to the absence of a compensatory counterpart in real terms. Halim claims that the three commentaries he refers to are unanimous on this interpretation of the verse.[17]

The position of the School also looks untenable on another score, one that is closely related to its 'no risk, no gain' gospel. The School maintains that interest is also prohibited for the reason that Islam does not grant a time value to money.[18] Some critics argue that not all interest is of the prohibited *ribā* type and that it is implicitly allowed in a large number of debt-based Islamic transactions. Money is a liquid asset and imposes disability on the creditor to the advantage of the debtor. So it is on the grounds of justice, that is, on the symmetrical treatment of parties, that Islam does allow a time value for money on a selective basis.

We shall examine the basis of this later. Presently, let us return to Halim's argument. Intuitively, one finds in his assertions a cover for the extensive use of deferred exchange contracts in Islamic banking. Malaysia presents an interesting illustration of the use of such contracts. Today, the country is regarded as a pioneer in Islamic banking and finance, and an example for much of the Muslim World to emulate. Some Muslim countries have fully transformed their banking system in accordance with Islamic requirements. However, Malaysia is operating Islamic banking side by side with the conventional system in a rather unique way.[19] The country has only two exclusive Islamic banks, one of them established as late as 1999. Its main strategy has been to allow the opening of Islamic windows in commercial banks, thus prompting competition for interest-free finance within the conventional system as well. The market share of the Islamic sector – exclusive plus mixed banking – in terms of assets owned is currently around 9.0 per cent. It is planned for this to become 20.0 per cent by the year 2010.

The constituents of the sector in the field are the usual sort of commercial banks, Islamic windows, finance companies, exclusive Islamic units and discount houses. The impact of opening Islamic windows in conventional institutions on the relative position of exclusive interest-free banks is clear from Table 1.1 below.

It is easy to see that the share of exclusive banks went down in all three aggregates – assets, deposits, and financing – more so in the last case, while that of mixed banking, combining conventional operations with Islamic windows, increased. Whether this trend augurs well for Islamic banks is worth considering. At the same time let us also have a look at the trend in the relative role of deferred contracts *vis-à-vis* PLS financing.

The data produced in Table 1.2 for the three years for which it was available

Table 1.1: Mixed versus exclusive Islamic banking in Malaysia (% share)

Category of transactions	*1999*		*2002*	
	Exclusive	*Mixed*	*Exclusive*	*Mixed*
Total Assets	32.4	67.6	29.6	70.4
Total Deposits	39.0	61.0	30.8	69.2
Total Financing	36.7	62.3	24.9	75.1

Source: The percentages are based on data in Bank Negara *Annual Reports* 2000, Table 4.14, p. 153, and 2002, Table 4.18, p. 156.

may not be adequate for indicating a reliable trend in the use of various modes of Islamic finance in Malaysia, but still it is quite revealing: the average share of PLS financing (entries 1 and 2) is a meagre 5.6 per cent, the remaining 94.4 per cent coming from deferred liability financing (entries 3 to 8). In fact, there is evidence of a falling trend in the share of PLS modes over time in aggregate financing. The trend is found all the more pronounced in the case of Bank Islam Malaysia, the oldest Islamic bank in the country, dating from 1983, whose former chairman was Abdul Halim, the writer cited earlier. The trends in other Islamic banks elsewhere are not dissimilar to those in Malaysia: they too seem to defy the principles of the Jeddah School that favours PLS financing.

Halim is finding more and more supporters for his stance, especially from the West. It is argued, for example in El-Gamal, that to equate *ribā* with the European notion of usury that raises the mental image of exploitative consumption loans is not appropriate. Much of the *ribā* used in pre-Islamic Arabia was for commercial and business purposes. Indeed, some controversial *fatāwā* recently

Table 1.2: Modes of Islamic financing in Malaysia (% share)

Modes of Finance	*2000*	*2001*	*2003**
1. *Al-Mushārakah*	1.4	0.7	0.5
2. *Al-Muḍārabah*	7.0	7.3	–
3. *Al-Istiṣnā'*	0.9	1.3	0.7
4. *Al-Ijārah*	4.3	3.0	1.4
5. *Al-Murābaḥah*	–	–	6.4
6. *Al-Bay' bi thaman al-ājil*	48.3	49.1	47.4
7. *Al-Ijārah thumma al-bay'*	22.2	23.3	27.9
8. Other Islamic contracts	15.9	15.3	15.7
9. **Total**	100.0	100.0	100.0

* Figures are as at November 2003.
Source: Bank Negara *Annual Reports* 2001, Table 4.18, and 2002, Table 4.17.

emanating from Egypt have gone to the extent of holding that conventional bank interest is a share in the profits of growth-inducing investment, and so does not constitute forbidden *ribā*.[20]

Again, some English translations of the last portion '*lā taẓlimūna wa lā tuẓlamūn*' of verse 2:279 dealing with *ribā* create the impression that the sole objective of prohibition is the avoidance of injustice, that is, the exploitation of the poor debtor by the rich creditor.[21] However, the meaning of that verse is claimed to be closer to 'if you turn back, then you should collect your principal without inflicting or receiving injustice'.[22] This implies that both increase and decrease in the principal amount at the time of repayment would be considered unjust.

Finally, the common position in Islamic economics that the School also shares is that Islam does not put a time value on money. The assertion is presently challenged as contradicting statements in all major schools of classical jurisprudence to the effect that 'time has a share in price' (*lil zamani hazzun fil thaman*).[23] Indeed, it is this juristic position that constitutes the fulcrum of all deferred obligations on which Islamic financial institutions tend to thrive. This is the basis of cost-plus sale (*murābaḥah*) with deferred receipt of the price, or leasing (*ijārah*).

Thus seen, *ribā* meaning addition is not prohibited in all cases.[24] *Ribā al-nasi'ah* is implicit in deferred contracts. Islamic banks operating in the US are obliged to reveal such implicit rates underlying *murābaḥah* or leasing contracts to their customers.[25] What Islam doubtlessly prohibits is *ribā al-faḍl* – trading like with like at more than a 1 to 1 ratio – not only in spot transactions but also when extended to future and forward contracts.[26]

CONCLUSIONS

The foregoing discussion demonstrates that today Islamic banking is at a crossroads. The problem, however, is not the juristic validity of what the Islamic financial institutions can do or are doing: all the instruments of financing listed in Table 1.2 above are equally permissible, and the list is likely to grow in future. Rather it is the reasons advanced to justify their permissibility that can be questioned, and the indiscreet way such financing methods are currently being used. Both have created much avoidable confusion in rationalising the theory for Islamic banking and finance, and have led its practice into suspect tracks. On the theoretical plane, the 'no risk, no gain' principle as the basis for eliminating interest from financial contracts is inadequate, though PLS contracts remain perfectly legitimate.

The profit–risk linkage of the classical era of small owner-operated firms competing in a rather open industry still lingers in the literature. However, the concept of risk has undergone a radical change since Frank H. Knight restricted the term to mean uncertainty that could be insured against at a cost.[27] The remaining uncertainty is a fact of human life like sun or rain: profit or loss is the consequence of opting to bear that uncertainty. Business being a *farḍ kifāyah*, obligatory duty, in Islam,[28] believers must accept the consequence simply as the will of God.

Economists, especially Islamic economists, continue to maintain the old profit–entrepreneur bond in the discipline more as a matter of tradition than reality. That bond has long vanished with the onset of modern corporations. Today it is difficult to identify the entrepreneur in a large multiproduct firm, let alone the functions he performs.[29] What goes to the entrepreneur, however defined, as profit is seldom possible to defend as equal to the value of his contribution to output: the Islamic criteria for a just reward.

Capitalism justifies interest on the ground that it is the expression of the difference between the present value of goods and their future value. This is the basis of allowing a time value for money, that is, interest. We have already mentioned that Islamic economists do not subscribe to this view. However, time is duly recognised as an element in price. Money provides command over real resources and has an opportunity cost. Islam allows this cost as part of the price. That is what imparts legitimacy to charging higher than cash prices in deferred contracts.

The permissibility of deferred contracts cannot of course be disputed. Nevertheless, the permission cannot perhaps be used without applying checks to safeguard the wider norms and objectives of Islamic law.[30] The use of deferred contracts in Islamic banking and finance seem to have been carried too far already: it is widely felt that it is time to apply the principle of *sadd al-dhara'* that closes the potential avenues for circumventing the law.[31] There is a growing feeling that deferred contracts provide the cover for interest-taking from the back door.[32]

It would be difficult to plead for an exclusive use of deferred contracts to promote Islamic banking. Such use would detract from the ability of these institutions to address more serious issues relating to wealth creation in the Muslim World. The instrument will mainly guide meagre financial resources of the community – as it is presently doing – into consumption channels. A market for venture capital will be hard to develop. To that extent the system is likely to work against capital formation for long-run growth, a basic need of Muslim countries. Most of these countries import consumer goods from abroad. Domestic demand may unwittingly enlarge external markets and aggravate local balance of payment problems. Islamic banks, like their mainstream counterparts, would work for private gain at public expense through distorting social priorities.

The main attraction of deferred contracts is that they bring in assured income at lower risk, thus enabling the Islamic system to compete with conventional banks. But the crucial question is how Islamic do the operations remain in the process? Are the banks interested in the promotion of Islamic objectives or norms in the area of finance? Probably they just want to exploit a safer profit-making opportunity that would not be available to them until existing banking laws were amended to make provision for the opening of Islamic windows.[33] Some countries such as Indonesia have resisted the temptation to follow the principle of exclusivity in the establishment of Islamic banking institutions. The contribution of windows to the achievements of Islamic banks being much larger than that of exclusive units, many may not be willing to take recent claims of faster growth and greater efficiency for Islamic banks at their face value.

We are not arguing against the use of deferred contracts in Islamic banking, but one can be ignorant of their limitations in achieving the broader Shari'ah objectives. The dismal performance of PLS financing over the years contributed to a rather liberal view of these contracts. A major source of the present discomfiture in Islamic banking is to be sought in the causes of this non-performance and in what could remedy the situation. The malady perhaps lies in PLS' structural mismatching with the goals of Islamic banking.

In principle, commercial banks – as their nomenclature suggests and practice confirms – were conceived for catering to the short-term liquidity needs of trade and commerce. Even when they ventured into long-term commitments their original perspective seldom changed. Keeping liquidity in their operations has ever been their guiding rule. The vast power they enjoy to create credit and the legal framework for their accounts embody this principle. Long- or medium-term financial needs have invariably called for establishing specialised financial institutions. Industrial banks, agricultural credit societies, housing development corporations, investment houses, import-export banks and refinance corporations are some of the leading examples. It is well to note that some progress on this front is now visible.[34] Islamic mutual funds and unit trusts are mushrooming, especially in the West,[35] and much more remains to be done.[36]

In summary, Islamic financial institutions have mostly been designed using the model of commercial banks in terms of their outlook, objectives, procedures, training and *modus operandi*. They are required, on the other hand, to undertake project financing of long-term risky ventures, and address social aspirations for development and wealth creation. They hardly have the aptitude, support or personnel to do what we expect them to do.[37] It is like providing shovels and baskets where excavators and trucks were needed for construction.

Opening Islamic windows in Western commercial banks causes an apparent mismatch between the provision of capabilities to them, and what they are expected to achieve. Even if established commercial banks want to enter the field of Islamic finance, it may be preferable for them to establish dedicated Islamic branches.

Islamic banking in the true sense of the term can rarely meet the vital Sharī'ah objective of raising a strong and prosperous Muslim *ummah* unless there is a complete break from tradition with reference to goals, sources and uses of funds, and operational methods. The planning authorities of a country, rather than its central bank, must prepare a blueprint for this purpose. Once the development is redirected along appropriate lines, one can hope that PLS schemes and deferred contracts will appropriately supplement one another in the balanced growth and efficient performance of the Islamic financial system.

Finally, Islamic finance, though important, is only a street under construction on a much larger Islamic roadmap. Its ultimate shape, carrying capacity and usefulness will depend on what happens in the bigger picture. Crucial for success in the matter are social conditioning and political will; everything else could then follow.

NOTES

1. On this point Halim (2001) quotes Siddiqi, Ahmed and Chapra, see pp. 60–1. Other evidence is not lacking.
2. Reference here includes the International Conference on Islamic Economics and Change, Islamic University Yogakarta of Indonesia held on 12–13 October 2002, and the Inauguration Ceremony of the Islamic Finance Services Board, Bank Negara, Kuala Lumpur 3–4 November 2002.
3. The three journals are: *Islamic Economic Studies* IRTI, King Abdulaziz University; *Islamic Economics* published by their Centre for Research in Islamic Economics; and *Review of Islamic Economics*, The Islamic Foundation, Leicester. The School exercises some ideological gatekeeping in each case.
4. Even in mainstream economics with its vast subject coverage, the award of the Nobel Prize does not make this sort of distinction.
5. There may, of course, be differences among individual adherents of the School on a particular point, yet nonetheless there seems to be overall agreement on the issues mentioned.
6. See Chapra (1985) p. 64 and p. 166.
7. See, for example, Siddiqi (1985) p. 9, Chapra (1985) p. 165, and also the supportive foreword by Khurshid Ahmad to the latter's book.
8. For further explanation see Hasan (2002) pp. 42 and 48–9.
9. See Hasan (1989), Section 2: Equality of Ratios Proposition, pp. 86–7.
10. See Hasan (1985) pp. 23–4.
11. See Khan (1995) p. 17 and p. 245.
12. The problem of Islamic financial institutions' surplus funds has now considerably eased for that reason, and not because of an increase in PLS investments.
13. See, for example, Ahmad (1985) p. 4.
14. Proponents of the School now concede the non-exclusive nature of the principle, but still maintain that the: 'PLS principle is the cornerstone of contractual transactions. Moreover, it is the most accepted in the Islamic legal literature.' See Hassan

(2003) p. 4. Incidentally, the authors provide no argument or documentation in support of their claim.

15. See Halim (2001), p. 66.
16. Here we have departed from Halim's explanation given on p. 25 (item 3) of his paper.
17. See also Kamali (1999) p. 102 for his observations on the verse.
18. See, for example, El-Gamal (2001) p. 3.
19. See Wilson (2002), the section: The Pioneering Malaysia, p. 35.
20. See the controversial *fatāwā* of Sheikh Tantawi (Al Ahram 1989) and the similar *fatāwā* by Sheikh Wasil (Al-Ittihad 1997)
21. El-Gamal (2001) p. 2.
22. Al-Imam Al-Tabari (1992), vol. 2 pp. 109–10.
23. This contradicts all claims of the School that Islam does not allow a time value for money; for, price is a money expression of value. For fuller references and quotations see, for example, Al-Misri (1997) pp. 39–48.
24. Whether the School calls this addition interest or not is a matter of taste, not of argument.
25. El-Gamal (2001) p. 6.
26. It is for this reason that interest on money loans is not allowed. See El-Gamal (2001) Section 1.3 p. 4 for a brief discussion of the nature of *ribā al-faḍl*. See also Kamali (1999) p. 102.
27. The 'no risk, no gain' precept completely ignores the well-recognised and vital distinction economists make between risk and uncertainty since Knight.
28. *Farḍ kifāya* is a social obligation placed on each Muslim and is deemed as performed by all of the community if performed by one or some of them in accordance with the Sharī'ah objective involved.
29. It is time for Islamic economics to take note of changes in business organisation and their impact on the heuristic concept of an entrepreneur and his functions. Who is the entrepreneur and what precisely is his role in a large corporation?
30. For a good discussion on these norms and objectives, see Kamali (1999) Chapter 20, pp. 395–409.
31. For details, significance and application of the rule, see Kamali (1999) Chapter 16 with translation 'Blocking the Means' pp. 310–20.
32. See Usmani (1998) p. 24.
33. It would be interesting to investigate what the proportion of Muslims is among the users of windows and what proportion Muslims constitute among all bank clients. For it is found that in the recent mushrooming of Islamic equity funds in the US, no more than one out of ten Muslims is using them. It is a question of invoking trust.
34. Failaka International Inc. *www.failaka.com* lists 100 Islamic bond and equity funds operating worldwide with details about fund name, manager(s), manager location, fund promoter(s), promoter location, inception date, minimum investment, sales load and annual fees. Most of these bonds/funds have been launched during the last 10 years.
35. Twenty-nine of these are global equity funds, North America has 10, Europe 5, Asia 4, Malaysia 14, emerging markets 12, and the remaining ones are scattered. Malaysia alone has launched 3 Islamic bond (*ṣukūk*) funds. Out of 100 fund managers, more than 60.0 per cent are located in the US and Europe. Among Muslim countries the

bulk is shared by Malaysia and Saudi Arabia.

36. Islamic banking has made good progress over the past two decades and managed to stand up to competition from the well-established conventional interest-based institutions. There are claims based on sophisticated econometric models that Islamic banks are more efficient than conventional banks. Such evidence is encouraging but must be treated with caution, not least because the small size of Islamic banks makes comparison with larger conventional banks problematic.
37. Interestingly, this important question is seldom raised in the literature. Rather one comes across explanation, even justification, for the overwhelming use of deferred contracts in Islamic banking: risk aversion was commonly indicated as the reason, but of late earning rates and dividend stability are also being mentioned. For instance, Hassan (2003) includes the two variables among the determinants of Islamic banks' concentration on short- or medium-term finance. But is not the causation in the reverse direction or bidirectional? The authors maintain silence on the point.

2

Islamic Banking Modes of Finance: Proposals for Further Evolution

Abdel-Rahman Yousri Ahmad

Due to the prohibition of interest in Islam, Islamic banking cannot depend on lending activities. When Islamic banking models were first proposed during the 1950s and later commenced operation, the pioneers of Islamic banking focused their efforts on turning traditional Islamic contracts of trade and partnership into practicable methods for finance. This may be termed as the first phase of the evolutionary process of Islamic banking. During the last thirty years a number of viable Sharī'ah-compatible financing methods have been developed. However, modes of finance based on classical Islamic contracts are not always sufficient in fulfilling the needs of modern banking. Like any other financial system, Islamic banking has to be viewed as evolving to meet modern requirements. In this chapter, an attempt is made to identify the need for a second phase of evolution in Islamic banking concepts.

INTRODUCTION

It was only during the 1960s and 1970s that the first Islamic banks were established in the Islamic World, starting in the Middle East, Malaysia and Pakistan. Thereafter, Islamic banks increased in both numbers and activity, spreading to many other parts of the world. Islamic banking could not, however, depend on lending activities alone. The banks had to search for modes of finance that did not depend on lending money or extending credit on interest. Equity finance is an obvious alternative, yet objections were raised against the modern practice of some familiar modes of equity finance, as they are not entirely separated or free from interest. Hence the pioneers of Islamic banks had a strong desire to revive the Islamic Sharī'ah and so focused their efforts on the renewal of traditional Islamic modes of finance. This may be termed as the first phase of the evolutionary process and it is discussed in the following section. These modes can be broadly divided into two main categories according to the nature of finance that they provide, direct or indirect. Modes that provide direct finance are *muḍārabah*, *mushārakah*, and *muzāra'ah* contracts. Others which provide indirect finance, that is, trade credit, are almost all in the form of 'sale contracts', such as *murābaḥah*, *bay' 'ājil*, *bay' salam* and *istiṣnā'*. This selection and modification process which conventional Islamic modes of finance had to undergo was not easy. These modes, as described and explained in traditional *fiqh* sources and practiced for centuries, were most suitable for trade finance on a bilateral basis either to cover short-run transactions or to establish unlimited liability companies among a small number of people. Finance granted by these modes depended on trustworthiness, a matter that was quite familiar and acceptable in traditional societies. Yet, trustworthiness under Islam depended not only on subjective or objective bases but also on ethical values derived from the Qur'ān and Ḥadīth.

Two main problems have to be faced with respect to the modern use of these conventional modes of finance. The first concerns selection of the most suitable for various economic activities and different needs. The second concerns modifications that have to be made so that they can be depended upon to run Islamic banking efficiently, particularly in an atmosphere that is characterised by strong competition from commercial banks. This warrants a second phase in the evolutionary process, and this will be discussed subsequently.

THE FIRST EVOLUTION

The evolution of Islamic modes of finance, which took place before the emergence of Islamic banks and continues till now, may be called the first growth stage. In this section, it is not our intention to give specific details of these Islamic modes of finance. Plenty of information on them is already available in Islamic economic literature and *fiqh* sources. Our purpose instead is to focus on the evolution process itself, how it was motivated, influenced and directed by practical matters, and how it was constrained by Shari'ah rules.

Mushārakah

The *mushārakah* contract had to be qualified to allow for a corporate form of organisation within a Sharī'ah framework. It should be noted that secular commercial laws in all contemporary Muslim countries endorse the joint stock limited liability company that was needed for establishing Islamic banks. It was not difficult, therefore, for Islamic economists and *fuqahā'* to find similarities between the basic principles of the joint stock company and those of Islamic *mushārakah*. Thus the joint stock company was accepted in principle but restricted by conditions to ensure adherence to the Sharī'ah. These conditions are: (1) it will totally depend on Islamic equity finance (that is, no debt finance); (2) all shares are common stock (that is, no preference or distinguished shares): each share represents proportionate ownership in the corporation and has a proportionate right in realised profit; (3) the transfer of shares' ownership through the market is allowed but, besides normal endorsement, will be subject to conditions that are necessary to keep the interests of the bulk of shareholders protected from the consequences of 'irrational speculation'. Conditions imposed in this respect may be flexible but they nevertheless mean restrictions on the right of the shareholder to sell shares in the market. The evolution of the *mushārakah* contract made it possible to use the form of the joint stock limited liability company in establishing Islamic banks, and later on in establishing corporations through these banks.

In establishing companies, the Islamic bank's participation (by means of *mushārakah*) in the equity of these companies may take one of two forms: (1) permanent *mushārakah*; or (2) diminishing *mushārakah*. The first is implemented mainly through the form of a joint stock company. The bank by subscribing in the company keeps its partnership in the company permanently. In the second form the bank establishes a company with a client upon his or her request. Thereby, the bank finances part or all of the capital which is required by the company by means of a special contract with the client who is a partner, but totally responsible for the company's organisation. The diminishing *mushārakah* contract provides for its termination after a specific period through the transfer of the bank's share in the company to its partner. In both forms the bank is entitled to profit, if and when achieved. Yet, in diminishing *mushārakah* the partner accepts that an extra payment will be assigned to the bank from any realised profits in return for progressively reducing its share in the company. In other words, the contract of diminishing *mushārakah* provides for progressively increasing the share of the bank's partner in the company until it becomes totally his or her property. This new development in a *mushārakah* contract has proved to be practical, opening doors to enhance the financing function of Islamic banks since resources withdrawn gradually from some companies can be employed in establishing new ones.

Muḍārabah

Among all forms of interest-free finance in Islamic jurisprudence, *muḍārabah* was considered the most suitable and practical mode for mobilising financial resources into Islamic banks. Yet, the traditional two-partners contract could not be depended upon for this purpose. Hence the contract had to be modified to allow for intermediation that could be established between large numbers of capital owners and users. A multiple-partnership *muḍārabah* was devised for this purpose. The Islamic bank would act as a capital user when receiving funds from clients and as a capital owner when financing businesses, whether by using clients' funds or its own resources. Funds mobilised by the bank are pooled together and employed through various modes in different projects that take different periods of time, but profit or loss is calculated for all projects, annually. Another feature of the multiple-partnership *muḍārabah* was its constraint-free nature. It should be noted that the Ḥanafī and Ḥanbalī schools of *fiqh* allowed the capital owner in *muḍārabah* to dictate conditions on his or her partner, the user of capital. The multiple-partner *muḍārabah* contract for the purpose of banking finance adopted only the view of the Mālikī and Shāfiʿī schools where no constraints should be imposed on the use of capital. This view was considered the most suitable for mobilising the funds of thousands of clients.

Hence, the *muḍārabah* contract was qualified to permit Islamic banks sufficient flexibility in mobilising funds from a large and unlimited number of capital owners. It also enabled the banks' resources to be employed for financing businesses in various economic activities, for definite or indefinite periods of time, without any constraints imposed on the modes of employment by the users of finance. The per capita risk involved in investment activities was thus significantly reduced in multiple-partnership *muḍārabah* as compared with two-partner *muḍārabah*.

Murābaḥah

A new *murābaḥah* contract was devised in the first evolutionary phase to allow for bank credit provisions. According to the modified contract, the Islamic bank would be ready to receive orders made by its clients to purchase for them specific goods on a *murābaḥah* basis. The bank would then be ready to respond to a purchase order made by the client after an agreement was reached with him on two matters, after knowing the purchase cost or current market price of the ordered good(s): (1) the profit margin (or mark-up) that would be added above the cost or the market price, as this represents the bank's gain from the deal; and (2) the mode which would be accepted by the client for payment of the final price to the bank after delivery was made. The new *murābaḥah* contract allowed for 'a deferred payment' in instalments at specific dates instead of payment on delivery as in the conventional contract. In this manner *murābaḥah* was transformed from a mere present or spot sale contract (immediate delivery against cash payment) to become a deferred-payment sale contract.

This reformation was considered essential for Islamic banking, since it established a method for extending trade credit on short- and long-term bases with limited risk to the bank. Giving the bank the right to take collateral against the *murābaḥah* could also further reduce this risk.

Salam

Qualifying the *salam* contract for banking purposes was not a difficult matter. Forward delivery sale is well known in markets and the mechanism that was suggested for its application by Islamic banks was simple. The Islamic banks would buy goods from their client on *salam* bases by paying their value as estimated and mutually agreed upon at the time. This provided trade credit to the client/seller, with the intention to resell these goods by the bank at a future known date after their receipt.

A profit can be obtained from *salam* provided that the resale value is greater than the purchasing value of the merchandise. The risk involved in *salam* is greater the larger the price fluctuation between the date of purchase and the date of reselling the merchandise after delivery is made to the bank. The cost of the operation is greater and the gain less the longer the time-lag is between delivery of the merchandise to the bank and its reselling. It was therefore suggested by some jurists that a parallel *salam* (hedging) could be made by the bank once it concluded a *salam* contract in order to minimise the risk and the cost of the operation. This proposal was not unanimously accepted by all jurists, some viewing a parallel *salam* contract as not permissible. According to them, the Shariʿah prohibits the selling of expected merchandise – in other words, merchandise which is not immediately to hand. Furthermore, this difference of opinion could not be settled by consensus.

Ijārah

Conventional leasing contracts had to be qualified for the purposes of Islamic banking. Under *ijārah* contracts the bank purchases real assets that are suitable for leasing and rents them to its clients. Yet to suit the financing nature of the bank, any asset can only be purchased as per the request and specifications provided by the client-lessee. The bank (lessor) and the client (lessee) then reach an agreement on the amount of rent, the terms of payment and maintenance being the bank's responsibility. On the other hand, the lessee gets the benefit (utility) of the asset and is responsible for any damage to it, if misused.

The *ijārah* contract as qualified in the above manner was not really practical. To suit all clients' demands for leasing, which may be quite diversified in terms of assets required and leasing periods, the bank is involved in multiple operations of purchasing, storing and maintenance besides leasing. Surely the long-run net return of such operations cannot be calculated with a significant degree of confidence, unless every lessee rents the real asset that is demanded for the whole of its durable economic life. More practical, therefore, was a new *ijārah* contract known as *ijārah wa iqtinā'*, that is, leasing ending with ownership. The main idea behind this new contract was to invite the client (lessee) to purchase from the bank (lessor) the leased asset by the end of the leasing period. The payment of rent and the terms of ownership transfer to the client are arranged in the contract. This form of *ijārah* opened the door to successful leasing activities by Islamic banks, but in practice the leasing contract has become more like a hire-purchase contract.

LESSONS FROM EXPERIENCE

The application of Islamic modes of finance in banking during the last 30 years has highlighted both the positive and negative aspects of these modes. The feedback from Islamic banks in this regard should therefore be taken into account earnestly. For the lessons derived from their application are expected to help in taking steps towards further reformation and development of these Islamic modes of finance. Relying on studies and analyses that have been undertaken on the Islamic banking experience,[1] the following lessons can be derived with respect to the employment of finance modes:

1. The development of *mushārakah* to include the joint stock limited liability company within Shari'ah constraints was not only indispensable for the establishment of Islamic banks but also for the extension of their direct investment activities in the modern manufacturing and service sectors. The participation of Islamic banks in establishing companies was, however, restricted in most, if not all, cases. Central bank regulations impose ceilings on banks' resources that can be invested directly. Islamic banks, therefore, managed to establish only a limited number of small- and medium-scale companies.

The diminishing *mushārakah* contract proved impractical for large and middle size firms. Large firms that have long depended either on their own sources or on financial resources obtained from commercial banks have not shown any significant signs of moving towards the Islamic banks for finance. New companies of a middle and large size followed the same pattern. *Mushārakah* contracts as offered by Islamic banks have not proved popular for such companies. New small-scale enterprises were, however, in a different situation, as they could never get sufficient finance for their investment either from commercial banks or capital markets. Diminishing *mushārakah* thus proved suitable and successful for these enterprises.

2. The new *muḍārabah* contract helped significantly in mobilising financial resources into Islamic banks. Available statistics published by Islamic banks show that their financial resources have grown during the last three decades (particularly during the 1970s and 1980s) at higher rates than time deposits in commercial banks. Although the capital fund is not guaranteed to its owner when invested on a profit and loss sharing basis, the new contract of multiple-partner *muḍārabah* has added much to security. By pooling all resources together, investing them in various activities with different degrees of risk and taking at the same time all necessary measures to avoid loss, multiple-partner *muḍārabah* has significantly reduced risk per capita in comparison to the conventional two-partner *muḍārabah*. Applying central bank regulations towards the normalisation of profit rates distributed annually by Islamic banks gave more confidence to holders of investment accounts and almost removed concerns about losses from their minds. The importance of reducing risk per capita should be seriously appreciated, since the competing commercial banks and all other interest-based

financial institutions guarantee the funds of their clients, besides interest.

Islamic banks' ability to employ the *muḍārabah* contract in financing business was a totally different story. According to most studies success was very limited. Indeed, probably no more than 3.0 to 5.0 per cent of Islamic banks' resources were employed using *muḍārabah*. It should be noted that the conventional two-partner *muḍārabah* contract has to be relied upon in financing any business person by the bank. This contract whose fulfilment depends on trustworthiness involves high risk to the Islamic bank. The first evolutionary stage of the *muḍārabah* contract could not deal with this matter, that is in how to administer the contract on the basis of personal trust in the *muḍārib* (the user of the capital). As the Muslim World has experienced major changes in its social, cultural and ethical environment during the past two centuries, trust cannot just be assumed in the *muḍārib* as in the earlier days of Islam when populations were smaller and personal and business relations were inexorably bound.

3. The new formula of *murābaḥah* that is dependent on deferred payment of the value of the merchandise purchased by the bank to the client has in practice proved to be the most important among all Islamic modes of finance. In fact, *murābaḥah* has been so excessively used that it has accounted for the employment of no less than 80.0 per cent of the Islamic banks' financial resources. One of the main advantages of the new *murābaḥah* contract is its flexibility in financing small or large transactions on a short- or even a relatively long-term basis. Yet the excessive employment of *murābaḥah* needs further explanation. Most of the managers recruited by Islamic banks in the early period (the 1970s and 1980s) were recruited from commercial banks. Those managers soon discovered that the structuring of *murābaḥah* finance was not really that much different from the interest-based finance which they previously practised. In fact some managers, out of their poor knowledge of Sharīʿah, besides their misunderstanding of Islamic banking ethics, committed gross mistakes in practice. This has clearly manifested itself in *murābaḥah*. The worst example in the early years of experience occurred when the manager, after accepting a certain request to purchase a known commodity and reaching an agreement on the final price (that is, the purchase price plus the mark-up) and terms of payment, allowed the client to withdraw the cash needed for purchase from the bank and do the job himself. This represented an outright *ribā* and not *murābaḥah* sale transaction since the bank client received a given amount of money and undertook to pay it back plus the mark-up, which here became exactly equal to an interest payment. This practice was sharply criticised by many Islamic economists and jurists, and was therefore terminated. Yet practices of *murābaḥah* sale have frequently been criticised for other reasons. For example, managers were frequently guided by the prevailing interest rate in fixing the *murābaḥah* mark-

up for each transaction. Furthermore, clients were obliged to fulfil the contract before actually receiving the merchandise, a matter that is against Sharīʿah law.

4. Leasing operations were limited in general. Managers of Islamic banks were clearly reluctant to take the risk of purchasing real assets of long durable economic life in order to lease them to their clients, at their request, only for months or even for a year or two. In fact, it was a new experience and the risks involved in such operations could not be calculated or estimated with any accuracy. Leases ending in ownership proved attractive to bank managers as well as to clients. Yet this new mode devised for Islamic banking cannot be treated on Sharīʿah grounds as proper leasing. It is more like a deferred payment sale contract or a deformed form of diminishing *mushārakah*. Leasing responsibilities and rights could not be clearly defined in *ijārah wa iqtinā'*, which has become in this way quite similar to hire-purchase contracts practised efficiently by non-Islamic institutions.

5. Reports issued by Islamic banks show that few activities were financed by *salam* contracts. Yet some Islamic banks, particularly in the Arab Gulf area, financed some major transactions in crude oil using this contract. Deals were made when petroleum prices were almost stable at low levels but expected to rise in the future. Some petroleum dealers were in need of advance monies and therefore accepted to deliver their product at a fixed date in the future at a current value which was (expectedly) less than what they could obtain if they waited for such a future date. The managers of Islamic banks were however quite aware that future oil prices may not necessarily be higher than current prices. Hence, a loss could well be expected. Dealers who requested a *salam* sale offered to compensate the banks in case of loss, a practice that does not conform with the principles of Islamic finance.[2]

6. Islamic modes of finance in general as applied by banks have proved practical and attractive to small enterprises. This outcome is very important for contemporary Muslim countries, which are all classified as developing economies and have significant small-scale enterprise sectors which may account for up to 20.0–35.0 per cent of their GDP. Small enterprises cannot normally secure finance from commercial banks or from the capital market for many reasons.[3] *Murābaḥah* and lease ending in ownership were employed quite successfully by some Islamic banks in financing small enterprises whether these were inside or outside the formal sector.

7. Lastly, any success that Islamic banks have managed to achieve in recent decades could not have been implemented without the adaptation of the major

modes of Islamic finance to serve modern requirements. Within a highly competitive financial market, where commercial banks, as well as other interest-based financial institutions, are posing a strong challenge to Islamic banks, these latter have been forced to adapt to survive and build market share. There remain a number of areas, however, in which Islamic banks cannot compete, notably in the provision of overdraft facilities. Thus efforts have to be made for a second evolution of at least some modes of Islamic finance with no delay and with no less vigour than the first evolution.

TOWARDS FURTHER EVOLUTION

The logic and principles of evolution

Islamic modes of finance should be understood correctly. They are not dogmas: their original forms existed and were practised by Arabs before Islam, and later on they were accepted by the Prophet (pbuh) as they were *ribā*-free.[4] In subsequent centuries they were revised, verified and subjected to strict conditions by *fuqahā'*, to guarantee that their contracts always remained *ribā*-free, fulfilled their functions effectively, were just and transparent, and never used to finance *ḥarām* activities. Muslim jurists of different schools of *fiqh* differed in some details about the terms of finance or these contracts' mechanisms but they were unanimous on their basic Sharī'ah principles.

For the sake of further clarification, Islamic modes of finance have 'constants' represented in a few principles which are directly derived from the Qur'ān and Sunnah, and 'variables' which are forms and mechanisms that developed over the centuries by *ijtihād* in response to the practical needs of Muslim societies.

A major obstacle that hinders the evolution of Islamic modes of finance in modern times originates from the mixing up of 'constant' and 'variable' elements in conventional modes of finance, or treating them equally. Constants cannot be touched, while all variables may be revised, qualified or even replaced altogether. Unfortunately the opposite happened in some cases. In *murābaḥah*, the form and the structure were superficially conserved while the principle of risk-sharing fell into ambiguity. In *ijārah wa iqtinā'*, the form in practice has turned out to be quite similar to hire-purchase arrangements which are offered by secular, interest-based institutions.

Once the nature of the Islamic modes of finance is understood correctly, they can be suitably employed within contemporary circumstances while their Islamic core remains intact. Consequently, some conventional contracts which have been used in very limited cases or neglected (for example, the two-partner *muḍārabah* contract, *muzāra'ah* and *istiṣnā'*) are likely to be effectively reformed and brought into employment to serve national economic interests.

The question that must also be raised here is why uneasiness or reluctance is shown on the part of contemporary Muslim scholars towards inventing new modes of finance to suit contemporary financial and economic needs. One explanation may be a misunderstanding of Islamic contracts, and how these contracts evolved during the transition from the pre-Islamic society to Islamic society and were modified several times by jurists to function suitably within Sharīʿah boundaries.[5]

In fact, shortcomings in the first evolution of Islamic conventional modes of finance mainly emerged from the concerns of the *fuqahāʾ* who were consulted about reformation of these modes to suit modern banking. These worries are appreciated but should not be exaggerated or left without treatment. Appreciated, because there were and still are serious attempts in the contemporary Islamic world to recognise the interest system as permissible on Sharīʿah grounds. There are also voices calling for the reformation but not for the revival of Islamic economics, although some of these advocate modernisation on a secular basis. On the other hand, the worries of *fuqahāʾ* should not be exaggerated since it is possible to meet practical needs while still preserving Islamic principles on transactions and finance. These principles include: (1) the prohibition of *ribā* in the form of interest or in any other form; (2) the observance of profit and loss sharing within Sharīʿah rules which implies justice and transparency; (3) the maintenance of the Islamic business ethics of benevolence[6] and honesty; (4) commitment to finance *ḥalāl* transactions and production only; (5) giving priority to the public interest where it conflicts with private interest; and (6) the avoidance of any inappropriate use or misuse of capital funds.[7]

These principles have to be interpreted correctly in our present circumstances and suitable mechanisms devised actually to carry their core into practice. For example, 'honesty' or trust cannot be based solely on personal information or on subjective motives as in former times. Suitable practical procedures and mechanisms built on an objective basis should be adopted to fulfil the target of 'honesty', or in other words to guarantee that honest behaviour will materialise. Dependence on profit and loss sharing does not mean that financiers will not take all the necessary measures to avert the risks involved in their operations. The avoidance of irrational use of financial resources requires careful scrutiny of the project that will receive finance to assess its economic viability, and careful examination of the user of finance to make sure of his or her skill, efficiency, achievement motivation and readiness to fulfil his or her undertakings. Public interest considerations also have to be translated in the Islamic World which is mostly poor, but developing, in conditions that encourage small-scale enterprises but deprive any activity from finance if it is detrimental to sustainable development.

Lastly, Muslims should not refrain from taking advantage from any secular laws or arrangements that are not contradictory to the Sharīʿah and to Islamic ethics in the process of evolution, now or in the future. Islam encourages the search for wisdom anywhere and recognises *ijtihād* as a source of Sharīʿah. The refusal of everything in the secular world without giving reason may then delay the evolution of finance and financial institutions in the Muslim World.

POSSIBILITIES FOR FURTHER REFORMATION

The mushārakah contract

As already approved by *fuqahā'*, *mushārakah* can be arranged in the form of a joint stock company. Islamic banks can still benefit from further evolution in this context much more than they did during the past three decades. One of the problems facing Islamic banks in establishing new companies through the securities market concerns their participation in direct investment, which should not exceed the ceiling fixed by the central bank. Compliance with secular regulations, which are more suitable to interest-based commercial banks, is inescapable until an Islamic financial system is fully established.

Although shares will be sold to the public, the bank should be keen to encourage its clients towards the purchase of new shares while keeping a minimum proportion of any issue to itself in order to be represented in the company's executive board. The role of the Islamic banks in establishing companies through the securities market will help in developing a secondary market in the majority of contemporary Muslim countries. Besides, by forming new companies in different activities and sectors, Islamic banks can actively help in achieving economic development along Islamic lines.

Ijtihād is needed, however, with respect to three matters, which have remained unsolved. These are: (1) the types of shares; (2) the right of holders to resell their shares in the market without restrictions; and (3) the need to issue bonds.

Types of shares

Only ordinary shares were approved in the first evolutionary phase but not preference shares. This matter should be given fresh consideration on new grounds. Preference shares should be rejected on Sharīʿah grounds in two situations: if they entail giving returns to their holders first, while no profit has been realised, because such returns will not be anything but *ribā*; or favouring their holders with profit realised while depriving other shareholders of dividends, because this is against the principles of justice and of profit and loss sharing. However, one of the most distinctive characters of conventional *mushārakah* is the allowance given in the contract to specify different proportions of any profit realised to partners irrespective of their shares in the total capital. Preferential treatment may therefore be given to some partners although their share in the capital may be smaller than others. Preference in this context is given with the consent of all partners, on the grounds that this particular partner has better entrepreneurial faculties or is more active than others in running the activities of the company. This spirit in conventional *mushārakah* has to be revived in the modern contract for it is of vital importance for the company's performance and efficiency in practice. Towards this end, we propose that the modern *mushārakah* contract should include a precondition that persons selected or appointed as executives or managers in the company and holding part of its common stock (one share or more) benefit from a premium, in terms of a reasonable fixed per cent, above the dividend distributed at any time from realised profits to shareholders. This preferential treatment has also to be extended to all the company's staff and workers who hold shares. Justification for the same is as follows. First, that partners in conventional *mushārakah* who were given preferential treatment in profit never worked as pure executives or managers. In fact, they most likely had to do other work linked with or attached to administration or management. They had in former times neither secretarial nor specialised staff to help them in carrying out the company's business. Second, this extension of preferential profit treatment is expected to bring about a positive effect in raising the efficiency of the company staff and labour. Preferential treatment of this type, which is derived from the spirit of Islamic *mushārakah*, would contribute significantly in making all the company, from the executives to the ordinary workers, keen to work for higher returns. Hence this would benefit all holders of the company's common stock.

Preferential treatment would therefore be geared to efficiency and productive effort, and not to wealth, as has always been the case in the Islamic system. It can be predicted that the greater the proportion of shares held by company employees, the smaller will be the need to resort to an 'efficiency wage' policy. Furthermore, the greater the willingness of executives and managers to acquire shares, the smaller will be the passive outcome which is predicted by the 'principal/agent' theory.

The right to sell shares

Dealing in shares mainly for speculative purposes has been judged to be against the Sharī'ah by the majority of *fuqahā'*. In the Sunnah, the manipulation of price in transactions where there is no intention finally to acquire a commodity is forbidden.[8] Secular economists may defend speculative activities, for one reason or another, yet experience has shown that such speculation may destroy real productive activities, a matter which is entirely rejected in Islamic economics. Yet, we should not let this matter impose heavily and unnecessarily on the right of any shareholder to sell his holding. Investors normally buy shares as a sort of package deal, that is, they accept the risk involved in profit and loss sharing, but with the right to sell their holdings at a suitable time to avoid capital loss or to realise capital gain. Thus, restrictions on speculation in themselves might have a detrimental effect on the promotion of joint stock companies which Islamic banks would be willing to establish. Besides, restrictions imposed on the right of any partner to withdraw from conventional *mushārakah* contracts was rational, as all these contracts were based on the simple unlimited liability partnership company form. The same rule cannot be applied to the limited liability joint stock company.

For these reasons, and taking into account the interests of the company, the only restriction on the right to sell shares in modern *mushārakah* contracts should be that provided for in the *shuf'ah* arrangement in Sharī'ah law.[9] Applying this *shuf'ah* rule in practice means that shareholders of any Islamic company, whenever they decide to sell their shares, should declare their intention to the company, directly or through the issuing Islamic bank. Unless the company, the bank or any of its shareholders are willing to buy these shares within a few days (say three days), they can be sold to any suitable buyer in the market.

Finally, it is possible that preferential treatment in profit allocation, as suggested previously, once manifested in a sizable portion of the company stock held by its management and employees, would reduce the size of speculation to an acceptable level that would not disturb its productive activity.

Issuing bonds

In modern Islamic companies some special types of bonds can be issued by the Islamic bank without infringing upon the Sharī'ah. Bonds traded in secular systems bear interest. Yet bonds can be issued on a non-interest basis to finance the purchase of land, buildings or capital equipment needed for the production activities of companies. Holders of such bonds will be the owner of a real underlying asset and accept to rent them to companies for a specified annual fee or two payments per year. Bondholders will, according to Sharī'ah rules, be responsible for the maintenance of all capital assets they own. Thus, the return (rent) given on bonds will be net, that is, after deducting maintenance costs. The Islamic bank in issuing this type of bond helps in financing the capital needed by firms, as well as satisfying a section of its clients who prefer stable and periodic returns on what can be viewed as secured capital.

The muḍārabah contract

The two-partner *muḍārabah* contract evolved to serve the Islamic banks' relationship with fund owners, but remained without any reformation with respect to the banks' relationship with fund users. Therefore it has either remained unused or employed in very limited cases, and with a high degree of risk.

The nature and mechanism of the two-partner *muḍārabah* shows high reliance on, and full trust in, the *muḍārib*, that is, in their personal character, sincerity, honesty and capability to run the business successfully. In the past such trust was fully supported by the strength of Islamic culture and the enforcement of Sharī'ah rules in transactions. Besides, full information was easily obtained about any person living within a tribe or in a village or small town. It can be deduced from this that the conventional *muḍārabah* contract could stand a fair chance of success if applied, even with minor modifications in the villages and small towns of contemporary Muslim countries. In fact, analysis of the first experience of an Islamic bank which was established in Egypt in the early 1960s at Mit Ghamr shows that the success achieved was due to the small-scale banking enterprise operating in a town to which the entrepreneur and the manager (the late Amad Al-Najar, the pioneer of Islamic banking in Egypt) belonged. Thus, close personal relations were established with known owners of small-scale enterprises in the town, and the bank funded them successfully by two-partner *muḍārabah* contracts. The same experience can be repeated if similar circumstances exist. Otherwise, the two-partner *muḍārabah* contract has to be qualified and modified to suit new circumstances in contemporary Muslim countries.

Societies have grown in number, with larger towns and cities, more substantial economic activities and huge financial markets. Businesses have grown in size and financial intermediaries have to deal with hundreds or thousands of people on non-subjective bases, at national and international levels. Thus: (1) objective criteria have to be used by Islamic banks for evaluating the capabilities of prospective users of funds (the *muḍārib*), that is, their enterprise facility, achievement motivation, managerial skill, previous experience, personal record and reputation. Sufficient information of this sort should be gathered as a preliminary step before trust can be assumed in the *muḍārib*; (2) sound economic criteria should be used for the evaluation of the investment project. The viability of the project has to be established through a careful feasibility study. Preference should be given to those projects promising higher profit rates at a reasonable or acceptable degree of risk; (3) the *muḍārabah* contract should include legal conditions and terms of finance based upon and derived from the approved feasibility study of the prospective project for the purpose of securing the best possible use of finance at minimum possible risk. This essential development means that the contract will endorse the standpoint of Ḥanafī and Ḥanbalī *fiqh* schools of restricted *muḍārabah*; (4) the *muḍārabah* fund should not be delivered in one single cash payment after the two partners make an agreement, as in former times. The new proposed contract, while stating agreement on the total amount of finance that will be given to the project, will arrange for the *muḍārib* to receive this amount in several payments scheduled in accordance with the project's progress at successive stages as outlined and described in the approved feasibility study; (5) the bank will maintain full rights to receive periodic progress reports from the *muḍārib*, to examine the accuracy and transparency of these reports and to halt or stop the flow of finance if the terms of finance are violated; (6) the *muḍārib* will undertake to refund the full amount of finance received from the bank in cases where the terms of finance stated in the contract have been violated. It should be noted that this undertaking takes place in compliance with the rules of 'restricted *muḍārabah*'; and lastly (7) in some cases, for example new firms or small enterprises expanding their business, the bank may require a third party of sound business reputation to guarantee the fulfilment of the *muḍārib*'s undertaking of giving a full refund in case of contract violation.

Financial resources held by Islamic banks in investment accounts are mobilised on a long-run basis. Yet they tend to be short-run and medium-run resources in practice because of the right given to clients to withdraw from their accounts at any time without restriction. This right has become a necessity because of the high degree of competition in a dualistic banking system. *Muḍārabah* finance is, in fact, needed in particular for relatively long-run investment projects and therefore should be of a long-run nature. The problem of suitable resources can be eliminated by issuing *muḍārabah* certificates of deposit for projects that the bank approves for finance, on the conditions mentioned above, for minimum periods of three or five years. These restricted *muḍārabah* certificates of deposit could be sold to holders of investment accounts at a discount. The bank could allow the transfer of the certificate of deposit's ownership from one holder to another, but would keep its right not to refund the value of the certificate issued before its period had elapsed. Only in exceptional circumstances stated in the contract should a refund be allowed and a penalty would then be imposed. By the end of the certificate's period it would be devalued in monetary terms, taking into account the market value of the existing project plus the total profit or loss that was realised throughout. Such *muḍārabah* certificates of deposit could provide an appropriate means of funding long-run projects by Islamic banks. But they will only gain popularity if it is proved in practice that higher rates of profit can be achieved in this manner, while the long-run value of the certificates remains fairly secured at minimum possible risk due to the restricted *muḍārabah* mechanism that would be applied.

The muzāra'ah contract

A suitable application of this contract, which has been almost totally neglected by Islamic banks, will be of particular importance to those Muslim countries with significant agricultural sectors. In employing *muzāra'ah* as a mode of finance, the role of the Islamic bank will be confined to the provision of current production requirements, such as seeds and fertilisers, in return for a share of output after harvest. In this contract neither labour services nor fixed capital equipments are eligible for finance. The bank receives requests from farmers or owners of agricultural land to finance given production requirements to produce known crop(s) during a given period of time.

Muzāra'ah, if practised to finance large-scale operations, should be extended on an objective basis and follow careful procedures along similar lines to those previously suggested for restricted *muḍārabah*. In practice, however, and for those Muslim countries where small-scale and often fragmented farms prevail, there are simpler alternatives for Islamic financing. First, as a prerequisite for agricultural finance, Islamic banks have to establish branches in villages and small towns. Second, banks' managers have to establish close relations with notable people of good reputation in rural areas and seek their advice with respect to the reputation of the local farmers and the size of finance demanded by them. These institutional and cultural factors are indispensable for the successful application of *muzāra'ah* finance. Third, farmers financed by *muzāra'ah* should undertake to pay back in cash the market value of the supplies which they have received financing for if these have been misused or if it is proved that cultivation of the land has been neglected.

According to the conventional *muzāra'ah* contract, the provision of production requirements by the financier and the payment of his share in the output after harvesting should be made in kind. For it is quite difficult to make these *muzāra'ah* transactions in money without the possibility of *ribā* emerging. In compliance with the Sharī'ah, a village Islamic bank branch would, therefore, be involved in purchasing production requirements for farmers as well as in selling crops in the market after each harvest. This would, however, be rather problematic unless the banks' branches employ specialists in the marketing of agricultural goods, and have warehouses available to store these goods whenever this is needed. This would not only be logistically complicated but may also be quite risky because of variations in the prices of stored agricultural produce. Secular banks that specialise in agricultural finance do not face such problems as they lend and receive money with interest. Yet these banks are often heavily criticised because of their unsympathetic attitude towards those farmers who fail to pay back their debts in time, frequently because of crop failure.

To minimise the efforts and risk involved in *muzāra'ah* finance, Islamic banks may seek the help of specialised agricultural trading companies. By contract, these companies would undertake to provide production requirements as directed by the bank, which would extend finance to them in return. These specialised companies may also, in return for a commission, take responsibility for the marketing of the products received from farmers and forward the revenue obtained to the bank. The cost of intermediation by these companies would be reflected, by the bank, in additional administration costs paid by those farmers who seek *muzāra'ah* finance. A further development may be for Islamic banks to establish agricultural trading subsidiaries whose activities could increase in parallel with the growth of *muzāra'ah* finance. Such subsidiaries could be financed by *muḍārabah* to implement the practical work related to *muzāra'ah* contracts as directed by the bank. The Islamic bank would get shares in profits realised from *muzāra'ah* and from *muḍārabah* as well. It should be noted that profits realised by these companies would be obtained from the bulk purchase of farm supplies and the marketing of crops and not from *muzāra'ah* financial operations.

The istiṣnā' contract

This mode of finance has also been neglected or used in only a limited number of cases, as the available records of Islamic banks show. We estimate that the revival of *istiṣnā'* in banking finance could play a significant role in the development of small-scale industries in developing Muslim countries. Manufacturers in these industries, in contrast to large- and medium-scale industries, face great difficulties in obtaining finance, and they may not even be getting as little as 1.0 per cent of their financial requirements from interest-based banks. These small manufacturing businesses often fail because of the financial problems they face as a result of borrowing from moneylenders, who are all too frequently 'loan sharks'.

To revive *istiṣnā'* through Islamic banking, a new mechanism has to be developed in which the bank would act only as an intermediary. The proposed procedures may run as follows: (1) the bank receives a request from a manufacturer to finance the manufacturing of a specific article(s) (of known quality and quantity) demanded by a certain buyer; (2) the bank contacts the buyer who demands the article to obtain full information on the terms of the contract which he and the manufacturer have mutually approved; (3) the bank investigates and examines the ability of both parties to fulfil the terms of the contract in practice; (4) once approval has been gained, the bank, as an intermediary, has to arrange for two contracts, one with the manufacturer and the second with the buyer. In the first contract, the bank undertakes to finance the specified manufacturing operation. In the second contract, the buyer undertakes to pay a down payment to the bank and then the remaining value of the manufactured item on delivery as required. Compared to a conventional contract, the benefit to the buyer is in relieving him from paying in advance the total costs of the demanded article to the manufacturer and bearing the risk of defective goods being produced or other problems arising that might delay or impede delivery. The benefit to the manufacturer is obvious, for this way he gets the finance he requires, interest-free as in conventional *istiṣnā'*. The benefit to the bank is the difference between cost, that is, finance given in advance to the manufacturer (in place of the buyer), and revenue, that is, the final price paid for the manufactured article by the buyer. The risk involved in *istiṣnā'* can be minimised by gathering accurate information on the manufacturer's business and technical reputation, as well as taking sufficient precautions towards securing the payments that will be made by the buyer of the manufactured article.

The use of *istiṣnā'* finance could cover the outsourcing by large corporations of manufacturing to reputable small companies, as well as the procurement by governments and local authorities of manufactured goods. This would not only help in extending interest-free finance to small manufacturers, but also in developing the small-scale industrial sector, a matter which is crucial for employment generation in Muslim countries.

The ijārah contract

The practice of *ijārah* by Islamic banks through the mode known as *ijārah wa iqtinā'* (hire-purchase) has been much criticised. Essentially, the contract has become a hybrid of leasing and ownership rights, and there is often ambiguity about the responsibilities of each of the parties. A possible solution to these problems, which is acceptable on Sharī'ah grounds, is to turn this contract into something of a diminishing *mushārakah*. Despite the change of legal status, there would be no significant practical difference to the size of finance advanced by the bank or in the benefits accruing to the partner.

The Islamic bank could, however, develop more liquid *ijārah* finance by issuing *ijārah* bonds and selling them to its clients (particularly to those who hold investment accounts) in order to establish and finance a specialised *ijārah* company. The bank could hold a share in the new company's capital. The owners of these bonds would most probably enjoy a relatively stable income from the company's leasing operations. The bank, by holding a share in the company's capital, would have the right to participate in its management and to receive a share of its dividends.

The murābaḥah contract

Use of the *murābaḥah* contract during the 1970s involved loopholes which were not consistent with Shari'ah law. However, *murābaḥah* in itself as a mode of finance should not be discredited or neglected as it can play a significant role in short- and long-run trade finance. It is therefore important to find a new structure for such financing that can avoid the present shortcomings.

It is argued here that buying and selling merchandise through *murābaḥah* contracts cannot strictly be accommodated in Islamic banking without violating the Sharī'ah or breaching the main banking function, that is, financial intermediation. Therefore, to maintain the benefits of *murābaḥah* finance a new mechanism based on the distinction between the two main parts of *murābaḥah*, namely trade and finance, is needed. The first part, the trading contract, could be assigned by the bank to specialised trading companies, on lines similar to those suggested previously in *muzāra'ah*. The second part, the finance, should be the responsibility of the bank. Thus, once a bank has approved a *murābaḥah* contract, the client would be directed to select the commodity demanded from a specialised trading company, which by agreement would cooperate with the Islamic bank. The *murābaḥah* contract would provide for the delivery of the commodity purchased to the client in the presence of an agent from the bank and the client would pay the purchase cost plus the *murābaḥah* mark-up to the bank in instalments over a given period of time, as mutually agreed. The bank paying the current price to the company would gain the mark-up for this advance. This mechanism means that Islamic banks can no longer be criticised for their role as buyers and sellers of the goods demanded on *murābaḥah* bases, as the specialised trading company would assume these responsibilities.

The cost of purchasing any commodity would be reduced to the client because the bank's administration costs of buying and reselling would be eliminated. A specialised trading company dealing with many of the bank's *murābaḥah* clients could also provide price discounts for clients because of its bulk purchasing power.

It is very important, however, to emphasise two points: first, the mark-up should be fixed on the basis of Islamic '*bay' ājil*', in which deferred payment is based purely on an estimation of the future market value of the commodity and not on the basis of interest. In other words, the mark-up should be fixed on a basis that is entirely different from that which fixes the cost of capital use. Islamic banks could employ marketing consultants to estimate the *murābaḥah* mark-up in different transactions. Second, although taking collateral or securing guarantees to reduce risk in *murābaḥah* contracts is permissible, this should only be called upon as a last resort in the case of default, as clients facing payments difficulties should be given time to remedy their situation.

The salam contract

The proposed evolution of this method of financing relies heavily on *salam* practice accompanied by a parallel *salam* contract.[10] As hedging through a parallel *salam* contract can be conducted by an Islamic bank in some but not all cases, it may be advisable to seek the help of specialised dealers to organise hedging and to avoid operations involving the storage or marketing of merchandise. This is especially important if actual delivery dates of the first and second *salam* contracts are not perfectly synchronised. Additional costs which result from such intermediation by specialised dealers are likely to be less than the losses that may result if the bank failed to organise hedging or to resell within a short period merchandise received by *salam*.

It is possible for Islamic banks to practice *salam* finance successfully at much lower risk in the international market. The bank on the one hand would be a purchaser of a specific merchandise deal at a known price to be delivered at a known date, and on the other hand a seller of the same deal at a fixed future date but at a higher known price. In an organised international commodity market such commercial deals can be conducted perfectly well. Yet the utmost care should be taken by the bank to make sure that actual delivery of *salam* goods occurs, since deals of this sort may be performed purely for speculative gain. If the actual delivery of merchandise does not take place, the *salam* transaction would be deemed invalid under Sharīʿah law.

It is safer for Islamic banks to purchase on a *salam* basis from known dealers in foreign markets goods that enjoy high and stable demand in the domestic market. A parallel *salam* contract could be made with other dealers in the domestic market to purchase these imported goods at higher fixed prices and at a known future date. To exclude any possible and unnecessary storage expenses, procedures could be arranged by contracts (first and second) that delivery of the merchandise to the bank, and then to the next *salam* purchaser, will be undertaken at the bonded warehouse after the arrival of the merchandise at the port of entry. Export deals can be arranged using a similar structure. The Islamic bank would purchase export goods produced at home on a *salam* basis from known suppliers and enter into a parallel *salam* contract undertaking the delivery of the same goods to importing firms in foreign markets. Transactions of this kind are usually better organised and allow a much better chance for *salam* financing to develop successfully. Such arrangements should promote export growth that can contribute to the economic development of Muslim countries.

CONCLUSIONS

Pioneers of Islamic banking during the 1960s and 1970s were enthusiastic about reviving traditional Islamic methods of financing. This revival needed *ijtihād* and innovative thinking. *Fuqahā'*, in cooperation with Islamic economists, managed to restructure some but not all of the traditional financing methods and apply these to modern banking. Yet in practice it appeared that one of the newly revived financing contracts, namely *murābaḥah*, was excessively used, while others were either neglected or little used in spite of their importance. Examples of the latter are *muḍārabah* for direct business finance or *muzāraʿah* in agricultural credit. Certainly the success that Islamic banks have achieved since the 1970s could not have materialised without the restructuring of traditional Islamic methods of financing. Yet many of the problems of Islamic banking could have been avoided if more of these methods of financing had been adapted to meet wider needs. This chapter shows that Islamic methods of finance are not inflexible, and that effective restructuring can be undertaken to improve banking efficiency while at the same time respecting the Shariʿah and Islamic principles.

NOTES

1. References are given in the References and Bibliography.
2. The author, when asked his opinion in this case, could not agree on the principle of compensation in the case of loss to any party of the *salam* contract, that is, in either case: whether the future value of the product is much less or much greater than the value actually paid at the time the *salam* contract was concluded. The Ḥadīth of the Prophet (pbuh) is quite clear on *salam* terms, which means that any *ijtihād* in this respect is totally unacceptable.
3. ILO (1991), *The Dilemma of the Informal Sector*, Report of the Director General, p. 11, Geneva, UNIDO (1992), *Global Report* 1992/1993, Vienna, Abdel-Rahman Yousri Ahmad, Tanmiyat el-Ṣinā'at Alsaghīra wa mushkilāt Tamwiliya (Development of Small Industries and Problems of their Finance) published by IRTI/IDB, Jeddah (in Arabic).
4. By the Prophet (pbuh)'s consent, they were included in his Sunnah and became part of the Sharī'ah.
5. In developing new modes of finance within the Islamic framework we learn from modern methods of finance in any system, anywhere in the world, as long as these do not contradict directly or indirectly Islamic ethics and its tenets. In the Ḥadīth of the Prophet (pbuh) the Muslim believer should search for wisdom and benefit from it, anywhere that it may be found.
6. For example, help should be given to young entrepreneurs and small enterprises, and patience should be practised when asking them to fulfil their financial obligations, particularly when they are facing substantial debts or unexpectedly difficult problems in business.
7. The Qur'ān exhorts 'and give not unto the foolish your property which Allah had made a means of support for you', (Sūrah al-Nisā:4). In the Ḥadīth, al-Mughira bin Shuba reported the Prophet (pbuh) as saying: 'Allah hated for you to waste wealth', that is by extravagance or by lack of wisdom and thinking (Al-Bukhari, vol. 3).
8. In the Sunnah the Prophet (pbuh) prohibited *najash*, which means that someone bids up a price against others without any intention of finally acquiring the commodity. This meaning can be applied to destabilising speculation. Buyers of shares whose intention is to keep them only till a capital gain is achieved, or sellers who bid share prices up or down to achieve capital gains, are in principle behaving in a manner which is really no different from that prohibited by the Prophet (pbuh).
9. *Shuf'ah* means giving priority in the purchase of property offered for sale to those most closely related, for example, a brother, kin, neighbour or partner. The Prophet (pbuh) also provided a ruling whereby: 'A person has no right to pre-emption against another partner if he preceded him in buying it, nor has a minor or an absentee such an option.'
10. Objections to a parallel or second *salam* contract should be overruled. The *salam* contract, the first or the second, entails selling goods which are not in the possession of the seller when the contract is concluded. A seller who sells goods which he normally produces and undertakes by *salam* to deliver later on, at a fixed future date, will be obliged by Sharī'ah rule, in case of failure to produce them, to buy goods of similar quality from the market and deliver them to the *salam* purchaser in time.

PART II

Islamic Retail Banking Issues

3

Wealth Mobilisation by Islamic Banks: The Malaysian Case

Sudin Haron and Badrul Hisham Kamaruddin

Since its inception in 1983, Bank Islam Malaysia Berhad (BIMB) has achieved considerable success in mobilising both Muslim and non-Muslim funds in Malaysia. As a consequence of BIMB's success in providing Islamic banking products and services, the government adopted policies to encourage the development of the Islamic banking and insurance system. In addition to Islamic banks, conventional financial intermediaries were also allowed to provide products based on Islamic principles. Among the institutions that are actively involved in promoting Islamic financial products is Bank Kerjasama Rakyat Malaysia Berhad. Using content analysis, this chapter highlights the similarities and differences between BIMB and Bank Rakyat in mobilising wealth. Issues relating to business strategies and management philosophies are also addressed.

INTRODUCTION

Many criticisms have been made against the means of wealth mobilisation by conventional banks. Kuran (1986) believes that the interest used by conventional banks only benefits certain sectors of the economy, as it transfers wealth from the poor to the rich. While Islam encourages legitimate trade and commerce, hoarding is however prohibited, and zakāh is imposed on unutilised wealth. Mannan (1986) claims that wealth created by Allah belongs collectively to the whole of society. Legal ownership by the individual, that is, the right of possession, enjoyment and transfer of property, is recognised and safeguarded in Islam. However, all ownership is subject to moral obligations. Even animals have the right to a share. In this regard, while making profit from business is acceptable, the accumulation of profit without its utilisation for the betterment of the community is forbidden. As a result of this teaching, Islamic banks are expected to be sensitive to the needs of society, promote social welfare programmes and activities, establish funds for social development and make a contribution towards the poor and the needy.

The objective of this chapter is to highlight the experience of two Islamic financial institutions in Malaysia, that is, Bank Kerjasama Rakyat Malaysia Berhad (Bank Rakyat) and Bank Islam Malaysia Berhad (BIMB), in mobilising wealth. These two institutions have been selected because of their distinctive differences in operations, target customers and usage of Sharī'ah principles in their activities. The chapter is divided into seven sections. An overview of Islamic banking in Malaysia is provided in section two. Section three elaborates on the history and development of Bank Rakyat and BIMB. The deposit and lending activities of Bank Rakyat and BIMB are reported in section four. Section five examines the other activities undertaken by both institutions. Section six highlights some issues and challenges facing both institutions. Finally, section seven presents some concluding remarks.

THE HISTORY AND DEVELOPMENT OF ISLAMIC BANKING IN MALAYSIA

Malaysia's Islamic banking system is considered to be more progressive as compared with the systems in other Muslim countries (Haron and Shanmugam 2001). The Malaysian government has aspired, through its Central Bank (Bank Negara Malaysia – BNM) to have a fully-fledged Islamic banking system operating side-by-side with the country's conventional banking system. This has led to the creation of a comprehensive Islamic financial system that encompasses the Islamic banking system, non-bank Islamic financial intermediaries and Islamic financial markets.

The history of Islamic banking in Malaysia began with the establishment of Bank Islam Malaysia Berhad (BIMB) in 1983, following the enactment of the Islamic Banking Act and the Government Investment Act. The bank recorded a strong growth only a year after its inception as total assets doubled from $US44.92 million (RM170.7 million) ($US = RM3.80) at the end of 1983 to $97.32 million (RM369.8 million) at the end of 1984, with a sharp increase in deposits from $23.95 million (RM91.0 million) to $72.34 million (RM274.9 million). Loans over the same period increased from $10.71 million (RM40.7 million) to $65.74 million (RM249.8 million). This provided the impetus for the introduction of the Islamic Banking Scheme (IBS) or Skim Perbankan Islam (SPI), also known as 'Islamic counters', in 1993. The Banking and Finance Act (BAFIA) (Sections 32 and 124) was amended for this purpose.

To facilitate the institutions that participate in the IBS in solving their liquidity and investment problems, an Islamic inter-bank money market was established in 1994. Its volume of transaction exhibited rapid growth from $0.55 billion (RM2.1 billion), transacted during the first year of its operation, to $73.68 billion (RM280 billion) in 2002. In 1996 new guidelines were implemented. First, the New Financial Disclosure or GP8 requires banking institutions participating in the IBS to follow the format prescribed by BNM in presenting financial data related to their Islamic operations. Second, instead of providing Islamic products through the 'Islamic counter' concept, conventional banks are allowed to set up fully-fledged (or 'green') branches that deal exclusively with Islamic products. Third, the National Sharīʿah Advisory Council (NSAC) was established to advise BNM on Islamic banking, to coordinate Sharīʿah issues and to analyse and evaluate Sharīʿah compliance for new products or schemes submitted by banking institutions.

In October 1999 the government granted a licence for a second Islamic bank in Malaysia – Bank Muamalat Malaysia Berhad. At the end of 2002 the Islamic banking system in Malaysia therefore comprised two Islamic banks regulated and supervised under the Islamic Banking Act 1983 (IBA); and 14 commercial banks, 9 finance companies, 3 merchant banks and 7 discount houses participating in the IBS, regulated and supervised under the BAFIA 1989. Islamic banking facilities are now available in 138 fully-fledged Islamic branches and 2,065 Islamic counters. There are approximately $14 billion (RM53 billion) deposits and $9.74 billion (RM37 billion) total loans extended under the Fakulti Pengurusan Perniagaan System.

Apart from the action undertaken by BNM to foster an effective Islamic banking system, attention has also focused on applying Islamic principles to the equity market. The Islamic equity market is reflected by the presence of Islamic stockbroking operations, Islamic indices, Islamic unit trusts and a list of the Sharīʿah-approved counters issued by the Securities Commission. The participation of non-bank financial intermediaries in the Islamic banking sector has also been encouraging. A very interesting development in the evolution of Islamic banking in Malaysia came from this category. Bank Rakyat, a leading credit cooperative institution, emerged as the second financial institution in the country to conduct an exclusively Islamic banking business.

It is estimated that investors from the Islamic World own assets worth up to $1.5 trillion (RM5.7 trillion) in conventional markets (*New Straits Times* 2002). The International Islamic Financial Market, centred at Labuan in Malaysia, is currently striving to provide the impetus for the development of global Islamic financial products by forming strategic alliances with other Islamic financial centres, as well as conventional partners, and then sell these products to all investors. In this way, Islamic funds can be put to profitable use. The inauguration of the Islamic Financial Services Board (IFSB) in Kuala Lumpur on 3 November 2002 could facilitate this activity, as the Board aims to obtain greater global recognition and acceptance of Islamic banking.

THE HISTORY AND DEVELOPMENT OF BANK RAKYAT AND BIMB

Bank Rakyat was initially registered as the Rural Cooperative Apex Bank of Malaya in 1954, renamed Bank Kerjasama Malaysia Berhad in 1967, and took its present name of Bank Kerjasama Rakyat Malaysia Berhad in 1973. The bank was first established to channel funds from the Malaysian government to farmers, and to promote thrift and savings among the rural population. Over the period 1960–6, owing to its small membership, the share capital of the bank remained limited and its loans portfolio fairly static. Hence, in 1967, Bank Rakyat was reorganised and its constitution amended to extend membership to both cooperative societies and individuals. Its operation expanded to that of carrying out banking activities and giving loans to cooperatives and individuals.

In 1973, Bank Rakyat adopted a more dynamic approach in its operations and embarked upon a rapid programme of expansion. Continuing its policy of diversification, the bank extended the scope of its operations to the financing of industry, housing, agriculture, investment, and the underwriting of shares allotted to the Bumiputera community. The bank was allowed to establish subsidiaries and even accept deposits from non-members. However, the approval of loans was still restricted to members, and the bank's rapid growth at that time in terms of deposits and fund management was not reflected in lending. As a result, accumulated losses amounted to $17.82 million (RM67.7 million) at the end of 1975. In 1976, the bank's management was reorganised and in the following year the government introduced the Bank Kerjasama Rakyat Malaysia Berhad (Special Provisions) Act 1978 to strengthen the bank's management and financial position. This Act also enabled the bank to give out loans to non-members. Total resources increased from $72.76 million (RM276.5 million) at the end of 1977 to $91.82 million (RM348.9 million) at the end of 1981, reflecting the mainly long-term loans received from the government to finance the bank's reorganisation programme. The accumulated losses of the bank were reduced from a peak of $24.71 million (RM93.9 million) at the end of 1979 to $10.53 million (RM40 million) at the end of 1982. Subsequently, this improved financial position enabled the bank to expand its scope of lending from traditional agricultural-related activities to the financial sector, including bridging finance and block discounting. As a result, the share of loans extended for agricultural purposes declined, constituting only 6.6 per cent of the total loans outstanding at the end of 1987, as compared with 19.5 per cent at the end of 1980.

As a result of this expansion in its operations, a total of $98.87 million (RM375.7 million), or 54.4 per cent of loans outstanding at the end of 1987, was directed to property development, bridging finance and commercial undertakings. At the end of 1987, Bank Rakyat's accumulated losses widened to $30.68 million (RM116.6 million). The Bank Kerjasama Rakyat Malaysia Berhad (Special Provision) Act of 1978 had placed the bank directly under the Minister responsible for Cooperative Development. In the interest of its members, the Minister of Finance and the Minister of National and Rural Development gave the necessary approval for Bank Rakyat to utilise its Capital Reserve of $25.45 million (RM96.7 million) to write off its accumulated losses of $22.79 million (RM86.6 million) in 1989. With the writing off of these accumulated losses, Bank Rakyat is now free from the restrictions imposed on it by the Act on matters pertaining to the declaration of dividend.

Recently, in February 2002, the bank came under a third Act, the Development Financial Institution Act (DFIA), which appoints BNM as the supervisory and regulatory authority. By virtue of this Act, risk management and tight internal controls became fundamental concerns to ensure improved future performance. Bank Rakyat is now the leading credit cooperative institution in the country operating on Islamic principles. The principal activities of the bank are those of a cooperative bank, accepting deposits and providing personal, leasing and other financing facilities to its members. The bank also pioneered the provision of an Islamic pawnbroking service using the principle of *qarḍ al-ḥasan* (beneficial loan). The bank introduced Islamic banking in 1993, and from 1 January 1997 became the second financial institution in the country to conduct only Islamic banking business. In 2001, the bank's Islamic assets represented 1.56 per cent of total assets of the whole banking industry, up from 0.96 per cent in 1998, 1.11 per cent in 1999 and 1.27 per cent in 2000. 80.0 per cent of the bank's business is in retail banking and the remainder in corporate banking. By February 2002, the bank had 95 branches spread all over the country.

Bank Islam Malaysia Berhad (BIMB) was incorporated by the IBA (No. 276) on 1 March 1983 and began its operations in July of the same year. With an authorised capital of $131.58 million (RM500 million) and a branch in Kuala Lumpur, the initial paid-up capital of $21.05 million (RM80 million) was distributed among the Malaysian government and five other institutions, namely State Religious Councils ($5.26 million) (RM20 million); Federal Agencies ($3.16 million) (RM12 million); State Religious Agencies ($0.79 million) (RM3 million); the Pilgrims Management and Fund Board ($2.63 million) (RM10 million); and the Muslim Welfare Organisation of Malaysia ($1.32 million) (RM5 million). The bank's authorised capital and paid-up capital have increased gradually, standing at $526 million (RM2 billion) and $148.16 million (RM563 million) respectively by 2000, to accommodate the growth of its assets and to position itself better to meet future expansion and growth. It is also noteworthy that the Malaysian government strongly backed the bank's establishment.

As provided in the IBA, BIMB carries out banking business similar to other commercial banks, but in conformity with Sharīʿah principles. The bank was listed on the main board of the Kuala Lumpur Stock Exchange (KLSE) on 17 January 1992. In terms of branch network, the bank has 82 branches nationwide that offer 45 innovative and sophisticated Islamic banking products and services that are comparable to those of their conventional counterparts. BIMB has several subsidiaries that specialise in family and general *takāful* (Islamic insurance) businesses, fund management, stockbroking (BIMB Securities), and the provision of leasing and nominee services, training, consultancy, research and development, and academic services. These have all contributed to the growth of BIMB, and by the end of 2002 its total assets were $3.18 billion (RM12.1 billion), while total deposits were $2.84 billion (RM10.8 billion) and total loans were $1.50 billion (RM5.7 billion).

THE DEPOSIT AND LENDING ACTIVITIES OF BANK RAKYAT AND BIMB

The analysis of Bank Rakyat and BIMB's performances was based on their achievements for the period 1998–2002. Like any other financial institutions, both Bank Rakyat and BIMB are dependent on the depositors' money as a major source of funds. Table 3.1 and Table 3.2 show the type of deposit accounts accepted from customers of Bank Rakyat and BIMB respectively. The growth in deposits over the period of both banks was probably due to public confidence and acceptance of Islamic banking, as well as rates of return on deposits that are comparable with the conventional banking industry (see Table 3.3). In addition, according to Wilson (1995), the concept of Islamic banking attracted Muslim depositors mostly from among those who already had accounts with conventional banks, rather than clients who had not acquired the banking habit. It is also noteworthy that according to the manager of the accounts and budget department of Bank Rakyat headquarters, the majority of depositors are Muslims. However, according to Haron et al. (1994), research findings indicate that not all Muslim depositors of Islamic banks are Islamically motivated.

Table 3.1: Composition of deposits ($) and annual growth (%), Bank Rakyat, 1998–2002

Deposits from Customers	*1998*	*%*	*1999*	*%*	*2000*	*%*	*2001*	*%*	*2002*	*%*
Al-Wadī'ah	121	16.35	141	16.53	168	19.15	202	20.24	223	10.40
Al-Muḍārabah/ Financing certificate of Bank Rakyat	811	71.74	1,247	54.76	1,688	35.36	2,315	37.14	2,722	17.58
Al-Rahnu Fund	0		0		0		10	–	9	(10)
Total	932	60.97	1,388	48.93	1,856	33.72	2,527	36.15	2,954	16.90

US$1=RM3.80
Source: Bank Rakyat Annual Reports, 1998–2002.

For Bank Rakyat, total deposits increased from $932 million in 1998 to $2,954 million at the end of 2002 (see Table 3.1). However, its yearly growth fluctuated for the reported period. It increased by 60.97 per cent in 1998 and 36.15 per cent in 2001, but continued to increase at declining rates for the years 1999, 2000 and 2002 (49.03 per cent, 33.62 per cent and 16.90 per cent respectively). As shown in Table 3.1, the amount of deposits increased from $121 million in 1998 to $223 million in 2002 for the *al-wadī'ah* savings account facility, and from $811 million in 1998 to $2,722 billion in 2002 for the *al-muḍārabah* (profit-sharing) general investment account facility. The yearly growth figures show that both deposit facilities increased at various rates, with *al-wadī'ah* savings accounts enjoying an upward trend for the years 1998, 1999, 2000 and 2001 (16.35 per cent, 16.53 per cent, 19.15 per cent and 20.24 per cent respectively). However, growth declined to 10.40 per cent in 2002. Unlike the *al-muḍārabah* general investment account, even though there was growth, this exhibited a decline for the years 1998, 1999 and 2000 (71.74 per cent, 54.76 per cent and 35.36 per cent respectively), but the trend reversed in 2001 when the percentage increase was 37.14. However, in 2002 the growth rate declined again to 17.58 per cent. This may be due to stiff competition from BIMB, Bank Muamalat and the IBS banks. The above reporting shows that the *al-wadī'ah* savings account has gained acceptance among depositors. The declining growth trend of these deposit accounts, particularly *al-muḍārabah*, will affect the ability of Bank Rakyat to mobilise wealth, as capital accumulation is a vital factor for Islamic banks. It is therefore important for Bank Rakyat to increase its resources by attracting savings depositors. Even though the bank itself has encouraged long-term rather than short-term deposits through its profit distribution policy on investment accounts (with lengthy periods, the rates of return compare very favourably with the interest paid by conventional banks – see Table 3.3), the bulk of *al-muḍārabah* are still short-term in nature. This affects the investment portfolio, thus affecting Bank Rakyat's ability to mobilise wealth.

Table 3.2: Composition of deposits ($) and annual growth (%), BIMB, 1998–2002

Deposits	*1998*	*%*	*1999*	*%*	*2000*	*%*	*2001*	*%*	*2002*	*%*
Current	226	(6.52)	334	48.32	324	(3.20)	406	25.31	522	28.68
Savings	189	(3.34)	195	3.51	201	2.99	235	17.03	270	14.52
Muḍārabah Fund	415	(23.32)	854	105.90	1,425	66.80	1725	21.06	2,107	22.17
Total	830	(15.05)	1,383	66.63	1,950	41.00	2,366	21.33	2,899	22.53

US$1=RM3.80
Source: Bank Islam Annual Reports, 1998–2002.

Table 3.3: Rates of return on 12-month deposits (%)

Year	*Commercial Banks*	*BIMB*	*Bank Rakyat*
1998	5.74	6.75	9.54
1999	3.95	4.66	5.98
2000	4.08	3.88	5.10
2001	3.71	3.77	4.60
2002	4.00	3.33	4.23

Sources: BNM, Monthly Statistical Bulletin; BIMB; Bank Rakyat.

For BIMB, total deposits increased from $830 million in 1998 to $2,899 million at the end of 2002. Similar to Bank Rakyat, growth in deposits, however, fluctuated for the reported period. It increased by 66.63 per cent in 1999, but continued to increase at declining rates for the years 2000 and 2001 (41.00 per cent and 21.33 per cent respectively). However, the trend reversed in 2002 when the percentage increase was 22.53.

As for the composition of deposit facilities, not many variations were found in the trend of growth rates. As shown in Table 3.2, the amount of deposits increased from $415 million in 1998 to $2,107 billion in 2002 for the *muḍārabah* facility; $226 million in 1998 to $522 million in 2002 for the current account facility; and $189 million in 1998 to $270 million in 2002 for the savings account facility. In terms of yearly growth figures, all the deposit facilities increased at various rates. For the *muḍārabah* facility (comprising savings accounts and investment accounts), the bank reported a contraction in 1998 of 23.32 per cent, and subsequently the annual growth continued to increase at declining rates for the years 1999, 2000 and 2001 (105.9 per cent, 66.8 per cent and 21.06 per cent respectively), with the trend reversing in 2002 when the percentage increase was 22.17. In the late 1990s both the savings and investment accounts that operate on the *muḍārabah* principle were lumped as one figure in the annual reports. From 2000 onwards the annual report gives a separate figure for each. According to an officer in charge of deposits in BIMB, even during the late 1990s until 2002, of *muḍārabah* deposits, investment accounts made up the bulk of the total. All the accounts reported a tremendous increase in growth in 2001, except for *muḍārabah* deposits. The weakening growth of the savings account (an increase by only 6.0 per cent from the 2000 figure as opposed to a 32.0 per cent increase for the investment account) probably contributed to lower growth in *muḍārabah* deposits in 2001. Bank Islam accepted *muḍārabah* deposits for periods ranging from six months to five years and over. It is relevant to note that the bulk of total *muḍārabah* deposits were for a period of one year or less.

Similar to Bank Rakyat, the deposit structure of BIMB did not favour equity

Table 3.4: Modes of financing (US$ million) and percentage of total financing of BIMB

Financing	*1998*	%	*1999*	%	*2000*	%	*2001*	%	*2002*	%
Bay' bi thaman al-ājil	561	69.00	618	65.70	684	62.40	808	56.30	915	58.44
Ijārah muntahiah bit tamlīk							76	5.30	46	2.87
Ijārah	34	4.10	37	4.00	37	3.30	28	2.00	29	1.87
Bay' al-'īnah									5.59	0.35
Mushārakah	3	0.40	5	0.50	5	0.50	47	3.30	57	3.65
Muḍārabah	5	0.60	5	0.50	3	0.30	5	0.30	11	0.68
Murābaḥah	173	21.20	233	24.70	304	27.70	343	23.90	399	25.48
Qarḍ al-ḥasan	24	3.00	28	3.00	54	5.00	111	7.70	131	8.36
Staff Financing	14	1.70	15	1.60	9	0.80	17	1.20	24	1.53
Total	814	100	941	100	1,096	100	1,435	100	1,612	100

US$1=RM3.80
Source: BIMB Annual Reports, 1998–2002.

financing, which is of a long-term nature. This affects the ability of both banks to mobilise wealth, now and in the future. It is also noteworthy that according to an officer in charge of deposits at the bank, the majority of depositors are Muslims. Previous studies on BIMB's performance for the period 1983–1993 indicated that most deposits with the bank were in the form of savings or investment accounts, rather than current accounts. According to Wilson (1995), clients viewed these accounts as a repository for precautionary and savings funds, rather than as transaction balances. The deposits tended to be regarded as long-term holdings, savings to cover, for example, the deposit on a house, the purchase of a major consumer item such as a car, education fees, pilgrimage expenses, payment for a marriage feast or the cost of health treatment in old age. However, the trend described above is slightly different during the reported period (1998–2002) as savings account deposits reported a slower growth than current account deposits (see Table 3.2). The preference for investment accounts remains stable, as in earlier periods.

Table 3.4 gives BIMB's modes of financing. These give us a picture of how well the bank has utilised its resources to generate revenues that in turn could mobilise wealth. BIMB's five most important modes of financing are *bay' bi thaman al-ājil*, *ijārah*, *muḍārabah*, *mushārakah* and *murābaḥah*.

As indicated in Table 3.4, BIMB's total financing and investment extended to its customers amounted to $1,612 billion in 2002, about two times the level reached in 1998 ($814 million). As for the composition of financing and investment facilities, there appear to be significant variations in terms of relative share in the total outlay for certain facilities. For instance, *murābaḥah* financing, second after *bay' bi thaman al-ājil* in terms of absolute and relative share, grew year after year in absolute terms, its relative share in total outlay also growing in 1998, 1999 and 2000 (21.2 per cent, 24.7 per cent, and 27.7 per cent respectively). However, the trend reversed in 2001 with a 23.9 per cent decline, but in 2002 the rate rose again to 25.48 per cent. *Mushārakah* (equity-participating partnership) investments showed a marked improvement in 2001 (3.3 per cent) and 2002 (3.65 per cent). In other words, its relative share in the total outlay increased remarkably from 0.5 per cent in 2000 to 3.65 per cent in 2002. The relative importance of *ijārah* was at a declining rate for the years 1998, 1999, 2000, 2001 and 2002 (4.1 per cent, 4.0 per cent, 3.3 per cent, 2.0 per cent, and 1.87 per cent respectively). The relative importance of *muḍārabah* also experienced a declining trend for the years 1998, 1999 and 2000 (0.6 per cent, 0.5 per cent and 0.3 per cent respectively), remained stable at 0.3 per cent in 2001 and its relative share increased to 0.68 per cent in 2002. Interestingly, the absolute and relative importance of *qarḍ al-ḥasan* has grown over time. Its share in the total increased during 1999, 2000, 2001 and 2002 (3.0 per cent, 5.0 per cent, 7.7 per cent, and 8.36 per cent respectively).

The most striking feature is the significance of *bay' bi thaman al-'ājil* (also referred to as *bay' al-mu'ajjal* in the literature), which accounted for the bulk of the total in terms of absolute and relative importance. Its share in the total increased at a declining rate during 1998, 1999, 2000 and 2001 (69.0 per cent, 65.7 per cent, 62.4 per cent and 56.3 per cent respectively). However, the trend

Table 3.5: Modes of financing (US$ million) and percentage of total financing of Bank Rakyat

	1998	%	*1999*	%	*2000*	%	*2001*	%	*2002*	%
Bay' 'al-'īnah	586	71.00	799	70.60	1,080	72.00	1,273	71.93	1,502	67.03
Al-Tarkhis	46	5.60	31	2.80	66	4.40	77	4.37	60	2.70
Al-Ijārah	1	0.10	5	0.40	1	0.10	1	0.06	66	2.93
Al-Istiṣnā'	19	2.30	18	1.60	15	1.00	18	1.03	–	–
Bay' bi thaman al-ājil	160	19.40	264	23.40	321	21.30	379	21.40	491	21.92
Ar-Rahnu	13	1.60	14	1.20	18	1.20	21	1.21	32	1.41
Qarḍ al-ḥasan									90	4.01
Total	826	100	1,131	100	1,501	100	1,770	100	2,241	100

Total financing – before provision for bad and doubtful financing.
Source: Bank Rakyat Annual Reports, 1998–2002.

reversed in 2002 with a percentage increase of 58.44. *Bay' bi thaman al-ājil* and *murābaḥah* are similar in their operations, except that the former recognises payment in instalments. They were once criticised because of the resemblance of their profit margin to interest, hence the term 'back door to *ribā*' *w*was applied. This could influence the borrower to shift to conventional modes of financing. It could also be a possible reason for the declining trend of *bay' bi thaman al-ājil* over the period 1998–2001.

As indicated in Table 3.5, Bank Rakyat's total financing and investment extended to its customers amounted to $2,241 million in 2002, nearly three times the level reached in 1998 ($826 million). As for the composition of financing and investment facilities, there also appear to be significant variations in terms of the relative share in the total outlay for certain facilities. The most striking feature is that *bay' al-'īnah* accounted for the bulk of total financing. This mode of financing grew year after year in absolute terms, but its relative share in the total outlay for the years 1998, 1999, 2000, 2001 and 2002 fluctuated over time (71.0 per cent, 70.6 per cent, 72.0 per cent, 71.93 per cent and 67.03 per cent respectively). *Bay' al-'īnah* is a type of financing based on the concept of buying and reselling to acquire immediate cash. With the *bay' al-'īnah* concept, customers receive immediate cash and repay the bank via instalments within a period agreed upon by both parties. That this represented the largest portion of the share of total financing indicates that Bank Rakyat played its role in helping the general public to acquire immediate cash for general purposes. The second largest share was attributable to *bay' bi thaman al-ājil*. Again, *bay' bi thaman al-ājil* grew year after year in absolute terms, but its relative share in total outlay also fluctuated over time for the years 1998, 1999 and 2000 (19.4 per cent, 23.4 per cent and 21.3 per cent respectively) and increased modestly in 2001 and 2002 (21.4 per cent and 21.92 per cent respectively).

Al-tarkhis financing grew year after year in absolute terms, but its relative share in total outlay fluctuated for the years 1998, 1999, 2000, 2001 and 2002 (5.6 per cent, 2.8 per cent, 4.4 per cent, 4.37 per cent and 2.7 per cent respectively). *Al-istiṣnā'* financing also fluctuated, both in absolute terms and relative share in total outlay for the years 1998, 1990, 2000 and 2001 (2.3 per cent, 1.6 per cent, 1.0 per cent, and 1.03 per cent respectively). Interestingly, *ijārah* financing declined drastically, both absolutely and relatively (from 0.4 per cent in 1999 to 0.06 per cent in 2001), but showed a marked increase in 2002, when it rose to 2.93 per cent. This implies that longer-term financing of one to five years through leasing was considered unfavourably by Bank Rakyat. Finally, *ar-rahnu* financing grew modestly in absolute terms, but its relative importance increased at a declining rate for the years 1998 and 1999 (1.6 per cent and 1.2 per cent respectively), but increased between 2001 and 2002 (1.21 per cent and 1.41 per cent respectively). With the introduction of *ar-rahnu* in 1993, the public, especially the poor, have benefited much from a bank scheme that enables them to pawn their jewels for immediate cash without having to pay any interest. Even though *ar-rahnu* showed only modest growth from 1998 to 2002, this facility demonstrates the bank's concern for the general public, and in particular its willingness to help those in difficulties so that they do not have to resort to usurious loans.

OTHER ACTIVITIES UNDERTAKEN BY BOTH BANKS

The methods of financing offered by Islamic banks are of a wider spectrum than conventional banks. Specifically, Islamic banks provide two kinds of services: economic services for individuals or companies, with some service charge approved by the Sharī'ah for banking services; and social services. Islamic banks try to maintain goodwill by helping those in need and establishing funds for social development. The goals of these two services should complement each other so that they benefit all. On the quantitative side, Islamic banks have generally done well in becoming profitable institutions, yet they have maintained the liquidity position of their depositors and shareholders. However, their contribution to socio-economic development has been limited.

Socio-economic activities

In order to determine how far Bank Rakyat and BIMB have contributed towards attaining socio-economic goals, an attempt is made to assess each bank's performance in terms of: (1) financing on the basis of *qarḍ al-ḥasan* (benevolent loans); (2) the distribution of each bank's financing; (3) each bank's *zakāh* contribution; and (4) overdrafts and activities associated with the preservation of Islamic culture. The analysis of Bank Rakyat and BIMB's performances was based on their achievements for the period 1998–2002, with 1998 chosen as the starting year for both banks in order to explain the performance of the two financial institutions after the Asian Financial Crisis. Also, Bank Rakyat became the second financial institution in the country to conduct Islamic banking business in 1997. Finally, these two financial institutions were chosen as they have been at the forefront of the Islamic banking system in Malaysia.

As indicated in Table 3.6, over the reporting period 1998–2002 *qarḍ al-ḥasan* was the only mode of financing disbursed by BIMB that exhibited an upward trend (3.0 per cent, 3.0 per cent, 5.0 per cent, 7.7 per cent and 8.36 per cent respectively). This represents a substantial rise compared to the performance of BIMB during the 1984–8 period when the relative share of *qarḍ al-ḥasan* in total financing was the lowest year after year, except from 1987 through 1988 where its relative share was double that of *muḍārabah* financing. Interestingly, in 2002 *qarḍ al-ḥasan* held the third-highest share of total financing. Zakariya Man

Table 3.6: Percentage of *qarḍ al-ḥasan* to total financing and growth rates of zakāh of BIMB and Bank Rakyat

	1998 $m	%	*1999* $m	%	*2000* $m	%	*2001* $m	%	*2002* $m	%
Qarḍ al-ḥasan										
Bank Islam	24	3.00	28	3.00	54	5.00	111	7.70	131	8.36
Bank Rakyat	13	1.60	14	1.20	18	1.20	21	1.21	122	5.42
Zakāh										
Bank Islam	0.21	50.25	0.32	233	1.05	(32.40)	0.71	(58.32)	0.30	n/a
Bank Rakyat	0.42	66.72	3.21	19	3.82	(16.71)	3.18	46.14	4.65	n/a

Source: Annual Reports.

(1987) evaluated BIMB's performance of *qarḍ al-ḥasan* for the period 1984–91 and found that the relative share of this method of financing to total financing was very minimal, in the range of 0.06 per cent to 0.1 per cent. Based on these earlier results, BIMB was accused of generating higher profits while neglecting its welfare-oriented operations.

For Bank Rakyat, over the 1998–2001 period the mode of financing that is based on the concept of *qarḍ al-ḥasan* is *ar-rahnu*. However, in 2002 the absolute figure as indicated in Table 3.6 comprised both *qarḍ al-ḥasan* and *ar-rahnu*. Out of the total financial advances of $122 million, *ar-rahnu* accounted for only $31.5 million. Even though there was yearly growth for the absolute figure, this facility's relative share to total financing declined over the years 1998 and 1999 (1.6 per cent and 1.2 per cent respectively), but increased over the years 2001 and 2002 (1.21 per cent and 5.42 per cent respectively). Bank Rakyat should have performed better than BIMB in providing this facility as it is not a commercial bank. A commercial bank has to cater for all sorts of financing needs, so it is not possible to finance all needs on the basis of *qarḍ al-ḥasan* or *ar-rahnu*.

Zakāh is meant to redistribute the wealth and the income of the rich to help the poor and the needy. Since BIMB and Bank Rakyat follow the rules of the Sharīʿah, they have to pay *zakāh* on their own resources. BIMB has been paying zakāh since its inception in 1984, while Bank Rakyat has paid *zakāh* since 1993. BIMB's *zakāh* contribution ranged from $0.21 million in 1998 to $0.30 million in 2002, depending on the profitability of its operations (Table 3.6). Bank Rakyat's *zakāh* contribution showed a growth only for the years 2000 and 2002 (19.0 per cent and 46.14 per cent respectively). However, in terms of yearly absolute figures, Bank Rakyat's contribution is larger. Bank Rakyat's *zakāh* contribution decreased slightly in 2001 to $3.18 million, but increased again in 2002 to $4.65 million.

The distribution of BIMB and Bank Rakyat's customer financing by sector

An examination of which sectors of the economy have benefited most from Bank Rakyat and BIMB's operations shows the extent of each bank's contribution towards mobilising wealth. Evidently, the allocation of funds disbursed by BIMB exhibited considerable diversity, covering nearly all sectors (see Table 3.7). Throughout the period 1998–2002, the largest percentage of financing went towards house purchases. Despite the Asian Financial Crisis, housing loans disbursed by BIMB (see Table 3.7) and Bank Rakyat (see Table 3.8) remained strong in 1997 and 1998 due mainly to the government's effort during the crisis to ensure the availability of funds for the housing sector and to promote home ownership. The second-largest sector the banks invested in was manufacturing, followed by real estate and construction. According to Wilson (1995), investments in manufacturing were much greater in proportion to most Islamic banks in other Muslim countries, largely reflecting Malaysia's aspiration to become a newly industrialised country by 2020.

BIMB's financing by sector is shown in Table 3.7. Throughout the reporting period, 1998–2002, more than 50.0 per cent of its financing was extended to consumer credit, largely reflecting Bank Rakyat's status as the main Malay consumers' choice of financing. This was followed by the real estate (purchase of landed property) sector, general commerce and the purchase of securities. The agriculture sector benefited very little from Bank Rakyat's financing. This is inconsistent with a statement made by the bank's managing director in 2001, whereby he claimed that Bank Rakyat would place added emphasis on the agriculture sector being promoted by the government, especially in boosting the nation's food production. In fact, throughout the period the relative share of financing for the agriculture sector was better for BIMB than Bank Rakyat. The

Table 3.7: Distribution by sector of BIMB's financing (%)

Sector	*1998*	*1999*	*2000*	*2001*	*2002*
Agriculture, mining and quarrying	4.81	5.25	4.67	7.23	4.18
Manufacturing	14.78	18.82	15.34	16.54	17.13
Real estate and construction	15.14	12.48	19.29	17.72	21.58
Housing	35.59	37.41	27.79	21.14	22.57
General commerce	10.40	8.41	3.26	1.54	3.58
Finance, insurance and business services	1.08	2.36	2.69	1.57	2.72
Consumption credit	4.03	5.37	5.62	9.04	5.59
Others	14.17	9.90	21.34	25.22	22.65
Total	100.00	100.00	100.00	100.00	100.00

Source: BIMB Annual Reports, 1998–2002.

Table 3.8: Distribution by sector of Bank Rakyat's financing (%)

Sector	*1998*	*1999*	*2000*	*2001*	*2002*
Agriculture, mining and quarrying	1.63	1.76	0.88	0.88	0.73
Construction	0.91	0.69	0.00	0.53	1.55
Purchase of landed property	16.08	16.92	11.93	17.61	19.24
General commerce	7.05	6.29	3.32	10.58	6.12
Purchase of securities	9.06	8.25	5.45	4.40	1.66
Purchase of transport vehicles	2.12	1.80	1.59	0.61	1.39
Consumption credit	62.69	63.16	67.01	62.94	67.85
Others	0.46	1.13	9.82	2.45	1.46
Total	100.00	100.00	100.00	100.00	100.00

Source: Bank Rakyat Annual Reports, 1998–2002.

latter's product, Skim Pembiayaan Ekonomi Desa (SPED) or Financing Scheme for the Rural Economy, a joint venture with a government agency, is slow at achieving its goals, possibly due to a lack of local political support. This scheme, which applies the *qarḍ al-ḥasan* principle, provides financing for working capital and the purchase of equipment to facilitate businesses that generate income for the rural economy. The low percentage uptake could also imply that farmers are still unaware of the facilities offered by Bank Rakyat. In addition, as Bank Rakyat has expanded its scope of operations from agricultural-based activities to encompass a wide range of other financing facilities including personal and property loans, as well as hire-purchase, leasing, bridging finance and mortgage facilities, it is not possible for the bank to focus its financing on one need alone.

ISSUES AND CHALLENGES

The fulfilment of socio-economic objectives

According to Khan (1983), the purpose of Islamic banks is to promote, foster and develop banking products and services based on Islamic principles. In addition, they are also responsible for promoting the establishment of investment companies, enterprises and concerns that will be engaged in business activities acceptable and consistent with the Sharī'ah. The main principles of Islamic banking comprise the prohibition of *ribā* in all forms of transactions, and the undertaking of business and trade activities on the basis of fair and legitimate profit. Islamic banks are to give *zakāh* and develop an environment that benefits society. Similarly, Ali (1988) believes that Islamic banks cannot be introduced merely by eliminating *ribā*; they also have to adopt Islamic principles of social justice and introduce laws, practices, procedures and instruments that facilitate the maintenance and dispensation of justice, equity and fairness. Like other business entities, Islamic banks are also expected to make profits from their operations because it is considered unjust by Islamic banks if they are unable to provide sufficient returns to the depositors who entrust their money to them (Mirakhor 1987).

The important point that can be concluded from the above is that Islamic banks have to incorporate both profit and morality into their objectives. In the context of mobilisation of wealth for Muslims by Islamic banks, we can associate morality with the socio-economic function. Even though the corporate objectives of Bank Rakyat and BIMB succinctly describe the aspiration of the banks to enhance the social development of the general public, in practice this aspiration is usually downplayed. Take for instance the positioning of this objective on each bank's list of corporate objectives. At Bank Rakyat, the objective is positioned third in a list of eight objectives. Obviously, this positioning implies the bank's seriousness in its concern for society's social development. Yet in practice, what was planned paled into insignificance for Bank Rakyat. BIMB, on the other hand, positioned the objective last on its list of six objectives. In the context of its fulfilment of the socio-economic function, BIMB, however, performed better than Bank Rakyat, especially in so far as its activities are predominantly commercial. In fact, BIMB's commitment towards fulfilling this objective has improved over time, as indicated in Table 3.4 illustrating the performance of *qarḍ al-ḥasan* in BIMB and Table 3.5 on the performance of *ar-rahnu* in Bank Rakyat during the period 1998–2002. The issue here is whether the strategies to achieve the objective are workable.

According to Razali (1995), the socio-economic activities offered by Islamic banks may be classified into two main categories. First is *qarḍ al-ḥasan*, as Islamic banks can offer *ribā*-free loans on such matters as education and medical expenses for some of their clients. Since its inception, the Jordan Islamic Bank has allocated some portion of its net profit to be used as a levy to be paid to Jordanian universities and funds for scientific research and vocational training. In addition, the Islami Bank Bangladesh and Bank Muamalat Indonesia are other Islamic banks that are actively involved in promoting social activities. Islamic banks can also offer their clients special facilities under the terms and conditions associated with *qarḍ al-ḥasan* such as the provision of overdraft facilities to customers who need to draw more funds than they have at the banks, but with an agreement not to exceed an upper limit. Usually, *qarḍ al-ḥasan* and overdrafts are provided for productive purposes in various fields in order to help bank customers raise their standard of living. The funds employed are usually part of the overall profits of the bank.

Second is funds for social purposes. To contribute to economic development by extra banking activities, Islamic banks may establish and administer special funds for various worthy social purposes. For instance, the *zakāh* fund. To reiterate the significance of the socio-economic function, it is important to mention that *zakāh* may well generate sufficient funds to ensure *niṣāb*, a minimum acceptable standard of living, for all members of the Muslim community, but its impact on narrowing income differentials may turn out to be negligible. In Islam, *zakāh* is not merely a contribution, but also a 'due' or a 'claim'. A person paying *zakāh* is not primarily doing a favour to the recipient or beneficiary of *zakāh*, but is rather meeting a claim on himself or herself by purifying wealth. Therefore, if both Bank Rakyat and BIMB claim that they have been paying *zakāh* since their inception and that they also perform a small portion of the distribution themselves apart from the main responsibility of the *Zakāh* Collection Centre or Pusat Pungutan *Zakāh* (PPZ), this is not enough to warrant any claim the two banks make about having fulfilled their socio-economic function.

Apart from the *zakāh* fund, Islamic banks can also participate in the process of long-term development by investing a modest proportion of their own resources from which they may not receive immediate returns, such as by contributing funds to cooperative ventures. For instance, in 2001 BIMB Holdings Berhad injected additional capital amounting to $526,000 (RM2 million) and $5.3 million (RM20 million) in two of its subsidiary companies, BIMB Venture Capital (BIMBVC) and BIMB *Mushārakah* Satu (BIMBMS) respectively. BIMBVC is the first Islamic venture capital company in Malaysia and BIMBMS is a fund company. The former was created in line with the government's increased effort to promote venture capital as an alternative mode of financing. It is a syndicate for large project financing, usually involving infrastructure, examples being the PUTRA LRT transportation system and Kuala Lumpur International Airport, KLIA. The BIMBMS is a fund company that facilitates joint venture financing in corporate and consumer financing. This fund company is expected to be the first of many more fund companies to be established in the future.

The commitment of Islamic banks towards fulfilling the socio-economic function varies from one Islamic country to another. In the case of Bank Rakyat and BIMB, they are operating in a competitive market environment of a mix of Islamic and conventional banking systems. In this regard, the business and socio-economic activities they undertake are used as an indicator of their commitment towards moral obligations. According to Algaoud and Lewis (2001), if the concept of Islamic banking takes hold in a significant way, the institutions need to provide a full range of commercial banking services while still conforming to Islamic rules and norms. For this purpose, the activities of the bank have to be commercial, as opposed to predominantly socio-economic. According to Wong (1995), BIMB has been accused of concentrating on profit maximisation, while neglecting its welfare-oriented operations. However, BIMB and Bank Rakyat have to compete with conventional banks to attract deposits and investments, as these are their main source of funds. In other words, Islamic banking is still in the making.

Religiosity attributes in the deposit and lending activities of Islamic banks

Religion does not appear to be the main, or even a major, motive prompting people to use an Islamic bank, as indicated by Haron et al. (1994). This issue is critical, as Malaysia is a country in which Muslims represent half of its population, and whose coalition government is led by UMNO, a Muslim-based party. In addition, according to Badrul and Rohani (2002), the Islamic religion has greater influence on the buying behaviour of Muslim consumers compared to other factors, such as age, gender, occupation, salary and education. What can be concluded from the above is that the influence of religion has positive implications on the deposit and lending activities of Islamic banks. In this regard, Islamic banks should stress their religious appeal, and not simply the efficiency of their operations and use of technology, in their strategy to attract customers.

Therefore, it is particularly important for the BNM and Islamic banks to raise awareness continually about the Islamic banking system among Muslims in Malaysia. Relevant verses from the Qur'ān in relation to an attribute can easily promote the system, as those verses educate Muslims on the benefits to be gained here and now, and hereafter. This is an effective and easy way to remind Muslims about their responsibility. According to Lewis and Algaoud (2001), some Muslim economists have argued that in a proper Islamic economic environment, Islamic religious ideology acts as its own enforcement mechanism. For instance, on the asset side of the balance sheet, the 'religious variable' may act as a counter to incentive difficulties. In effect, this minimises the transaction costs arising from incentive issues.

For business clients the religious appeal could have important implications for two types of financing contracts offered by Islamic banking, namely *muḍārabah* and *mushārakah*. To date, because knowledge of Islamic banking among Muslims in Malaysia is shallow, Islamic banks have failed to use *muḍārabah* and *mushārakah* as their main business products. As lending has been the traditional approach in banking, Muslims thought that only *murābaḥah* and *bay' bi thaman al-ājil* serve as the best alternative to lending. With an in-depth understanding of Islamic banking, Muslims will also realise that leverage is no longer an attractive method of wealth creation and also be able to understand the impact of leverage on risk-sharing. As Islam teaches mankind to uphold justice, in the economics of production this principle has put labour on a par with capital. For instance, in *muḍārabah*, the worker or *muḍārib* will not receive a fixed wage, but instead a share in the profits generated from the venture. This shows the importance given to labour as an indispensable input that can absorb risk and therefore has the right to profit.

CONCLUSIONS

This chapter highlights several issues and challenges related to the mobilisation of wealth by Islamic banks in Malaysia. Even though the Islamic banking system in Malaysia is recognised to be more progressive as compared with the systems operating in other Muslim countries, it should not be viewed in isolation, but should be seen in the context of the overall Islamic reform that has been taking place in Malaysia. The majority of the depositors in BIMB and Bank Rakyat are Muslims, and their patronage of the Islamic banking system is important to expand the deposit base; which in turn could boost financing and investment, and eventually the ability to mobilise wealth for Muslims. It is worth reiterating that there is much more to Islamic banking than the elimination of *ribā*. Even though BIMB belongs to the commercial charter, it cannot run away from its moral obligations to serve the *ummah*. The same applies to Bank Rakyat. Both banks have been trying to fulfil their socio-economic responsibility, but their efforts have been modest and fall short of the level required. In order to enhance their performance in this area, it is suggested that the banks should depend more on non-government organisations. It is also recommended that both banks should strive to find out what the banking needs of the community are and devise the means to meet those needs within the framework of the Sharīʿah. When this situation prevails, society will be confident that Islam is a religion that promotes moral obligation not only between mankind and God, but also between human beings. Realising the superiority of the Islamic banking system in promoting the welfare of mankind, the whole of society will ultimately adopt the Islamic banking system not only as an alternative to the conventional banking system, but also as the main choice in their banking transactions.

According to Chapra (1985), Islamic banking transactions should not be solely profit-oriented, but instead be aimed at the needs of the Islamic society overall. He suggests the introduction of a comprehensive Islamic financial system in order to achieve these twin goals. He envisages that there are differences in the functions, scope and responsibilities of the institutions concerned. Most importantly, each of the institutions is seen as an essential component of the integrity of the system and as such is necessary for the fulfilment of the twin goals, particularly socio-economic goals. As Malaysia already has such a system, the wealth mobilisation of Muslims' responsibility can be dispersed to all levels of the system, rather than concentrating it on the Islamic banks and the dual-counter banks. Bank Rakyat is still in its infancy as a fully-fledged Islamic bank, and moreover it works under considerable handicap as three existing acts govern its operations.

Past experience has shown that many patrons of BIMB have no qualms about shifting their funds between Bank Islam and interest-based conventional banks, depending on which bank pays more (Ariff 1988). Even marginal changes in the rate of return seem to have resulted in substantial movements of funds. The implication is that not all depositors of BIMB are Islamically motivated. In a situation where funds are highly sensitive to even small changes in rates of return and mobile in response to small differentials in rates of return, it would be hazardous for the bank to commit deposit funds in long-term portfolios such as *mushārakah* and *muḍārabah*. To put it differently, the market for *mushārakah* seems somewhat limited, while that for *muḍārabah* is beset with pitfalls. BIMB lacks the management skills needed for project evaluation, supervision and control of *muḍārabah* deals (Wong 1995). In this regard, the non-bank financial institutions that are ancillary institutions of the Islamic banking sector can take the role of supplementing BIMB and Bank Rakyat by mobilising capital through equity participations and profit-sharing deposits for investment purposes.

Apart from mobilising capital, as these institutions are different from each other according to the nature of the financing activity undertaken, those projects and sectors of the economy that might not be attractive to BIMB and Bank Rakyat, but which are nevertheless important for the mobilisation of Muslims' wealth, could be financed by specialised credit institutions. Their fields of operation could include farmers, artisans and other small businesses and entrepreneurs. Therefore, this communal role (that is, the dispersal of social welfare responsibilities and religious requirements to all levels of the financial system) explicitly adds an extra parameter to the objective function of the Islamic financial agent. In support of the above, theoretically, one of the main selling points of Islamic banking, unlike conventional banking, is its concern for the viability of the project and the profitability of the operation, rather than the size of the collateral. Sound projects that might be turned down by conventional banks for lack of collateral could be financed (if not by BIMB and/or Bank Rakyat) by other financial intermediaries on a profit-sharing basis. This communal role is important, as it could stimulate private-sector activities in Malaysia, as so far the Islamic banks have been less successful in playing this catalytic role.

4

Managing and Measuring Customer Service Quality in Islamic Banks: A Study of the Kuwait Finance House

Abdulqawi Radman Mohammed Othman and H. Lynn Owen

This chapter introduces the alternative measures of service quality (SQ) proposed in the literature and examines their performance in the Islamic banking industry using the Kuwait Finance House (KFH) as a case study. It suggests a new model to measure SQ called CARTER which is based on 34 items. The study shows that all CARTER items that have appeared in both important items' weights and percentages were significant. The strong link between SQ and customer satisfaction is apparent and the study identifies this through a system of CARTER-items processes inputs and overall satisfaction output. Finally, the study suggests a scenario plan for KFH to adopt SQ and emphasises the importance of training for its implementation.

INTRODUCTION

An historical lack of interest in services can be partly explained by the fact that there was little understanding of the differences between the management of services and the management of manufacturing organisations. Although basic management principles are similar for both types of companies, services have some characteristics that require a different emphasis by managers. The characteristics that differentiate services from manufacturing in terms of quality have been described by many writers (Bitran and Lojo 1993; Parasuraman et al. 1993; Zeithaml et al. 1996) and can be summarised as follows:

1. The nature of products: these are basically intangible in services including a tangible action, so customer satisfaction in services is not only influenced by objective measures of performance but also by intangible aspects during the service performance.

2. Heterogeneity: this creates another challenge for quality management in services, because quality in service is not just ensuring conformity to standards, but taking into account the service diversity of customers while the service delivery is taking place, the behaviour and expectations of the customer being

served and to customise the service delivery accordingly.

3. Simultaneity: most services are produced and consumed at the same time. This represents a difficulty in the quality management of services because it is not usually feasible actively to monitor all service deliveries that are taking place and the service cannot be inspected before its consumption.

4. Human contact: services are often characterised by the existence of human contact between employee and customer.

Practitioners and researchers have devised many concepts of quality. These include Total Quality Management (TQM), Quality Control (QC) and Service Quality (SERVQUAL). Samuel (1999) quoted the International Standards Organisation (ISO) definition of quality as: 'the totality of features and characteristics of product or service that bear on its ability to satisfy or imply customers' needs'. He noted that in Total Quality Management, 'Total' means that everyone linked with the company is involved in continuous improvement (including its customers and suppliers if feasible); 'Quality' indicates that customers' expressed and implied requirements are met fully; and finally, 'Management' signifies that executives are fully committed.

The majority of researchers on SQ, such as Buzzel and Gale (1987: 111) support the following definition: quality is 'what the customer says it is'. Thus, how could Islamic banks know whether they give services which are judged one hundred per cent satisfactory by one hundred per cent of their customers? They would have to ask, observe, find out from the customers themselves, see whether they recommend the bank to others or not, and so on. Therefore, a focus on customers is the key to adopting and delivering total SQ management, or total service quality management (TSQM) as John Peters (1999) named it.

By contrast, Parasuraman, working with Zeithaml and Berry (1985: 46), concentrated from the outset on SQ. Their so-called 'Gap' school defined SQ as the 'degree and direction of discrepancy between customers' perceptions of service and expectations'.

The other way to think about quality is operational efficiency, which means that if the bank can discover the most efficient ways to produce products and services, without wasting time and materials, and replace unsatisfactory services, it will also become more successful. In other words, the quality of bank services may be defined as the measure of success of its operations in providing excellent products and service as viewed by the customer receiving the products and service. So it is an agreed measurement, to a defined standard, of the bank's response to the customer's request for the service that it is delivering. SQ tends today to play an important role in many service industries, such as banking services, because excellent quality of services in the banking industry is not an optional competitive strategy which may, or may not, be adopted to differentiate one bank from another, but it is essential to corporate profitability and survival for many banks around the world.

The development of SQ dimensions

Many researchers have recognised the need to develop valid and distinct measures of SQ, given the rise of service development in the last few decades. Gronroos (1984) tried to explain in his model of SQ how customers perceived SQ based on three points. First, functional quality or how the service is performed and delivered (concerned with the outcome of the service encounter); second, building the image of the firm during buyer-seller interactions (a reflection of the corporate image of the service organisation); and finally, the overall perception of quality as a function of the customers' evaluation of the service (the process of service delivery). In his 1988 work, Gronroos developed five key dimensions of SQ: (1) professionalism and skills; (2) reputation and credibility; (3) behaviour and attitudes; (4) accessibility and flexibility; and (5) reliability and trustworthiness.

Le Blanc et al. (1988) stated that Lethtinen identified three dimensions of quality: first, physical quality (equipment, premises, tangibles); second, corporate quality (image and profile organisation); and finally, interactive quality (customer contact with service personnel and other customers). The study found that among the most popular assessment tools of SQ in the literature was SERVQUAL, which was designed by the market research team of Parasuraman et al. (1985, 1988, 1990, 1991, 1993, 1994) to measure the quality in service industry. They began their work with qualitative research, which suggested ten dimensions of SQ (reliability; responsiveness; competence; access; courtesy; communication; credibility; security; understanding/knowing the customer; and tangibles), and through various qualitative researches they evolved a set of five dimensions, namely Tangibles, Reliability, Responsiveness, Assurance and Empathy (see Appendix 1), which have been consistently ranked by customers to be most important for SQ, regardless of the service industry.

The SERVQUAL model

The model developed into a 22-item instrument (see Appendix 2) for measuring customers' expectations and perceptions (EX and PS) of the five dimensions listed above. The measurement is managed using two different forms, one to measure expectation and the other to measure perception.

The basic assumption underlying the SERVQUAL scale is that performance below expectations (obtaining a negative score) leads to a perception of low SQ, while exceeding expectations (obtaining a positive score) leads to a perception of high SQ. Therefore, perceived SQ is the result of the customer's comparison of expected service with the service received. Le Blanc and Nguyen identify the differences between customers' expectations and perceptions using three possible scenarios to define how customers perceive SQ:

1. Expectations of SQ are exceeded (quality exceeds expectations)
   PS>EX or PS-EX>0

2. Expectations of SQ are met (quality is acceptable)
   PS=EX or PS-EX=0

3. Expectations of SQ are not met (quality is unacceptable or less than satisfactory)
   PS<EX or PS-EX<0

Parasuraman's approach represents the customer entertaining expectations of performance on the service dimensions, observing performance and later forming performance perceptions. Thus, the SERVQUAL instrument illustrates the core of what SQ may mean, namely a comparison to excellence in service by customers.

The SERVQUAL model identifies five opportunities for quality failure, or what are called 'gaps', which can be perceived as a process for the design of a service. Essentially, four gaps stand in the way of delivering a service perceived by customers as being of high quality:

1. Gap one: Customer expectations – management's perceptions.
2. Gap two: Management's perceptions – SQ specifications.
3. Gap three: SQ specifications – service delivery.
4. Gap four: Service delivery – external communications.
5. Gap five: Perceived service gap.

Customers' perceived quality of a bank's products and services is affected by gaps one to four, which belong to the bank's service side. The bank's management can identify causes of service quality problems by examining each gap. Gap five is an overall measure of SQ from the customer's point of view. It is the difference between perceived and expected levels of service.

The SERVQUAL instrument has been widely used since the mid-1980s and the Gap model was designed to be applicable for all industries, but it has also been widely criticised. Researchers such as Francis Buttle (1996) argued the SERVQUAL model has some critics in terms of theories and operations. In terms of theories, he noticed that SERVQUAL fails to draw on established economic, statistical and psychological theory, and there is little evidence that customers assess SQ in terms of PS-EX gaps. He added that SERVQUAL focuses on the process of service delivery, not the outcome of the service encounter. Finally, SERVQUAL's five dimensions are not universal. Operational critics focused on the following areas: first, the term expectation is polymeric because SERVQUAL fails to measure absolute SQ expectations, second, item composition is questionable because four or five items cannot capture the variability within each SQ dimension; third, the problem of moments of truth (MOT). Customers' assessments of SQ may vary from MOT to MOT; fourth, the seven-point Likert scale is flawed; and finally, two administrations of the instrument cause boredom and confusion.

Furthermore, Cronin and Taylor (1992; 1994) criticised Parasuraman et al. for their uncertainty in defining perceived SQ in attitudinal terms, even though Parasuraman et al. (1988) had earlier claimed that SQ was 'similar in many ways to an attitude'. Cronin and Taylor observe: 'Researchers have attempted to differentiate SQ from consumer satisfaction, even while using the disconfirmation format to measure perceptions of SQ ... this approach is not consistent with the differentiation expressed between these constructs in the satisfaction and attitude literatures.'

Cronin and Taylor (1992) developed a measurement model based on the performance measure of SQ (SERVPERF). They tested this model in some industries (banking, dry cleaning and fast foods) and the findings showed that SERVPERF explained more of the variance in an overall measure of SQ than did SERVQUAL. However, SERVPERF is composed of the 22 perception items in the SERVQUAL scale, and therefore excludes any consideration of expectations. In a later defence of their argument for a perceptions-only measure of SQ, Parasuraman et al. (1994) admit that it is possible for researchers to infer consumers' disconfirmation through arithmetic means (the PS-EX gap) but that 'consumer perceptions, not calculations, govern behaviour'. Thus, SERVQUAL has indeed proved to be the most popular instrument for measuring and managing SQ.

WHY SQ IN ISLAMIC BANKS?

There are several reasons why SQ in Islamic banks is important. First, Islamic banks' products and services are expected to be of high quality by customers because, in Islam, work, and the quality of that work, are considered to be a type of worship. The Prophet said: 'Whoever finds himself at nightfall tired from his work, God will forgive his sins.' Additionally, Abu Hurairah reported that the Prophet said:

> Charity (*ṣadaqah*) is due upon every joint of a person on every day that the sun rises. Administering justice between two people is an act of charity; and helping a man concerning his riding beast by helping him on to it or lifting his luggage on to it, is an

act of charity; a good word is charity; and every step which you take to prayer is charity; and removing that which is harmful from the road is charity. (Abdul Hameed 2001)

The Prophet also said: 'Allah loves to see one's job done at the level of *itqān*' (Sabeq 1988). *Itqān* means to arrange and dispose of things in a professional way in order to obtain the most perfect results, or in other words to undertake work in a high-quality manner with wisdom.

Second, adopting SQ in Islamic banks has become important because of its apparent relationship to costs (Crosby 1979), profitability (Buzzell and Gale 1987; Rust and Zahorik 1993; Zahorik and Rust 1992), customer satisfaction (Bolton and Drew 1991; Boulding et al. 1993), customer retention (Reicheld and Sasser 1990) and positive word of mouth. SQ is widely regarded as a driver of corporate marketing and financial performance in banking (Kwon and Lee 1994; Wong and Perry 1991).

In addition, the measuring and evaluation of SQ in banking, including the Islamic banking industry, has become very important because of the changes in the banking environment. Banking has become globally integrated, there is much competition and it is important for banks to know what, when, where and how they will provide services and how their customers perceive products and services.

Finally, SQ has become particularly important for Islamic banks in general and KFH in particular for several reasons. First, there is a lack of knowledge and research on management in general and SQ in particular in this industry. Second, the industry grows annually between 10.0 per cent and 15.0 per cent. Third, the consequent increase in competition between non-Islamic and Islamic banks has made SQ a key differentiating factor for Islamic banks to improve their market share and profit position. New entrants to the market in Kuwait, which provide the same Islamic products and services as KFH, are increasingly based on the delivery of quality service to customers, such as Investment Dar, which was successfully granted the ISO certificate for International Quality Standards 9001.

AN HYPOTHESISED MODEL FOR THE ISLAMIC BANKING INDUSTRY

Since the purpose of this study is to develop and test a theoretical model for Islamic banks to manage service quality, the difficulties and challenges expressed in the previous section are explicitly accounted for in our hypothesised theory. However, since the model is to be applied to the Kuwait Finance House (KFH), it is appropriate to give a brief profile of KFH first.

Kuwait Finance House (KFH)

KFH is a Kuwaiti public shareholding company established in 1977 with a capital of KD10 million. It engages principally in providing banking services, including internet banking, the purchase and sale of properties, leasing, project construction for its own account as well as for its customers, and other trading activities without practising usury. Its main aim is to develop and promote Islamic banking worldwide and become one of the leading Islamic banks.

KFH's growth has been significant in the last decade, as its assets increased from KD1.05 billion in 1991 to KD2.02 billion in 2000, its capital increased to KD61.3 million in 2000 from KD31 million in 1991 and profits increased to KD115 million from only KD27 million in 1991. KFH's mission is to offer a distinctive service to its customers. It has improved its information technology sector, particularly its management information systems. A central customer database was commissioned, and the communications network upgraded. The KFH internet website now provides banking, investment and commercial services online, with consequently greater exposure both locally and worldwide.

The model's main dimensions (CARTER)

Based on the discussion above, researchers studying different service categories, such as banking, telephone services, securities brokers and credit card companies, have identified SERVQUAL dimensions on the bases of the firm's culture, products and services, technology, and so on. Therefore, new studies in SQ might rightly be based on the original ten dimensions together with the five evolved dimensions, which can then be merged and subsequently modified to be suitable for each industry by defining and examining new dimensions. That is, because of the existence of cultural differences between countries, regions, religions or ethnic groups which reinforce the importance of building different dimensions, an additional dimension for SQ in the Islamic banking industry is proposed to meet the above requirements. Therefore, while the set of quality dimensions defined for our study is based on previous research, Islamic banks' internal and external environment and culture have guided the researchers to add a new dimension called 'Compliance with Islamic law' to Parasuraman's five dimensions. This dimension includes such items as run on Islamic law and principles, no interest paid nor taken on savings and loans, the provision of Islamic products and services, the provision of interest-free loans and the provision of profit-sharing investment products.

Hence, the following dimensions (D), compliance, assurance, reliability, tangibles, empathy and responsiveness (CARTER), were conceptualised as a proposed framework for this study (see Appendix 3):

D1: Compliance (items 1–5 items) means the ability to comply with Islamic law and operate under the principles of Islamic banking and economy.
D2: Assurance (items 6–10) is the knowledge and courtesy of employees and their ability to convey trust and confidence. It also includes verbal and written communication between bank staff and customers.

D3: Reliability (items 11–15) entails the ability to perform the promised service, dependability and accuracy.
D4: Tangibles (items 16–20) mean the appearance of physical facilities, equipment, personnel and communication materials.
D5: Empathy (items 21–28) equates with caring, and the individualised attention that the Islamic bank provides for its customers.
D6: Responsiveness (items 29–34) is the willingness to help customers and provide a prompt service.

CARTER *supporting factors*

Customers of Islamic banks perceive service quality in relation to the CARTER dimensions. However, in order to achieve customer satisfaction, it is not enough for Islamic banks to deliver high-quality service, for they should also successfully shape the customers' expectations. In other words, they should establish a quality culture inside the bank. The following will discuss the customer satisfaction and service encounter because of their positive relationship with service quality.

Customer satisfaction

Oliver (1993) noted that satisfaction loosely means 'enough' or 'enough to excess'. Thus, customer satisfaction can be defined as the customer's fulfilment response. It has also been described by Rust and Oliver (1994) as a process, and the most widely adopted of process theories is that of expectancy disconfirmation in which satisfaction is viewed as largely based on meeting or exceeding expectations.

Researchers such as Cronin and Taylor (1992) recognised that customer service satisfaction occurs at various levels in the organisation, including satisfaction with the contact person or front office staff (service encounter), satisfaction with the core service experienced and overall satisfaction with the organisation. Thus, overall satisfaction is viewed as customer satisfaction with a multiple of experiences or encounters with the organisation.

Customer contact – employees

In the banking industry, including Islamic banks, most personal contact between the customer and the bank occurs through employees at a low level in the hierarchy, such as bank tellers. No matter how low these employees are in the hierarchy, it is usually their performance that determines the customers' perception of the quality of service provided. Therefore, satisfied employees have a positive outlook and can take pride in their work. This has the potential for their being able to deal positively with customers. Well-treated customers are more likely to remain customers of the bank and not move to another institution. In other words, when employees understand and regard the customers as the reason for their jobs, they will treat customers with dignity and serve them quickly. Thus, employees should have a working environment in which they feel highly motivated, and a quality-training programme to provide high-quality services.

The service encounter

The service encounter is defined as the period of time in which the consumer and service firm interact in different ways, including the telephone and media. It is the interaction that takes place where the service is delivered to the customer, and during this interaction customers' perception of the bank service is shaped. Therefore, the service encounter is considered to be the most critical moment for the success of the bank, the moment of truth.

In order to manage the quality of the service being provided by the Islamic bank, six phases of service encounter are presented below:

1. Customer access: there are a number of ways through which customers can gain access to the bank service (for example, telephone, walk in, ATM, making an appointment, the internet, and so on).

2. Customer check-in: this is where customers identify themselves. It can be through name, opening an account by filling in an application form, and so on. It is important at this stage for the bank to make customers feel welcome and important.

3. Diagnosis: the bank here identifies customers' needs, and the reason why they have come. This phase is also important because the bank has the opportunity to sense the customers' overall expectations of its service and decide the best way to serve them.

4. Service delivery: this is critical for overall satisfaction because customers' needs and perceptions are met and shaped during this time.

5. Disengagement: this is to make sure that all customers' needs have been fulfilled during the service encounter. This is the assessment phase to correct eventual mistakes that might be made during service delivery and obtain feedback from customers about the service they received.

6. Follow-up: this is important because improved service quality follows from customers' complaints and suggestions.

Thus, elements of the service encounter are waiting time, personal interaction, customers' expectations and perceptions.

STUDY METHODOLOGY

A questionnaire was chosen as the method by which the survey was completed. The questionnaire measured actual and desired expectations, and perceptions of service quality, as well as overall feelings towards the relevant bank, in terms of satisfaction. The Systematic Random Sampling (SRS) system was used to select the study samples for customers. 500 questionnaires were distributed to customers and 360 were returned to the researchers, which is a sufficient number for statistical reliability. Customers were contacted in their offices, homes and in the front offices of KFH and its 22 branches. The sample reflects the life stage of KFH customers (gender, age, education, income, marital status, nationality, occupation and place of work).

Personal details of sample respondents showed that 81.0 per cent were male and 19 per cent of them female, 82.0 per cent were married and more than 65.0 per cent were between 30 and 50 years old. Their incomes were very high because 48.0 per cent said they received more than KD12,000 (nearly US$39,000) annual income, and 28.0 per cent said their annual incomes were between KD7,212 and KD12,000. Also, 67.0 per cent held Kuwaiti nationality and 71.0 per cent had university degrees. Their employment fields were: 22.0 per cent professionals, 14.0 per cent administrative, 16.0 per cent academic and education, 15.0 per cent own businesses, 8.0 per cent marketing and sales, and 5.0 per cent were clerks or in the police and army. The responses showed that 42.0 per cent worked in the private sector, 37.0 per cent in the public sector, 12.0 per cent were self-employed and 3.3 per cent worked for semi-government agencies.

These questions were organised under a framework based on the SERVQUAL model, with a compliance with Islamic law dimension added to complete the picture of Islamic banking SQ dimensions. The CARTER model includes a 34-item instrument that was customised for Islamic banks. Findings from a qualitative study were used to establish quality service standards (Avkiran 1994). Each item was surveyed directly on the five-point Likert scale starting at (1) not important, (2) less important, (3) neutral, (4) rather important, and (5) very important.

The coefficient a was calculated to measure the reliability of the survey based on internal consistency (Peter 1979). Avkiran (1994) suggests that the 'Coefficient alpha sets an upper limit to the reliability of tests constructed in terms of [the] domain-sampling model. If it proves to be very low, either the test is too short or the items have very little in common.' In fact, alpha for the model showed very high reliability (0.95) and the alpha for CARTER dimensions were also high (0.70, 0.81, 0.79, 0.89, 0.77 and 0.79 respectively), which supports the reliability of these instruments.

ANALYSIS OF THE FINDINGS

KFH customers were asked about the importance of the proposed quality items model, which were based on the CARTER six dimensions as shown in Appendix 3. Respondents, in essence, ranked the CARTER dimensions by rating the importance of each item and their satisfaction and dissatisfaction with overall services and quality. They were particularly consistent in their assessment because they clearly judged Compliance, Assurance and Responsiveness as the most important, while Tangibles, Reliability and Empathy were the least important (see Appendix 5).

As shown in Appendix 3, KFH customers placed more emphasis on the Compliance dimension (3.95 average scale) because 93.0 per cent of them said that it was important for KFH to be run on Islamic legal principles. The provision of Islamic products and services was also shown to be highly important for 91.0 per cent of respondents, while 73.0 per cent said it was important that KFH should neither pay nor take interest on savings and loans. Finally, the item concerned with the provision of profit-sharing investment products was seen as important by 68.0 per cent of respondents. The provision of interest-free loans was the least important (28.0 per cent) because KFH does not provide this service to its customers.

Relative importance weights were calculated for all 34 items and six dimensions based on the highest scale point, 5, as shown in Appendices 4 and 5. For KFH customers all items are important, the minimum weight being 53 for overdraft privileges on current accounts. Almost 30.0 per cent of the customers said overdrafts were important but, because KFH dose not provide overdrafts, most customers who were interviewed were surprised by the question, asking: 'What is this product?'

Appendix 4 indicates whether the CARTER items represent process or outcome issues. This clearly shows that the model includes 80.0 per cent 'Processes' and 20.0 per cent 'Outcomes', which illustrates the expected pattern that service customers attach considerably more significance to the process elements of the bank than to outcomes when judging quality.

Customer satisfaction and the service encounter

Two facts regarding customer satisfaction in this study should be highlighted. When respondents were asked whether KFH came up to their expectations as a good bank, 75.0 per cent were satisfied with this phrase. When asked if KFH was close to being the ideal bank, only 34.0 per cent were satisfied with this phrase. The results of measuring overall customer satisfaction in KFH show that the majority of customers were satisfied with its products, services and its profits, whereas only 46.0 per cent were satisfied with the time spent to finish the service encounter and only 39.0 per cent were satisfied with the waiting time before being served. However, customers rated their satisfaction with KFH profits positively and as a consequence there is satisfaction with overall performance.

Putting together a special team to talk with customers and to evaluate the bank's existing practices brings about new visibility of the customer's requirements into the bank. If such efforts are successful, service designers can expect to develop new customer services. This creates satisfied and loyal customers, produces a more efficient organisational structure and establishes a competitive advantage framework for the bank.

Essentially, service quality and customer satisfaction can be defined as a system of CARTER-items, notably processes inputs and overall satisfaction outputs. In this way, a service quality programme based on customers' overall satisfaction and feedback may help the bank develop its methods of operation and provide new products and services to satisfy customer needs.

Management implications

Islamic bank managers can use the CARTER model and its dimensions to examine the following issues:

1. To identify those areas where improvement should be made and resources can be allocated. For instance, management needs to know the level of quality in their banks so that they can make improvements in quality performance. They can use benchmarking to compare their performance with that of other banks that have already implemented quality programmes to help prioritise quality management efforts.

2. There is a growing worldwide demand for Islamic banking products and services, and customers are usually aware of whether their banks follow Islamic principles in all transactions or not. Therefore, the Islamic bank management must ensure that all products and services offered by their institutions, processes and procedures are compliant with Islamic laws. The study suggested that it may be appropriate for Islamic banks to provide their customers who are in need with interest-free loans, as this will enhance the banks' image.

3. The findings show the need to reduce the time allocated to each process, to increase work intensity and to expand service capacity in KFH. Hence, the implementation of quality programmes in Islamic banking may help the bank management to achieve those aims.

4. The importance of redesigning the front offices and counters with attractive layouts has emerged from the tangibles variable results.

Another key issue revealed in the findings is the need for balance between a general understanding of customers' needs and an internal understanding related to the bank's operations, specific services, geographical locations or counter designs. The CARTER approach attempts to develop a protocol that is scalable and yet also useful for internal planning and decision-making. Therefore, the results can be used for both diagnostic and comparative purposes. They were able to identify specific service areas that needed further improvement. At the same time, the bank management may develop an understanding of how their institutions compare to similar institutions and how the CARTER assessment relates to other large-scale assessment efforts they have in place.

The understanding of service quality in an Islamic bank will possibly lead its management to develop not only an understanding of preferred and best service practices but also towards widespread recognition of standards for service quality, especially the extent to which customers have an overreaching preconceived notion of bank quality. For example, as customers expect Islamic banks to provide all products and services under the umbrella of Islamic laws and principles, so standards should build on the bases of those principles.

Finally, the findings reported in the point of process and outcome above and their implications have far-reaching consequences for the future of Islamic banks and their evaluation and assessment. Islamic bank service quality is a concept that is becoming increasingly recognisable and actionable. As standardised procedures like CARTER are emerging and flourishing side-by-side with local implementations emphasising quality improvements, there is a distinct possibility that Islamic banks will be in a position to develop a better understanding of what constitutes and determines various levels of quality.

SCENARIO PLAN FOR KFH TO ADOPT SQ

As observed by the authors and as a result of interviewing managers, KFH has not adopted or implemented any kind of quality system or programme since its establishment in the late 1970s. No department responsible for quality measure or control was found in its organisational structure. Thus, there is a lack of quality knowledge and practice in both its managerial and operational sides. The following scenario provides a plan for KFH to adopt SQ and develop quality culture in its divisions, departments and branches. This plan must include the following stages in the first tier inside the bank:

1. KFH Board of Directors or the Management Committee might take a decision to adopt and implement SQ within a defined period of time and pass it to the General Manager.

2. The General Manager will announce the establishment of the Quality Leadership Team (QLT). Quality literature should stress the importance of strong leadership, commitment and support by top management to ensure the success of the quality effort. The QLT should be involved with the General Manager and/or one of his assistants and the division and some department managers. Its primary role is to ensure that quality is integrated into management processes and into the provision of products and services to customers. This will help to establish quality not as a separate initiative, but rather through the way every employee's job is done each day. The QLT's activities include:

- Leading quality programmes and teaching managers and employees quality values.
- Developing strategic quality initiatives and guiding the creation of division goals and work units, teams, and individual objectives and measurements.
- Ensuring the development and implementation of quality training programmes aligned with the bank's Mission, Vision and Quality Excellence initiatives.
- Ensuring the development and maintenance of quality documentation.
- Developing a quality performance indicator report.
- Making sure that the programmes will lead to continuous improvement in terms of satisfaction for internal and external customers, performance, productivity and profitability.

3. The QLT must take decisions first to train managers in different divisions, departments and branches on conducting self-assessment tests using well-known criteria, such as the International Standards Organisation (ISO) or any other award, second to perform quality leadership using the ideal criteria, and third to establish self-assessment committees or teams to complete and analyse quality leadership and develop strategies from addressing the results. Self-assessment might include BEST and SWOT analyses. Finally, short- and long-term self-assessment improvement must be identified.

4. In the light of self-assessment, it is time to define KFH's SQ, its objectives and the benefits of their implementation. Quality teams could be identified, their remit being to develop a systematic approach that will enable and integrate quality into operations. All team objectives and goals should be identified.

5. The QLT should introduce quality initiative programmes to divisions, departments and branch managers, and through them to all the staff in the bank, and discuss it in the planned meetings with the General Manager or one of his assistants. Divisions, departments and branches should set goals for the quality programme that must be accepted by the QLT.

6. Quality teams should conduct employee and customer satisfaction surveys

from time to time. When they believe quality has improved, they might let an external body assess the quality programme.

7. In all these stages, the QLT must engage some quality experts and professionals to consult them and to train managers and employees in how to implement this programme.

In the second tier, administrative SQ can be measured by designing the CARTER positive and negative questionnaires to record customers' expectations and perceptions and to find out whether or not the level of quality is satisfactory.

An evaluation of the quality programme must be carried out after every single action on the basis of a plan-action-check system. An overall evaluation must be undertaken after SQ measurement results, and productivity and profitability analyses should be carried out in order to measure the level of improvement that might be achieved.

CONCLUSIONS

As mentioned above, the banking industry today is moving towards the goal of integrated financial services because of the strong competition and quick changes in technology. Islamic banks must, therefore, pay attention to this movement and start to think strategically by providing high-quality products and services to satisfy their customers. This study indicates that it is important for Islamic banks to put cultural differences to the fore when adopting SQ, and suggests a new model to measure SQ, called CARTER, based on 34 items. The study shows that all CARTER items that have appeared in both important items' weights and percentages were significant. The strong links between SQ and customer satisfaction are apparent and the study has identified this through a system of CARTER-items processes inputs and overall satisfaction outputs. Finally, the study suggests a scenario plan for KFH to adopt SQ and emphasises the importance of training for its implementation.

5

The Lending Policies of Islamic Banks in Iran

Nezamaddin Makiyan

Since 1984, when all Iranian banks were required to operate under Islamic principles, banks have been able to increase their lending significantly. In this chapter, descriptive analysis and an error-correction model are used to investigate the lending activities of Iranian banks. The results indicate that many factors have affected lending policies. These include rate of return, inflation and state intervention, of which government directives on managing funds have played the most important role.

INTRODUCTION

This chapter is concerned with the dynamics of loans in the Iranian banking system, which operates under Islamic principles. It studies the operations of all Iranian banks and analyses lending policies. The investigation covers the period 1984–2000 using data from the Central Bank of Iran.

The central feature in an Islamic banking system is the prohibition of *ribā*. The Islamic financial system relies on equitable profit/risk-sharing between the provider of capital and the entrepreneur. Islamic law, while rejecting the concept of interest, permits an undetermined rate of return based on profit.

Islamic banks have been established in most Muslim countries in recent years. In the case of Iran, after the Islamic Revolution in 1979, the process of Islamisation from an interest-based to a non-interest banking system went through three distinct stages. The first stage was the nationalisation of the banking system implemented by the Revolutionary Council during the summer of 1979.[1] Thereby, commercial and specialised banks were merged and allowed to continue their operation under government supervision.[2] Foreign banks' representative offices were closed in 1980. However, some of these banks were later reopened with limited operations. They were then allowed to establish representative offices for advisory services – mainly to benefit importers and other Iranian banks.

Following nationalisation, the Iranian authorities took steps to bring the operations of the banking system into compliance with the requirements of Islamic law. In February 1981, the Central Bank eliminated interest from banking operations. Consequently, interest on all asset operations, or loans, was replaced by a 4.0 per cent maximum service charge and by a 4.0–8.0 per cent minimum expected profit rate depending on the kind of activity. For example, 4.0 per cent was charged for housing financing, farming and manufacturing and 8.0 per cent for services. Interest on the liability side was also replaced by a minimum profit return for savings and time deposits set at 7.5 to 8.0 per cent.[3] Meanwhile, the authorities, academic scholars and *fuqahā'* prepared the first draft of a law to make the entire operations of the banking system conform with the Sharīʿah.

The second stage began in 1982 and continued until 1986. During this stage legislation was introduced in order to adopt and implement a clearly conceptualised model of Islamic banking. The law on interest-free banking was passed in August 1983 and came into effect on 20 March 1984. It gave the banks a deadline of one year to convert their deposits so that they conformed with Islamic principles. It also asked the banks to convert the asset side of their operations, or loans, within three years from the date of the law's approval. The law also specified the types of contracts that must constitute the basis for banking assets and liabilities, with several modes of financing provided to cater for the needs of bank clients.[4]

The third (present) stage began in 1986. During this stage the banking system was considered as an integral part of the Islamic government, and with the reduction in oil revenues plus the political intent behind ceasing to rely on external financial sources, this meant that the banking system would have to play a role broader than that of pure intermediary. Therefore, the banking system was used as a government instrument for restructuring the economy.

This chapter evaluates the rate of return on loans after the basis of bank operations was transformed by the introduction of Islamic principles. The methods employed to analyse the data are descriptive, with use made of an error-correction model. To this end, the model correlates the supply of loans with the rate of return to banks, total deposits and the rate of inflation. The problems that have impeded, or could impede, the efficiency of the system are explained.

CHARACTERISTICS OF BANK LIABILITIES

According to the law on interest-free banking in Iran, liabilities incurred by the banks are basically of two kinds: *qarḍ al-ḥasan* deposits, which constitute current accounts; and savings deposits. These are similar to those of conventional banks except that they cannot earn any return. Current *qarḍ al-ḥasan* deposits are similar to demand deposits or current accounts in conventional banks, as customers are offered chequebooks. They can withdraw their money at any time without notice. This account, from the point of view of customers, is simply a means of making transactions and payments. The other type of deposit is the *qarḍ al-ḥasan* savings account. In this account depositors are offered non-fixed prizes and bonuses in cash or kind. Other incentives for this type of account include depositors' exemption from fees or commissions, and priority in the use of banking facilities. *Qarḍ al-ḥasan* savings deposits are the main sources of *qarḍ al-ḥasan* loans.

The second category of deposits which banks are authorised to provide are investment deposits. These could be short-term or long-term investment deposits. These deposits differ with respect to the time period to maturity. The minimum time limit for short-term deposits is three months, and for long-term deposits the period can be one, two, three, four or even five years. No fixed amount or rate of return can be guaranteed to depositors in advance. In practice, banks pay profits to depositors provisionally on a quarterly basis, with a condition for final adjustment at the end of the financial year. Depositors can withdraw their money from long-term investment deposits before the agreement's termination provided they give notice in advance. In this case, the basis for the calculation of the profit is the next-lowest category of deposits, according to the time when the money has been deposited. Withdrawal from short-term deposits is possible at any time without notice.

CHARACTERISTICS OF BANK ASSETS

The law forbidding interest in Iran provides for various financing contracts between banks and customers. A brief description of these modes follows.

Muḍārabah (profit-sharing)

Banks provide the initial capital to the commercial sector, both individuals and traders, who engage in trade and business. By prior agreement, the profits from undertakings are divided at the end of the contract.

Mushārakah (partnership)

The law recognises two different forms of partnership, namely civil and legal. Civil partnership is project-specific for short- and medium-term financing. It is defined as the combination of capital from a bank with that from a partner or partners (in cash or kind) on a joint-ownership basis for a specific purpose. A legal partnership is a joint venture of long duration. In this case, the bank provides a portion of the total equity of a newly established firm, or purchases a proportion of the shares of an existing company.

Direct investment

Banks can invest directly in any economic activity for a long period. The possibilities for direct investment by banks only exists in the public sector through the creation of companies where legal partnership is not possible. Direct investment cannot be made in projects involving the production of luxury commodities, but rather the banks must consider government priorities for the country's economic development.

Mark-up or deferred payment sale (murābaḥah)

Banks are authorised to purchase raw materials, machinery, equipment, spare parts and other supplies and inputs for industry, farming, mining and services and resell them on a short-term instalment basis. The cost of this financing covers cost plus an agreed profit margin. Banks are not permitted to purchase items unless on the orders of a specific customer.

Purchase with deferred delivery (salaf or salam purchase)

Banks can purchase goods from productive enterprises in order to provide them with working capital. Thus, instead of lending money, the bank buys some proportion of the future product at an agreed price that must not exceed the market price of the product at the time of the contract.

Lease-purchase (ijārah bi sharṭ al tamlīk)

In this mode of financing, banks buy real property or other assets needed by enterprises or individuals and lease the assets to them. The price of the asset is determined on a cost-plus basis. Ownership of the property is transferred to the lessee at the end of the contract. The period of repayment of the assets cannot exceed their useful life.

Ju'ālah (transactions based on commission)

This is an undertaking by the bank (or the customer) to pay a specific sum in return for a service as specified in the contract. *Ju'ālah* is a short-term facility which may be granted for the expansion of production, commercial and service activities. The service to be performed and the fee to be charged must be determined at the time of the contract.

Qarḍ al-ḥasan (benevolent loan)

This is a non-commercial facility without any expectation of profit. *Qarḍ al-ḥasan* loans are usually made to small producers, farmers, small-scale businesses and those who through no fault of their own are unable to find the finance to cover personal needs, perhaps because of illness. The ability of banks to grant *qarḍ al-ḥasan* loans depends on the supply of *qarḍ al-ḥasan* savings deposits, the limit to cover personal needs being 2 million Iranian rials. The period of repayment for such loans is two to three years. The administrative expenses of such loans are borne by borrowers as service charges.

Table 5.1: Financing by Iranian banks

Transactions	*Production*						*Commercial*				*Services*
	Industry	*Mining*	*Agriculture*		*Building*		*Internal*	*Export*	*Import*		
			Arable	*Live-stock*	*Fact-ories*	*Hous-ing*			*Pri. Sec.*	*Pub. Sec.*	
1 *Muḍārabah*							*	*		*	
2 Civil partnership	*	*	*	*	*	*	*	*	*	*	*
3 Legal partnership	*	*	*	*	*	*	*	*	*	*	*
4 Direct investment	*	*	*	*	*	*					
5 Mark-up	*	*	*	*	*	*					*
6 *Salaf*	*	*	*	*	*	*					
7 Leasing	*	*	*	*	*	*					*
8 *Ju'ālah*	*	*	*	*	*	*	*	*	*	*	*
9 *Muzāra'ah*			*								
10 *Musāqah*			*								
11 *Qarḍ al-ḥasan*	*		*	*	*	*					*

Other financing methods such as *muzāra'ah* and *musāqah* are used to a limited extent for agriculture. Debt-purchasing was provided for in the law for interest-free banking, but this is no longer used as the Council of Guardians of the constitutional law declared that this method of financing could involve elements of *ribah*.[5] Table 5.1 provides a summary of the financing methods used by Iranian banks. As in conventional banking, most financing by Islamic banking in Iran is directed to services.

DESCRIPTIVE ANALYSIS OF LENDING OPERATIONS BY IRANIAN BANKS

As part of the implementation of interest-free banking in Iran, Bank Markazi, the Central Bank of Iran (CBI), established the minimum and maximum expected rates of return in various economic sectors, and also for each method of financing for the lending activities of banks. These rates ranged from 4.0 per cent to 25.0 per cent, depending on the year and the type of contract between banks and clients. Table 5.2 illustrates the ranges of the expected rates of return from various economic sectors.

Table 5.2 shows that the lowest rate of return was set for the agricultural sector, while the highest rate was set for the trade and service sectors. The latter were regarded as more profitable, and less in need of credit subsidy, but agriculture was given soft loans in order to help employment creation in rural areas and prevent excessive rural to urban migration. These rates of return on bank loans were generally less than the inflation rate, which rose from 7.6 per cent in 1985 to an average of 24.0 per cent over the 1986–8 period before falling

Table 5.2: Sector rates of return for bank financing (%)

Year/Sector	*1984–9*	*1990*	*1991*	*1992*	*1993–4*	*1995–2000*
Agricultural	4–8	6–9	6–9	9 (minimum)	12–16	13–16
Industry	6–12	11–13	11–13	13 (minimum)	16–18	17–19
Housing	8–12	12–14	12–16	12-16	12–16	15–16
Trade	8–12	17–19	17–19	17-24	18–24	22–25
Services	10–12	17–19	17–19	17-24	18–24	22–25
Export	8 (minimum)	–	–	–	18 (minimum)	18

Source: Bank Markazi (Central Bank of Iran).

temporarily to 8.6 per cent in 1990 as the supply shortages resulting from the Iran-Iraq War eased. High government spending on postwar reconstruction during the early to mid-1990s exacerbated inflationary pressures once again, however, with the rate peaking at almost 50.0 per cent by 1995, but subsequent attempts to curb government spending and the easing of import restrictions as a result of higher oil and gas revenue resulted in inflation falling to 9.3 per cent by 2000. Given that the average rate of inflation from 1984 to 2000 was 20.9 per cent per annum, this implied borrowers on average benefited from a 6.2 per cent subsidy on their bank borrowings.

In other words, the market rates of return were not applied to lending. Instead, lending rates were heavily influenced by government policy and regulation rather than market information, though the latter could have led to a more appropriate allocation of financial resources. Government policy was influenced by the need to mitigate the effects of external shocks, notably the war with Iraq, sanctions and reduction in oil revenues. Government intervention provided a situation whereby borrowers have benefited by obtaining loans from banks at rates that were lower than the rate of inflation. This, together with the discriminatory lending rates set for different sectors, created economic distortions. The authorities were of course aware of this problem, but their justification was the long-term social benefits of such loans to support the financial needs of various sectors of the economy.

THE ERROR CORRECTION MODEL FOR ANALYSING LENDING OPERATIONS

To analyse the determinants of banks' lending, an error-correction model is employed. The model regresses the supply of loans in Iranian banks against the average rate of return, total deposits and the rate of inflation during the first decade (1984–94) of Islamic banking experience in Iran. The reason for consideration of this period is that in 1993 the authorities realised that the policy of pressurising banks to offer low-cost loans was unsustainable. Subsequently, they permitted the banks to set market-determined rates for returns on loans.

In the model that is used here, it is expected that the supply of loans has a positive relationship with rates of return and the size of total deposits in banks and a negative relationship with the rate of inflation.[6] In equation (1) these behavioural assumptions require that coefficients β_1 and $\beta_2 > 0$ and $\beta_3 < 0$.

$$SLt = \beta_0 + \beta_1 R_t + \beta_2 TD_t + \beta_3 I_t + \varepsilon \quad (1)$$

Where SL_t = Supply of loans in period t,
R_t = Average rate of return on loans in period t,
TD_t = Total deposits in banks in period t,
I_t = Rate of inflation in period t.

The results of the unit root test show that all the series, that is, the supply of loans, average rate of return on loans,[7] total deposits and the rate of inflation, are integrated to order one, or I(1). The co-integration test using Johnson methodology leads us to the long-run relationship of the chosen vector, which is:

$$SL_t = -5950 + 294.1\ R_t + 1.278\ TD_t + 88.41\ It \quad (2)$$

Having found an appropriate co-integrating vector, the short-run dynamic Error Correction Model (ECM) is employed. This short-run dynamics model can be generated as follows:

$$\Delta SL_t = \beta_0 + \beta_1 \Delta R_t + \beta_2 \Delta TD_t + \beta_3 \Delta I_t + \sum_{i=1}^{n} \alpha_i \Delta SL_{t-i} + \sum_{i=1}^{m} \lambda_i \Delta R_{t-i} + \\ + \sum_{i=1}^{j} \gamma_i \Delta TD_{t-i} + \sum_{i=1}^{k} \eta_i \Delta I_{t-i} + \beta_4 EC(-1) + \varepsilon_t \quad (3)$$

The ECM for the loan supply is then estimated, the results of which are shown in Table 5.3.

The results show the sign and probability of the coefficient of the error term are as expected. In other words, the coefficient of the error term is negative and significantly different from zero. The speed of adjustment (the coefficient of the error term) is 0.30, which indicates a relatively rapid adjustment towards long-run equilibrium.

Following the above estimation, three more ECM-causality equations are estimated to find the exogeneity or endogeneity of the variables. The results are shown in Table 5.4.

In Table 5.4, the figures in columns 2 to 5 represent the number of lag length(s) of the variables at the head of each column, which appeared in the ECMs for

Table 5.3: Estimation of the supply of loans

Dependent Variable is $D(SL_t)$			
Variable	*Coefficient*	*t Statistic*	*Probability*
D(R)	17.32096	0.481935	0.6331
D(TD)	0.228957	4.185879	0.0002
D(I)	33.43566	2.073116	0.0463
D(SL(-1))	0.297459	3.610730	0.0010
D(SL(-4))	0.532199	4.250384	0.0002
D(R(-4))	–70.16207	–2.114172	0.0424
EC(-1)	–0.309308	–3.602068	0.0011
R-squared	0.948358		
Adjusted R-squared	0.938675		
Durbin-Watson stat.	1.911871		
F-statistic	97.94190		
Prob (F-statistic)	0.000000		

D(SL), D(TD), D(R) and D(I) are changes in the supply of loans, total deposits, rate of return and inflation rate. The table shows that D(R) is not significant.

causality findings.[8] The term EC(-1) is the lagged error-correction term. The t-statistics of the EC terms are given in parentheses below them. The sixth column shows the adjusted R^2. The last column is related to the LM test (which is a $\chi 2$ test with 1 degree of freedom). The figures in the square brackets are the probabilities of the LM tests.

The error-correction term can show the exogeneity or endogeneity of a variable and its long-run causality in terms of the indirect relationship between the variables. The causal variable in this framework is described in the literature as being weakly exogenous.[9] The ECM for the supply of loans shows that the error-correction term has a negative sign and is significantly different from zero. This means that the supply of loans is only weakly determined by the other

Table 5.4: Summaries of the ECMs for causality findings

DV	*DSL*	*DR*	*DTD*	*DI*	*EC(-1)*	*Adj.R2*	*LM*
ΔR	1	0	0	0	2.93E–05 (0.43)	0.04	0.096 [0.75]
ΔTD	4	2	1,5,6	0	–1.482 (–4.34)	0.91	1.31 [0.25]
ΔI	0	0	0	1	0.0001 (1.14)	0.58	0.32 [0.57]

variables. The subsequent equations, which are summarised in Table 5.4 for causality findings, indicate that only the error-correction term for the variable of total deposits is negative and significant. This indicates that total deposits are also only weakly determined by the other variables, that is, the supply of loans, the rate of return and the rate of inflation. These causal relationships indicate that both the supply of loans and total deposits are determined by the rate of return and the rate of inflation. Thus, the rate of return and the rate of inflation are weakly exogenous for the supply of loans and also for total deposits in the long run. To put it another way, it is changes in these two variables that generate changes in the supply of loans and of total deposits. The ECM also passed the diagnostic tests for the residuals. The estimated ECM can be written as:

$$\Delta SL_t = 17.32 \times \Delta R_t + 0.22 \times \Delta TD_t + 33.43 \times \Delta I_t + 0.29 \times \Delta SL_{t-1} + 0.53 \times \Delta SL_{t-4} - 0.70 \times \Delta R_{t-4} - 0.30 \times EC(-1) \quad (4)$$

From the result of the ECM implemented for the supply of loans (see Table 5.3), it can be seen that the changes in the average rate of return on loans, D(R), is not significant. This means that the supply of loans had no relationship to the rate of return in the period considered. The other explanatory variables, namely the changes in total deposits D(TD), changes in the rate of inflation D(I) and changes in the time-lag of variables, are significant. The sign of the variable of changes in the inflation rate D(I) is also positive, which is contrary to the theory of fund supply in an inflationary situation.

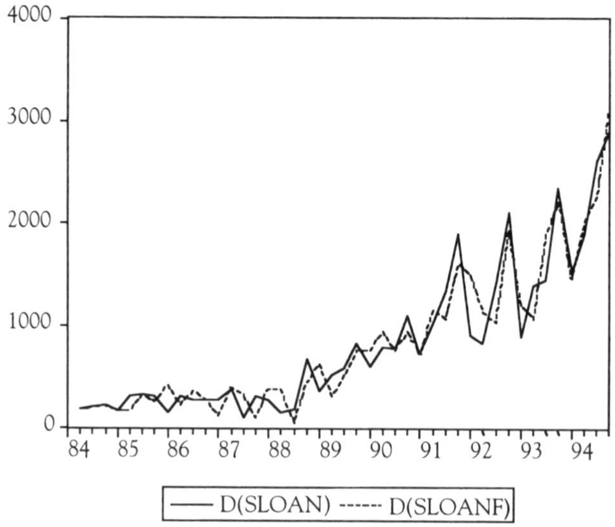

Figure 5.1: Actual and fitted values of the changes in the supply of loans

CONCLUSIONS

The study indicates that government financial management and intervention largely determined lending policy and the supply of funding rather than the returns to the banking system. Given the financial needs of the economy, the constraints imposed by the government on banks to grant low-cost loans and inflationary pressures, it is not surprising that the rate of return on loans is insignificant, and that there is a positive relationship between changes in the supply of loans and changes in the rate of inflation that emerges from the ECM analysis. The evidence on indirect causality observed from the ECM analysis shows that the weak exogenous variables are the rate of return and the rate of inflation for both the supply of loans and total deposits. This indicates that changes in the rate of return and the rate of inflation generate changes in the level of loans and total deposits. Moreover, despite the fact that banks were reluctant to offer loans in an inflationary situation, the positive sign of the inflation variable in the ECM analysis indicates that the supply of loans was affected by the financial needs of the economy.

It can be said that independence of the banking system from government in terms of the market determination of rate of return can result in the payment of a suitable return to depositors, and thus capital accumulation for developing the economy. A further step for the improvement of the banking system could be to allow the establishment of private financial institutions. Although some steps have been taken towards the establishment of a few private banks in recent years, more needs to be done. Development of the existing stock market can also serve as a main source of capital, both internal and external, to industry and the government. These steps will lead to the improvement of banking services and also help market forces to determine loans and deposits, thus improving the efficiency of financial intermediation.

NOTES

1. R. K. Ramazani, 'The Constitution of Islamic Republic of Iran', in *The Middle East Journal*, Washington, D.C., vol. 34, no. 2, September 1980. Article 44 of the Islamic Republic of Iran's constitutional law divides the economy into three parts, namely the public, cooperative and private sectors. The public sector includes all large-scale and basic industries, foreign trade, major mineral resources, banking and insurance.
2. Commercial banks include the following institutions: Melli, Sepah, Saderat, Tejarat, Mellat and Refah-e Kargaran. The specialised banks are: Keshavarzi (Agricultural Bank), Maskan (Housing Bank), San'at-wa-Ma'dan (Industrial and Mining Bank) and Touse'ah-e Saderat (Export Development Bank).
3. *Economic Report and Balance Sheet of Iran*, Tehran, The Central Bank of Iran, 1984, p. 452.
4. They are *qarḍ al-ḥasan* deposits (both saving deposits and demand deposits) for the

liability side. The financing modes, *muḍārabah*, *mushārakah*, mark-up, leasing, *salaf*, *ju'ālah*, *muzāra'ah*, *musāqāt* and *qarḍ al-ḥasan* loans, are used for the asset side.

5. *Rībah* derives from *rayb*, which literally means doubt or suspicion. It refers to the income which is similar to *ribā* or which raises doubt in the mind about its rectitude.
6. Carter, H. and Partington, I. (1979), *Applied Economics in Banking and Finance*, Oxford: Oxford University Press.
7. In determining the expected rates of return on different financing modes, an average rate between the maximum and minimum expected rates of return is calculated. The outcome is then weighted by the share of various modes of financing in total loans.
8. For example, the average rate of return on loans as a dependent variable is only significant when lagged by one period when the variable of the supply of loans is incorporated in the equation.
9. Enders, Walter (1995), *Applied Econometric Time Series*, pp. 315–16.

PART III

Measuring Islamic Banking Efficiency

6

Efficiency in Arabian Banking

Idries Al-Jarrah and Philip Molyneux

This chapter investigates the efficiency levels of the Jordanian, Egyptian, Saudi Arabian and Bahraini banking systems. It also highlights the role of economic and financial reforms that have taken place in these countries in recent years. The chapter uses the stochastic frontier and Fourier-flexible form to estimate cost and profit efficiency levels. The cost efficiency averaged around 95.0 per cent over the 1992–2000 period. Estimates of standard and alternative profit functions reveal technical efficiency on average at around 66.0 per cent and 58.0 per cent respectively. Islamic banks are found to be the most cost and profit efficient, while investment banks are considered the least so. Larger banks appear to be relatively more cost and profit efficient. Geographically, Bahraini banks are the most cost and profit efficient, while Jordanian banks are the least efficient. There is little evidence to suggest that economic and financial reforms have had a noticeable impact on improving banking sector efficiency.

INTRODUCTION

Financial sectors in developing countries, including the Arabian systems, have traditionally been characterised by relatively high levels of government control. Regulatory authorities maintained a protected banking environment that inhibited competition. However, market conditions in banking have undergone extensive changes over the last two decades or so. On the demand side, customer preferences have changed substantially, becoming more sophisticated and price conscious. On the supply side, the globalisation of financial markets has been accompanied by governmental deregulation, financial innovation and automation. Both factors imply an increase in the number of competitors, followed by reductions in costs and narrowing of profit margins. In addition, progress in communications technology, especially phone-based and internet banking, has enabled the larger financial institutions to extend their activities beyond narrow national boundaries and to increase their market share both within national and overseas markets by providing competitive products at lower prices. New suppliers of retail banking products, such as retailers, automobile manufacturers and so on, have entered the market. As such, banks are now faced with strong competition from both banks and non-bank institutions.

To assist banks in confronting the new challenge, financial authorities throughout the world have become more aware of the importance of financial deregulation to promote competition in the market, the aim being to increase both the efficiency and soundness of banking systems. In this respect, Arabian countries, including those under study – namely Jordan, Egypt, Saudi Arabia and Bahrain – have passed a substantial body of legislation (over the last few years) aimed at liberalising their financial systems. This liberalisation process has been accompanied by financial deregulation, reduction of government control and upgrading of prudential regulations. The main objective of these reforms concurs with the views of McKinnon (1973) and Shaw (1973); namely that liberalised financial systems direct scarce economic resources to the most efficient uses that impact favourably on the growth of the national economy. Recent studies by Levine (1997), Levine and Zervos (1998), Rajan and Zingales (1998) and Demirguc-Kunt (2000) also emphasise the importance of financial sector growth and efficiency in fostering economic development.[1]

The process of deregulation has some important implications for banks. First, deregulation removes or reduces collusive and/or restrictive practices, promoting competition between banks and thereby increasing the banks' risk. Second, changes arise from the ability of banks to seek new business in much wider fields of activity, such as loan purchases and off-balance sheet transactions. Moves into new business areas and an increased competitive environment change the nature of banks' risks and substantially increase the cost of funds to the established players, thus reducing their competitive advantage. This induces banks to pay greater attention to pricing and upgrading the quality of their products. Therefore, banks become more concerned about analysing and controlling their costs and revenues, as well as dealing with risks taken to produce acceptable returns. In this context, maximising shareholders' wealth and promoting improvements in productive efficiency have become much more important strategic targets for banks. A number of studies have shown that efficient banks have substantial competitive advantages over those with average or below average efficiency (Sinkey 1992; Berger et al. 1993; Gardner 1995; Molyneux et al. 1996).

Given the inextricable link between financial liberalisation and efficiencies, it is interesting to highlight the impact of economic and financial reforms in various Arabian markets on the efficiency levels of the financial institutions operating in these countries (as suggested by Berger and Humphrey 1997). It should be noted, however, that the limited literature on the impact of financial deregulation on banking sector efficiency is mixed (Berger and Humphrey 1997). Some studies find that financial sector deregulation has brought about higher levels of efficiency (Berg et al. 1992; Zaim 1995; Bhattacharya et al. 1997; Leightner and Lovell 1998). Others argue that there was no noticeable impact from banking sector deregulation (Bauer et al. 1993; Elyasiani and Mehdian 1997; Griffell-Tatjé and Lovell 1997; Humphrey and Pulley 1997).

Despite the extensive literature that has examined productive efficiency, especially in the US banking system and other European markets (see Berg et al. 1993; Berg et al. 1995; Bergendahl 1995; Pastor et al. 1995; Allen and Rai 1996; European Commission 1997a), empirical research on financial sectors in developing countries, including Arabian countries, is limited.

The aim of this chapter is to explore efficiency levels in various Arabian banking industries and to examine the impact of economic and financial reforms which have taken place in these countries over the past two decades. There are various reasons for examining efficiency levels in Arabian banking systems. First, little empirical work has been undertaken to investigate efficiency levels in Arabian banking and as such an empirical investigation may yield interesting insights that could be of use to policy makers operating in these countries and to the financial institutions themselves. Second, such a study should help in assessing the impact of the economic and financial reforms that have taken place in the countries under study. In addition, assessing the impact of financial reforms on banking sector efficiency should provide useful policy information. Furthermore, this paper aims to provide empirical evidence about efficiency differences across various Arabian banking industries (and across various types of financial institutions operating in these countries, such as commercial, investment and Islamic banks). The study further seeks to assess whether there is a link between a bank's size, and cost and profit efficiency levels. Furthermore, this study attempts to reveal the determinants of Arabian banks' efficiency by examining various factors that help explain Arabian banking sector efficiency and reveal characteristics of efficient banks. In particular, the chapter evaluates whether such factors as asset quality, capital levels and other environmental variables (such as bank size, market characteristics, geographic position and liquidity ratios) influence banks' efficiency levels (see Mester 1996a; Berger and Mester 1997; Berger and DeYoung 1997; Altunbas et al. 2001a,b). This chapter also presents some methodological suggestions as to how productive efficiency is best evaluated.

METHODOLOGY: MEASURES OF EFFICIENCY AND PRODUCTIVITY

The stochastic frontier, with the Fourier-flexible functional form, is the main methodology employed to derive efficiency measures in the countries under study. While the translog functional form has probably been the more widely utilised to derive efficiency estimates, the Fourier-flexible functional form has received more focus in recent efficiency literature. This section presents the main features of the Fourier-functional form and shows how to derive scale economies and scale inefficiencies estimates using this functional form.

The most widely used functional form in bank efficiency literature is the translog. However, it is subject to certain limitations, especially in so far as it does not necessarily fit well the data that are far from the mean in terms of output size or mix. In addition, McAllister and McManus (1993) and Mitchell and Onvural (1996) show that some of the differences in results of scale economies across studies may be due to the bad fit of the translog function across a wide range of bank sizes, some of which may be underrepresented in the data. The translog functional form for a cost function represents a second-order Taylor series approximation of any arbitrary, twice-differentiable cost function at a given (local) point. This restrictive property of the translog form is part of White's (1980) appraisal, which led Gallant (1981) to propose the Fourier-flexible functional form (FF) as a preferred alternative. The methodology was later discussed by Elbadawi, Gallant and Souza (1983), Chalfant and Gallant (1985), Eastwood and Gallant (1991) and Gallant and Souza (1991), and applied to the analysis of bank cost efficiency by Spong et al. (1995), Mitchell and Onvural (1996) and Berger et al. (1997). It has been shown (Tolstov 1962) that a linear combination of the sine and cosine function, namely the Fourier series, can exactly fit any well-behaved multivariate function.

The Fourier-flexible functional form is preferred over the translog because it better approximates the underlying cost function across a broad range of outputs as suggested by Spong et al. (1995) and Mitchell and Onvural (1996). The semi-nonparametric Fourier-flexible functional form has desirable mathematical and statistical properties because an infinite Fourier series is capable of representing any function exactly, and even truncated Fourier series can approximate a function reasonably well throughout its entire range. When using the Fourier-flexible functional form, one avoids holding any maintained hypothesis by allowing the data to reveal the true cost function through a large value of fitted parameters.

Besides, Berger and Mester (1997) note that the local approximations of the translog may distort scale economy measurements since it imposes a symmetric U-shaped average cost curve. This aspect of the translog might not fit very well data that are far from the mean in terms of output size or mix. The FF alleviates this problem since it can approximate any continuous function and any of its derivatives (up to a fixed order). Any inferences that are drawn from estimates of the FF are unaffected by specification errors (Ivaldi et al. 1996; Carbo et al. 2000) which indicate that since the FF is a combination of polynomial and trigonometric expansions, the order of approximation can increase with the size of the sample. This is due to the mathematical behaviour of the sine and cosine functions that are mutually orthogonal over the [0, 2p] interval and function space spanning.

Finally, the FF has several appealing properties in terms of modelling bank cost or profit structures, as pointed out by Williams and Gardener (2000). Unlike other commonly used functional forms such as the translog, the FF form is unaffected by specification errors. Furthermore, it has been widely accepted that global property is important in banking where scale, product mix and other inefficiencies are often heterogeneous. Therefore, local approximations (such as those generated by the translog function) may be relatively poor approximations to the underlying true cost (or profit) function. Specifically, the Fourier-flexible functional form augments the translog by including Fourier trigonometric terms.

The Fourier-flexible functional form

The stochastic cost model for a sample of N firms can be written as:

$$\ln TC_i = TC(y_i, w_i, z_i; B) + u_i + v_i, \; i = 1, \ldots, N,$$

where TC_i is observed cost of bank i, y_i is the vector of output levels and w_i is the vector of input prices for bank i. z_i represents a vector of control variables which in the case of our estimates includes the quality of a bank's output (q_i), the level of its financial capital (k_i) and the time trend (T_i). B is a vector of parameters, v_i is a two-sided error term representing the statistical noise (assumed to be independently and identically distributed and to have a normal distribution with mean 0 and variance σ^2_v). u_i are non-negative random variables that account for technical inefficiency.

In order to estimate our cost and profit efficiencies, we adopt the two approaches suggested by Battese and Coelli (1992 and 1995). In the case of Battese and Coelli's 1995 model, u_i are assumed to be independently distributed as truncations at zero of the N (m_i, σ^2_u) distribution. $m_i = \delta_i d)$, where d_i is a set of environmental variables (defined in the previous section) which are employed to control for a firm's specific factors that may contribute to explain the differences in the efficiency estimates, and d is a vector of parameters to be estimated. For the Battese and Coelli 1992 model, u_i are assumed to be truncations at zero of the N (μ, σ^2_u) distribution.

For ease of exposition, the following outlines the model specification for estimating cost functions.[2] The translog functional form for the cost frontier is specified as:

$$\begin{aligned}\ln(C/w_3) &= \alpha + \sum_{i=1}^{2} B_i \ln(w_i/w_3) + \sum_{k=1}^{3} \gamma_k \ln y_k + \sum_{r=1}^{3} \psi_r \ln z_r \\ &+ \frac{1}{2}\left[\sum_{i=1}^{2}\sum_{j=1}^{2} B_{ij} \ln(w_i/w_3)\ln(w_j/w_3)\right] + \frac{1}{2}\left[\sum_{k=1}^{3}\sum_{m=1}^{3} \gamma_{km} \ln y_k \ln y_m\right] \\ &+ \frac{1}{2}\left[\sum_{r=1}^{3}\sum_{s=1}^{3} \psi_{rs} \ln z_r \ln z_s\right] + \sum_{i=1}^{2}\sum_{k=1}^{3} \eta_{ik} \ln(w_i/w_3)\ln(y_k) \\ &+ \sum_{i=1}^{2}\sum_{r=1}^{3} \rho_{ir} \ln(w_i/w_3)\ln(z_r) + \sum_{k=1}^{3}\sum_{r=1}^{3} \tau_{kr} \ln y_k \ln z_r + u_{it} + v_{it}\end{aligned}$$

By augmenting the previous translog form by Fourier trigonometric terms, we get the Fourier-flexible functional form written as:

$$
\begin{aligned}
\ln(C/w_3) = {} & \alpha + \sum_{i=1}^{2} B_i \ln(w_i/w_3) + \sum_{k=1}^{3} \gamma_k \ln y_k + \sum_{r=1}^{3} \psi_r \ln z_r \\
& + \frac{1}{2}\left[\sum_{i=1}^{2}\sum_{j=1}^{2} B_{ij} \ln(w_i/w_3)\ln(w_j/w_3)\right] + \frac{1}{2}\left[\sum_{k=1}^{3}\sum_{m=1}^{3} \gamma_{km} \ln y_k \ln y_m\right] \\
& + \frac{1}{2}\left[\sum_{r=1}^{3}\sum_{s=1}^{3} \psi_{rs} \ln z_r \ln z_s\right] + \sum_{i=1}^{2}\sum_{k=1}^{3} \eta_{ik} \ln(w_i/w_3)\ln(y_k) \\
& + \sum_{i=1}^{2}\sum_{r=1}^{3} \rho_{ir} \ln(w_i/w_3)\ln(z_r) + \sum_{k=1}^{3}\sum_{r=1}^{3} \tau_{kr} \ln y_k \ln z_r \\
& + \sum_{n=1}^{8} \left[\phi_n \cos(x_n) + w_n \sin(x_n)\right] + \\
& \sum_{n=1}^{8}\sum_{q=n}^{8} \left[\phi_{nq} \cos(x_n + x_q) + w_{nq} \sin(x_n + x_q)\right] \\
& + \sum_{n=1}^{8} \left[\phi_{nnn} \cos(x_n + x_n + x_n) + w_{nnn} \sin(x_n + x_n + x_n)\right] + u_{it} + v_{it}
\end{aligned}
$$

where *lnC* is the natural logarithm of total costs (operating and financial); $ln\ y_i$ is the natural logarithm of bank outputs (that is, loans, securities, off-balance sheet items); $ln\ w_i$ is the natural logarithm of *i*th input prices (that is, wage rate, interest rate and physical capital price); the x_n terms, n=1,…,8 are rescaled values of the $\ln(w_1/w_3)$, i=1,2, $\ln(y_k)$, k=1,2,3, and $\ln(z_r)$, r=1,2,3, such that each of the x_n span the interval $[0, 2\pi]$, and π refers to the number of radians here (not profits), and α, β, γ, ψ, ρ, τ, η, δ, ω, ϕ and *t* are coefficients to be estimated.

Since the duality theorem requires that the cost function be linearly homogeneous in input prices, and continuity requires that the second order parameters are symmetric, the following restrictions apply to the parameters of the cost function in the equation above: $\sum_{i=1}^{3}\beta_j = 1$; $\sum_{i=1}^{3}B_{ij} = 0$; $\sum_{i=1}^{3}\eta_{ij} = 0$; $\sum_{i=1}^{n}\rho_{ij} = 0$ for all *j*. Moreover, the second order parameters of the cost function must be symmetric, that is $B_{ij} = B_{ji}$ and $\eta_{ik} = \eta_{ki}$, for all *i*, *k*. The scaled log-output quantities x_i are calculated as in Berger and Mester (1997) by cutting 10.0 per cent off each end of the $[0, 2\pi]$ interval so that the z_i span $[0.1 \times 2\pi, .9x\ 2\pi]$ reduces approximation problems near endpoints. The formula for z_i is $[0.2\pi - \mu \times a + \mu$ x variable], where [a, b] is the range of the variable being transformed, and $\mu \equiv (0.9 \times 2\pi + 0.1 \times 2\pi/\ (9b-a))$. This study applies Fourier terms only for the outputs, leaving the input price effects to be defined entirely by the translog terms, following Berger and Mester (1997). The primary aim is to maintain the limited number of Fourier terms for describing the scale and inefficiency measures associated with differences in bank size. Moreover, the usual input price homogeneity restrictions can be imposed on logarithmic price terms, whereas they cannot be easily imposed on the trigonometric terms.

The maximum-likelihood estimates for the parameters in the Fourier-flexible stochastic frontier for Cost, Standard and Alternative profit efficiency functions, that include efficiency correlates, are estimated using the computer program FRONTIER Version 4.0 (see Coelli 1996). This program uses three steps to obtain the maximum-likelihood estimates. The first step involves obtaining ordinary least squares (OLS) estimates of the equation. These estimates are unbiased because of the non-zero expectation of u_{it}. The second step involves evaluating the log-likelihood function for a number of values of γ between zero and one. During this procedure d_i, are set to zero and the values of B_0 and σ^2 are adjusted according to the corrected ordinary least squares formulae for the half-normal model. The estimates corresponding to the largest log-likelihood value in this second step are used as starting values in the iterative maximisation procedure in the third and final part of the estimation procedure.

In addition to estimating cost efficiencies, we also estimate alternative profit efficiency and standard profit efficiency using the same methodology. For the case of the standard profit function, we specify variable profits in place of variable costs and take output prices as given but allow output quantities to vary. On the other hand, the alternative profit function employs the same dependent variable as the standard profit function and the same exogenous variables as the cost function, but it measures how close a bank comes to earning maximum profits given its output levels rather than its output prices.

DATA

Our data comprises a representative sample of the banks operating in Jordan, Egypt, Saudi Arabia and Bahrain. It consists of 82 banks over the 1992–2000 period. This sample represents around 78.0 per cent, 88.0 per cent, 63.0 per cent and 55.0 per cent of the financial systems of these countries (excluding the assets of foreign branches and central banks). Table 6.1 below shows the details.

Our sample represents the major financial institutions that have consistently published their financial statements over the last ten years in the countries under study. The relative size of Bahrain's banks looks small, the reason being that the financial system in this country has been dominated by offshore banking units which are excluded from the sample as these belong to large international financial institutions and their data are unavailable. In Saudi Arabia, specialised government institutions, while important, do not publish detailed financial statements and so these are not included in the sample.

Table 6.2 shows the specialisation of the banks included in the sample. The number of commercial banks comprises around 66.0 per cent of the total sample. The per cent of commercial banks operating in each country varies, ranging from 44.0 per cent in Bahrain to 77.0 per cent in Saudi Arabia.

Table 6.1: Size of the sample relative to the banking sectors of Jordan, Egypt, Saudi Arabia and Bahrain over the 1992–2000 period (US$ million)

Country	*Bahrain*			*Egypt*			*Jordan*			*Saudi Arabia*		
Year	*Sample Assets*	*Total Banking Assets*	*%*	*Sample Assets*	*Total Banking Assets*	*%*	*Sample Assets*	*Total Banking Assets*	*%*	*Sample Assets*	*Total Banking Assets*	*%*
1992	34,200	77,500	44	52,200	62,500	84	6,900	9,100	75	77,600	129,600	60
1993	34,300	68,400	50	54,300	60,900	89	7,100	9,600	74	82,700	142,800	58
1994	37,000	73,700	50	57,200	62,300	92	8,000	10,700	75	85,400	146,300	58
1995	40,000	73,700	54	63,900	69,800	92	9,100	11,900	77	89,600	150,100	60
1996	42,500	76,600	55	67,600	77,100	88	9,800	12,500	79	93,900	156,400	60
1997	44,900	83,500	54	77,200	89,100	87	11,100	13,700	81	105,000	163,900	64
1998	48,700	99,400	49	82,600	97,300	85	12,000	14,800	81	111,500	171,400	65
1999	55,200	102,100	54	88,700	103,300	86	13,000	16,300	80	121,700	172,200	71
2000	57,400	106,400	54	93,800	103,600	90	14,500	18,900	77	131,900	181,300	73
Average	43,800	84,600	52	70,800	80,600	88	10,200	13,100	78	99,900	157,100	63

Sources: The total assets were extracted from the annual financial reports of the monetary agencies in the countries under study (the consolidated financial statements of the banks), while the sample was drawn from the London Bankscope database (January 2000 and 2002).

Table 6.3 shows that the size of total assets of all the banks included in the present study increased from about US$180 billion in 1992 to about US$310 billion in 2000 and averaged about US$235 billion over the whole period. Dividing these financial institutions into nine size categories, the share of the largest banks (with assets size greater than US$5 billion) constituted around 70.0 per cent of the total assets of all the banks over the period 1992–2000.

This study employs the intermediation approach for defining bank inputs and outputs. Following Aly et al. (1990), the inputs used in the calculation of the various efficiency measures are deposits (w_1), labour (w_2) and physical capital (w_3). The deposits include time and savings deposits, notes and debentures, and

Table 6.2: Specialisation of banks under study, 1992–2000

% of total	*Bahrain*	*Egypt*	*Jordan*	*Saudi Arabia*	*All*
Commercial	44	76	57	77	66
Investment	28	8	29	8	16
Islamic	17	5	7	0	7
Other	11	11	7	15	11
Total Number	18	37	14	13	82

Source: Bankscope (January 2000 and 2002).

Table 6.3: Distribution of banks' assets in Jordan, Egypt, Saudi Arabia and Bahrain, 1992–2000

	1992 %	*1993* %	*1994* %	*1995* %	*1996* %	*1997* %	*1998* %	*1999* %	*2000* %	*Avg. US$m*
1–99.9	0.11	0.08	0.14	0.16	0.14	0.10	0.06	0.02	0.02	202
100–199.9	1.16	1.05	0.78	0.35	0.31	0.18	0.21	0.29	0.27	1,073
200–299.9	1.76	1.35	1.10	1.78	1.04	0.80	0.67	0.36	0.32	2,173
300–499.9	3.78	4.08	3.47	2.79	2.92	2.75	2.49	2.04	1.58	6,422
500–999.9	2.56	2.73	4.64	4.57	4.51	3.53	3.67	3.47	3.29	8,569
1,000–2,499.9	11.87	11.50	9.89	13.09	10.02	11.31	11.84	10.51	10.15	25,911
2,500–4,999.9	8.29	8.56	4.68	4.94	7.12	6.65	6.50	7.66	8.26	16,470
5,000–9,999	18.22	19.28	24.51	26.23	24.40	26.82	14.88	19.13	9.28	46,196
10,000+	52.26	51.37	50.78	54.22	49.54	47.85	59.67	56.53	66.83	129,190
Total Assets (US$m, nominal values)	179,033	186,975	197,046	213,044	225,426	250,325	267,943	292,855	313,209	

Source: Bankscope (January 2000 and 2002).

other borrowed funds. The price of loanable funds was derived by taking the sum of interest expenses of the time deposits and other loanable funds divided by loanable funds. Labour is measured by personnel expenses as a per cent of total assets.[3] Bank physical capital is measured by the book value of premises and fixed assets (including capitalised leases). The price of capital is derived by taking total expenditures on premises and fixed assets divided by total assets. The three outputs used in the study include total customer loans (y_1), all other earning assets (y_2), and off-balance sheet items (y_3), measured in millions of US dollars.

The off-balance sheet items (measured in nominal terms) were included as a third output. Although the latter are technically not earning assets, these constitute an increasing source of income for banks and therefore should be included when modelling the banks' cost characteristics; otherwise, total banks' output would tend to be understated (Jagtiani and Khanthavit 1996). Furthermore, these items are included in the model because they are often effective substitutes for directly issued loans, requiring similar information-gathering costs of origination and ongoing monitoring and control of the counterparts, and presumably similar revenues, as these items are competitive substitutes for direct loans.

Table 6.4: Descriptive statistics of the banks' inputs and outputs for Jordan, Egypt, Saudi Arabia and Bahrain, 1992–2000

Variables	*Description*	*Mean*	*St. Dev.*	*Min.*	*Max.*
TC	Total cost (includes interest expense, personnel expense, commission expense, fee expense, trading expense, other operating expense) (US$ millions).	170	300	0	1,720
W1	Price of funds (%) (total interest expense/ total customer deposits [demand, saving and time deposits]).	0.07	0.09	0.00	1.98
W2	Price of labour (%) (total personnel expense/total assets).	0.02	0.01	0.00	0.21
W3	Price of physical capital (non-interest expense/average assets).	0.01	0.01	0.00	0.21
Y1	The US$ value of total aggregate loans (all types of loans) [US$ millions].	1,260	2,280	1	15,060
Y2	The US$ value of total aggregate other earning assets (short-term investment, equity and other investment and public sector securities [US$ millions]).	1,390	2,470	1	13,600
Y3	The US$ value of the off-balance sheet activities (nominal values, US$ millions).	1,320	3,510	1	26,740
P1	Price of loans (%) (total earned interest/total loans).	0.15	0.07	0.01	0.87
P2	Price of other earning assets (%) (trading income and other operating income, excluding commission and fees income/other earning assets).	0.05	0.04	0.01	0.33
P3	Price of off-balance sheet items (%) (commission and fees income/ off-balance sheet items).	0.01	0.02	0.00	0.20

Source: Bankscope (January 2000 and 2002).

The definitions, means and standards of deviation of the input and output variables used in the stochastic frontier estimations are reported in Table 6.4. The table shows that the average bank had US$1.26 billion in loans, US$1.39 billion in other earning assets and US$1.32 billion of off-balance sheet items over the period 1992–2000. The cost of input variables averaged about 7.0 per cent for purchased funds, 2.0 per cent for labour and 1.0 per cent for physical capital over the period 1992–2000. On the other hand, the prices of banks' output averaged about 15.0 per cent for loans,[4] 5.0 per cent for other earning assets and 1.0 per cent for off-balance sheet items over the same period.

In addition to the above input and output variables, the present study employs a variety of control and environmental variables[5] to rule out the effect of other factors that might explain differences among efficiency estimates for the banks under study. The three control variables included in our model are the size of loan loss reserves as a per cent of a bank's credit portfolio, the capital adequacy ratio, and a time trend (see Table 6.5 below for details). The loan loss reserves as a proportion of gross loans ranged between 0.01 and 19.68 per cent, the latter figure suggesting that some banks faced substantial credit quality problems. The total banks' capital as a percentage of total assets averaged around 14.0 per cent with a standard deviation of 12.0 per cent, which reflects sizable differences in the capital adequacy of the banks under study.

The size of loan loss reserves as a proportion of gross loans is added to the model to control for the bank's risk structure. It is also used as a measure of the bank's asset quality and as a measure of the bank's management efficiency in monitoring the credit portfolio. A lack of diversity in a bank's asset portfolio may be associated with increases in problem loans without sufficient provisioning, exposing the bank's capital to risk and potential bankruptcy that might be closely related to the quality of bank management. Banks facing financial distress have been found to carry large proportions of non-performing loans (Whalen 1991). Furthermore, studies on bank failures suggest a positive relationship between operating inefficiency and failure rates (see for example, Cebenoyan, Cooperman and Register 1993; Hermalin and Wallace 1994; Wheelock and Wilson 1995). Barr, Seiford and Siems (1994) found that this positive relationship between inefficiency and failure is evident a number of years ahead of eventual failure. Kwan and Eisenbeis (1994) report that problem loans are negatively related to efficiency even in non-failing banks. Berger and DeYoung (1997) found a link between management quality and problem loans by reporting that an increase in management quality reduces the bank's problem loans.

Hughes et al. (1996a,b) and Mester (1996) included the volume of non-performing loans as a control for loan quality in studies of US banks, and Berg et al. (1992) included loan losses as an indicator of loan quality evaluations in a DEA study of Norwegian bank productivity. Whether it is appropriate to include non-performing loans and loan losses in banks' cost, standard and alternative profit functions depends on the extent to which these variables are exogenous. Such variables would be exogenous if caused by negative economic shocks, 'bad luck', but they could be endogenous either because management is inefficient in managing its portfolio, 'bad management', or because it has made a conscious decision to reduce short-run expenses by cutting back on loan origination and monitoring resources, 'skimping'. Berger and DeYoung (1997) tested the bad luck, bad management, and skimping hypotheses and found mixed evidence on the exogeneity of non-performing loans.

Another important aspect of efficiency measurement is the treatment of financial capital. A bank's insolvency risk depends on the financial capital available to absorb portfolio losses, as well as on the portfolio risks themselves. Even apart from risk, a bank's capital level directly affects costs by providing an alternative to deposits as a funding source for loans. On the other hand, raising equity typically involves higher costs than raising deposits. If the first effect dominates, measured costs will be higher for banks using a higher proportion of debt financing; if the second effect dominates, measured costs will be lower for these banks. Large banks depend more on debt financing to finance their portfolios than small banks do, so failure to control for equity could yield a scale bias. The specification of capital in the cost and profit functions also goes part of the way towards accounting for different risk preferences. Therefore, if some banks are more risk averse than others, they may hold a higher level of financial capital than maximising profits or minimising costs. If financial capital is ignored, the efficiency of these banks would be measured incorrectly, even though they behave optimally given their risk preferences. Hughes et al. (1996a,b, 1997) and Hughes and Moon (1995) tested and rejected the assumption of risk neutrality for banks. Clark (1996) included capital in a model of economic cost and found that it eliminated measured scale diseconomies in production costs alone. The cost studies of Hughes and Mester (1993) and the Hughes et al. (1996a, 1997) profit studies incorporated financial capital and found increasing returns to scale at large-asset-size banks. A possible reason is that large size confers diversification benefits that allow large banks to have lower capital ratios than smaller banks. Akhavein et al. (1997a) controlled for equity capital and found that profit efficiency increases as a result of mergers of large banks. Banks' capital is also included in the model of Berger and Mester (1997), who find that well-capitalised firms are more efficient. This positive relationship between capital and efficiency may indicate that inefficient banks with lower capital have less to lose in taking more risky projects than an efficient bank. This is consistent with moral hazard and agency conflict between managers and shareholders, where less-monitored managers with lower equity have incentives to expense preference.

The environmental variables (or efficiency correlates) were also added to the model to investigate the reason for the differences in efficiency scores across banks under study. These include variables that control for market structure and organisational characteristics, geographical segmentation and bank liquidity. We identify variables to account for bank specialisation, bank size and concentration in the respective banking industries. Financial institutions in each country are divided into four categories; commercial, investment, Islamic and other financial institutions (that perform various bank functions). Furthermore, we employ the three-firm asset concentration ratio that is widely used to test for monopoly characteristics. We also include a dummy variable to control for bank geographical (country) location. Table 6.5 shows descriptive statistics of the control and environmental variables

The total assets variable is used to control for bank size where bank size should be strongly associated with efficiency as size may be required to utilise scale and (maybe) scope economies (if large banks are more diversified).

Table 6.5: Descriptive statistics of the banks' control and environmental variables for Jordan, Egypt, Saudi Arabia and Bahrain, 1992-2000

Variables	*Description*	*Mean*	*St. Dev.*	*Min.*	*Max.*
The Control Variables					
K	Capital adequacy (%) (Total Equity/ Total Assets)	0.14	0.12	0.01	0.72
S	Asset quality (Loan Loss Reserve/Gross Loans)	0.22	0.81	0.01	19.68
T	Time trend	5.00	2.58	1.00	9.00
The Environmental Variables					
TA	Total Assets (US$ millions)	2,881	4,966	35	26,700
B	Dummy variable for Bahrain	0.22	0.41	0.00	1.00
J	Dummy variable for Jordan	0.17	0.38	0.00	1.00
E	Dummy variable for Egypt	0.45	0.50	0.00	1.00
Com.	Dummy variable for commercial banks	0.66	0.47	0.00	1.00
Inv.	Dummy variable for investment/ securities banks	0.16	0.37	0.00	1.00
Isl.	Dummy variable for Islamic banks	0.07	0.26	0.00	1.00
L	Liquidity ratio (%) (Total Liquid Assets/Total Assets)	0.14	0.16	0.00	0.71
3-FCR	Three-firm concentration ratio (%) (the largest 3 banks' Total Assets /Total Assets of all banks in the bank country for the respective years)	0.62	0.14	0.48	0.81
MS	Bank assets market share (%) for each year	0.05	0.10	0.00	0.68

Source: Bankscope (January 2000 and 2002).

Furthermore, larger banks may have more professional management teams and/ or might be more cost conscious due to greater pressure from owners concerning bottom line profits (Evanoff and Israilevich 1991). Berger et al. (1993) found that most of the efficiency differences among large banks were on the output side, as larger banks might be better able to reach their optimal mix and scale of outputs. On the other hand, Hermalin and Wallace (1994), Kaparakis et al. (1994) and DeYoung and Nolle (1996) found significant negative relationships. Other studies, such as Aly et al. (1992), Cebenoyan et al. (1993), Mester (1993), Pi and Timme (1993), Mester (1996b), Berger and Hannan (1995), Berger and Mester (1997) and Chang et al. (1998), report no significant relationship between bank size and efficiency.

The three-firm concentration ratio and market share variables were included to control for oligopoly behaviour along the lines of the traditional structure-conduct-performance paradigm (see Molyneux et al. 1996) and as an indicator of the characteristics of the respective banking industry structures. The Cournot model of oligopolistic behaviour suggests that there is a positive relationship between concentration and profitability. Consistent with this model, some studies have found a positive relationship between market concentration and profitability (Berger and Hannan 1997; Berger and Mester 1997). The market power that prevails in less competitive markets enables some banks to charge higher prices for their services and make supernormal profits. Banks may exert their own market power through size as noted by Berger (1995). Therefore, we include a market share variable to control for what Berger refers to as 'relative market power'.

Dummy variables for bank specialisation are also included in the model so as to control for product diversity, as efficiency might be associated with a firm's strength in carefully targeting its market niches. The cost of producing various products might be lower when specialised banks produce them rather than when a single bank produces all the products due to diseconomies of scope. There are a number of studies that have examined the impact of product diversity on efficiency. Aly et al. (1990) found a negative relationship between product diversity and cost efficiency. Ferrier, Grosskopf, Hayes and Yaisawarng (1993) found that banks with greater product diversity tend to have lower cost efficiency. Chaffai and Dietsch (1995) compared the efficiency of universal versus non-universal (more specialised) banks in Europe and found the former to be less cost efficient.

Finally, the liquidity ratio is included to account for banks' liquidity risk. Banks that hold more liquidity may be expected to have lower liquidity risk but may be less profit efficient as liquid assets tend to yield lower returns. By contrast, as liquid assets are controlled in outputs, one would expect banks with higher liquid assets (all other things being equal) to be more cost efficient.

RESULTS: COST AND PROFIT EFFICIENCIES

This section reports the main results derived from estimates of 'preferred' cost, standard and alternative profit models.[6] The Fourier-truncated model excluding control variables (capital, risk and time trend) but including all the efficiency correlates is our preferred cost function model and the parameter estimates are shown in Appendix 6. The preferred model for both the standard and alternative profit functions is the Fourier-truncated model that includes both the control variables (capital, risk and time trend) as well as the efficiency correlates. (Parameter estimates are available from the authors on request.)

Estimated levels of cost and profit efficiency

Inefficiency estimates for the cost, standard and alternative profit efficiency, derived from the preferred models, are summarised in Tables 6.6 to 6.8 below.

In terms of the preferred cost function, efficiency estimates for banks in the countries under study averaged 95.0 per cent, and these estimates have slightly varied over time from 95.0 per cent in 1992 to 94.0 per cent in 2000. This suggests that the same level of output could be produced with approximately

95.0 per cent of current inputs if banks under study were operating on the most efficient frontier. This level of technical inefficiency is somewhat less than the range of 10.0–15.0 per cent for the 130 studies surveyed by Berger and Humphrey (1997)[7] and Berger and DeYoung (1997). These results are also less than the level of inefficiency found in European studies, including Carbo et al.'s (2000) whose findings for a sample of banks from 12 countries show a mean cost inefficiency of around 22.0 per cent for the period 1989–96.

Referring to Table 6.6, the average efficiency based on bank specialisation ranged from 93.0 per cent for investment banks to 98.0 per cent for Islamic banks. The efficiency scores based on geographical location ranged from 89.0 per cent in Jordan to 99.0 per cent in Bahrain. Finally, based on asset size, the differences among technical efficiency scores are not significant where optimal bank size is between US$2.5 and 5.0 billion and the largest banks seem to be more efficient. These results are noticeably different from Carbo et al.'s (2000) findings on European savings banks, who find that the least X-efficient banks were the largest in asset size.

As indicated earlier, the bank efficiency literature considers the estimation of both cost and profit efficiencies to reveal more accurate information about firm-level performance (see Berger and Mester 1999). Referring to Tables 6.7 and 6.8, the standard and alternative profit functions results show average technical efficiency estimates are around 66.0 per cent and 58.0 per cent respectively over the period 1992–2000. It should be noted that this level of efficiency is somehow similar to the typical range of profit efficiency found in US studies, which is about half of the industry's potential profits, according to Berger and Humphrey (1997). Profit inefficiencies in Arabic banking are less than those found in European banking. For instance, William and Gardener (2000) estimate profit efficiency to have been 79.7 per cent in European banking during the 1990s. The mean profit efficiency given the standard profit function suggests that banks under study lose around 34.0 per cent of profits that could be earned by a best practice institution. The profit efficiency given both the standard profit and alternative profit function has witnessed volatility over the period 1992–2000. While over the period 1993–9, the efficiency estimates derived from both profit function specifications fluctuate slightly around their average, in 2000 there was a fall in profit efficiency across the banks under study. This might reflect the response of economic and financial activities to instability in oil prices and to political instability aroused from recent conflict aggravation in Palestine and the Gulf.

In the case of the standard profit function, profit efficiency ranged from around 61.0 per cent in Jordan to 68.0 per cent in Bahrain. Based on specialisation, the results show that the efficiency scores ranged from 56.0 per cent for investment banks to 75.0 per cent for Islamic banks (see Table 6.7 for details).

Table 6.6: Cost efficiency in Jordan, Egypt, Saudi Arabia and Bahrain banking, 1992–2000

	1992	*1993*	*1994*	*1995*	*1996*	*1997*	*1998*	*1999*	*2000*	*All*
Bahrain	100	100	100	100	100	99	99	99	99	99
Egypt	94	94	94	94	94	93	93	93	93	94
Jordan	90	89	89	89	89	89	89	88	88	89
Saudi Arabia	97	97	97	97	97	97	97	97	96	97
Commercial	95	95	95	95	94	94	94	94	94	94
Investment	93	93	93	93	93	93	93	93	93	93
Islamic	98	98	98	98	99	99	98	98	98	98
Other	97	96	96	96	96	96	96	96	96	96
All	95	95	95	95	95	94	94	94	94	95
Asset Size (*US$ million*)	*1–199*	*200–299*	*300–499*	*500–999*	*1,000–2,499*	*2,500–4,999*	*5,000–9,900*	*10,000+*		*All*
Bahrain	100	99	100	99	99	99	99	99		99
Egypt	95	94	94	94	94	93	92	90		94
Jordan	88	87	88	91	90			91		89
Saudi Arabia				98	98	98	98	95		97
All	95	93	94	95	95	96	96	94		95
Asset Size (*US$ million*)	*1992*	*1993*	*1994*	*1995*	*1996*	*1997*	*1998*	*1999*	*2000*	*All*
1–199	94	94	95	95	96	96	95	96	95	95
200–299	93	94	92	93	92	92	95	95	95	93
300–499	95	95	95	95	94	94	92	92	91	94
500–999	96	94	94	94	94	95	96	95	96	95
1,000–2,499	96	96	95	96	96	94	94	94	94	95
2,500–4,999	95	96	99	96	96	96	96	96	96	96
5,000–9,999	98	98	97	96	96	96	95	96	95	96
10,000+	95	95	94	94	94	93	94	93	94	94
All	95	95	95	95	95	94	94	94	94	95

Source: Adapted from Al-Jarrah and Molyneux (2003).

This result might explain the increase in Islamic banking activities especially in Bahrain over the past few years, as the cost of funds for Islamic banks is relatively less. Islamic banks in general do not pay interest, but rather a mark-up that is a profit margin based on the way in which the funds are utilised. In terms of geographic location, Jordan is a relatively much poorer country as compared with Saudi Arabia and Bahrain (oil-producing countries) and banks may be able

Table 6.7: Standard profit efficiency in Jordan, Egypt, Saudi Arabia and Bahrain banking, 1992–2000

	1992	*1993*	*1994*	*1995*	*1996*	*1997*	*1998*	*1999*	*2000*	*All*
Bahrain	69	78	67	71	66	72	67	68	57	68
Egypt	66	64	66	70	66	64	65	73	63	66
Jordan	84	60	61	61	63	56	56	59	50	61
Saudi Arabia	67	68	66	69	69	65	59	63	63	65
Commercial	70	67	68	72	69	65	62	68	62	67
Investment	65	69	55	55	48	51	57	60	43	56
Islamic	83	73	78	79	75	80	67	67	76	75
Other	64	58	57	61	64	73	74	78	55	65
All	70	67	65	68	66	65	63	68	59	66
Asset Size *(US$ million)*	*1–199*	*200–299*	*300–499*	*500–999*	*1,000–2,499*	*2,500–4,999*	*5,000–9,900*	*10,000+*		*All*
Bahrain	75	67	71	62	66	66	78	56		68
Egypt	74	59	60	70	69	70	58	72		66
Jordan	53	66	56	73	53			68		61
Saudi Arabia				43	62	65	68	68		65
All	70	63	62	68	65	67	67	67		66
Asset Size (US$ million)	*1992*	*1993*	*1994*	*1995*	*1996*	*1997*	*1998*	*1999*	*2000*	*All*
1–199	72	68	75	70	65	70	76	70	56	70
200–299	65	75	60	65	62	60	57	63	44	63
300–499	71	65	60	60	58	63	59	64	55	62
500–999	61	66	62	76	71	64	63	75	66	68
1,000–2,499	78	62	64	66	65	67	66	67	56	65
2,500–4,999	59	49	79	79	78	63	64	77	62	67
5,000–9,999	65	73	71	72	64	60	61	70	64	67
10,000+	70	73	64	73	76	71	60	61	63	67
All	70	67	65	68	66	65	63	68	59	66

Source: Adapted from Al-Jarrah and Molyneux (2003).

to sell higher profit generating products in these markets. This might explain why Jordanian banks are relatively less profit efficient than the banks in other countries under study.

In terms of the size of assets, apart from the smallest banks (US$1–199 million) that are the most profit efficient, larger banks seems to be more profit efficient, in general. This result supports the theory that large banks enjoy

Table 6.8: Alternative profit in Jordan, Egypt, Saudi Arabia and Bahrain banking, 1992–2000

	1992	*1993*	*1994*	*1995*	*1996*	*1997*	*1998*	*1999*	*2000*	*All*
Bahrain	58	72	60	66	58	64	51	61	58	61
Egypt	65	58	60	62	59	60	56	68	55	60
Jordan	59	51	54	53	49	39	42	52	46	49
Saudi Arabia	56	56	54	51	61	59	51	61	61	57
Commercial	60	59	61	63	63	58	53	62	56	60
Investment	55	61	52	50	43	46	46	62	44	51
Islamic	76	57	60	64	54	63	51	55	78	62
Other	69	62	47	53	48	63	56	67	47	57
All	61	60	58	60	58	57	52	62	55	58

Asset Size *(US$ million)*	*1–199*	*200–299*	*300–499*	*500–999*	*1,000–2,499*	*2,500–4,999*	*5,000–9,900*	*10,000+*		*All*
Bahrain	63	66	59	54	55	59	86	68		61
Egypt	59	55	54	63	64	61	64	78		60
Jordan	42	46	46	59	43			74		49
Saudi Arabia				23	50	65	56	63		57
All	56	55	54	59	57	62	61	69		58

Asset Size (US$ million)	*1992*	*1993*	*1994*	*1995*	*1996*	*1997*	*1998*	*1999*	*2000*	*All*
1–199	61	47	57	68	49	62	63	55	48	56
200–299	56	72	47	58	57	45	46	59	46	55
300–499	58	64	56	52	50	57	44	53	44	54
500–999	62	53	55	61	63	55	51	70	56	59
1,000–2,499	70	57	63	54	49	57	50	64	53	57
2,500–4,999	58	50	66	66	64	52	55	73	66	62
5,000–9,999	58	55	67	64	64	58	63	65	56	61
10,000+	62	80	62	74	84	77	60	62	68	69
All	61	60	58	60	58	57	52	62	55	58

Source: Adapted from Al-Jarrah and Molyneux (2003).

several advantages as compared with small banks. These advantages include the ability of large banks to utilise more efficient technology with less cost, the ability of these banks to prepare more specialised staff for the most profitable activities, and their ability to provide higher-quality output resulting in higher prices.

Similar results are obtained from the alternative profit function estimates, where profit efficiency ranges from 49.0 per cent in Jordan to 61.0 per cent in

Bahrain. Based on specialisation, Islamic banking is again the most profit efficient while investment banking is the least efficient. Based on asset size, the largest banks seem to be the most efficient. Overall, the results of both the standard and alternative profit function, while varying in absolute efficiency levels, are exactly identical in terms of profit efficiency ranking in terms of country, specialisation and bank asset size.

CONCLUSIONS

A major aim of this study was to estimate efficiency levels in various Arab banking sectors by applying statistical analyses to a data set on Jordan, Egypt, Saudi Arabia and Bahrain. As pointed out by Berger and Humphrey (1997), there have been many studies that investigate banking sector efficiency using varying data periods, methodologies and countries, but there is no consensus on the sources of the sizable variation in measured efficiency. The undue variations in the bank efficiency studies undertaken so far make it impossible to determine how important the different efficiency concepts, measurement techniques and correlates used are related to the outcomes of these studies.

This study employs three distinct economic efficiency concepts (cost, standard profit and alternative profit efficiencies), using a number of different measurement methods (including the stochastic frontier approach, specification of the Fourier-flexible functional form versus the translog form, and the inclusion of banks' asset quality and financial capital in a number of different ways) to a single data set. In choosing the 'preferred' cost and profit models, we follow the recent efficiency methodologies that proceed by testing various model specifications to arrive at the preferred model. Based on these preferred models for cost, standard profit and alternative profit, different efficiency measures are reported for the banks in the countries under study. In the case of cost efficiency, the preferred model is the Fourier-truncated form that excludes the control variables (capital adequacy, asset quality and the time trend) but includes all the environmental variables. In the case of the standard and alternative profit function, the preferred model is the Fourier-flexible that includes the control as well as the environmental variables.

Overall, this main finding is that efficiency levels differ according to the three various efficiency concepts that are used (cost, profit and alternative profit), and each method adds some informational value. A somewhat interesting result is that the choices made concerning the efficiency measurement method lead to somewhat similar model specifications.

In terms of the preferred model, cost efficiency averaged around 95.0 per cent over the 1992–2000 period. In the case of the standard and alternative profit function, technical efficiency averaged 66.0 per cent and 58.0 per cent respectively over the same period. Islamic banks are found to be the most cost and profit efficient, while investment banks are the least cost and profit efficient. In terms of bank asset size, larger banks seem to be relatively more cost and profit efficient. Geographically, Bahrain is the most cost and profit efficient, while Jordan is the least cost and profit efficient country. It should be noted that these results, in general, are similar to those found in other US and European banking studies. The results for scale efficiency also suggest that larger banks are the more cost and profit efficient. Saudi Arabian, and to a lesser degree Egyptian, banks are found to be the most cost and profit efficient.

Another major finding of this chapter is that there is little evidence to suggest that the economic and financial reforms undertaken in Jordan, Egypt, Saudi Arabia and Bahrain over the last decade have had a noticeable impact on improving banking sector efficiency. Given this finding, it seems that more reforms may be needed to improve their profit efficiency in particular. Perhaps the move to create a single Gulf Cooperation Council market may help to facilitate these developments, as the creation of a similar European single market appears to have had a positive impact on European bank efficiency (see the European Commission 1997). The main policy recommendation from this study, therefore, is that these countries need to continue the reform process in order to enhance financial sector performance.

NOTES

1. Also see Levine et al. (1999) and Levine and Loyaza (2000).
2. For the standard profit function, we specify variable profits in place of variable costs and take variable output prices as given but allow output quantities to vary. On the other hand, the alternative profit function employs the same dependent variable as the standard profit function, and the same exogenous variables as the cost function, but it measures how close a bank comes to earning maximum profits given in its output levels rather than in its output prices.
3. As staff numbers were not available for the banks in the sample, we used this measure instead. This measure for staff costs has been used in various previous studies, including Altunbas et al. (1996) and (2001a,b).
4. This may be an overstatement, as interest earned on bonds is also included in this figure.
5. The control variables enter into the stochastic frontier model in the same way as the input variables (as betas) and these variables are fully interactive with other parameters of the model. On the other hand, the environmental variables are not interactive with other model parameters and are added to the model as deltas.
6. There are three stages undertaken to arrive at the preferred model for our cost function estimates. The first stage involves utilising Battese and Coelli's (1995) approach that allows us to include the efficiency correlates directly in the model estimation. The second stage involves utilising Battese and Coelli's (1992) time-varying efficiency approach that gives flexibility to examine different assumptions

concerning the distribution of efficiency terms, comparing time-variant versus time-invariant models, but it does not allow for the inclusion of efficiency correlates in the model. Finally, stage 3 compares the best specified models in stage 1 and stage 2 to arrive at a single preferred model from the two stages and provides the basis for the model choice.

7. Of these, 60 parametric studies found that the mean technical inefficiency is smaller that 15.0 per cent.

7

Determinants of Islamic Banking Profitability

M. Kabir Hassan and Abdel-Hameed M. Bashir

This chapter analyses how bank characteristics and the overall financial environment affect the performance of Islamic banks. Utilising bank level data, the study examines the performance indicators of Islamic banks worldwide during the period 1994–2001. A variety of internal and external banking characteristics have been used to predict profitability and efficiency. Controlling for macroeconomic environment, financial market structure and taxation, the results indicate that high capital and loan-to-asset ratios lead to higher profitability. Other things remaining equal, the regression results show that implicit and explicit taxes affect the bank performance measures negatively, while favourable macroeconomic conditions impact performance measures positively. In general, our analysis confirms previous findings on the determinants of banks' profitability. The only unusual result is that a strong positive correlation is found between profitability and overhead expenses.

INTRODUCTION

The steady expansion of Islamic banks has been the hallmark of the Muslim World financial landscape during the 1980s and 1990s. With a network that spans more than 60 countries and an asset base of more than $166 billion, Islamic banks are now playing an increasingly significant role in their respective economies. Based on their charters, Islamic banks have the flexibility of becoming shareholders and creditors of firms, as well as the advantage of providing investment banking services. In this respect, Islamic banks are rapidly gaining market shares in their domestic economies.[1] In retrospect, the presence of Islamic banks signifies the viability and success of eliminating fixed interest payments from financial transactions.

Indeed, consolidation among banks, rising competition and continuous innovation to provide financial services, all contribute to a growing interest in a critical evaluation of Islamic banks. Evaluating the performance of Islamic banks is essential for managerial as well as regulatory purposes. While managers are keen to determine the outcomes of previous management decisions, bank regulators are concerned about the safety and soundness of the banking system, and also about preserving public confidence and identifying banks that are experiencing severe problems. Without persistent monitoring of performance, existing problems can remain unnoticed and could lead to financial failure. Depositors may also be interested in knowing the performance of their bank(s), since they are not entitled to fixed returns and the nominal values of their deposits are not guaranteed. Most importantly, performance evaluation is needed to provide answers to key policy questions such as: Should Islamic banks be held to the same set of regulations as conventional banks? Are they relics of a bygone era, propped up by subsidies and distorting financial sector competition? Or, are they efficient and focused financial institutions that could, if unleashed, eventually dominate the retail financial landscape?

Previous attempts to study Islamic banks (Ahmed 1981; Karsen 1982) focused primarily on the conceptual issues underlying interest-free financing. The issues surrounding the viability of Islamic banks and their ability to mobilise savings, pool risks and facilitate transactions did not receive enough coverage in the literature. Some studies, however, have focused on the policy implications of eliminating interest payments (Khan 1986; Khan and Mirakhor 1987; Bashir 1996). In fact, the lack of complete data impeded any comprehensive analysis of the experience during the last three decades. For example, the empirical work done so far has yielded inconclusive results (see Bashir, Darrat and Suliman 1993; Bashir 1999; Zaher and Hassan 2001; Hassan 1999). Meanwhile, the recent trends of financial liberalisation and deregulation have created new challenges and new realities for Islamic banks. The integration of global financial markets has put Islamic banks in fierce competition with traditional banks. To compete in local and global deposit markets, Islamic banks have to design and innovate Islamically acceptable instruments that can cope with the continuous innovations in financial markets. In addition, Islamic banks should find investment opportunities (for fund mobilisation and utilisation) that offer competitive rates of return at acceptable degrees of risk. Equally, banks' management must carefully consider interactions between different performance measures in order to maximise the value of the bank.

This chapter identifies some financial and policy indicators that impact the overall performance of Islamic banks. Specifically, the purpose of the study is to examine closely the relationship between profitability and banking characteristics, after controlling for economic and financial structure indicators. The intention is to decide which, among the potential determinants of performance, appear to be important. By studying the relationship between Islamic banks' performance and efficiency indicators, this chapter contributes to the ongoing discussion on the effects of deregulation and liberalisation on the performance of the banking sector. The chapter attempts to add to the existing literature in several ways. First, utilising bank level data, the paper provides summary statistics pertaining to Islamic banks' sizes and profitability. Second, the paper uses regression analysis to determine the underlying determinants of Islamic banks' performance.[2] To this end, a comprehensive set of internal characteristics is examined as determinants of banks' profitability.[3] These internal characteristics include bank size, leverage, loans, short-term funding and overheads. Third, while studying the relationship between banks' internal characteristics and performance, the work controls for the impact of external factors, such as the macroeconomic, regulatory and financial market environment. Among the external factors controlled, reserves, taxes and market capitalisation were not included in previous studies of Islamic banks. Moreover, some of the determinants were also interacted with the country's GDP per capita to check whether their impacts on bank performance differ with levels of income. Finally, the results show that it is possible to conduct a meaningful analysis in spite of the substantial differences in regulation and financial development between the countries in the sample.

The rest of the chapter is organised into four sections. Section 2 identifies the data sources, and defines and highlights the variables benchmarking Islamic banking performances. In Section 3 we formulate the model and discuss the possible links between bank performance and the set of internal and external indicators. Section 4 provides the empirical results, while the conclusions are stated in Section 5.

DATA AND VARIABLES

The data used in this study are cross-country bank level data compiled from the income statements and balance sheets of Islamic banks in 21 countries for each year during the period 1994–2001. Table 7.1 gives the country-wise and year-wise breakdown of these Islamic banks. The main data source is the BankScope database. In so far as possible, the BankScope database converts the data to common international standards to facilitate comparisons. Other data sources include the International Monetary Fund's International Financial Statistics (IFS), World Development Indicators (2001) and Global Development Finance (2001).

Let us begin our review with an initial assessment of the banking sector of the selected Islamic countries by analysing some accounting ratios as given in Table 7.2 without controlling for the other variables that are also important. We will move into deeper analysis gradually.

Columns 1 through 4 of Table 7.2 present the averages of four macroeconomic variables, which are GDP per capita, growth, inflation and real interest rate. Per capita GDP measured in 1995 US dollars is highest in Qatar ($19,907) followed by UAE ($17,988) and then by Brunei ($17,675). Sudan has the lowest per

Table 7.1: Number of banks by country and by year

Country\Year	*1994*	*1995*	*1996*	*1997*	*1998*	*1999*	*2000*	*2001*
Algeria		1	1	1	1	1	1	1
Bahamas					1	1	1	1
Bahrain	3	3	3	4	5	5	4	4
Bangladesh	1	1	1	1	1	1	1	2
Brunei Darussalam	2	2	2	3	3	3	3	
Egypt	1	2	2	2	2	2	2	1
Gambia				1	1	1	1	
Indonesia			1	1	1	1	1	
Iran	1	1		3	3	3	3	
Jordan	1	1	1	1	2	2	2	2
Kuwait	1	1	1	1	1	1	1	1
Lebanon	1	1	1	1	1	1		
Malaysia		2	2	2	3	3	3	3
Mauritania					1	1	1	
Qatar	1	2	2	2	2	2	2	2
Saudi Arabia	1	1	1	1	1	-1	1	
Sudan	2	2	3	3	3	3	1	1
Tunisia	1	1	1	1	1	1	1	
United Arab Emirates	1	1	1	1	2	2	2	2
United Kingdom	1	1	1	1	1	1	1	
Yemen			1	1	2	2	2	2
Total	18	23	25	31	39	39	34	22

Source: BankScope (2002).

capita GDP ($284). Bangladesh, Gambia and Yemen all have per capita GDP within the range of $300 to $360. Growth rates of GDP vary within the sample countries from the highest of 5.77 per cent per year in Sudan and the lowest of 0.98 per cent in Indonesia. Inflation is highest in Sudan (49.44 per cent per year) followed by Indonesia (24.40 per cent) and Iran (23.15 per cent). It is lowest in Jordan at 1.82 per cent, followed by 1.98 per cent in UAE. The real interest rate is highest in Gambia (20.80 per cent) and lowest in Algeria (-1.66 per cent). Therefore, the Islamic banks that we are about to study operate around the world at different levels of development. The economic structures, historical backgrounds, social norms and cultural values of these countries are also diverse in many respects.

Columns 5 to 7 of Table 7.2 show reserves to deposit ratios, bank to GDP ratios, and tax ratios. These ratios are indicators of financial market structure. The reserves to deposit ratio is highest in Jordan at 46.69 per cent, followed by Iran at 31.64 per cent and then by Sudan at 26.03 per cent. The ratio is lowest

Table 7.2: Economic and institutional indicators (for countries where there are Islamic banks)

All variables, except deposit insurance, are averaged over the period 1994-2001 (or the available years). The deposit insurance variable takes value 1 if the country has explicit insurance deposit coverage (as of 2001) and zero otherwise. Number of banks is the number of banks with at least three years of complete information in a given country.

Country	*GDP Per Capita (US$ 1995)*	*Growth (%)*	*Inflation (%)*	*Real interest (%)*	*Reserves/ deposits (%)*	*Bank/ GDP*	*Tax (%)*	*Deposit insurace*	*Concen- traction- (%)*	*Number of banks*[a]	*Credit*[b] *(%)*
Algeria	1,536	2.69	16.88	–1.66	1.97	29.48	14.12	0	65.92	4.86	10.84
Bahrain	10,175	3.57	0.36	11.62	7.58	54.97	–7.87	1	83.84	13.71	2.69
Bangladesh	344	5.03	3.98	10.16	12.21	30.48	57.23	1	9.13	21.25	64.90
Brunei	17,675	n.a.	n.a.	n.a.	n.a.	n.a.	35.17	0	n.a.	3.00	n.a.
Egypt	1,134	4.96	5.63	8.18	19.72	77.61	3.65	0	47.77	30.07	59.95
Gambia	357	5.45	3.27	20.80	16.44	22.63	3.27	0	40.14	2.25	49.02
Indonesia	1,034	0.98	24.40	2.31	15.88	56.71	45.28	0	38.36	69.20	63.02
Iran	1,574	3.20	23.15	n.a.	31.64	20.91	75.81	0	49.23	6.94	56.71
Jordan	1,613	3.75	1.82	9.74	46.69	78.43	44.74	0	75.41	11.00	17.60
Kuwait	15,056	1.55	6.49	4.09	1.76	100.52	0.27	0	26.25	9.57	18.44
Lebanon	2,840	4.42	6.67	14.84	16.38	127.40	14.72	1	31.92	63.33	29.68
Malaysia	4,600	4.94	3.04	5.09	16.79	117.47	68.17	0	27.58	45.43	34.58
Mauritania	489	4.27	7.42	n.a.	11.73	11.35	n.a.	0	96.68	3.67	87.63
Qatar	19,907	n.a.	n.a.	n.a.	4.93	72.14	n.a.	0	79.44	6.71	37.28
Saudi Arabia	6,836	1.55	5.15	5.35	6.05	46.37	n.a.	0	50.26	13.86	82.95
Sudan	284	5.77	49.44	n.a.	26.03	0.01	68.19	0	59.83	6.05	45.20
Tunisia	2,254	4.88	3.76	n.a.	6.22	57.09	5.04	0	38.98	16.13	73.02
UA Emirates	17,988	1.95	1.98	n.a.	16.25	61.69	n.a.	0	43.29	20.16	52.68
Yemen	306	4.47	13.95	6.79	25.40	8.72	n.a.	0	60.44	6.40	44.20

[a] Number of banks includes commercial banks, Islamic banks and non-banking credit institutions.

[b] Credit is Domestic credit to private sector / Total assets banking system.

in Algeria (1.97 per cent). The bank to GDP ratio, which is the ratio of the deposit money divided by GDP, is highest in Lebanon (127.40 per cent), followed by Malaysia (117.47 per cent) and then by Kuwait (100.52 per cent). Sudan has the lowest deposit money to GDP ratio of 0.01 per cent and is preceded by Yemen (8.72 per cent) and then Mauritania (11.35 per cent). The tax ratio is highest in Iran (75.81 per cent), followed by Sudan and Malaysia, both just over 68.0 per cent. It is lowest in Bahrain at –7.87 per cent.

In column 8 of Table 7.2 we present the deposit insurance dummy variable. It takes a value of 1 if such an insurance scheme is present, and otherwise it takes 0. We can observe that only Bahrain, Bangladesh and Lebanon have such schemes. In column 9 we present the concentration ratios defined as the ratio of the three largest banks' assets to total banking sector assets. We can see that the concentration ratio is very high in Mauritania (96.68 per cent), followed by Bahrain (83.84 per cent) and then by Qatar (79.44 per cent). It is lowest in Bangladesh (9.13 per cent). For other countries included in the sample this ratio ranges from 66.0 to 26.0 per cent. This is high indeed. This indicates lack of competition within the banking sector. The last column of Table 7.2 presents the credit variable, which is defined as the domestic credit of the private sector over total assets of the banking system. Mauritania has the highest credit ratio of 87.63 per cent, followed by Saudi Arabia (82.95 per cent) and then by Tunisia (73.02 per cent).

Financial institutions in general and banks in particular are exposed to a variety of risks. The extent of these risks depends on the portfolio characteristics of individual banks (IMF 2001). The variety of risks to which banks are exposed justifies looking at aspects of bank operations that can be categorised under the CAMEL framework.[4] Recent studies have deepened our understanding of the financial soundness indicators that are more relevant for the analysis of financial stability. Studies have focused on the contemporaneous indicators of financial health. No consensus has yet emerged, however, on a set of indicators that is more relevant to assessing financial soundness or to building effective early warning systems. Nonetheless, the literature provides some empirical justifications for the use of most of the variables that have been identified as prudential indicators of financial soundness (IMF 2000).

Table 7.3 presents the comparative performance indicators of Islamic banks and commercial banks in countries where Islamic banks operate side by side with conventional banks. The importance of the indicators listed in Table 7.3 stems from the fact that they help bank regulators assess bank performance. To facilitate comparison, the commercial banks and Islamic banks selected are similar in size, where size is measured in terms of total assets. Specifically, we select all commercial banks that are in the third quartile, in terms of size, in each country. Table 7.3 also summarises the time averages of some important ratios. The value of each ratio represents the average over the period 1994–2001. All ratio definitions for asset quality, capital, operations and liquidity are from BankScope database. Similarly, data on GDP, population and interest rates have been derived from International Financial Statistics (IFS).

To analyse the performance measures presented in Table 7.3, we start with asset quality ratios. Monitoring asset quality indicators is important since risks to the solvency of financial institutions often derive from impairment of assets. The most useful asset quality indicator is the financial leverage ratio (measured by the ratio of asset to capital). Poor asset quality is perceived to cause capital erosion and increase credit and capital risks. Asset quality depends on the quality of credit evaluation, monitoring and collection within each bank, and could be improved by collateralising the loans, having adequate provisions against potential losses, or avoiding asset concentration on one geographical or economic sector.[5] Any analysis of asset quality needs to take into account indicators of the likelihood of borrowers to repay their loans. It is particularly important to monitor whether the increase in indebtedness in the economy is concentrated in sectors that are vulnerable to shifts in economic activity. Loan concentration in a specific economic sector or activity (measured as a share of total loans) makes banks vulnerable to adverse developments in that sector or activity. Hence, the quality of financial institutions' loan portfolios is closely related to the financial health and profitability of the institutions' borrowers, especially the non-financial enterprise sector (IMF 2001). In this context, monitoring the level of household and corporate indebtedness is useful.

In comparing the asset quality ratios for equal-sized commercial and Islamic banks, we observe a significant difference in the ratio of loan loss reserve to gross loans. Commercial banks in our sample tend to have more loan loss reserve – relative to the total loans – than Islamic banks. Since high-performing banks tend to restrain their credit risk, they tend to have lower loan loss provision ratios. The comparison between the two groups of banks indicates that Islamic banks have a better quality of loan portfolio. Another significant difference is found when comparing the ratio of impaired loans over total loans. As in the previous case, Islamic banks have better asset quality compared to commercial banks. Finally, a significant difference exists in the percentage of net charge-off (NCO) to gross loans. The net charge-off indicates the percentage of loans written off the books. With a zero per cent, Islamic banks are out-performing their peers in the sample. In summary, when compared to commercial banks of similar size, Islamic banks seems to have better asset quality than their counterparts.

The second entry in Table 7.3 includes capital adequacy ratios. Capital adequacy and availability ratios indicate the robustness of financial institutions to shocks to their balance sheets. Usually actual capital adequacy ratios are lagged

Table 7.3: Benchmark performance measures of Islamic banks *vis-à-vis* conventional banks (a)

The average number of commercial banks with a similar asset size in the countries where Islamic banks are present. All commercial banks are selected the third quartile by size in each country in 2001. The value of each ratio represents the average in the period 1994–2001.

	Mean			
	Commercial	*Islamic*	*Difference*	*P–value*
Asset Quality				
Loan Loss Res / Gross Loans	5.31	2.19	3.12	0.02
Loan Loss Prov / Net Int Rev	58.44	16.44	42.00	0.13
Loan Loss Res / Impaired Loans	236.48	379.65	–143.17	0.25
Impaired Loans / Gross Loans	4.84	0.76	4.08	0.03
NCO / Average Gross Loans	0.96	0.00	0.96	0.03
NCO / Net Inc Bef Ln Lss Prov	54.44	0.30	54.15	0.16
Capital				
Equity / Tot Assets	7.89	12.22	–4.33	0.03
Equity / Net Loans	15.13	25.13	–10.00	0.04
Equity / Cust & ST Funding	9.83	19.79	–9.96	0.01
Equity / Liabilities	8.62	14.20	–5.58	0.04
Cap Funds / Tot Assets	8.18	12.23	–4.05	0.04
Cap Funds / Net Loans	15.68	25.16	–9.48	0.05
Cap Funds / Cust & ST Funding	10.20	19.81	–9.61	0.02
Cap Funds / Liabilities	8.94	14.21	–5.28	0.05
Subord Debt / Cap Funds	3.65	0.17	3.48	0.00
Operations				
Net Interest Margin	3.31	2.51	0.80	0.14
Net Int Rev / Avg Assets	2.92	2.00	0.92	0.06
Oth Op Inc / Avg Assets	1.93	0.88	1.04	0.01
Non Int Exp / Avg Assets	4.11	2.00	2.10	0.01
Pre–Tax Op Inc / Avg Assets	0.96	0.60	0.36	0.64
Non Op Items & Taxes / Avg Ast	0.38	–0.02	0.40	0.00
Return On (Avg) Assets (ROA)	0.58	0.62	–0.04	0.95
Return On (Avg) Equity (ROE)	5.93	5.26	0.68	0.95
Dividend Pay–Out	29.61	32.65	–3.04	0.84
Inc Net Of Dist / Avg Equity	–3.30	3.76	–7.06	0.42
Non Op Items / Net Income	7.53	–34.45	41.97	0.03
Cost To Income Ratio	56.87	56.39	0.48	0.93
Recurring Earning Power	2.40	0.93	1.47	0.02
Liquidity				
Inter–bank Ratio	191.96	426.72	–234.76	0.15
Net Loans / Tot Assets	53.24	49.91	3.33	0.29
Net Loans / Cust & ST Funding	66.25	79.13	–12.89	0.01
Net Loans / Tot Dep & Bor	62.91	66.42	–3.51	0.35
Liquid Assets / Cust & ST Funding	30.61	41.45	–10.85	0.01
Liquid Assets / Tot Dep & Bor	29.07	34.53	–5.46	0.10

Table 7.4: Benchmark performance measures of Islamic banks *vis-à-vis* conventional banks (b)

The average number of commercial banks with a similar asset size in the countries where Islamic banks are present. All commercial banks are selected the third quartile by size in each country in 2001. The value of each ratio represents the average in the period 1994–2001.

	Mean			
	Commercial	*Islamic*	*Difference*	*P–value*
Asset Quality				
Loan Loss Res / Gross Loans	7.53	2.19	5.34	0.03
Loan Loss Prov / Net Int Rev	71.63	16.44	55.19	0.25
Loan Loss Res / Impaired Loans	215.38	379.65	-164.27	0.09
Impaired Loans / Gross Loans	5.59	0.76	4.83	0.02
NCO / Average Gross Loans	1.20	0.00	1.20	0.08
NCO / Net Inc Bef Ln Lss Prov	15.74	0.30	15.45	0.01
Capital				
Equity / Tot Assets	6.39	12.22	–5.83	0.02
Equity / Net Loans	12.76	25.13	–12.37	0.03
Equity / Cust & ST Funding	7.79	19.79	–12.00	0.01
Equity / Liabilities	7.03	14.20	–7.17	0.02
Cap Funds / Tot Assets	6.71	12.23	–5.52	0.03
Cap Funds / Net Loans	13.38	25.16	–11.78	0.04
Cap Funds / Cust & ST Funding	8.18	19.81	–11.64	0.01
Cap Funds / Liabilities	7.38	14.21	–6.84	0.02
Subord Debt / Cap Funds	2.51	0.17	2.34	0.06
Operations				
Net Interest Margin	2.77	2.51	0.26	0.75
Net Int Rev / Avg Assets	2.52	2.00	0.52	0.48
Oth Op Inc / Avg Assets	1.57	0.88	0.69	0.00
Non Int Exp / Avg Assets	4.69	2.00	2.69	0.05
Pre–Tax Op Inc / Avg Assets	–0.43	0.60	–1.03	0.55
Non Op Items & Taxes / Avg Ast	0.31	–0.02	0.33	0.09
Return On (Avg) Assets (ROA)	–0.75	0.62	–1.36	0.39
Return On (Avg) Equity (ROE)	–85.65	5.26	–90.90	0.21
Dividend Pay–Out	23.87	32.65	–8.78	0.41
Inc Net Of Dist / Avg Equity	–99.15	3.76	–102.91	0.20
Non Op Items / Net Income	7.76	–34.45	42.20	0.03
Cost To Income Ratio	79.86	56.39	23.47	0.31
Recurring Earning Power	1.75	0.93	0.83	0.23
Liquidity				
Interbank Ratio	191.56	426.72	–235.16	0.15
Net Loans / Tot Assets	50.87	49.91	0.97	0.81
Net Loans / Cust & ST Funding	61.45	79.13	–17.68	0.00
Net Loans / Tot Dep & Bor	58.25	66.42	–8.17	0.11
Liquid Assets / Cust & ST Funding	31.90	41.45	–9.56	0.06
Liquid Assets / Tot Dep & Bor	30.16	34.53	–4.37	0.30

indicators (historic) of already existing banking problems. Yet, an adverse trend in these ratios may signal increased risk exposure and possible capital adequacy problems. According to the Basle Committee on Banking Supervision, the most commonly used indicator in this group is the risk-based capital ratio (measured as the ratio of capital to risk-adjusted assets). Simple leverage ratios (ratio of assets to capital) usually complement this ratio.[6] In addition to capital adequacy, it is important also to monitor other capital quality indicators, which may reflect the bank's capability of absorbing losses.

When capital ratios are compared for the banks in our sample, several systematic variations between Islamic banks and commercial banks are observed. One noticeable difference is the variation in capital-asset ratios. Although both types of bank (on average) maintain the Basle Committee's uniform standard of capital adequacy of 8.0 per cent, Islamic banks tend to maintain much higher capital-asset ratios than their commercial peers. Except for one ratio (subordinated debt over capital funds), Islamic banks seem to be better capitalised than commercial banks of similar size. The subordinated debt ratio indicates the per centage of total capital provided in the form of subordinated debt. The lower this ratio the better it is. In summary, Islamic banks have better capital adequacy ratios than commercial banks of similar size.

The third group of ratios presented in Table 7.3 is operation ratios. Generally, banks are increasingly involved in diversified operations that involve some aspect of market risks. The most important components of market risk, which significantly impact the assets and liabilities of financial institutions, are interest and exchange rate risks.[7] Virtually all financial institutions are subject to interest rate risk and, therefore, it is considered a market indicator.

Most of the operation ratios presented in Table 7.3 are significantly larger for commercial banks as compared with Islamic banks in our sample. These include net interest income or revenue over total (average) assets, other operating income over total assets, non-operating items and tax over total assets, non-operating items over net income and recurring earning power. Usually, better-performing banks have larger operations ratios. In our case, commercial banks have significantly larger operations ratios.

The last group of indicators in Table 7.3 is liquidity ratios. Liquidity is generally not a major problem for sound banks in a reasonably competitive banking system. However, liquidity can change rapidly, requiring frequent updating of relevant indicators. The recent banking crises suggest that in many cases liquidity crises have their roots in solvency problems. It is, therefore, extremely important to monitor liquidity indicators because poor management of short-term liquidity may force solvent banks towards closure.[8] An important indicator of liquidity is inter-bank credit, whereby a high dispersion in inter-bank rates signals high risk. Banks may control their inter-bank positions by using quantitative controls.

In comparing the liquidity ratios for our sample banks, the two ratios that are significantly different between commercial banks and Islamic banks are net loan over customer and short-term funding, and liquid assets over customers' short-term funding. These ratios tend to be higher for high-performing banks. The liquidity ratios show that commercial banks are more liquid than Islamic banks.

We find almost similar results when we compare Islamic banks' performance ratios with those of conventional commercial banks according to deposit base. These results are reported in Table 7.4.

DETERMINANTS OF ISLAMIC BANKS' PROFITABILITY AND SPREAD

In this section we formulate the model used to examine the relationship between the performance of Islamic banks and the set of internal and external banking characteristics. Since the ultimate objective of management is to maximise the value of shareholders' equity, an optimal mix of returns and risk exposure should be pursued in order to increase the profitability of the bank. Hence, a comprehensive plan to identify objectives, goals, budgets and strategies should be developed. The planning should encompass both internal and external performance dimensions. Because of increasing innovation and deregulation in the financial service industry, internal and external competitiveness is becoming a critical factor in evaluating performance. While internal performance is evaluated by analysing financial ratios, external performance is best measured by evaluating the bank's market share, regulatory compliance and public confidence.

The operating efficiency and profitability measures used as criteria for performance are specified below. Whereas capital, leverage, overhead, loan and liquidity ratios were used as proxies for the banks' internal measures, macroeconomic indicators, taxation, financial structure and country dummies were used to represent the external measures. A linear equation relating the performance measures to a variety of financial indicators is specified.[9] The subsequent regression analysis starts from estimating the following basic equation:

$$I_{ijt} = \alpha_0 + \alpha_i B_{it} + \beta_j X_{jt} + \gamma_t M_{tj} + \delta_j C_j + \varepsilon_{ijt} \quad (1)$$

where I_{ijt} = is the measure of performance (either non-interest margin or before tax profit margin) for bank i in country j at time t; B_{it} are bank variables for bank i at time t; X_{jt} are country variables for country j at time t; M_{jt} are the financial structure variables in country j at time t, and C_j are country dummy variables.[10] α_0 is a constant, and α_i, β_j, γ_i and δ_j are coefficients, while ε_{ijt} is an error term. Although the primary focus of this chapter is the relationship between performance and bank internal variables, the inclusion of macroeconomic variables, financial structure variables and the country dummies is meant to control for cyclical factors that might affect bank performance. Several specifications of equation (1) are estimated.

Measures of performance

Evaluating bank performance is a complex process that involves assessing interaction between the environment, internal operations and external activities. In general, a number of financial ratios are usually used to assess the performance of financial intermediaries. The primary method of evaluating internal performance is by analysing accounting data. Financial ratios usually provide a broader understanding of the bank's financial condition, since they are constructed from accounting data contained on the bank's balance sheet and financial statement. Another key management element that many studies have found to be a primary factor in assessing bank performance is operating efficiency. In measuring efficiency, both *ex ante* and *ex post* spreads can be used to provide information on cost control. Generally speaking, *ex ante* spreads are calculated from the contractual rates charged on loans and rates paid on deposits. In contrast, however, the spread for the Islamic banks can be calculated from the rates of return generated from various non-interest banking activities, including participation in direct investment. As an efficiency indicator, we use the *ex post* spreads consisting of revenues generated from Islamic banking operations such as mark-up (*murābaḥah*), rent-to-own (*ijārah*), deferred sale (*bay' mu'ajjal*) and service charges, minus the expenses of carrying out such activities.[11] Accounting values from the banks' financial statements were used to compute the *ex post* spread and profitability measures employed in this study.

Four measures of performance are used in this study: the net non-interest margin (NIM), profit margin (BTP/TA), return on assets (ROA) and return on equity (ROE). The NIM is defined as the net income accruing to the bank from non-interest activities (including fees, service charges, foreign exchange and direct investment) divided by total assets. Non-interest income is growing in importance as a source of revenue for conventional banks. Some of the fastest-growing non-interest income items include ATM surcharges, credit card fees, and fees from the sale of mutual funds and annuities (see Kidwell, Peterson and Blackwell 2000). For Islamic banks, non-interest income, NIM, makes up the lion's share of total operating income and captures the banks' ability to reduce the risk of insolvency. Moreover, since the returns on Islamic banks' deposits are contingent on the outcome of the projects that banks finance, NIM reflects the management's ability to generate positive returns on deposits. If banks were able to engage in successful non-loan activities and offer new services, non-interest income will increase overtime (Madura 2000). Goldberg and Rai (1996) used the net non-interest return as a rough proxy for bank efficiency.[12]

The bank's before-tax profit over total assets (BTP/TA) is used as a measure of the bank's profit margin. This measure is computed from the bank's income statement as the sum of non-interest income over total assets minus overhead over total assets minus loan loss provision over total assets minus other operating income. BTP/TA reflects the banks' ability to generate higher profits by diversifying their portfolios. Since large size (scale) enables banks to offer a large menu of financial services at lower costs, positive relationships between BTP/TA and the explanatory variables in equation (1) will give support to the efficient-structure hypothesis (Smirlock 1985).

Other alternative measures of overall performance are ROA and ROE. Both measures are closely tied to the key item in the income statement: net income. ROA and ROE have been used in most structure-performance studies and are included here to reflect the bank's ability to generate income from non-traditional services. ROA shows the profit earned per dollar of assets and, most importantly, reflects management's ability to utilise the bank's financial and real investment resources to generate profits. For any bank, ROA depends on the bank's policy decisions as well as uncontrollable factors relating to the economy and government regulation. Many regulators believe return on assets is the best measure of bank efficiency. ROE, on the other hand, reflects how effectively a bank management is in using shareholders' funds. A bank's ROE is affected by its ROA as well as by the bank's degree of financial leverage (equity/asset). Since returns on assets tend to be lower for financial intermediaries, most banks utilise financial leverage heavily to increase return on equity to a competitive level.

Bank characteristics

To assess the relationship between performance and internal bank characteristics, our analysis utilises several bank ratios. These supplemental measures are particularly useful for comprehensive understanding of the factors underlying a bank's net margins and the quality of bank management. The set of ratios used comprises fund source management (CSTFTA), funds use management (OVRHD/TA and NIEATA), and leverage and liquidity ratios (EQTA and LOANTA). Each one of these determinants was also interacted with per capita GDP to capture the effects of GDP on bank performance. Capital ratios have long been a valuable tool for assessing the safety and soundness of banks. Bank supervisors use capital ratios as rules of thumb to gauge the adequacy of an institution's level of capital. Since capital management is related to dividend policy, banks generally prefer to hold the amount of capital that is just sufficient to support bank operations. Starting 1988, the Basel Accord has prescribed uniform capital ratio standards on banks internationally.

Previous studies of the determinants of bank profitability in the US found a strong and statistically significant positive relationship between EQTA and profitability. This supports the view that profitable banks remain well-capitalised; or the view that well capitalised banks enjoy access to cheaper (less risky) sources of funds with subsequent improvement in profit rates (Bourke 1989). A positive relationship between the ratio of bank loans to total assets, LOANTA, and profitability was also found from using international databases (Demirguc-Kunt and Huizinga 1997). Bank loans are expected to be the main source of revenue, and are expected to impact on profits positively. However, since most of the Islamic banks' loans are in the form of profit and loss sharing (loans with equity features), the loan-performance relationship depends significantly on the expected change of the economy. During the upturn of the business cycle only a small per centage of the PLS loans will default, and the bank's profit will rise. On the other hand, the bank could be severely damaged during a downturn in the economy, because borrowers are more likely to default on their loans. Ideally, banks should capitalise on favourable economic conditions and insulate themselves during adverse conditions.

Since the bulk of the earnings of Islamic banks come from non-interest activities, the ratio of non-interest earning assets to total assets, NIEATA, is expected to have a positive impact on profitability. The ratio of consumer and short-term funding to total assets, CSTFTA, is a liquidity ratio that comes from the liability side. It consists of current deposits, saving deposits and investment deposits. Since liquidity holding represents an expense to the bank, the coefficient of this variable is expected to be negative.

The ratio of overhead to total assets, OVRHD, is used to provide information on variation in operational costs across the banking system. It reflects employment and total costs of wages and salaries, as well as the cost of running branch office facilities. A high OVRHD ratio is expected to impact performance negatively because efficient banks are expected to operate at lower costs. On the other hand, the usage of new electronic technology, like ATMs and other automated means of delivering services, has caused the wage expenses to fall (as capital is substituted for labour). Therefore, a lower OVRHD ratio may impact performance positively. Meanwhile, the interaction variable OVRGDP captures the effects of both overhead and GDP on the performance measures. The sign of the coefficient of this variable is not restricted.

The control variables

To isolate the effects of bank characteristics on performance, it is necessary to control for other factors that have been proposed in the literature as possible determinants of profitability. Three sets of variables are expected to be external to the bank: the macroeconomic environment, the financial market structure and the taxation indicator variables. The economic conditions and the specific market environment would obviously affect the bank's mixture of assets and liabilities. We introduce these indicators in order to see how they interact with each other and how they affect bank performance. Two indicators are used as proxies for macroeconomic conditions: GDP per capita (GDPPC) and the real interest rate (RI). The GDP per capita variable is expected to have an effect on numerous factors related to the supply and demand for loans and deposits. It is hypothesised in this chapter that GDPPC affects performance measures positively. Since most of the countries in the sample are characterised as low- or middle-income countries, banks in these economies are expected to operate less competitively and are, therefore, expected to generate higher profit margins.

Previous studies have also revealed a positive relationship between real interest rate (RI) and bank profitability (Bourke 1989). For conventional banks, high real interest rates generally lead to higher loan rates, and hence higher revenues. However, in the case of Islamic banks, real interest rates may impact performance positively if a larger portion of Islamic banks' profits accrues from direct investment, shareholding and/or other trading activities (*murābaḥah*). Yet, real interest rates may have a negative effect on bank profitability if higher real interest rates lower the demand for loans.

One of the most important industry characteristics that can affect a commercial bank's profitability is regulation. If regulators reduce the constraints imposed on banks, banks may take on more risk. If banks taking on the higher degree of risk are profitable, then depositors and shareholders gain. If, on the other hand, the banks fail, depositors lose. To incorporate the impact of prudential surveillance and supervision, we used the required reserves of the banking system (RES), and its interactions with GDP, RESGDP, as proxies for financial regulation. Although prudential supervision of Islamic banks is just as necessary and desirable as it is in conventional banks, the traditional regulatory measures are not always applicable to Islamic banks. Many Islamic economists argue that Islamic banks should not be subject to reserve requirements because required reserves do not generate any income to the bank. Nonetheless, we use reserve requirements as proxies for regulation because almost all Islamic banks operate in an environment where these traditional supervisory measures are used. Both implicit and explicit taxes are expected to impact profits negatively.[13]

Studies of financial structure for the banking industry relate bank performance to several market constraints. Competition from other providers of financial services and from the stock market may influence banks' operations (Fraser et al. 2000). In this study we use the ratio of total bank deposits to GDP to measure the influence of the financial market, despite the fact that financial and capital markets are still at the initial stages of development in the countries in our sample. The size of the banking system (BNK), comprising the ratio of total assets of the deposit money bank to GDP, is used to measure the importance of other financial competitors in the economy. Both variables are expected to impact performance negatively. Furthermore, BNK is also interacted with GDP. Moreover, the number of banks (BANKS) is used to show the impact of competition on Islamic bank profitability. Finally, total assets (ASST) is used to control for cost differences related to bank size and for the greater ability of larger banks to diversify. The first factor may lead to positive effects if there are significant economies of scale, while the second may have negative effects if increased diversification leads to higher risks and lower returns.

EMPIRICAL RESULTS

This section analyses the regression results. The data from a sample of 43 Islamic banks are pooled for all eight years (1994–2001) and used to extend earlier research. Different specifications of equation (1) were estimated. As stated above, in addition to bank-level variables, the explanatory variables used include control variables like financial structure variables, taxation variables and macroeconomic indicators. The estimation technique used is panel data methods, and the White (1980) procedure is used to ensure that the coefficients are heteroskedastic.[14]

Tables 7.5 through 7.8 report the estimated coefficients of the panel regressions for ROA, ROE, Net Profit Before Taxes (NPBT) and Net Non-Interest Margin (NNIM) respectively. The results reported are for two sets of models: the fixed effects (FE) model and/or the random effect (RE) model, depending on the result of the Hausman specification test at the 5.0 per cent level. The tables show the estimated coefficients for bank characteristics, macroeconomic indicators, taxation and financial structure. Four possible econometric specifications (for each performance measure) were estimated. We denote them as specification 1, 2, 3 and 4 respectively. The first regression in each table is a benchmark, including the bank characteristics indicators only and excluding all other explanatory variables. In the second regression we add the macroeconomic indicators, while the third regression adds the taxation variables. Finally, the fourth specification includes all the above variables plus the financial structure variables. The estimation technique is robust-covariance matrix in generalised least squares (GLS).

The first bank characteristic variable is book-to-value equity divided by total assets lagged one period (Equity/TA (t-1)). As with Demirguc-Kunt (1997) and Berger (1995), we find a statistically significant positive relationship between Equity/TA (t-1) and Net Non-Interest Margin. Unlike the above-mentioned studies, we find a statistically significant inverse relationship between the equity variable and ROE, indicating that high capital ratio reduces the returns on the equity of Islamic banks. Further, our results show an almost lack of correspondence between the capital ratio variable and the return on assets (ROA). However, when controlling for the macro variable, taxation and finance variables, we find a significant negative relation when the dependent variable is profitability (Table 7.7, specification 4).

In the regressions, the Equity/TA (t-1) variable is also interacted with per capita GDP (measured in thousands of dollars of 1995) to see the effect of the capital ratios on bank performance in countries with different levels of income. The results indicate that the interaction variable has negative and statistically significant effects on the net interest margin alone, indicating that the Equity/TA (t-1) variable does not have a strong impact on bank performance in countries with different levels of income. The effect of the interaction variable on profit before tax, ROE and ROA are all statistically insignificant.

Next, there is an inverse and statistically significant relationship between the non-interest earning assets variable (NIEATA) and the performance measures. Note that the coefficient of the non-interest earning variable interacted with GDP is positive and statistically significant in the NNIM (specification 1), PBT (specification 1 and 3), and all columns of both ROA and ROE specifications. The coefficient of Loan/TA variable is negative and statistically significant for ROE, ROA and profitability, and negative but insignificant for Non-Net Interest Margin only. When the Loan/TA is interacted with GDP per capita, we find a significant positive impact in specification 1 for NNIM, and specification 2 and 3 in ROA and ROE.

Our results also show that the coefficients of Customer and Short-Term Funding over Total Assets (CSTFTA) on Net Interest Margin (all specifications) and profitability (specification 2 and 4 only) are negative and significantly different from zero. It does not have any impact on ROE and ROA. The interaction of CSTFTA with GDP has no meaningful relationship with the bank's performance measures. The next characteristic variable considered in these regressions is overhead. Our results show that overhead (OVRHD) is directly and significantly related to the Non-Interest Margin. But it does not have any significant coefficients in ROA, ROE and profitability specifications. When overhead is interacted with GDP per capita, the results show a significant positive relationship in only specification 3 and 4 of profit before taxes. Therefore, the conclusion remains ambiguous.

The final bank characteristics variable, Total Liabilities over Total Assets (LATA), has a significant positive correlation on NNIM and specification 1 of ROE and ROA. However, its impact on the other performance variables and other specifications is not significant. Its interaction term with GDP enters the NIM equations significantly and negatively. It does not have other significant variables.

We now discuss the effects of macroeconomic variables. Per capita GDP has

Table 7.5: Determinants of return on assets (ROA)

The regression is estimated using the GLS estimation pooling bank level across 21 countries where there are Islamic banks for the 1994–2001 period. Regression also includes country dummies, which are not reported. The dependent variable is return on assets, which is defined as net income (profit after taxes) over total earning assets. Standard errors are given in parentheses.

	1	2	3	4
Bank Characteristics				
EQTA(–1)	0.022 (0.014)	–0.029 (0.057)	–0.023 (0.051)	–0.031 (0.051)
EQAGDP(–1)	0.001 (0.006)	0.004 (0.010)	0.004 (0.010)	0.004 (0.010)
LOANTA	–0.015** (0.008)	–0.022*** (0.008)	–0.024*** (0.008)	–0.018** (0.007)
LONGDP	0.004 (0.003)	0.007* (0.004)	0.007* (0.004)	0.005 (0.004)
NIEATA	–0.039*** (0.015)	–0.056*** (0.020)	–0.056*** (0.018)	–0.058*** (0.015)
NIEAGDP	0.019*** (0.006)	0.019* (0.011)	0.022* (0.011)	0.021* (0.012)
CSTFTA	–0.006 (0.013)	–0.019 (0.016)	–0.018 (0.016)	–0.020 (0.016)
CSTFGDP	–0.001 (0.003)	–0.001 (0.003)	0.000 (0.003)	0.000 (0.003)
OVRHD	–0.090 (0.179)	0.016 (0.124)	0.008 (0.129)	–0.033 (0.138)
OVRGDP	0.031 (0.045)	0.030 (0.045)	0.054* (0.030)	0.051* (0.029)
LATA	0.052* (0.031)	0.020 (0.097)	0.027 (0.087)	0.042 (0.085)
LATAGDP	–0.006 (0.007)	–0.004 (0.016)	–0.004 (0.015)	–0.006 (0.015)
Macro Variables				
GDPPC		–0.012 (0.020)	–0.008 (0.021)	–0.005 (0.022)
GDPGR		0.247* (0.143)	0.397** (0.166)	0.397*** (0.128)
INF		–0.017 (0.015)	–0.010 (0.014)	0.013 (0.016)
INFGDP		0.004 (0.003)	0.005** (0.003)	0.006 (0.005)
Financial Structure				
RES			0.051 (0.106)	0.050 (0.109)
RESGDP			–0.051 (0.040)	–0.045 (0.037)
TAX			–0.005 (0.003)	–0.005* (0.003)
TAXGDP			0.002*** (0.001)	0.002*** (0.000)
BANK				0.041 (0.036)
BANKGDP				0.002 (0.007)
NUMBER				0.000 (0.000)
CONCEN				0.056** (0.024)
CREDIT				–0.042** (0.020)
ASST				0.000* (0.000)
C	–0.002 (0.020)	0.047 (0.096)	0.023 (0.097)	–0.008 (0.100)
Adjusted R^2	0.28	0.33	0.40	0.46
N	157	143	143	143

*, ** and *** indicate a significance level of 10.0, 5.0 and 1.0 per cent respectively.

Table 7.6: Determinants of return on equity (ROE)

The regression is estimated using the GLS estimation pooling bank level across 21 countries where there are Islamic banks for the 1994–2001 period. Regression also includes country dummies, which are not reported. The dependent variable is return on assets, which is defined as net income (profit after taxes) over total earning assets. Standard errors are given in parentheses.

	1	2	3	4
Bank Characteristics				
EQTA(–1)	–0.611* (0.338)	–0.696 (0.861)	–0.753 (0.780)	–0.923 (0.715)
EQAGDP(–1)	0.059 (0.093)	0.060 (0.150)	0.065 (0.148)	0.053 (0.146)
LOANTA	–0.316** (0.139)	–0.352** (0.135)	–0.353*** (0.124)	–0.265** (0.114)
LONGDP	0.079 (0.058)	0.092** (0.046)	0.086* (0.046)	0.061 (0.044)
NIEATA	–0.985*** (0.301)	–0.909*** (0.329)	–0.862*** (0.302)	–0.880*** (0.278)
NIEAGDP	0.337** (0.139)	0.347* (0.193)	0.372* (0.205)	0.347* (0.206)
CSTFTA	–0.056 (0.233)	0.061 (0.244)	–0.023 (0.241)	–0.080 (0.229)
CSTFGDP	–0.059 (0.049)	–0.061 (0.044)	–0.045 (0.040)	–0.041 (0.037)
OVRHD	–0.440 (1.772)	0.475 (1.781)	0.767 (1.747)	0.465 (1.670)
OVRGDP	–0.299 (0.453)	–0.304 (0.380)	–0.376 (0.416)	–0.477 (0.409)
LATA	1.184** (0.534)	1.806 (1.977)	1.683 (1.717)	1.759 (1.588)
LATAGDP	–0.088 (0.124)	–0.149 (0.287)	–0.137 (0.273)	–0.176 (0.265)
Macro Variables				
GDPPC		–0.075 (0.313)	–0.052 (0.336)	–0.064 (0.331)
GDPGR		1.075 (1.434)	1.609 (1.526)	2.143* (1.150)
INF		0.074 (0.173)	0.069 (0.160)	0.275 (0.185)
INFGDP		0.034 (0.037)	0.055 (0.039)	0.133 (0.092)
Financial Structure				
RES			–0.876 (1.336)	–1.001 (1.403)
RESGDP			–0.350 (0.565)	–0.261 (0.531)
TAX			–0.026 (0.046)	–0.023 (0.044)
TAXGDP			0.006 (0.007)	0.005 (0.007)
BANK				0.235 (0.436)
BANKGDP				0.118 (0.103)
NUMBER				–0.006 (0.006)
CONCEN				0.576** (0.225)
CREDIT				–0.430** (0.191)
ASST				–0.004* (0.002)
C	–0.268 (0.370)	–0.912 (1.838)	–0.564 (1.724)	–0.715 (1.647)
Adjusted R^2	0.28	0.29	0.29	0.35
N	157	143	143	143

*, ** and *** indicate a significance level of 10.0, 5.0 and 1.0 per cent respectively.

Table 7.7: Determinants of profit before taxes (PBT)

The regression is estimated using the GLS estimation pooling bank level across 21 countries where there are Islamic banks for the 1994–2001 period. Regression also includes country dummies, which are not reported. The dependent variable is return on assets, which is defined as net income (profit after taxes) over total earning assets. Standard errors are given in parentheses.

	1	2	3	4
Bank Characteristics				
EQTA(–1)	0.000 (0.015)	–0.108 (0.072)	–0.096 (0.059)	–0.109* (0.056)
EQAGDP(–1)	0.002 (0.006)	0.008 (0.009)	0.007 (0.009)	0.007 (0.009)
LOANTA	–0.015* (0.009)	–0.024** (0.009)	–0.027*** (0.009)	–0.019** (0.008)
LONGDP	0.002 (0.004)	0.004 (0.004)	0.005 (0.004)	0.003 (0.003)
NIEATA	–0.053*** (0.019)	–0.080*** (0.026)	–0.080*** (0.022)	–0.081*** (0.017)
NIEAGDP	0.018*** (0.006)	0.016 (0.011)	0.019* (0.011)	0.018 (0.011)
CSTFTA	–0.008 (0.017)	–0.036* (0.021)	–0.032 (0.020)	–0.033* (0.020)
CSTFGDP	–0.002 (0.003)	–0.002 (0.003)	–0.001 (0.003)	–0.001 (0.003)
OVRHD	–0.152 (0.259)	0.043 (0.156)	0.026 (0.155)	–0.022 (0.157)
OVRGDP	0.033 (0.056)	0.023 (0.056)	0.060** (0.028)	0.055** (0.027)
LATA	0.044 (0.035)	–0.017 (0.104)	–0.002 (0.093)	0.009 (0.093)
LATAGDP	–0.004 (0.007)	–0.002 (0.016)	–0.003 (0.015)	–0.005 (0.015)
Macro Variables				
GDPPC		–0.013 (0.021)	–0.009 (0.020)	–0.004 (0.022)
GDPGR		0.381* (0.214)	0.600** (0.255)	0.599*** (0.199)
INF		–0.026 (0.022)	–0.015 (0.019)	0.018 (0.021)
INFGDP		0.004 (0.003)	0.006 (0.004)	0.007 (0.006)
Financial Structure				
RES			0.097 (0.115)	0.103 (0.113)
RESGDP			–0.070 (0.048)	–0.065 (0.042)
TAX			–0.006 (0.005)	–0.006* (0.004)
TAXGDP			0.003*** (0.001)	0.003*** (0.001)
BANK				0.065 (0.045)
BANKGDP				0.000 (0.007)
NUMBER				–0.001 (0.001)
CONCEN				0.076** (0.036)
CREDIT				–0.060* (0.031)
ASST				–0.0005* (0.0003)
C	0.012 (0.022)	0.106 (0.108)	0.060 (0.101)	0.025 (0.105)
Adjusted R^2	0.21	0.31	0.44	0.53
N	157	143	143	143

*, ** and *** indicate a significance level of 10.0, 5.0 and 1.0 per cent respectively.

Table 7.8: Determinants of net non–interest margin (NNIM)

The regression is estimated using the GLS estimation pooling bank level across 21 countries where there are Islamic banks for the 1994–2001 period. Regression also includes country dummies, which are not reported. The dependent variable is return on assets, which is defined as net income (profit after taxes) over total earning assets. Standard errors are given in parentheses.

	1	2	3	4
Bank Characteristics				
EQTA(–1)	0.073** (0.036)	0.182** (0.076)	0.254*** (0.091)	0.238** (0.095)
EQAGDP(–1)	–0.001 (0.005)	–0.012* (0.007)	–0.016** (0.007)	–0.015** (0.008)
LOANTA	–0.014 (0.015)	–0.025 (0.016)	–0.024 (0.016)	–0.019 (0.015)
LONGDP	0.008* (0.004)	0.008 (0.005)	0.008 (0.006)	0.006 (0.006)
NIEATA	–0.105* (0.057)	–0.108** (0.053)	–0.074 (0.049)	–0.084* (0.049)
NIEAGDP	0.017*** (0.006)	0.005 (0.008)	–0.005 (0.009)	–0.006 (0.009)
CSTFTA	–0.169*** (0.062)	–0.153** (0.063)	–0.111** (0.054)	–0.119** (0.055)
CSTFGDP	0.011** (0.004)	0.007 (0.005)	0.002 (0.004)	0.004 (0.005)
OVRHD	2.665*** (0.769)	2.907*** (0.826)	2.906*** (0.732)	2.959*** (0.763)
OVRGDP	–0.126 (0.094)	–0.140 (0.103)	–0.124 (0.094)	–0.130 (0.094)
LATA	0.241*** (0.085)	0.554*** (0.178)	0.655*** (0.183)	0.622*** (0.179)
LATAGDP	–0.018*** (0.007)	–0.049*** (0.016)	–0.055*** (0.016)	–0.054*** (0.016)
Macro Variables				
GDPPC		0.035** (0.015)	0.044** (0.017)	0.034 (0.022)
GDPGR		0.250 (0.164)	0.512*** (0.177)	0.471** (0.195)
INF		–0.015 (0.042)	–0.017 (0.040)	–0.014 (0.052)
INFGDP		0.006 (0.005)	0.005 (0.004)	0.008 (0.008)
Financial Structure				
RES			0.095 (0.254)	0.009 (0.293)
RESGDP			0.004 (0.058)	0.022 (0.062)
TAX			0.026** (0.013)	0.026** (0.013)
TAXGDP			–0.002 (0.002)	–0.002 (0.002)
BANK				–0.091 (0.105)
BANKGDP				0.011 (0.011)
NUMBER				0.001 (0.001)
CONCEN				0.025 (0.050)
CREDIT				–0.020 (0.043)
ASST				–0.001 (0.001)
C	–0.087* (0.047)	–0.398*** (0.149)	–0.573*** (0.183)	–0.517** (0.199)
Adjusted R^2	0.56	0.58	0.63	0.62
N	157	143	143	143

*, ** and *** indicate a significance level of 10.0, 5.0 and 1.0 per cent respectively.

a significant positive coefficient in NNIM (specification 2 and 3). It does not have a significant coefficient in profitability, ROE and ROA. Next we discuss the growth rate of the GDP (GDPGR) variable. It has a significant positive relation with NNIM (specification 3 and 4), in all specifications of profitability and ROA, and specification 1 for ROE. As regards the inflation rate (INF) and its interaction term with GDP, the only significant variable is observed in specification 3 of ROA. Therefore, the impact of these variables on the profitability measures is not conclusive.

Next we present the effect of taxation variables. We observe that the reserve variable (RES) and its interaction term with per capita GDP (RESGDP) have no significant relation with any of the performance measures. Our results also show that taxation (TAX) has a meaningful positive impact on all the specifications of NNIM. Its coefficient is significant only in specification 4 of profitability and ROA. In the rest of the specifications the impact is not statistically significant. We can cautiously conclude that there is some statistically meaningful relationship between taxation and profitability in Islamic banks.

For the financial structure variables, our results indicate that the total assets of the deposit money banks divided by GDP, its interaction term with GDP and a number of banks does not have a significant coefficient in any of the specifications. Concentration has a significant impact on profitability, ROE and ROA. Credit has a significant and negative correlation on profitability, ROE and ROA. Bank total assets (ASST) has a negative and significant and non-zero correlation on profitability and ROA. This implies a negative association. This negative correlation implies that to some extent large size tends to be associated with less profitability in Islamic banks. Although it affects the other two profitability measures (ROA and Before Tax Profit) positively, the impact is not significantly different from zero.

CONCLUSIONS

The preceding empirical analysis allows us to shed some light on the relationship between banking characteristics and performance measures in Islamic banks. First, Islamic banks' profitability measures respond positively to increases in capital and negatively to loan ratios. The results reveal that a larger equity to total asset ratio leads to more profit margin. This finding is intuitive and consistent with previous studies. It indicates that adequate capital ratios play an empirical role in explaining the performance of Islamic banks. Islamic banks' loan portfolio is heavily biased towards short-term trade financing. As such, their loans are low risk and only contribute modestly to bank profits. Bank regulators may use this as evidence for prompt supervisory action. Second, the results also indicate the importance of consumer and short-term funding, non-interest earning assets and overhead in promoting banks' profits. A high CSTF to total asset ratio is shown to lead to low non-interest margins. The counter-intuitive finding about the association between NNIM (Net Non-Interest Margin) and overhead suggests that high profits earned by banks may be appropriated in terms of higher wages and salaries. It seems that the expense preference behaviour appears to be holding in the Islamic banking market. Third, the results suggest that regulatory tax factors are important in the determination of bank performance. However, our findings seem to suggest that reserve requirement does not have a strong impact on profitability measures. Fourth, a favourable macroeconomic environment seems to stimulate higher profits. A higher growth rate of GDP seems to have a strong positive impact on performance measures. However, per capita GDP seems to have a limited effect on performance. Furthermore, the inflation rate and its interaction term with GDP does not seem to have a significant impact on performance. Finally, the size of the banking system has a negative impact on profitability, except the Net Non-Interest Margin.

NOTES

1. Their market share has grown from around 2.0 per cent during the 1970s to around 15.0 per cent during the 1990s, see Aggarwal and Yousef (2000).
2. Since both shareholders and depositors in Islamic banks are the residual claimants of the bank's profits, profitability is the designated measure of bank performance.
3. The literature divides bank profitability determinants into internal and external measures. Internal factors are areas of bank management that the officers and staff of the bank have under their immediate control. By contrast, external factors are environmental aspects of the bank's market over which management has no direct control (Bourke 1989; Molyneux and Thornton 1992).
4. Most bank supervisors have broadly adopted the CAMEL method of assessing bank performance: *c*apital adequacy, *a*sset quality, *m*anagement quality, *e*arnings and *l*iquidity.
5. A large concentration of aggregate credit in a specific economic sector or activity, especially commercial property, may signal an important vulnerability of the financial system to developments in the sector or activity. Many financial crises in the past (including the Asian crises) have been caused or amplified by downturns in particular sectors of the economy spilling over into the financial system via the concentrated loan books of financial institutions (IMF, OP no. 192, April 2000).
6. Financial institutions' leverage increases when bank assets grow at a faster rate than capital, and is particularly useful as an indicator for institutions that are primarily involved in lending.
7. Large open foreign exchange positions (including foreign exchange maturity mismatches) and a high reliance on foreign borrowing (particularly short-term maturity) may signal a high vulnerability of financial institutions to exchange rate swings and capital flow reversals (IMF, OP no. 192, April 2000).

8. Acute liquidity problems could potentially lead to widespread solvency problems if banks are forced to liquidate their assets at a significant loss. These effects would have grave consequences for borrowers, lenders and the economy at large.
9. No specification test is used here to support using the linear function. However, the linear functional form is widely used in the literature and produces good results (see Bourke 1989).
10. We ran Hausman specification tests for both fixed and random coefficient effects within a pooled cross-section time-series model. We report the correctly specified panel data model.
11. The *ex post* spreads on conventional banks consist of the difference between banks' interest revenues and their actual interest expenses.
12. Since the operations of Islamic banks are generally risky, any change in the perceived risks faced by the bank will necessarily be reflected in this margin.
13. Theoretically, Islamic banks' deposits are not supposed to be subject to reserve requirements. Therefore, the direction of effect of RES on profitability is unclear.
14. The use of panel data has a number of advantages. First, it provides an increased number of data points and generates additional degrees of freedom. Second, incorporating information relating to both cross-section and time-series variables can substantially diminish the problems that arise from omitted variables.

8

Allocative and Technical Inefficiency in Sudanese Islamic Banks: An Empirical Investigation

Abd Elrhman Elzahi Saaid

In 1989, all the operations of Sudanese banks were required to conform to Islamic principles. Previous investigations have shown that subsequently the banks grew rapidly in terms of assets and liabilities despite difficult economic conditions. An analysis of their financial operations revealed that they made substantial profits despite relatively high risks and severe economic sanctions. However, this success does not always imply managerial efficiency. This chapter investigates the allocative and technical inefficiency (X-inefficiency) of Sudanese Islamic banks. For this purpose the basic stochastic frontier approach (SFA) is used. The results show that those Sudanese Islamic banks investigated were allocatively and technically inefficient. This implies that Islamic banking principles may have impacted on the performance of the banking industry in Sudan. The results have important implications both for the Sudanese government and Sudan's Islamic banks' management.

INTRODUCTION

In recent years the Sudanese Islamic banking industry has experienced widespread change. In 1989, all banking operations in the country were converted so as to conform with Islamic principles. These changes had implications for the efficiency of Sudanese Islamic banks. Such banks first started their operations in 1979, but this was unfortunately the start of the most difficult economic and political period for the country, which inevitably had serious implications for the performance of Sudanese Islamic banks. Factors impacting negatively on banking included a deteriorating infrastructure, inconsistent monetary policies, economic mismanagement in the public sector, drought, desertification, famine, the disparate distribution of income and resources among different regions of the country, and a continuous civil war (Elzahi 2002). These factors put severe economic pressures on Islamic banks, leading to a high level of non-performing investments. Despite these difficulties, Islamic banks in Sudan grew rapidly in terms of assets and deposits and maintained high profit levels, as shown by their balance sheets and income statements (Elzahi 2002).

The evidence also shows that Islamic banks in Sudan have contributed positively to social responsibility and the eradication of poverty, as reflected by the distribution of the large amount of *zakāh* given to the poor and needy (Elzahi 2002). Sudanese Islamic banks have applied equity finance in their financial operations widely. *Mushārakah* constitutes more than 50.0 per cent of the total financing. Other instruments widely used by Sudanese Islamic banks include *murābaḥah*, *salam* and *muḍārabah*. *Salam* has become an especially popular method of financing for the Sudanese agricultural and livestock sectors (Elzahi 2002).

Sudanese banks have, however, faced many difficulties in using Islamic finance. Due to the government policy of self-reliance adopted at the beginning of the 1990s, most finance was directed towards the agricultural sector. *Salam* financing, however, presupposes that Islamic banks receive the produce in kind. This in turn requires the banks to maintain large warehouses to store these commodities before selling them. Moreover, the banks have difficulty in selling these products abroad due to the economic sanctions imposed against the country. Such factors have thus impacted adversely on banks' revenue and caused an increase in their overhead costs due to the long storage periods involved.

This chapter investigates the allocative and technical inefficiency (X-inefficiency) of the Sudanese Islamic banks by using the stochastic frontier approach (SFA). Although the studies of efficiency using frontier approaches were introduced long ago, their application in evaluating the performance of banks did not start until Sherman and Gold (1985) initiated their study. They applied the frontier approaches to the banking industry by focusing on the operating efficiency of the branches of a savings bank. Since then, numerous studies have been conducted using frontier approaches to measure the efficiency in banking. A recent survey found that 130 studies have applied frontier approaches or frontier efficiency analysis to financial institutions in 21 countries worldwide (Berger and Humphrey 1997). The frontier approach represents a very powerful tool, as it permits individuals with very little institutional knowledge or experience to identify the best banking practices within the industry.

REVIEW OF THE LITERATURE

Numerous studies have been conducted on Islamic banks throughout the world during the last 20 years. Samad (1999) used financial ratios to evaluate the efficiency of Bank Islam Malaysia Berhad (BIMB). His study revealed that BIMB is less efficient compared with its conventional counterparts. Despite this result, he concluded that Bank Islam has performed better than conventional banks in terms of loan recovery. Bashir (1999) used financial ratios and regression to examine the scale effect on the two Sudanese Islamic banks. By using data from these banks he discovered that Islamic banks in Sudan became more profitable as they increased in size and that large size is economically efficient. Shahid Ebrahim and Joo (2001) studied Islamic banking in Brunei. Despite the limited information on the banking system of Brunei, their investigation revealed that Islamic banks performed well during their first phase and were able to capture 11.5 per cent of the market share.

Unfortunately, many of these empirical studies were constrained either by the relatively short time periods for which data was available or the limited size of the samples. Many writers complained about data deficiencies (Elzahi 2002). Moreover, the methodology used in these studies to evaluate the performance and efficiency of Islamic banking has been relatively unsophisticated as compared with those used for some studies of conventional banks. Most of the work on Islamic banks has involved descriptive analysis using financial ratios, and only a few of the empirical studies have investigated scope and scale efficiency. However, evidence has shown that X-efficiency dominates the product mix and scale efficiencies in the banking sector (Berger and Humphrey 1991).

Recent literature has concluded that scale and scope efficiencies are not found to be important in banking (Berger and Humphrey 1993). The evidence suggests that X-efficiency, or in other words managerial ability to control costs, is of much greater magnitude and represents at least 20.0 per cent of banking costs. This means that on average, banks may have costs about 20.0 per cent higher than the industry minimum for the same scale and scope. By comparison, the scale effects generally account for less than 5.0 per cent of costs and the scope efficiency only reduces the bank's costs by 5.0 per cent or less when multiple products are produced jointly.[1] Hence cost improvements are more likely to be generated by an improvement in X-efficiency or better management of resources, rather than through improvement in efficiencies of scale or scope.

METHODOLOGY AND TECHNIQUES

In any firm, outputs are taken to be the function of a large number of inputs. The outputs may deviate from the optimum due to the availability of observable inputs, but such deviation must be random. If this deviation comes as a result of excessive use of inputs it is described as technical inefficiency, but if it is a result of sub-optimum combination between inputs and outputs it is designated as allocation inefficiency. This study adopts the SFA procedure to measure the allocation and technical inefficiency in Sudanese banks. Error terms are identified and estimated, and subsequently decomposed into a one-side error term and asymmetric error term, because the basic stochastic cost frontier model states that a firm's observed cost will deviate from the cost frontier due to random noise, ν_i, and possible inefficiency, μ_i. Thus, the cost function may be written as:

$$\text{In } TC = f(y_i, w_i) + \varepsilon \qquad (1)$$

where TC is the observed cost of firm^i, y_i and w_i are the vectors of output levels and input prices respectively. The function $f(y_i, w_i)$ is the predicted natural log cost function of a cost-minimising firm operating at output level y_i and input prices w_i. Once the model is estimated, inefficiency measures are calculated using the residuals. Hence, technical efficiency (*TE*) can be captured by decomposing the error term into two parts as follows:

$$\varepsilon_i = \nu_i + \mu_i \qquad (2)$$

The first component ν_i is a normal error term with $\nu \approx N(0,\sigma_\nu^2)$ representing pure randomness and μ_i is a non-positive error term exponential or half normally distributed[2] representing technical inefficiency. The non-positive u_i reflects the fact that each firm's cost must lie on or below its frontier. Any deviation is the result of factors under the firm's control such as technical inefficiency. Technical efficiency is estimated by decomposing the error term based on the random effects model. In this approach, one-sided random deviations are allowed in order to characterise inefficiencies. Estimated efficiency can be obtained directly if the following procedures are pursued.

To begin with, let $\bar{\varepsilon}_i = \Sigma\hat{\varepsilon}_i$ where $\hat{\varepsilon}_i$ is the obtained residual from equation (1) (see Simmer 1991 for details). Then we define $\hat{\zeta}_i$ = max $\bar{\varepsilon}_i - \bar{\varepsilon}_i$ where the maximum is introduced in order to provide a positive value of the $\hat{\zeta}_i$'s. Hence the estimation of the efficiency of the ith bank is given by:

$$TE = eff_i = exp\,(-\hat{\zeta}_i) \qquad (3)$$

Banks are assumed to be technically inefficient if $exp\,(-\hat{\zeta}_i)$ is less than 1. Thus the optimal value of $exp\,(-\hat{\zeta}_i)$ provides a measure of technical efficiency (*TE*). If $exp\,(-\hat{\zeta}_i)$ is positive but less than 1, it implies that the production unit under investigation is technically inefficient or not efficient at the 100 per cent level. The overall efficiency level (*OE*) may be obtained by averaging the $-\hat{\zeta}_i$. Finally, the solutions to the equation (3) and *OE* are used to derive the allocative efficiency (*AE*) as follows:[3]

$$AE = OE/TE \qquad (4)$$

ECONOMETRIC SPECIFICATION

The translog specification of the generalised cost function as given in equation (1) is:

$$\ln C = \alpha_0 + \sum_{j=1}^{3}\alpha_j \ln W_j + \sum_{i=1}^{3} \beta_i \ln Y_i + \tfrac{1}{2}\sum_{i=1}^{3}\sum_{k=1}^{3}\phi_{ik} Y_i Y_k$$

$$+ \tfrac{1}{2}\sum_{j=1}^{3}\sum_{k=1}^{3}\gamma_{jk} \ln W_j \ln W_k + \sum_{i=1}^{3}\sum_{j=1}^{3}\delta_{ij} \ln W_j \ln Y + \varepsilon_i \qquad (5)$$

where the subscripts are as follows:
Y_m = *mushārakah*
Y_r = *murābaḥah*
Y_s = *salam*
W_1 = the price of capital
W_2 = the price of labour
W_3 = the price of deposits

The cost-share S_j is derived through Shephard's lemma as,

$$S_j = \alpha_j + \sum_{k=1}^{3}\gamma_{jk} \ln W_k + \sum_{i=1}^{3} \delta_{ij} \ln Y_i \qquad (6)$$

For any cost function to be sensible, it must satisfy the linear homogeneity in input prices which requires:

$$\sum_{j=1}^{3}\alpha_j = 1, \; , \; \sum_{j=1}^{3}\gamma_{kj} = \sum_{k=1}^{3}\gamma_{jk} = 0 \; , \; \sum_{j=1}^{3}\delta_{Yj} = 0 \qquad (7)$$

Additional regularity conditions that the cost function must satisfy in order to correspond to well-behaved production technology are monotonicity and concavity in factor prices. Sufficient conditions for these to hold are positive fitted cost shares (α_j) and negative semi-definiteness of the bordered Hessian of the cost function (Abdullah and Elzahi 2003).

For econometric estimation, the cross-equations equality and the linear homogeneity restrictions defined in (7) are imposed *a priori* on the translog cost function (5), and on the cost-share equations (6). This allows us to drop arbitrarily any one of the three cost-share equations. In this study, the cost-share equation of capital was omitted. The estimates of the coefficients of this equation are obtainable by using the parameter relationships of the linear homogeneity restrictions once the system of the remaining cost-share equations has been estimated. Given this set of conditions, the Iterative Seemingly Unrelated Regression (ISUR) method is used for estimation.

DATA SOURCES AND VARIABLES SPECIFICATIONS

The data used to estimate the multiproduct cost function were gathered from six Sudanese Islamic banks' annual reports for the years 1992–2001. These years were chosen due to data availability and also because these years witnessed the transformation of conventional Sudanese banks into fully-fledged Islamic banks. The definitions of the cost, prices and output variables were made based on how and what banks produce.[4] There are two different views on the determination of input and output variables. These are the intermediation approach and the production approach.

The intermediation approach views banks as using deposits together with physical inputs to produce various types of bank assets as measured by their currency value. Berger and Humphrey (1997) suggest that the intermediation approach is the most appropriate for evaluating firm level efficiency, the reason being that the intermediation approach is superior for measuring the importance of frontier efficiency to the profitability of the financial institution since the minimisation of total costs, not just production costs, is needed to maximise profit.[5] By contrast, the production approach views banks as using only physical inputs such as labour and capital to produce deposits and other types of bank liabilities and assets. The production approach is appropriate for evaluating the efficiency of financial institutions' branches. This is because branches initially process customers' services for the whole institution and branch managers have little influence over the bank's funding and investment decisions. Therefore, the bank's outputs are both investments and various loans if we follow the intermediation approach or loans, investments and various types of bank deposits if we follow the production approach. Since we used banks' level data, the intermediation approach is the most suitable for this study.

Under the Islamic banking system, all Sudanese banks practised only interest-free financing modes. As a result, the outputs available were *mushārakah* (Y_m), *murābaḥah* (Y_r) and *salam* (Y_s). While fixed assets (X_1), labour (X_2) and core deposits (X_3) are treated as factor inputs, total expenses on furniture, equipment and premises divided by their book value (W_1), salaries and wages divided by number of employees (W_2) and the return on deposits divided by the total deposits (W_3) are the prices of X_1, X_2 and X_3 respectively.

THE EMPIRICAL RESULTS

Table 8.1 shows the data summary and its statistical descriptions for the six Sudanese banks. Table 8.2 presents the estimated results of the translog cost function using the Iterative Seemingly Unrelated Regression method. The R^2 for the cost function and the two cost-share equations, namely labour and

Table 8.1: Data summary

Variables	*Observations*	*Mean*	*Maximum*	*Minimum*	*Std. Dev.*
Y_m	60	1386914	6787000	17191	1691722
Y_r	60	2339910	24265000	36700	4936490
Y_s	60	504711	4044000	1000	925196
X_1	60	2007902	15987656	12938	3131714
X_2	60	710	2208	258	438
X_3	60	43596663	891000000	2154	13600000
W_1	60	1.086	16.95	0.02295	2.09993
W_2	60	1485	14727	2.10	2449.98
W_3	60	10.79	641.27	3.48	82.77
TC	60	2800036	16008478	22943	3118575

Note: The variables are *mushārakah* (Y_m), *murābaḥah* (Y_r), *salam* (Y_s), capital (X_1), labour (X_2), deposits (X_3), price of labour (W_1), price of capital (W_2), price of deposits (W_3). All variables are measured in millions Sudanese pounds except X_2, which is number of employees. The numbers of the cross-sections are six banks. *TC* = total cost of the three inputs.

deposits, were 0.78, 0.38 and 0.42 respectively, indicating a fairly good measurement of goodness of fit for the model. Table 8.2 also shows that 15 out of the 21 estimated parameters were significant either at the 5.0 per cent or 10.0 per cent level. The parameters that measure the output and the interaction between the output and input prices are also generally significant. The estimated cost elasticity equation for physical capital, labour and deposit inputs were 0.535, 0.181 and 0.284 respectively. The absolute summations of the inputs' coefficients are equal to one. This shows that the model satisfies the symmetry and linear homogeneity conditions that were imposed prior to the estimation.

In this study, multi-inputs multi-outputs cost frontier analysis is used to evaluate six Sudanese Islamic banks' X-inefficiency. The concept of frontier is consistent with the theory of optimisation and gives a bank a chance to customise and adjust its objectives if its efficiency deviates from the optimal point. The study estimates the technical and allocative inefficiencies (X-inefficiency) of the six Sudanese Islamic banks for the period 1992–2001. Traditional cost regressions are normally interpreted on the hypothesis that all banks operate at the lower frontier of the cost function. This behaviour, however, is not found in practice because the banks, which incur higher costs than the minimum at a given scale and scope due to allocative inefficiency or technical inefficiency, are behaving less efficiently than theoretically assumed (Shaffer 1993).

Consistent with input efficiency studies, we find considerable technical inefficiency. This can be seen from Table 8.3, in which the estimated technical

Table 8.2: Coefficients of the multiproduct, translog cost function

Coefficients	*Estimate*	*T–statistic*	*Probability*
α_1	0.535	–1.854	0.071
α_2	0.181	2.134	0.039
α_3	0.284	–5.256	0.000
β_{ym}	–0.241	–2.066	0.046
β_{yr}	0.269	1.798	0.080
β_{ys}	0.0034	0.0409	0.967
φ_{mr}	0.152	0.922	0.362
φ_{ms}	–0.234	–2.131	0.040
φ_{rs}	0.192	1.798	0.080
γ_{w12}	0.706	–1.048	0.301
γ_{w13}	–0.431	–2.147	0.038
γ_{w23}	0.162	2.764	0.008
$\delta_{w1\,ym}$	0.796	1.830	0.075
$\delta_{w1\,yr}$	–0.279	–0.474	0.637
$\delta_{w1\,ys}$	0.016	0.063	0.950
$\delta_{w2\,ym}$	0.120	2.109	0.041
$\delta_{w2\,yr}$	–0.157	–2.335	0.025
$\delta_{w2\,ys}$	–0.031	–1.142	0.260
$\delta_{w3\,ym}$	0.056	1.909	0.064
$\delta_{w3\,yr}$	0.133	2.755	0.009
$\delta_{w3\,ys}$	–0.105	–4.688	0.000
	DW 1.82	SE = 0.6630	
			R^2
	Cost function		78
	Labour share equation		38
	Deposits share equation		42

Method: Seemingly Unrelated Regression, Total Panel Observations are 60.
Note: The coefficient for capital was obtained using parameter restrictions of linear homogeneity. A one-cost share equation, namely capital, was dropped prior to the estimation.

efficiency registered a value of less than 1 for all the investigated banks. This implies that Sudanese Islamic banks in the sample used their input resources excessively when they were on the frontier. This is consistent with the results in Berger et al. (1993), Sathye (2001) and Elzahi (2002).

Table 8.3 also demonstrates that the Saudi Sudanese Bank, Tadamon Islamic Bank and Faisal Islamic Bank were more technically efficient than the Al-Shamal Islamic Bank, Sudanese Saving Bank and Sudanese Islamic Bank. This suggests that the first group were better able to control costs than the latter during the period under investigation.

Table 8.3: Technical inefficiency

Banks	*Technical Efficiency*	*Technical Inefficiency*
Sudanese Saving Bank	84%	19%
Faisal Islamic Bank	91%	10%
Sudanese Islamic Bank	77%	30%
Saudi Sudanese Bank	96%	4.2%
Tadamon Islamic Bank	96%	4.2%
Al-Shamal Islamic Bank	89.7%	11.5%
Overall Efficiency	88.9%	12.5%

Technically, inefficiency relates to the banks' inputs productivity. Hence, Sudanese Islamic banks in the sample need to improve the productivity of the three inputs (capital, labour and total deposits) included in the study. That is to say, banks need to reduce their capital assets ratios and shed excess labour. The banks have already started reducing their staff, as the number of employees fell from a maximum of 2208 to 258 during the period investigated. Sudanese banks also need to use deposits in producing outputs such as *mushārakah, murābaḥah* and *salam* in a more efficient way. Producing these products without managing the usual high risk has made a significant contribution to their technical inefficiency. The experience in Sudan has shown that non-performing investments were on the high side, with *mushārakah, murābaḥah, salam* and *muḍārabah* at 62.0 per cent, 56.0 per cent, 30.0 per cent and 27.0 per cent respectively (Elzahi 2002). Moreover, to minimise the cost, Sudanese Islamic banks need to introduce more advanced banking technologies. Evidence shows that telephone and internet banking are cost-effective ways for the delivery of financial services (Sathye 2001). To date no Islamic bank in the Sudan provides such services.

The banks in the sample are also found to be allocatively inefficient (see Table 8.4), which means that the Sudanese Islamic banks' management did not combine the three inputs (capital, labour and deposit) in the right proportion.

Table 8.4: Allocative inefficiency

Banks	*Allocative Efficiency*	*Allocative Inefficiency*
Sudanese Saving Bank	75%	33%
Faisal Islamic Bank	81%	24%
Sudanese Islamic Bank	69%	45%
Saudi Sudanese Bank	85%	18%
Tadamon Islamic Bank	85%	18%
Al-Shamal Islamic Bank	79.7%	26%

As we have seen in Table 8.2, some coefficients of the input variables such as capital were high. This indicates that the Sudanese Islamic banks in the sample overused this input. Not surprisingly, the labour input coefficient was low, which indicates that the banks underused it. Alternatively, we can say that the Sudanese Islamic banks in the sample used more labour than they actually needed.

Allocative inefficiency implies that the Sudanese Islamic banks' management might not allocate their inputs in the right proportion due to internal factors such as lack of managerial expertise, as well as external factors such as economic sanctions imposed during the 1990s. This may also imply that the management in the country's banking industry was busy in managing high risks rather than optimising their inputs mix (Elzahi 2002).

Table 8.3 also shows that the overall efficiency (*OE*) was 88.9 per cent. This means that 12.5 per cent of the cost was inefficiently used when these banks were on the efficient frontier. Alternatively, we can say that Sudanese Islamic banks were 12.5 per cent away from the optimum cost frontier. Although the results demonstrate that those Sudanese Islamic banks investigated were X-inefficient, the main source of overall inefficiency in this study was the allocative component rather than technical efficiency. This conclusion is inconsistent with the results in Elzahi (2002). Elzahi (2002) studied the X-efficiency of 12 Sudanese Islamic banks for a period of 10 years from 1989 to 1998 and found that technical components were the major source of Sudanese banks' inefficiency. However, since this study investigates a more recent period (1992–2001), this trend may imply that slight improvement has occurred on the technical side.

CONCLUSIONS AND POLICY IMPLICATIONS

In this chapter a multiproduct cost function is estimated for the first time with usual linear homogeneity and symmetry conditions imposed to arrive at the allocative and technical inefficiency of six Sudanese Islamic banks. The results show that the Sudanese Islamic banks in the sample are technically and allocatively inefficient. With the estimated technical efficiency (*TE*) being 77.0 per cent, 84.0 per cent, 89.7 per cent, 91.0 per cent, 96.0 per cent and 96.0 per cent for Sudanese Islamic Bank, Sudanese Saving Bank, Al-Shamal Islamic Bank, Faisal Islamic Bank, Saudi Sudanese Bank and Tadamon Islamic Bank respectively, this indicates that these banks have not optimised their inputs usage. Alternatively, one can say these banks are technically inefficient. Their technical inefficiency is 30.0 per cent, 19.0 per cent, 11.5 per cent, 10.0 per cent, 4.2 per cent and 4.2 per cent for Sudanese Islamic Bank, Sudanese Saving Bank, Al-Shamal Islamic Bank, Faisal Islamic Bank, Saudi Sudanese Bank and

Tadamon Islamic Bank respectively. The main source of this technical inefficiency seems to be over-utilisation of physical inputs. This result is consistent with previous findings. Elzahi (2002) found that the over-utilisation of capital input indicates that the banks expanded operations by setting up new branches. This strategy may have diverted their capital to unproductive fixed assets in less profitable branches. Sudanese Islamic banks might have chosen this approach given that they are not able to exploit new technologies such as automated telling machines (ATMs) and banking solutions due to the economic sanctions imposed by the US and UN. Economic sanctions may also have adversely impacted on the Sudanese banking training programme. This may have caused the under-utilisation of labour in Sudanese Islamic banks. Another reason could be the appointment or recruitment policy of Sudanese Islamic banks where employment is based on political and religious connections. Hence the officers appointed may not be the best in executing their jobs efficiently (Elzahi 2002).

The study also estimates the allocative efficiency (*AE*) of these banks. The results show that the investigated banks were allocatively inefficient and, in contrast to previous studies, this allocative inefficiency appears to be increasing. The implications are very important if further improvements in the Sudanese banking industry are to be gained. In particular, the *OE* indicates this improvement as compared with previous investigations (Elzahi 2002).

NOTES

1. Allen N. Berger and David B. Humphrey (1993).
2. J. Jondrow et al. (1982).
3. J. Sengupta (2000).
4. Karlyn Mitchell and Nur M. Onvural (1996).
5. Allen N. Berger and David B. Humphrey (1997).

PART IV

Islamic Mortgages, Insurance and Risk Management

9

Islamic Mortgages in the United Kingdom

Humayon A. Dar

The ownership of a house is a major aspiration for most families. For Muslim communities in Western countries, this poses a difficult problem because all conventional mortgage products involve interest, which is prohibited in Islam. Some alternative products are now available. This chapter discusses three such products being offered in the UK market and compares them with conventional mortgages. The study argues that though these products do not involve paying interest and hence are acceptable from an Islamic point of view, in the price-determining process of these products there is a link with interest, which is used as the benchmark. The chapter proposes another product, a Shared Appreciation Mortgage, which has no link with interest and hence in the author's opinion is better than the existing Islamic products from a Sharīʿah perspective.

INTRODUCTION

Purchasing a house is perhaps the single most important financial commitment a household makes during their lifespan. In the UK, there are 25.5 million dwellings (2002 figure published in UK 2004 Yearbook) and, with an increase in population and a decrease in family size, there is a steady increase in demand for housing in the country. Every year, thousands of houses are purchased, mostly due to people moving home, but first-time buyers also account for significant demand for housing. Most house purchases in the UK are through mortgage loans. In 2002, 76.0 per cent of loans for home purchases were obtained through banks and 17.0 per cent through building societies, with 7.0 per cent through other lenders (UK 2004 Yearbook).

The housing market has been buoyant in the recent past, pushing the average UK dwelling price in July 2004 to over £154,000, a 20.0 per cent increase on the previous year and about four times the average price ten years earlier. Consequently, home ownership is increasingly becoming more and more difficult, especially for lower-income households. In other words, although the size of mortgages has risen with an increase in house prices to record levels, there are many who are excluded from the market.

The approximately two million Muslims in the UK now have a growing number of options available for home purchase through Sharīʿah-compliant mortgage loans. There are at least seven providers of Islamic mortgages in the country, including Ahli United Bank, United National Bank, HSBC Bank, West Bromwich Building Society, Ansar Foundation, Islamic Bank of Britain and ABC International Bank.[1] Other banks are also contemplating entering into this niche market, one that is currently worth less than £50 million, but it is estimated could be worth more than £4.5 billion by 2006 (Datamonitor 2002). It is expected that the demand for Islamic financial services in general, and Islamic mortgages in particular, will grow as more and more providers enter into this market.

This chapter critically evaluates the provision of Islamic mortgages in the UK and discusses some challenges facing providers that have implications for future developments in this area. While there are many who argue that there is significant pent-up demand for Islamic mortgages (following Datamonitor's above referred projection), there are some who are not so optimistic about the growth in the market, especially if little is done to create awareness of Islamic finance in the Muslim community. There is anecdotal evidence that Muslims tend to associate Islamic finance with ethical values involving equity and economic justice, and that they reject the models of Islamic banking and finance based on the notion of the maximisation of shareholders' value, especially if it adversely affects other stakeholders, particularly customers. As the provision of Islamic mortgages in the UK is by profit-oriented banks, this may mean that demand for such mortgages is over-estimated by the market research firms employed by banks and building societies thinking of entering into this market.

The next section surveys the Islamic mortgages on offer in the UK, delineating their salient features, and how they compare with conventional interest-based mortgages. Section 3 discusses the problems associated with existing mortgage products and offers some suggestions for product development and delivery. Section 4 provides some conclusions.

ISLAMIC MORTGAGES ON OFFER IN THE UK

The first attempt to offer Islamic mortgages in the UK was an experiment by the Al-Baraka Bank during the late 1980s. The bank surrendered its banking licence to the then regulator, the Bank of England, in the early 1990s when Islamic mortgages ceased to exist in the UK. A second attempt was made by the then United Bank of Kuwait (now Ahli United Bank or AUB in short) through its subsidiary, the Islamic Banking and Investment Unit, which has been offering Islamic mortgages since 1997. The West Bromwich Building Society later joined hands with AUB to cater for the needs of Muslims located in the

West Midlands. The United National Bank and HSBC started offering Islamic mortgages in the summer of 2003, and two new players, the Islamic Bank of Britain (soon to be the first fully fledged British Islamic bank) and ABC International Bank, are almost ready to offer retail Islamic banking services, including Islamic mortgages. There are some non-bank financial institutions, like the Manchester-based Ansar Finance, which follow a cooperative model to offer Islamic home finance to their members.

Broadly, there are three principles on which UK Islamic mortgages are based: *murābaḥah*, *ijārah wa iqtinā'* (IWI) and diminishing *mushārakah* and *ijārah* (DMI). *Murābaḥah* is a form of mark-up financing in which the bank buys a property, identified by its customer, to sell it on credit to the customer at a price higher than the purchased price. The difference between the sale and purchase price makes up the bank's profit. The *Manzil Murābaḥah* Plan offered by AUB follows this principle. The IWI principle, however, is the most popular way of structuring Islamic mortgages. *Manzil Ijārah*, HSBC *Ijārah* and the Islamic mortgages offered by United National Bank, Islamic Bank of Britain and ABC International Bank all follow the IWI model. Only cooperative institutions like Ansar Finance use DMI as a guiding principle for their mortgages.

IWI-based mortgages combine features of deferred payment sale and leasing so that the bank customer rents a house that the bank specifically buys for the customer on their advice. Although the customer 'promises' to purchase the house at a future date (or during an agreed period), the arrangement between the bank and the customer is effectively that of a deferred payment sale, in which the bank sells the property on credit to the customer at the same price that it pays to the vendor. As there is no profit or loss sharing (that is, sharing of the appreciation or depreciation in the property value), there are no elements of diminishing partnership in such an arrangement even though some providers of such mortgages claim so.

In DMI-based mortgages, the mortgage provider and the customer share in the appreciation or depreciation in the value of the property that the customer occupies for the duration of the mortgage. Although closer to the ideal of Islamic profit and loss sharing, this scheme is limited in scope in the current legal and regulatory framework in the UK. The DMI model requires the bank and customer jointly to own the property, allowing the latter to occupy the property and gradually increase their equity in it to eventually become its sole owner. This essentially requires creating a partnership that should own the property, with the bank and the customer owning shares in it. The partnership should delineate a mechanism for share ownership and 'exit' options for the bank and the customer. The model suits a cooperative structure more than limited liability companies – hence it is less popular in practice.[2]

The DMI model shares similarities with a conventional shared ownership scheme, which allows people to part buy and part rent homes developed by registered social landlords (RSLs), like housing associations in the UK. The scheme allows people to increase their share of ownership in their homes over time. A 'Do-It-Yourself Shared Ownership Scheme' is a similar arrangement in which local authorities in partnership with RSLs fund people to buy a house in the private market to part own and part rent the property. The RSL shares ownership of the house with the household. Another scheme, called Homebuy, allows people to buy a home in the private market with an equity loan from an RSL for 25.0 per cent of the value of the property. The loan is payable, at 25.0 per cent of the current market value, when the home is sold. The Shared Appreciation Mortgages (SAM), offered by Bank of Scotland and Barclays for a short time before they were withdrawn in the mid-1990s, had similar structures.

Islamic mortgages vis-à-vis conventional mortgages

Islamic and conventional mortgages are comparable in terms of prices and their response to market changes. *Murābaḥah*-based mortgages, although based on

Table 9.1: HSBC Amānah and HSBC capital repayment (interest-based) mortgages compared as at July 2004

	HSBC Amānah	*HSBC capital repayment*
Loan-to-value	90%	95%
Standard variable rate	5.99%	5.49%
Rate guarantee	No more than 2.5% above the Bank of England base rate during the mortgage term	No more than 1% above the Bank of England base rate during the mortgage term
Overpayments (without penalty)	Yes	Yes
Payment composition by order of preference	Rent, charges (e.g. insurance) and on account payments	Interest, charges (e.g. insurance) and capital repayment
Rate calculation	Bi-annually	Daily
Loan	£100,000	£100,000
Monthly payment	£635.00	£613.83
Term	25 years	25 years
Total rent/interest (at the current rate)	£90,369.00	£84,320.80
Total amount payable	£190,369.00	£184,320.00

Source: *http://www.hsbc.co.uk*.

different legal documentation, are similar to fixed interest rate mortgages, with the exception that perhaps the former are more flexible as they allow and indeed encourage overpayments without unnecessarily penalising customers. IWI-based mortgages, again drawn on different documentation than conventional mortgages, are similar to their conventional counterparts in terms of pricing and their response to market changes. Being profit-oriented banks, the providers of Islamic mortgages price their products so as to earn returns on equity comparable with that of conventional banks. As Islamic mortgages are at an initial stage of development and have yet to experience economies of scope and scale, they tend to be costlier than their conventional counterparts.[3] This, along with the emphasis on maximisation of the shareholders' value, has resulted in Islamic mortgages being in general more expensive than their interest-based equivalents. Table 9.1 compares the cost of HSBC Amānah and HSBC Buyer (interest-based) mortgages for a loan of £100,000.

This comparison of HSBC Amānah and conventional mortgages is only for illustrative purposes. The story is not much different for other Islamic mortgages on offer in the UK; a comparable Manzil Ijārah mortgage, for instance, costs £675 a month – even more expensive than the HSBC Amānah. The next section discusses why Islamic mortgages are so expensive.

ISLAMIC MORTGAGES – PROBLEMS AND CAUSES

The providers of Islamic mortgages offer a number of reasons for the high costs of their products. These include the higher cost of capital (due to the 100.0 per cent risk weighting requirement for *ijārah*-based mortgages as opposed to 50.0 per cent for conventional mortgages), diseconomies of scale and scope, and the higher costs of documentation. These are certainly genuine problems and one can hope that their removal will make Islamic mortgages more competitive in the years to come. The UK government, particularly the Financial Services Authority and the Treasury, have been supportive, as is evidenced by the recent abolition of double stamp duty on Islamic mortgages.

Probably a more compelling reason for such steep pricing is competitive pressure on the providers of Islamic mortgages. AUB's Islamic Investment and Banking Unit and HSBC Amānah Finance are subsidiaries of large and highly profitable groups that require these subsidiaries to keep pace with the overall performance indicators of the group. Thus, management of such subsidiaries have to price Islamic mortgages so as to maintain the required level of profitability and return on shareholders' equity. If true, then while buyers of Islamic mortgages are required to pay a premium for their religious commitment, the shareholders of the institutions providing these mortgages seem unwilling to accept lower returns.[4] This is perhaps the most important problem facing Islamic finance. Without addressing this issue, it is overoptimistic to assume that demand for Islamic mortgages will grow dramatically.

Another related problem is the lack of commitment from shareholders and the management of Islamic financial institutions to ethical investment and social responsibility. In general, they consider it sufficient to give reference to the prohibition of interest to show their commitment to the Islamic Sharīʿah. However, indifference to social responsibility and an overemphasis on shareholders' value are not entirely in line with what Muslims in the UK perceive as Islamic finance.

A proposal

Islamic mortgages, although not interest-based, are in a way still interest-linked through benchmarking with interest (LIBOR or Bank of England base rate). While Sharīʿah scholars pronounce these mortgages as *Sharīʿah*-compliant, there is a definite aversion among ordinary Muslims to the link with interest. Dar (2002) suggests some changes in *ijārah*-based mortgages to make them less dependent on changes in interest rate. He proposes that the rent should be determined as a fraction of the appreciation in property value rather than with reference to the market rental or by benchmarking with market interest rates. This chapter goes a step further by suggesting that Islamic mortgages should be structured completely independently of interest rates and that some elements of profit and loss sharing should be incorporated to make them fairer and more Islamic in outlook and spirit. The idea is quite close to Shared Appreciation Mortgages (SAM), briefly used by Bank of Scotland and Barclays in the 1990s, but with some important differences.[5]

Table 9.2: Average house price inflation in the UK

Period	*Average house price inflation (%)*
1970–94	12.1
1971–95	11.8
1972–96	11.5
1973–97	10.2
1974–98	9.2
1975–99	9.3
1976–2000	9.7
1977–2001	13.7
1978–2002	10.0
1979–2003	10.0

Source: Office of Deputy Prime Minister (*http://www.odpm.gov.uk*).

The proposed structure relies on the historical data on house price inflation in the UK to price a mortgage. For ease of reference we may call it an Islamic Shared Appreciation Mortgage or ISAM. The historical data on house price inflation suggests that house prices increase by about 10 times over a period of 25 years.[6] The average increase in house prices for any block of 25 years for the last 10 years (starting from a year and going back 25 years in the past) ranges between 9.2 and 13.9 per cent as shown in Table 9.2.

We suggest that the ISAM should be based on an expected rate of return determined by the expected value of the property at the end of the mortgage period. For example, it is in line with historical trend to assume that a property worth £100,000 today will be worth about £1,000,000 in value in 25 years' time. The bank's expected share in the appreciated value may be calculated as α x FV, where α is a weight (less than 1) 3–5 points higher than the 25-year average house price inflation in the recent past, and FV is the future value of the property. Thus, if a bank wishes to use a weight of 5 points higher than the 1979–2003 average house price inflation (10.0 per cent), *a* will be 0.15. If the future value of the property after 25 years is £1,000,000, a bank may use £150,000 as a benchmark for pricing the ISAM. Figure 9.1 explains how an ESAM mortgage should work and Table 9.3 provides some key statistics using a hypothetical example. Figures 9.2 and 9.3 compare the proposed product with the HSBC Buyer Mortgage.

The data is based on the assumption that a property worth £100,000 today will continue appreciating in accordance with the previous year's monthly price inflation. We use the Nationwide House Price Index for this purpose. Based on this assumption, the proposed product generates a schedule of payments over the 25 years, which is slightly higher than the HSBC Buyer Mortgage. However, our calculations suggest that the bank may in fact earn the expected return on the ISAM mortgage in 23 years, rather than the full term of 25 years. Therefore, we suggest that the return to be received by the bank in the last two years should be reimbursed to the customer in the first two years of the mortgage to make it more attractive for customers. The ISAM with the provision of money-back is depicted in Figure 9.3. As Figures 9.2 and 9.3 suggest, the proposed product requires higher monthly payments after an initial period of four years. Although some may consider this a disadvantage, this structure provides relief in payments at the tail end.

It must be noted that the bank's and the customer's shares in the property value are used only for the purpose of the next year monthly payments; they do not represent ownership rights for the two parties. They are, however, used in determining the amount of unpaid loan at the time of termination of contract before the end of the term. We propose a formula that should treat both parties fairly. To ensure that ISAM does not favour the lender unduly, we suggest that

Table 9.3: Hypothetical example of an ISAM mortgage

Year	*Monthly payment* (£)	*Annual payment* (£)	*Appreciation in the price property value* (%)	*Estimated price of property* (£)	*Bank's share in the property value value*	*Customer's share in the property value*(%)
1	500	6000	15.10	100,000	76	24
2	454	5448	15.01	115,099	73	27
3	471	5652	14.96	132,385	70	30
4	486	5832	14.9	152,188	68	32
5	502	6024	14.86	174,872	66	34
6	518	6216	14.82	200,859	64	36
7	535	6420	14.79	230,628	62	38
8	553	6636	14.76	264,730	61	39
9	571	6852	14.73	303,795	60	40
10	589	7068	14.71	348,544	59	41
11	608	7296	14.69	399,804	58	42
12	626	7512	14.67	458,520	57	43
13	644	7728	14.65	525,777	56	44
14	660	7920	14.64	602,816	56	44
15	674	8088	14.62	691,057	55	45
16	684	8208	14.61	792,128	55	45
17	689	8268	14.60	907,894	54	46
18	684	8208	14.60	1,040,492	54	46
19	665	7980	14.59	1,192,368	53	47
20	624	7488	14.58	1,366,326	53	47
21	544	6528	14.58	1,565,581	53	47
22	399	4788	14.57	1,793,816	53	47
23	126	1512	14.57	2,055,257	53	47
24	126	1512	14.57	2,354,752	53	47
25	126	1512	14.57	2,697,875	53	47
Total		156,696				

Figures are rounded and may not add up to the exact total.

the unpaid loan should be determined by the difference in the bank's expected share in appreciation and the total payments made by the customer up to a given point in time, weighted by their respective share in the property value. For example, if the customer wishes to remortgage with another lender after 10 years, the amount of unpaid loan should be determined as shown in Table 9.4.

Out of the £62,148 paid by the customer by the end of year 10, only £28,127 could be considered as 'capital repayment', with the remaining £34,021 going to the bank as its share in the appreciation in the property value.

Figure 9.1: ISAM mortgages: how should they work?

- A customer identifies a property, negotiates its price with the vendor and agrees to buy it.
- They then arrange for a deposit (minimum 5.0 per cent of the property price).
- They then apply to a bank offering ISAM mortgages.
- The bank, satisfied with the credibility of the application, accepts the application.
- The customer is advised that ISAM mortgages are *completely* interest free, that is, that the monthly payments will not be affected by changes in the Bank of England base rate or any other market rate of interest.
- The bank makes it clear that although the customer will be the legal owner of the house, the bank, being the financier of the house purchase, will have a right to share appreciation in the property value during the term of the mortgage.
- The bank explains how property prices have changed in the area over the past 25 years (assuming that the mortgage term is 25 years). For example, if the property is located in the East Midlands, the bank should use a relevant regional house price index.
- The bank should inform the customer of the total increase in property value in the relevant region in the last 25 years. It should also inform them of the annual increase in house prices in the region during the last 25 years.
- If house price inflation has been ten-fold in the past 25 years and the annual increase in average house prices has be 10.0 per cent in the last 25 years, the bank should explain that it expects to receive 15.0 per cent (5.0 percentage points higher than the average annual increase in house prices in the region) of the expected house price at the end of 25 years (the mortgage term). For example, if the property is worth £100,000 today, it is expected to go up to £1,000,000 after 25 years. The bank expects to receive £150,000 as its share in the property value (including its initial investment).
- The bank should clarify that it is only an expected return, and that the actual return will be determined by changes in property prices over the course of 25 years.
- Other provisions, like ending the contract, overpayments, moving mortgage to another lender and so on, should be explained.
- Monthly instalments should be reviewed on an annual basis to incorporate changes in the relevant home price index over the last 12 months.
- Monthly instalments are calculated using a formula incorporating previous payments by the customer, appreciation in the property value over the last 12 months and the respective shares of the bank and the customer.
- The contract ends either at the end of the mortgage period or during it, depending on the relevant redemption clauses.

Table 9.4: Calculation of the unpaid loan (after 10 years)

Bank's expected share in the appreciation (at the start)	£150,000
Total payments by the customer to date	£62,148
Difference	£87,852
Bank's share in the property value	59%
Unpaid loan	£87,852 x 59% = £51,833

Benefits

The ISAM type of a structure is completely interest-free: neither interest-based nor interest-linked. At no stage in the development or delivery of the product is reference made to an interest rate of any kind. This is possibly the purest form of an Islamically permissible interest-free mortgage and, hence, should be acceptable to religiously motivated Muslims. Although it incorporates some elements of profit and loss sharing, it does not allow the banks to take a major share of the appreciation in the value of the house. This was certainly a criticism of the SAM offered in the US and the UK. The proposed product addresses this criticism and ensures that it is priced fairly.

Given that interest rates and property prices in general tend to move in opposite directions (see Figure 9.4), the ISAM type of product should provide a tool for diversification to lenders. At the same time, it is expected to serve as an attractive option available to customers during high interest rate periods.

CONCLUSIONS

Although there are a growing number of providers of Islamic mortgages in the UK, a completely interest-free mortgage has yet to emerge. This chapter provides some thought on how to construct such a mortgage by using historical house price inflation data instead of benchmarking with interest. The model presented here explains the idea in a simple way by using a mix of hypothetical and real data. As the treatment is explanatory, it does not apply sensitivity analysis to find out how the proposed product would react to changes in different variables such as interest rates and house prices. This is left for future research and for those readers who are keen to develop the idea further.

Figure 9.2: ISAM and HSBC Buyer Mortgage: monthly payments

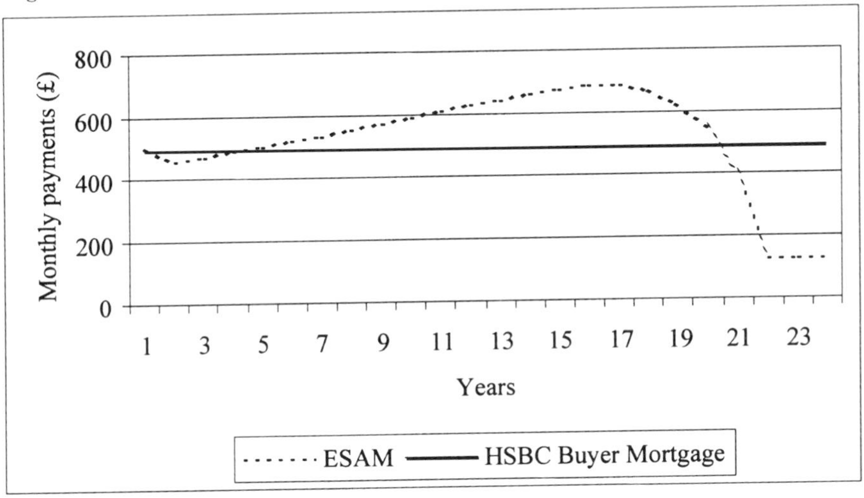

- HSBC Buyer Morgage with interest rate of 4.49 per cent (July 2004).
- ISAM based on a rate of return based on expected appreciation in the property value.

Figure 9.3: ISAM (with money-back) and HSBC Buyer Mortgage: monthly payment

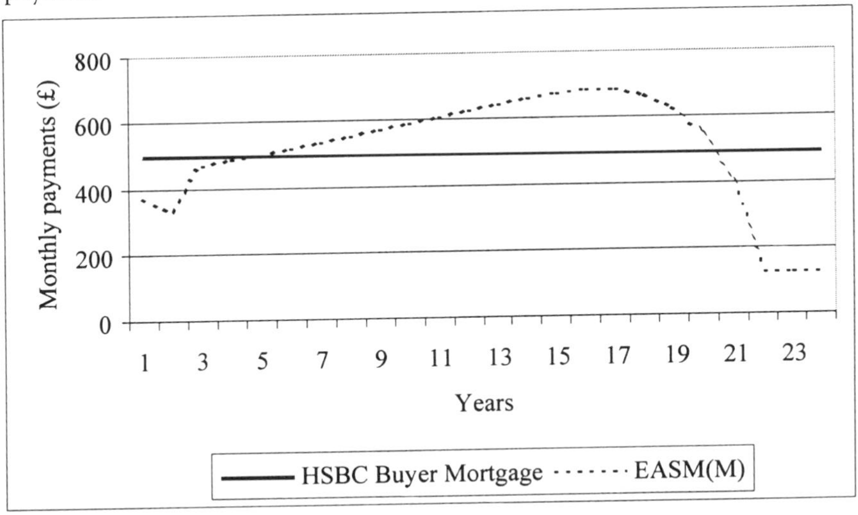

- HSBC Buyer Morgage with interest rate of 4.49 per cent (July 2004).
- ISAM based on a rate of return based on expected appreciation in the property value.

Figure 9.4: House price inflation and standard variable rates

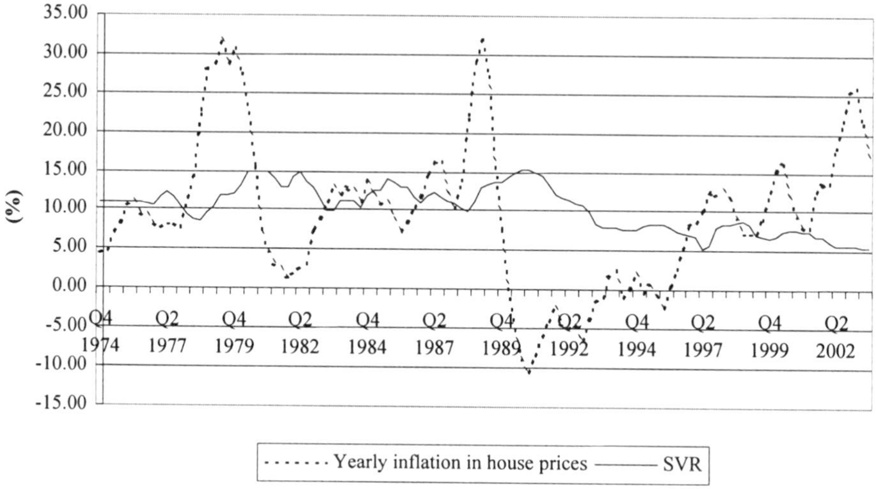

Source: Nationwide and the Bank of England.

NOTES

1. The Islamic Bank of Britain and ABC International Bank's Al-Burraq (provider of Islamic retail banking services) were not in operation at the time of submission of this manuscript for publication.
2. The new limited liability partnership structure may be used to design mortgages on the DMI principle.
3. Although the issue of double stamp duty has now been resolved, Islamic mortgages still face 100 per cent capital weighting, as opposed to 50.0 per cent capital weighting for conventional mortgages.
4. If that is not the case, then the provision of Islamic mortgages is perhaps inefficient at present; the inefficiency is expected to decrease with the passage of time.
5. The SAM may be structured completely interest-free or interest-plus-share-based. The interest-free version allows the customer to borrow any proportion up to 25.0 per cent of their home's current value, in return for a share of the house price appreciation amounting to three times the initial loan-to-value (LTV) rate. A borrower may be required to pay up to 75.0 per cent of the house appreciation if they take a mortgage with an LTV of 25.0 per cent. In the interest-plus-share version, the borrower must pay an interest rate (usually around two-thirds of the current market rate) in addition to a proportion in the house appreciation up to a maximum of 75.0 per cent, but normally equal to the initial LTV. The SAM product offered by the Bank of Scotland had no set term: the borrower was required to pay back only when they sold the house, or upon the death of the last surviving joint borrower.
6. Although there are some regional variations, the aggregated data on the UK averages at the figure of a ten-fold increase in house prices.

10

Wealth Creation through *Takāful* (Islamic Insurance)

Mervyn K. Lewis

Despite continued growth of *takāful*, with over 50 companies operating in 22 countries, there is a relative lack of study of their contribution to savings in the Muslim World. Insurance products have long been recognised as major vehicles for savings in Western countries. This chapter examines different ways in which insurance products act as vehicles for savings and then goes on to consider the distinctive form of wealth creation via *takāful* operations. The chapter analyses the basis of *takāful* business and compares this with conventional insurance. While considerable differences exist between *takāful* and traditional insurance, similarities are found between *takāful* and some of the newer insurance products. Finally, the chapter outlines the challenges facing the development of *takāful* business and considers how its wealth creation role could be enhanced.

INTRODUCTION

A major development in the financial markets of the major industrial countries in recent decades has been the increasing dominance of institutional investors. Life insurance companies, pension funds, investment funds and other similar financial institutions have been growing in size dramatically. Total institutional assets in the OECD area rose from $3.2 trillion in 1981 to $24.3 trillion in 1995 (OECD 1998). In 1997, the proportion of household wealth managed by institutional investors was 53.0 per cent in the UK, 45.0 per cent in the US, 44.0 per cent in France and 43.0 per cent in Germany (Aglietta 2000).

Life insurance companies are the largest of the institutional investors group, with 36.0 per cent of institutional investment funds in 1995 under their management (OECD 1998), and they are often seen as being a particularly suitable vehicle for promoting long-term savings given the long-term motive of the contractual arrangements (OECD 1992). Many life insurance products have always embodied elements similar to those of traditional types of savings products, and a life insurance contract can be looked upon as an insurance arrangement that also allows the formation of investments to the extent that it guarantees the payment of a capital sum either to the policyholder or the beneficiaries named. In this way, in addition to the insurance and savings elements, it performs a social role by providing future incomes that may make a contribution to the economic wellbeing of the beneficiaries of the policy.

By comparison with their Western counterparts, the amount of investments brought to the market by Islamic insurance companies is negligible relative to the vast investment holdings of Western insurance companies and pension funds. While *takāful* is an important part of the Islamic financial system, it has been somewhat neglected in favour of Islamic banking, which has received considerable attention because of its worldwide expansion and strong growth. Yet, judged by the market position of conventional insurance, there is a considerable potential for Islamic insurance – especially life insurance – to increase Islamic assets under management (Taylor 2002). This chapter considers the challenges that need to be met if this potential is to be realised. In order to examine these challenges, the chapter provides an explanation of *takāful*, its differences from conventional insurance, and the nature of wealth creation under *takāful*.

THE BASIS OF *TAKĀFUL*

Takāful is a noun stemming from the Arabic verb *kafal* meaning to take care of one's needs. It is descriptive of a practice whereby participants in a group agree jointly to guarantee themselves against loss or damage. If any member or participant suffers a catastrophe or disaster, they would receive financial benefit from a fund to help meet that loss or damage. The amount is drawn out of a common pool created with the individual contributions of participating members. There are thus some similarities with the concept of mutuality in insurance, in that members are the insurers as well as the insured.

Essentially, the concept of *takāful* is based on solidarity, responsibility and brotherhood among members, where participants agree to share defined losses to be paid out of defined assets. It is based on the Qur'ānic concept of *ta'āwun* (mutual assistance). In Malaysia, for example, Section 2 of the *Takāful* Act 1984 defines *takāful* as 'a scheme based on brotherhood, solidarity and mutual assistance which provides for mutual financial aid and assistance to the participants in case of need whereby the participants mutually agree to contribute for that purpose', and *takāful* business as a 'business of *takāful* whose aims and operations do not involve any element which is not approved by the Sharī'ah'. The Act established the Syarikat *Takāful* Malaysia Sendirian Berhad in 1985. Its Memorandum of Association states: 'The business of the company will be transacted in accordance with Islamic principles, rules and practices.' To this end, there is a Sharī'ah Supervisory Council to make sure that this objective is fully realised.

In order to conform to Islamic rules and norms, four features, which are well established in the literature (for a recent survey, see Lewis and Algaoud 2001), must be followed in investment behaviour. These four aspects are as follows:

Ribā

Perhaps the most far-reaching feature of Islamic economics from a Western financial perspective is the prohibition of interest (*ribā*). The payment of *ribā* and the taking of interest as occurs in a conventional financial system is explicitly prohibited by the Qur'ān, and thus investors must be compensated by other means. The prohibition of *ribā* is mentioned in four different verses in the Qur'ān (Sūrah al-Rūm, verse 39; Sūrah al-Nisā', verse 161; Sūrah Āle 'Imrān, verses 130–2; Sūrah al-Baqarah, verses 275–81). The first emphasises that interest deprives wealth of God's blessings. The second condemns it, placing interest in juxtaposition with wrongful appropriation of property belonging to others. The third enjoins Muslims to stay clear of interest for the sake of their own welfare. The fourth establishes a clear distinction between interest and trade, urging Muslims, first, to take only the principal sum and, second, to forego even this sum if the borrower is unable to repay. The ban on interest is also cited in unequivocal terms in the Ḥadīth and Sunnah.

Although for most Muslims this clear prohibition is sufficient, the Islamic ban on *ribā* – literally 'increase', but widely understood in this context to mean all predetermined interest payable on a loan of any kind – is well grounded in the Islamic theory of property rights. Islamic law recognises two types of individual claim to property: (1) property which is a result of the combination of an individual's creative labour and natural resources; and (2) property the title of which has been transferred by its owner as a result of exchange, remittance of rights, other benefits, grants and inheritance. Money represents the monetised claims of its owner to property rights created. Lending money, in effect, is a transfer of this right, and all that can be claimed in return is the principal (Murvat 1992). Funds are used either productively or unproductively. In the first case, when funds are combined with creative labour, the lender may ask for a portion of the created wealth but may not ask for a fixed return, irrespective of the outcome of the enterprise. In the second case, the money lent, even if legitimately acquired, cannot claim any additional property rights, since none are created.

Zakāh

Islamic financial institutions must establish a *zakāh* fund. According to the Qur'ān, God owns all wealth and private property is seen as a trust from God. Property has a social function in Islam, and must be used for the benefit of society. A mechanism for the redistribution of income and wealth is inherent in Islam, so that every Muslim is guaranteed a fair standard of living, *niṣāb*. *Zakāh* is the most important instrument for the redistribution of wealth. This almsgiving is a compulsory levy, and constitutes one of the five basic tenets of Islam. The generally accepted amount of *zakāh* is a one fortieth (2.5 per cent) assessment on assets held for a full year (after a small initial exclusion, *niṣāb*), the purpose of which is to transfer income from the wealthy to the needy. *Zakāh* is neither a welfare programme nor a tax. A tax in a modern society is an obligation of individuals and other entities towards the state, whereas *zakāh* is an obligation of a Muslim not only to society and the state, but also to Allah. In other words, *zakāh* is not merely a 'contribution', it is also a 'due' or 'claim'. A person paying *zakāh* is not primarily doing a favour to the recipient of *zakāh*, but is rather meeting a claim on himself by purifying wealth. Of course, the same is true of a Muslim who eschews interest. Neither obligation can be judged in earthly terms alone.

Ḥarām

A Sharī'ah Supervisory Council consisting of Muslim jurists acting as independent Sharī'ah auditors and advisers ensures that a strict code of 'ethical investments' operates. Hence, Islamic financial institutions cannot finance activities or items forbidden (that is, *ḥarām)* in Islam, such as trading in alcoholic beverages and pork meat. Furthermore, as the fulfilment of material needs assures a religious freedom for Muslims, Islamic institutions are encouraged to give priority to the production of essential goods that satisfy the needs of the majority of the Muslim community.

Gharar/Maysir

Prohibition of games of chance is explicit in the Qur'ān (Sūrah al Mā'idah 5:90–1). It uses the word *maysir* for games of hazard, implying that the gambler strives to amass wealth without effort. Gambling in all its forms is forbidden in Islamic jurisprudence. Along with explicit forms of gambling, Islamic law also forbids any business activities that contain any element of gambling (Siddiqi 1985). In the interests of fair, ethical dealing in commutative contracts, unjustified enrichment through pure chance should be prohibited.

Another feature condemned by Islam is economic transactions involving elements of speculation, *gharar* (literally hazard). While *ribā* and *maysir* are condemned in the Qur'ān, condemnation of *gharar* is supported by a ḥādith. In business terms, *gharar* means to undertake a venture blindly without sufficient knowledge or to undertake an excessively risky transaction. By failing or neglecting to define any of the essential pillars of contract relating to the consideration or measure of the object, the parties undertake a risk that is not indispensable for them. This kind of risk was deemed unacceptable and tantamount to speculation due to its inherent uncertainty. Speculative transactions with these characteristics are therefore prohibited. *Gharar* also applies to investments such as trading in futures on the stock market; indeed, *gharar* is present in all future (*muḍāf*) sales. Such a contract is therefore null and void.

The rejection of *gharar* has led to the condemnation of some or all types of insurance by Muslim scholars, since insurance involves an unknown risk. Further, an element of *maysir* arises as a consequence of the presence of *gharar*. In addition, many forms of life insurance are merely thinly disguised investment methods, and the majority of insurance companies conduct their business by investing collected premiums and reinsuring with other insurers, thereby contravening the Islamic laws regarding *ribā* along with *gharar* and *maysir*. These issues are now explored more fully.

PROBLEMS WITH CONVENTIONAL INSURANCE

The basic objection is that this type of insurance is effectively a gamble upon the incidence of the contingency insured against, because the interests of both parties are diametrically opposed, and both parties do not know their respective rights and liabilities until the occurrence of the insured events. From the viewpoint of Islamic law, there are three main problems with conventional, especially life, insurance.

First, standard insurance violates the prohibition of *gharar* (uncertainty), since the benefits to be paid depend on the outcome of future events that are not known at the time of signing the contract. It would appear that the *gharar* or uncertainty objected to by certain scholars is from the aspect of the delivery of the subject matter, with uncertainty as to whether the insured will get the compensation which has been promised, how much the insured will get, and when the compensation can be paid. This prohibition in particular nullifies a conventional whole-of-life policy contract because this type of policy is based on a time frame, the lifetime of the insured, which is not known and cannot be known until the event (death) itself occurs. *Gharar* is objected to in any transaction because it is said to undermine the element of consent necessary for a valid contract. There cannot be mutual consent when one party, because of inadequate information, does not have the correct impression of the material aspects of the contract. It would not be fair to expect that party to consent to something of which the essential elements are not known. Mutual consent and the truthfulness of the parties to a contract is therefore a moral obligation and a basic requirement for a valid contract in Islam.

Second, insurance is regarded as *maysir* (gambling) because policyholders are held to be betting premiums on the condition that the insurer will make payment (indemnity) consequent upon the circumstance of a specified event. For example, when policyholders take out a pure endowment policy they are taking a gamble that they will still be alive by the end of the term of the policy to receive the benefits stated in the contract. According to one writer (Ismail 1998, p. 3):

> There are similarities between the conventional insurance contract and gambling. The amount insured is paid back to the insurer when certain events occur. If the event never occurs, the insurance company keeps the premium. It's like putting money in a pot and rolling the dice, the lucky winner takes the pot. In the case of conventional insurance companies, they play the role of the 'House' and the insuree plays the role of the gambler by placing a bet. The gain for the 'House' is always certain, while the gain for the gambler is doubtful; the person may gain or lose. Overall, the 'House' is against the gamblers, and the insurance company is against the insured, the 'House' and the insurance company are always winners.

Third, all insurance policies (including general insurance) have a significant savings element built into them, as the insurer invests prepaid premiums on behalf of those insured. Consider, for example, term insurance. Life offices could offer one-year contracts, with annual premiums rising sharply in line with the age of the life covered. Although it is possible to buy term insurance (or temporary life insurance) on this basis, this is not the usual way. Under the standard form of a term life insurance policy, a contract period of a number of years' duration is specified and a constant annual premium is determined. If the person whose life is the subject of cover then dies during the contract period, and if the various other terms of the contract have been complied with, the insurer pays out the sum specified in the contract, and no further premiums are payable. If at the end of the contract period the relevant person is still alive, the obligations of the insurer simply end.

The fact that a constant annual premium for term insurance is being levied when the likelihood of a claim arising on the policy is in fact increasing from one year to the next means that, during the early years of the contract, premium monies are being paid in excess of what would have been necessary to secure the same cover under one-year term policies for those years. In effect, then, the insurer is providing the insured with two distinct sets of services: death cover over the contract period via a sequence of one-year term policies (each with its own appropriate premium rate); and a 'premium-equalisation' service consisting of the management of a balance of prepaid premiums on behalf of the insured. The insurer invests these balances.

With whole-of-life policies the same principle applies, but on a larger scale, because the contract period is not a specified number of years: it is the remaining lifetime of the person whose life is the subject of the cover, with a constant annual premium rate again being the norm. In the early years, when few claims are made, the insurer must be accumulating the funds necessary for coping with the more rapid flow of claims in later years. The funds held are, in effect, an aggregate of a set of 'prepaid premium deposits' – one deposit per policy still in force. The insurer invests and manages these deposits and simultaneously provides each insured with death cover. Whole-of-life insurance has undergone considerable development in recent years with the growth of adjustable life, universal life and variable life (or unit-linked policies), but these changes merely serve to bring this product closer to traditional financial products.

The other standard types of life insurance contracts in existence can be regarded as outgrowths of these two basic products, and all in one way or another bundle together life cover with a substantial 'savings bank' type facility. For example, endowment insurance policies require the insurer to manage an accumulating balance of the insured's savings. Annuities require the insurer to manage a decumulating balance of the annuitants' savings (Covick and Lewis 1997).

Since in most cases the underlying investment activities of the insurance company contracts are *ribā*-based, conventional insurance policies, therefore, contravene the Sharī'ah. For example, interest-rate bonds and securities accounted for about 80.0 per cent of the assets of US life insurance companies in 1988 (Lewis 1992), and in 2000 still accounted for 61.0 per cent of assets (ACLI 2001).

Insurance, it must be said, remains a controversial matter within the Muslim community. Some argue that the calculation of probability involved might be seen as an act of defiance against *taqdīr*, God's predestination of events. House insurance, for example, is virtually unknown in some Arab countries. Muslehuddin (1982) surveys the *fatāwā* (religious rulings) for and against the contract of insurance. As recently as 1995, Sheik Al-Azhar Al-Sheikh Jad-al Haq Ali Jad al-Haq of Egypt declared all life insurance to be prohibited under the Sharī'ah (Wahib 1999; Billah 2001). Other scholars, however, argue that a system of life insurance can be worked out, based on mutuality, which avoids the presence of *gharar*, *ribā* and *maysir* in conventional life insurance. This is the essence of *takāful* insurance.

TAKĀFUL INSURANCE

The type of insurance that would appear to be lawful according to the Sharī'ah is mutual (or 'joint-guarantee') insurance. The OIC Islamic Fiqh Academy, at its second session held in Jeddah on 10–16 Rabi'll, AH (22–28 December 1985), resolved as follows:

1. The commercial insurance contract with the fixed premium offered by commercial insurance companies is a contract that contains excessive and, hence, contract-invalidating *gharar*. Therefore, it is *ḥarām* (forbidden) by the Sharī'ah.

Table 10.1: Takāful (Islamic insurance) institutions

Country	*Organisation*[1]
Australia	Australia Takāful Association Inc
Bahamas	Islamic Takāful ReTakāful, Bahamas (DMI Group) – 1983
Bahrain	Al-salam Islamic Takāful Company – 1992
	Islamic Insurance & Re-insurance Co. (Al-Baraka Group)
	Takāful International Company (formerly Bahrain Islamic Insurance Company (Bahrain Islamic Bank) – 1989
	Takāful Islamic Insurance Co. EC (DMI Group)
Bangladesh	Bangladesh Islamic Insurance Co. – 2000
Brunei	Insurans Islam Taib Sendiran Berhad II TSB (Perbadanan Tabung Amānah Islāmī Brunei) – 1993
	Takāful Ab Birhad – 1993
Ghana	Metropolitan Insurance Company Ltd
Indonesia	PT Asuransi Takāful Keluarga (Bank Muamalet Indonesia) – 1994
	PT Asuransi Takāful Umum (Bank Muamalet Indonesia)
	Takāful Asuransi
	PT Syarikat Takāful Indonesia (Bank Mu'āmalāt)
Jordan	Islamic Insurance Company plc (Jordan Islamic Bank for Finance and Investment)
Kuwait	Al-Auwaly Litamin Ataqafuly (Kuwait Finance House) – 2000
	Al-Takāfuliah Litamin – 2000
Luxembourg	International Takāful Co.
	International Takāful Co. Takāful SA (DMI Group) – 1982
Malaysia	Asean ReTakāful International (Labuan) Ltd (Bank Islam Malaysia Berhad) – 1997
	Syakirat Takāful Malaysia Berhad (Bank Islam Malaysia Berhad) – 1984
	Takāful Nasional Sdn. Berhad (MNI Holdings) – 1993
Nigeria	The African Alliance Insurance Co. (Takāful window) – 2003
Oman	Oman Insurance Company
Saudi Arabia	Arab-Eastern Insurance Co. Ltd[2]– 2002
	Arabian Malaysian Takāful Co.
	International Islamic Insurance Co.
	Islamic Arab Insurance Co. (Al-Baraka Group) – 1979
	Islamic Corporation for the Insurance of Investment and Export Credit (Islamic Development Bank) – 1994
	Islamic Insurance Co. Ltd, Riyadh
	Islamic Insurance and Reinsurance Co. Bahrain (Al-Baraka Group) – 1985
	Islamic International Company for Insurance, Salamat – 1985
	Islamic Rajhi Co. for Cooperative Insurance, Al-Aman – 1985

Country	*Organisation*[1]
	Islamic Takāful & ReTakāful Company (DMI Group) – 1986
	National Company for Cooperative Insurance – 1986
	Takāful Islamic Insurance Company, Riyadh (DMI Group)
	Takāful Ta'āwuni Division, Bank Al-Jazira – 2002
Singapore	AMPRO Singapore
	Syarikat Takāful Singapura – 1995
Senegal	Sosar Al Amane (Al-Baraka Group) – 1998
Sri Lanka	Amānah Takāful Ltd – 1999
Sudan[3]	Al Baraka Insurance Co. (Al-Baraka) –1984
	Sheikhan Takāful – 1979
	The National Reinsurance Company (Sudan) Ltd – 1968
	The United Insurance Company (Sudan) Ltd – 1968 (1992)
	Watania Cooperative Insurance Co. (Islamic Cooperative Development Bank) – 1989
Trinidad	Takāful T & T
Tunisia	BEIT Ladat Ettamine Tounsi Saudi (BEST) – RE (Al-Baraka group)
Turkey	Ihlas Sigorta As
Qatar	Qatar Islamic Insurance Co. – 1994
UAE	Islamic Arab Insurance Co. (Al-Baraka group)
	Oman Insurance Company, Dubai
UK	Takāful (UK) Ltd[4] – 1983

Source: Directory of Islamic Insurance (*Takāful*) 2000, *New Horizon* (various issues).
Notes: [1] The name of any Islamic Bank with a full or part share ownership, along with the date of establishment, where known, is shown in parentheses.
[2] A composite insurance company registered in Bahrain and operating in Jeddah providing family *takāful*.
[3] All insurance companies in Sudan have been deemed to operate on an Islamic basis since 1992.
[4] The marketing arm of the sister DMI Group company *Takāful* SA (Luxembourg).

2. An alternative contract that meets Islamic principles for transactions is a cooperative insurance contract based on voluntary contributions and cooperation. The same applies to re-insurance based on cooperative insurance.
3. Islamic countries should be called upon to set up cooperative institutions of insurance and re-insurance … (cited in Dhareer 1997, p. 57).

Such views have led to the development of *takāful* (cooperative) insurance which operates in accordance with Islamic financial principles. There are now over 50 *takāful* companies providing Islamic insurance. Table 10.1 shows the countries in which *takāful* companies operate, and the organisations engaged in *takāful* business. Islamic banks established many of these organisations wholly or partly, and the table indicates the associated bank, along with the date of formation (where known). Although most *takāful* companies are akin in structure to a proprietary life office or general insurance company, which is wholly owned either by shareholders or by another company, the *takāful* company's main purpose and the way it operates and distributes its excess or profits makes it more like a mutual or cooperative life office.

Unlike its banking counterpart, Islamic insurance has been largely neglected in the literature for reasons that seem difficult to explain other than the specialised nature of insurance as a subject. The major contributors are Muslehuddin (1982) and Siddiqi (1985). Anwar (1994) provides a later commentary (and critique), while Wahib (1999) gives a practitioner's guide. BIMB Institute of Research and Training (1996) and the Institute of Islamic Banking and Insurance (1999) focus on the operational aspects.

Takāful, according to jurists, is acceptable in Islam for the following reasons:

1. The policyholders cooperate among themselves for their common good.
2. Every policyholder pays his or her subscription in order to assist those of them who need assistance.
3. It falls under a donation contract which is intended to divide losses and spread liability according to the community pooling system.
4. The element of uncertainty is eliminated in so far as subscription and compensation are concerned.
5. It does not aim at deriving advantage at the cost of other individuals.

There are two basic building blocks to the *takāful* contract: the concepts of *tabarru'* and *muḍārabah* (Sharif 2000). *Tabarru'* means donating, contributing, offering or granting. In the context of *takāful*, what it means is a voluntary specific amount of donation made among participants and managed by the *takāful* operator. The pooled fund is then utilised to help the unfortunate members. The spirit embodied in the concept of *tabarru'* is that the participants are not thinking only of their own protection, but that they should also be thinking of helping other participants. Without the concept of donation, the transaction would be that of the buying and selling of insurance, that is the purchase of a promise that some form of benefit will be paid in the event that the insured faces a misfortune. The promise may or may not be fulfilled, depending on whether or not the event insured against occurs. Should there be no claim, the insurers will stand to earn the premium paid. However, in the case of *tabarru'* the risk is equally shared by the participants, as the *takāful* operator is not the owner of the fund but just its custodian. This distinction and other differences from conventional insurance are summarised in Table 10.2.

Table 10.2: Takāful and conventional insurance compared

	Conventional	*Takāful*
Contract	Insurance is a buy-sell contract. Policies are sold and buyers are the policyholders.	Participants in principle own the insurance funds, managed by the company. Participants give up individual rights to gain collective rights over contributions and benefits.
Guarantees	The company guarantees certain benefits, especially death benefits.	No contractual guarantees are given by the company. Joint indemnity between participants is a prerequisite of participating in a *takāful* scheme.
Company	Relationship between the company and the policyholders on a one-to-one basis.	Company acts as a trustee and entrepreneur.
Profits	Legally, insurance surplus belongs to shareholders.	Insurance surplus belongs to the participants. Shareholder returns come out of margins in management fees for the insurance and investment activities of the *takāful* fund.
Funds	Funds belong to the company, though separation of assets is maintained between shareholders and policyholders.	Funds belong to the participants on a collective basis and are managed by the company for a fee.
Benefits	Paid from funds legally belonging to the company.	Paid from defined funds under joint indemnity borne by the participants.
Sales Distribution	Sales on both commission and salaried basis.	Sales normally through salaried staff is preferred.
Regulations	Statutory only.	Statutory with Islamic principles through a Sharīʿah Committee.
Investments	Invested freely in interest-based assets and other activities prohibited under the Sharīʿah.	Invested in accordance with Sharīʿah guidelines. Investment returns must not be driven by interest and by unethical commercial activities.
Accounting	Several methods used, i.e. cash, deferred, embedded values, etc.	Cash accounting is mostly preferred.

Source: Adapted from Bhatty (2000).

Sharif argues that the concept of *tabarru'* will also eradicate the element of gambling perceived by the Islamic jurists as existing in insurance. Take, for example, a participant with a contribution of, say, $1,000 who participates in a particular *takāful* scheme. After some time this participant faces a misfortune which incurs a claim of, say, $20,000. A jurist might look at this situation and conclude that this participant gained $19,000, which can be interpreted to be somewhat like a gambling transaction. Moreover, the source of the compensation is unclear. The *tabarru'* element can explain and correct both problems. Since every participant donates the contribution for the benefit of all members of the pool, the extra $19,000 comes from those donations consented by the participants, and furthermore, it is transparent as to the source of the fund. In this case, the *tabarru'* element addresses the issues of both *gharar* and *maysir*.

Another major component in a *takāful* transaction is the *muḍārabah*. Under this concept two parties, basically the participant or capital provider (*rabb al-māl*) and the entrepreneur or *takāful* operator (*muḍārib*), operate on a joint-venture basis.

The *takāful* operator invests the capital and if any surplus emerges from this activity it is shared at a fixed agreed ratio. For the *muḍārabah* contract to be permissible, a number of elements need to be present: the capital provider/participant; the entrepreneur/*takāful* operator; capital; an appropriate activity; profit and loss sharing; and offer and acceptance. In the event of a loss, it is the duty of the capital provider to top up. The *muḍārabah* contract can be annulled, and upon cancellation all cumulative capital plus profit must be returned to the capital provider less administrative expenses. Also, the capital provider will have to give consent to appoint the entrepreneur to work on his behalf. Of course, when investing the funds the instruments used should be Sharī'ah compliant. Table 10.3 lists the types of assets that can be used.

Three types of *takāful* products are on offer:

1. General *takāfuls* (Islamic general insurance): these offer protection or coverage against risks of a general nature for companies or individuals (participants). Some of the products are motor insurance, fire and allied perils, worker compensation, marine cargo, engineering insurance, property, transport, and so on.

2. Family *takāfuls* (Islamic life insurance): these provide coverage for participation by individuals or corporate bodies on a long-term basis and the maturity period generally ranges from 10 to 40 years. Some of the products are medical and health plans, education, accident, marriage, ḥajj and *'umrah* plans, lump sum investments, savings plans, retirement plans, mortgages, and so on.

3. *Retakāful* coverage (Islamic reinsurance): there are only eight companies in this field and they are located in the Bahamas, Bahrain, Malaysia, Saudi Arabia,

Table 10.3: Comparing investments of conventional insurance and *takāful* funds

Liabilities	*Assets*	
	Conventional	*Takāful*
Working capital requirements	Bank deposits and cash managed through money markets. Interest gained on overnight and short-term deposits.	Overnight deposits not available. Weekly commodity *murābaḥah* provides the liquidity, with risk similar to bank deposits.
Contractual short-term liabilities	Government stocks provide fixed returns on the face value at maturity.	Trade finance, lease and rental instruments provide fixed returns at maturity. Not as liquid as government stocks but would be acceptable. These are *ijārah*, *bay' salam* and *bay' istiṣnā'* contracts.
Longer-term guarantees	Debentures, preference shares and commercial paper.	Lease and rental instruments of longer duration, including instruments related to real estate-financing similar to closed-end property unit trusts.
Long-term capital growth	Established company equities.	Ample possibilities exist with good returns. Islamic instruments written as *muḍārabah* and *mushārakah* contracts or invested in equities or equity financing.
Income generation for long-term liabilities	High-yield fixed interest securities, high-risk commercial paper, institutional (bank) loans.	Real estate funds could be used. Islamic bonds are possible in the future.
Overall investment performance	Overseas and emerging market equities.	Opportunities exist similar to conventional ones.
	Property.	Same, under *muḍārabah* and *mushārakah* contracts.
	Venture capital investments.	Same, under *mushārakah* contracts.

Source: Based on Institute of Islamic Banking and Insurance (2000).

Sudan and Tunisia. The *retakāful* companies offer coverage for *takāful* companies against risks, loss or dilution of capital and reserves resulting from high claim exposures.

General *takāfuls* are short-term contracts for the protection of potential material losses from specified catastrophes. Members' premiums are called *tabarru'* (contribution, donation). The *takāful* company invests these on a *muḍārabah* basis, with profits allocated between the *tabarru'* fund and the management. Any surplus, after indemnity, reserves and operational costs are deducted, is then shared between either all participants or those who did not make a claim, depending on the company concerned. In short, the similarity with conventional insurance comes from the entire contribution of members being invested, like premiums, in a *tabarru'* fund; the differences come from the *muḍārabah* investment basis and the entitlement of participants to any surplus in the *tabarru'* fund.

In the case of life (family) insurance, the basic objective of *takāful* is to pay for a defined loss from a defined fund which is set up mutually by policyholders but is managed by a *takāful* company. There are three features. First, the policy is not so much to insure one's own life but is a financial transaction that relies on the principles of mutual cooperation for the welfare of the insured and/or their dependants. In the case of a general *takāful*, it is obvious that all of the funds collected are mainly used for this purpose. There is a slight difference in family *takāful* as the contribution of the participants is segregated into two accounts, namely the participant account (PA) and the participants' special (*takāful* or *tabarru'*) account (TA). In *takāful* convention, practitioners consider the TA as the donation account, whereas the PA is the investment account. Second, elements of *gharar* can be avoided if the policy operates on the principles of *muḍārabah*, as a profit-sharing contract between the provider(s) of the fund, that is, the policyholders and the entrepreneur, namely the *takāful* company, under defined profit-sharing ratios. Third, each policy also has a fixed period or term such as, say, 10 or 15 years, so as to eliminate uncertainty in the contract period and prevent it from being a whole-of-life policy.

THE OPERATION OF *TAKĀFUL* LIFE INSURANCE

So as to better understand how a *takāful* life policy works, it is instructive to look at some of the newer products in conventional insurance – in particular, unit-linked or variable life policies – for *takāful* family insurance is an ingenuous adaptation of these policies to meet the special needs of the Islamic community.

Unit-linked or investment-linked policies, as they are called in the UK, were introduced in the 1960s and have become very popular, largely displacing the traditional US-style policies such as term, whole-of-life, and so on. Linked policies are those where the value of the saver's fund is directly linked to the value of the assets in which the fund is invested. Instead of bundling together death cover and a savings-type account, unit-linked or investment-linked policies package the insurance cover with a unit trust (mutual fund) or a special management fund. Premiums are collected over the length of the contract and a

Figure 10.1: Structure of an individual *takāful* life policy

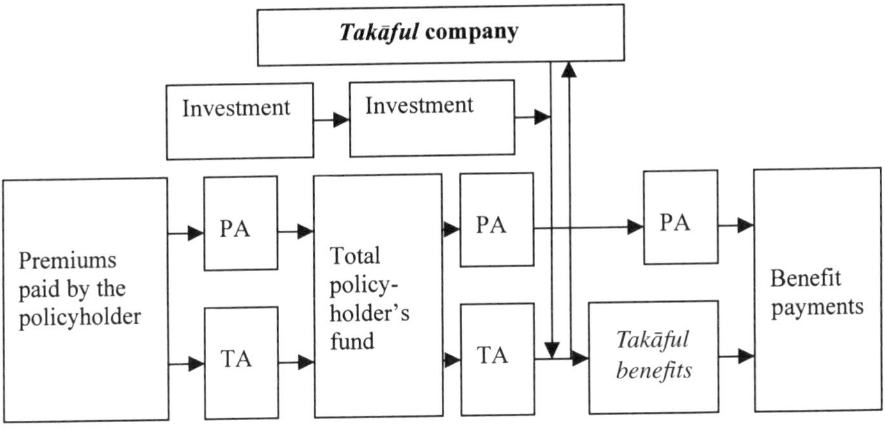

Source: Wahib (1999).
Notes:
PA Portfolio account.
TA Tabarru' (*takāful*) account.

determined minimum death benefit may be guaranteed (based upon an assumed but very modest rate of return on assets). A part of the premium goes to pay for the insurer's expenses and another part can be regarded as going to provide the minimum life cover. The balance, rather than being invested in the normal life insurance fund, is used to buy units (shares) in a mutual fund or in one of the office's special funds consisting, say, of common stocks. Both funds contain assets that can be expected to increase in nominal value year by year and thus provide a hedge against inflation. When the policy matures or the person dies, all units credited to the policy are sold, with the value of the proceeds depending upon the growth of performance in the interim of the underlying fund or investment pool.

In the UK, around two-thirds of policies are generally linked, whereas in the US variable life policies (as investment-linked are called) account for about one-eighth of the total. This difference translates into vastly different investment patterns between US and UK insurers.

This distinction between the US style and the UK style of life insurance is important for understanding family *takāfuls* (life insurance). *Takāful* life insurance is very different in operation to standard life insurance, but it is closer to the unit-linked policy than to the traditional. Figure 10.1 shows the structure. Premiums paid by the participants are divided into a *takāful*, also called *tabarru'*, account (TA) and participants' *muḍārabah* investment portfolio account (PA).

Usually, depending on the formula used, which sometimes varies according to the age and participation period of the participants, between 2.5 per cent and 10.0 per cent of instalments go to the *tabarru'* fund and the balance goes to the *muḍārabah* portfolio account of the participants. Insurance benefits are paid from the *tabarru'* fund. Profits from *muḍārabah* investments are shared between the participants and the companies in pre-agreed ratios, for example, 6:4, 7:3, 8:2, and so on. Participants are entitled to reimbursements (of PA premiums and investment earnings and share of net surplus) upon maturity, withdrawal (PA funds only) and, in some cases, upon disablement. Upon death of a participant, his heirs are entitled to *takāful* benefits, along with PA funds, which are reimbursed according to Islamic inheritance laws.

There are obvious similarities between the family *takāful* and the unit-linked policy. In particular, both types of policy deduct a proportion of the premiums paid and credit it into a separate account, namely a TA for the *takāful* policy and a special management fund for the unit-linked policy, to cover the cost of any guarantees. Furthermore, the sum assured for both policies depends on the investment performance of the remaining portion of the premiums, subject to a minimum guaranteed sum assured on death.

There are also important differences. Most obviously, all the activities of *takāful* must be in line with Sharī'ah principles and investments, and an independent body called the Sharī'ah Supervisory Council generally supervises the implementation of *takāful* practices. A *takāful* operation may be held void if any aspect of its operation is proven to be contrary to Sharī'ah principles, and a *takāful* policy can at any time be called into question should either party (operator or participant) be able to prove breach of good faith in the disclosure of material matters. The duty to reveal relevant facts rests on both operator and participant alike.

At the operational level too there are some different practices:

1. Under unit-linked policies, only the remaining portion, which is put into a unit fund, is invested in a portfolio of assets, whereas under *takāful*, both accounts, PA and TA, are invested.

2. There are no bid and offer values under *takāful* like the ones used under a unit-linked policy.

3. Under *takāful* there is a fixed minimum premium that is the same for all policyholders of all ages, normally from 18 to 55. *Takāful* companies are not allowed to make a profit from favourable mortality experience, and the policies taken out are regarded more as a means of the family saving for the future rather than as a means to obtain compensation in the event of death (or on the survival) of the policyholder.

4. Conventional life companies usually charge an extra premium in addition to

the normal amount for policyholders (for example, smokers, those with dangerous jobs) who are deemed to pose extra risk and hence have higher mortality rates than average. *Takāful* companies generally still charge the same fixed minimum premium.

5. Conventional insurance companies may not pay claims from death due to suicide or other unnatural causes. *Takāful* companies, by contrast, have to pay out the benefits regardless of the way any policyholder dies and this includes death by suicide or being killed while committing a crime. Muslims believe that God ultimately determines the death of all creatures, no matter how the creature dies.

6. Finally, under the terms of the *muḍārabah* investment arrangement, participants cannot interfere with portfolio selection as the management assumes full authority and the investment is made under utmost good faith, which may exclude firm contracts. However, if a loss occurs due to disrespect of *muḍārabah* conditions, the *takāful* companies will bear those losses.

In summary, *takāful* differs from conventional insurance in the sense that the company is not the 'insurer' insuring the participants. The persons participating in the scheme mutually insure one another. The *takāful* company simply handles matters of investment, business and administration. In principle, the *takāful* company operates on much the same basis as mutual insurance companies or an indemnity-type club. In mutual insurance the insured themselves are the insurers. The income from premiums is used to cover the cost of operations and to pay claims. The balance, if any, is returned to the members. The major difference between *takāful* and mutual insurance is that under *takāful* contributions (premiums) are not invested in interest-earning schemes and un-Islamic businesses, but instead are Sharīʿah-compatible.

Islamically-acceptable investments are:

1. Stocks and shares of screened corporate bodies, partnerships and other firms not guaranteeing any fixed returns.
2. Participation accounts, including profit-sharing certificates and deposits, mutual funds and unit trusts, and other similar instruments on a profit and loss sharing basis.
3. Those directly involved in trade, commerce and industry, including hire-purchase leasing operations as approved by the Sharīʿah.
4. Real estate.
5. Any other instrument, transaction or manner conducted on an interest-free basis.

Note that in order to comply with local legal requirements, certain investments may be made in interest-bearing deposits and instruments, but the income derived from such deposits and instruments must be distributed to authorised charities and not utilised for the benefit of the shareholders or the policyholders.

CHALLENGES TO THE SYSTEM

The first *takāful* company was established in 1979. Since then many others have been established, especially in recent years (see Table 10.1), but the industry still has not obtained a market presence which parallels that of Islamic financial institutions as a whole. According to Fisher (2002), since 1972 over 35 Islamic banks, 115 Islamic financial institutions and 50 Islamic mutual funds have been formed, with paid-up capital in excess of $7.3 billion. For the *takāful* insurance sector, the global base of paid-up capital is nearly $300 million; while for *retakāful* companies the capital base is $70–100 million. In recent years, the strongest growth has been in Malaysia. There, insured assets under the *takāful* system are about 5.0 per cent nationwide, and the Financial Sector Master Plan target for the *takāful* sector is for it to attain a 20.0 per cent market share of the Malaysian insurance industry by 2010. Note also that the investment portfolio of Syarikat Takāful Malaysia Berhad for 2002 identified 90.0 per cent of its business as being in terms of family *takāful*, where it has been a leader in product innovation with family, educational, mortgage and women-only plans. Elsewhere, however, growth has been slower. What then are the problems?

INSURANCE PENETRATION

An MBA instructor set his class the question of where a new shoe shop should be established in the local city. Participants spent hours examining income distribution statistics, demographics, travel and transport grids, home versus work shopping habits, etc, etc. None met with the instructor's approval. The simple answer he was seeking was: next to other shoe shops. A problem facing the *takāful* industry is the absence of insurance 'shopping' in certain locations, especially the Middle East which might otherwise be seen as a natural catchment area given the high GDP in countries such as Kuwait, Saudi Arabia and UAE. In fact, expenditure on life insurance in Saudi Arabia in 2000 was $1 per head and $68 per head in UAE, whereas life premiums per capita in the UK were $2503, USA $1447 and Switzerland $2914. Much the same pattern emerges for general insurance (Bhatty 2001). Some possible reasons for the low insurance density and penetration in some of these countries include a greater reliance on social welfare, the extended family system and attitude to risk. But the upshot is that *takāful* family business has made little inroad in the Middle East (as compared to Malaysia, where it is the backbone of the *takāful* industry and its recent growth). Family *takāful* was only introduced in Qatar in 2001, and in Bahrain in 2002. One of the main reasons for this low penetration is the underdevelopment of life insurance in all forms. It means that expansion of the *takāful* industry is tantamount to one of raising the awareness of the value of insurance generally.

Sharīʿah acceptability

A related factor is the poor reputation of insurance among many Muslims. For generations, Muslims around the world have grown up with the suspicion that insurance (life insurance especially) contravenes basic Islamic tenets. Objections have been raised on the grounds that taking out a *takāful* policy or a family *takāful* policy is against *tawakkul* (relying and depending totally on the will of Allah). As jurists (for example, Yaquby 2000) have pointed out, they forget the Prophet Muhammad's famous ḥadīth: tie your camel, then depend on Allah. Taking precautions in future planning for one's life is not against *tawakkul* but, on the contrary, is a prerequisite, because it is a financial transaction for protecting widows, orphans and other dependants, rather than leaving them needy and having to ask others for help.

Supporting structures

A number of conditions need to be put in place to facilitate the development of *takāful* business. These include a cohesive regulatory and legal framework that emphasises transparency and consumer protection, uniform accounting standards, and a higher degree of consensus on the interpretation of Sharīʿah principles in the context of *takāful* operations.

Reward structure

Takāful rests on a clear segregation between participant and operator, but the operator must be rewarded either on a profit-sharing (*muḍārabah*) basis or on a fee-for-services (*wakālah*) basis. Although at least one *takāful* company has adopted the *wakālah* model, this needs to be structured carefully to ensure appropriate incentives and risk-sharing from a Sharīʿah viewpoint. Most operators use the *muḍārabah* approach, but at present there are differences on the issue of whether the *muḍārib* or entrepreneur can deduct operational expenses prior to the distribution of the surplus (Ismail 1998; Yusof 2001). Greater harmonisation on the reward structure may aid industry development.

Reinsurance

Reinsurance on Islamic principles is known as *retakāful*. The problem has been one of the lack of *retakāful* companies in the market. This has left *takāful* companies with the dilemma of having to reinsure on a conventional basis, contrary to the customer's preference of seeking cover on Islamic principles. Sharīʿah scholars have allowed dispensation to *takāful* operators to reinsure on a conventional basis when no *retakāful* alternative is available. In the Middle East up to 80.0 per cent of risk is reinsured on a conventional basis. While a number of large conventional reinsurance companies from Muslim countries take on retrocession, there is a lack of capacity within the *takāful* industry worldwide (Bhatty 2001).

Flexibility

We noted earlier the similarities between family *takāful* and unit-linked policies in the West, and that *takāful* companies operate on the basis of 'non-interference' in terms of portfolio selection. This non-interference feature differs from conventional unit-linked policies, under which provision for switching between funds is a feature. An office issuing unit-linked policies may provide a policyholder with a choice of, say, five different funds. There may be a specialised equities fund, a property fund for real estate investments, a fund of international shares, a fund of money market deposits (essentially a money market mutual fund) and a fund of longer-term fixed interest securities. Frequently, one switch per year is allowed free of charge. The companies are able to offer this switching flexibility to savers by conducting their own capital market, selling the units purchased from one saver to another saver switching into that fund. As the *takāful* market develops, this is a feature that may well be adopted without departing from the *muḍārabah* principle, since each separate fund's investments would remain at the *muḍārib*'s discretion. Yet, at the same time, it would add to product variety, which is regarded as a problem for *takāful* companies (Wahib 1999).

Investment avenues

As well as product variety, one of the other difficulties facing *takāful* insurance has been in finding *ribā*-free investments. Avenues of investment must be in accordance with Sharīʿah principles and these can be limited. Widening the range of investment instruments and products that are Sharīʿah acceptable remains a high priority, particularly in the area of Islamic project finance and infrastructure financing so important for Muslim countries. At the same time, with the move to unit-linked policies, many conventional insurers' investments have become more equity-oriented, whereas in the past they have been predominantly interest-based (and still are in the US). This trend ought to suit *takāful* insurers, but a suitable portfolio requires knowledge of the degree of *ribā* involved in a company's operations on a company-by-company basis. Such knowledge can be tedious and costly to obtain for the many companies that trade shares on exchanges. Further developments in Islamic investment funds in terms of filters, screening and purification would help (Hassan 2001).

Mutuality

Islamic insurance is based on the principle of mutuality, in that members are both the insured and the insurers themselves. The members themselves share all the losses and thus no transfer of risk is involved. Unfortunately, as El-Gamal (2000) observes, most of the *takāful* companies established in Muslim countries are in fact similar in ownership structure to stock or proprietary insurance companies. This perception may limit the acceptability of the concept of *takāful* in the Islamic community. Certainly, a mutual insurance company that invested its funds in Islamically acceptable ways would satisfy all of the conditions laid down by jurists as a valid alternative to conventional insurance.

CONCLUSIONS

Insurance products have long been recognised as major vehicles for savings in Western countries. However, in the Islamic financial industry, unlike its banking counterpart, Islamic insurance has been largely neglected in the literature for reasons that seem difficult to explain other than the specialised nature of insurance as a subject. In practice also, most Muslim countries have a very low insurance density compared to international standards. Some possible reasons for the low insurance density and penetration in these countries include some Sharīʿah objections to the practice of insurance which have not yet been fully resolved and the socio-cultural milieu in Muslim countries including a greater reliance on social welfare, the extended family system and attitude towards risk. This situation is somewhat changing. Over 50 *takāful* companies have now been established in 22 countries.

While considerable differences exist between *takāful* and traditional insurance, similarities are found between *takāful* and some of the newer insurance products. *Takāful* differs from conventional insurance in the sense that the company is not the insurer insuring the participants. The persons participating in the scheme mutually insure one another. The *takāful* company simply handles matters of investment, business and administration. In principle, the *takāful* company operates on much the same basis as mutual insurance companies or an indemnity-type club. The major difference between *takāful* and mutual insurance is that under *takāful*, contributions (premiums) are not invested in interest-earning schemes and un-Islamic businesses, but instead are Sharīʿah-compatible. There are still several challenges facing the development of *takāful* business, some of which have been highlighted here along with some discussion as to how its wealth creation role could be enhanced.

11

Towards Optimal Risk Management for Profit-Sharing Finance

Seif I. Tag El-Din

It is commonly alleged that the risks of profit-sharing make *muḍārabah* financing less appealing than fixed return modes. However, the workings of the fixed return modes imply similar potential risks as those borne by *muḍārabah*. The appeal of fixed return (FR) modes is attributable to the conventional banking vision that seems to have inspired the practitioners of Islamic banking. The same banking culture of money capital pricing and cost-of-credit accounting has been structured into FR-modes. However, FR-modes are becoming less appealing in the present-day variable and floating rate culture. It is high time for Islamic banking to revitalise its core vision of profit sharing through a shift from seeking conventional banking returns to seeking real trade profits. Many effective hedging tools are already known and commonly practised, which are closer to the spirit of the Sharīʿah than interest-like FR-modes. In this chapter, two specific tools for the management of profit-sharing in Islamic finance are proposed: an appropriately adapted forward *istiṣnāʿ* contract and a put trade option.

INTRODUCTION

Risk is an unpleasant fact of life that people seek to reduce as much as possible through better financial structuring, better project management and better market regulation. It has been rightly appreciated by contemporary scholars of Muslim jurisprudence that the deliberate restructuring of traditional modes is necessary in order to develop bankable Islamic modes. This is reflected in the fact that all the current Islamic banking products have no exact counterparts in Muslim jurisprudence. It is no wonder, therefore, that the story of Islamic banks has been one of developing efficient financial structures – where maximum possible return is achievable at minimum possible risk – subject to the juristic rules. The fundamental jurisprudence postulate to which risk management must conform is the ruling 'no damage, to give or to take' (*lā ḍarara wa lā ḍirār*).

This chapter addresses the question of efficient financial structuring in relation to profit-sharing *muḍārabah*, which is typically characterised by two parties contracting for any profitable project: a capital provider (*rabb al-māl*) and a manager or entrepreneur (*muḍārib*). What distinguishes *muḍārabah* from forbidden interest-rate financing is that *rabb al-māl* can only be rewarded in terms of a pre-specified profit-sharing ratio with the *muḍārib*. In case of loss, it is totally borne by the *rabb al-māl*, while the *muḍārib* loses only his or her work effort. In this respect, *muḍārabah* is distinct from profit and loss sharing (PLS) *mushārakah* where all the parties are capital providers, and hence share between themselves profit as well as loss. The focus here is on profit-sharing *muḍārabah*, since it is particularly relevant to the demand for banking finance. At least in principle, banks' clients are assumed to be a 'deficit' group with little funds to participate with banks, which explains why the basic theory of an Islamic bank has been developed along the principles of *muḍārabah* (Uzair 1955). The economic appeal of profit-sharing, as opposed to fixed interest rate financing, has been elaborated upon in the current Islamic literature; see for example Siddiqi (1983, 1996, 2000), Masood (1984), Chapra (1985), Mohsin Khan (1987) and Tag El-Din (2002).

However, the current Islamic banking practice of efficient financial structuring is most manifest in the commonly known fixed return structures of *murābaḥah*, *ijārah*, *istiṣnā'* and *salam*. Although to a limited extent profit-sharing is also adopted, it is mostly forced into the basic structure of fixed return modes (FR-modes).[1] Accordingly, the real potentials of profit-sharing are far from being reaped, justifying the search for a more efficient financial structure for *muḍārabah*.

The need for optimally managed muḍārabah

The current restructuring experience of Islamic banking tends to associate with any Islamic mode of finance what we may conveniently refer to as the contract-specific-structure of risks (CSSR) for that particular mode. In *murābaḥah*, for example, the CSSR relates to the way commodity risk is allocated between seller and buyer at the time of the contract. In *ijārah* it relates to the way responsibilities towards the rented asset are shared between the lessor and lessee. In *istiṣnā'*, it is reflected in the bank's liability to produce the required product as per the technical specifications demanded by the client.

The CSSR of *muḍārabah* relates to the sharing of risk between *rabb al-māl* and the *muḍārib*. More specifically, it requires risk to be fairly shared between the two financing parties. The *rabb al-māl* cannot throw all risk on the *muḍārib's* shoulder to have his capital or profit share secured. He will have to share with the *muḍārib* whatever profit accrues to the latter subject to a pre-specified ratio. In a nutshell, *muḍārabah* financing implies that risk is shared in exactly the same ratio as profit (Tag El-Din 2002).

The basic principle we shall shortly derive from the current Islamic banking experience is that Islamic contracts can be suitably restructured in an effort to minimise financial risk, subject to the preservation of their contract-specific structures of risks. Non-Islamic elements will only creep into the restructuring process when that process violates the CSSRs given by the jurisprudence of any particular financial mode. The underlying idea is to preserve the CSSR while eliminating all non-essential risks associated with the traditional mode. However, this principle seems to have been adopted most liberally in the efficient structuring of fixed return modes, with too little attention to profit-sharing finance. Hence, our main objective is to adopt the same principle for the efficient structuring of *muḍārabah*.

One important implication of fair risk-sharing in a *muḍārabah* structure is that risk is acknowledged as an undesirable fact of life, which is the same thing as saying that both financier and financee are risk-averse.[2] Interestingly, this is the same behavioural postulate that is explicitly adopted in modern financial theory. Thus, the need for optimal management is re-emphasised by the negative attitude towards risk that already underlies the jurisprudence of *muḍārabah* financing. The Islamic principle of *iḥsān* implies that an optimally managed low-risk *muḍārabah* is better than a poorly managed high-risk one.[3]

THE QUESTION OF VISION

Many authors grappled with the problem of 'informational asymmetry' and the consequent 'moral hazard problem' on the grounds that these are the primary obstacles to a fully-fledged profit-sharing system; see for example Abalkhail et al. (2002), Bashir (2001), Habib (2002) and Khalil (2002). However, we believe that the problem in implementing a profit-sharing system in Islamic banking reflects more on the lack of strategic vision rather than on simply being a technical problem. This hypothesis will be tested through a critical appraisal of the current Islamic banking experience in order to see whether or not useful lessons can be learned.

In the first place, sharing real trade profits is totally alien to the conventional banking culture where money capital pricing, cost-of-credit accounting and preset cash inflows are the key factors. Islamic FR-modes are most dominant, it is argued, because they are consistent with such a debt-based banking vision. This may partly explain a history of painful struggle by the advocates of debt-oriented Islamic banking in their efforts to acquire Sharīʿah approval. In a nutshell, Islamic FR-modes have been developed as means to provide a credit facility comparable to that of conventional banking, while the real trade hedging tools are considered beyond the scope of the banking agenda.

On the other hand, the adoption of *muḍārabah* involves a significant shift of vision from conventional debt-based banking to one that is governed by the dynamics of real trade; a shift from the targeting of conventional banking returns to the targeting of real trade profit. The key point is that *muḍārabah* is not a credit facility, and hence does not match the conventional banking culture. Naturally, a new horizon of risk management would automatically emerge for Islamic banks if they became sufficiently motivated to target real trade profits. It will soon be realised that trade hedging tools are already available for the management of profit-sharing risks.

The deliberate emphasis on trade hedging tools is intended to exclude other financial engineering products that involve currency and money market security products, as they are commonly utilised as tools of capital market hedging by conventional banks (for example, currency futures, options and swaps). These products, which may violate certain norms in Islamic jurisprudence, do not concern us here since they do not conform to the hedging of real trade profit. Yet, at the outset we must ask the question: why profit-sharing (*muḍārabah*)? We shall then be led to the second question: why has the current Islamic experience focused primarily on the risk management of fixed return 'sale-contract' modes (*murābaḥah*, *ijārah*, *istiṣnā'* and *salam*) and paid little attention to profit-sharing? Against this background, this chapter will draw some useful lessons from the current Islamic practice of financial structuring and risk management.

WHY *MUḌĀRABAH*?

There are at least three main factors to justify the special appeal of *muḍārabah* from the viewpoint of Islamic economics. First, *muḍārabah* is ideally suited to the financial intermediary function. Like conventional interest-based finance, it is a pure financing mode, where the financier cannot interfere in the client's work or be engaged in the running of the financed project. Although the availability of a broad range of alternative FR-modes is often considered a healthy sign of financial flexibility to meet a broad range of clients' needs, flexibility is ideally attainable through the provision of pure cash at the clients' own disposal. Indeed, this is the fundamental reason why *muḍārabah* has traditionally been highlighted as the Islamic alternative to interest rate financing, and that the earliest theoretical model of an Islamic bank (Uzair 1955; Siddiqi 2000) has been defined as a symmetric two-tier *muḍārabah* model.

Second, unlike capital market credit tools, including the interest rate and its close Islamic FR substitutes, *muḍārabah* financing relates to trade in real goods and services. While it is the length of time that matters in credit facilities, it is the actual trade profit that matters in *muḍārabah* at a given point of time. Ironically enough, the FR-modes are originally traditional 'sale' contract structures, but the banking restructuring process rendered them more responsive to changes in the money market interest rate than to changes in the real trade profit rate. Thus, apart from offering a better financial intermediary function than the one currently practised, *muḍārabah* makes the Islamic bank more sensitive to commodity trade dynamics than those of the money market. In this sense, profit-sharing financing is ideally suited to integrate the financial sector with the real trade sector, tilting the Islamic financial sector away from a debt-perpetuating culture towards greater equity participation.

Third, it has been repeatedly recognised in the current literature that the future progress of Islamic banking is bound by the ability to tap the full potential of the profit-sharing system (see for example Khan 1995; Siddiqi 2000; Iqbal 2001; Warde 2000; Tag El-Din 2002). It is believed that the tendency to dwell upon FR-modes will thwart the progress of Islamic banking, most particularly within a global financial environment where fixed income contracts are gradually giving way to risk-sharing and floating rate incomes. There is an increasing awareness in the current literature of the strategic need to reorientate Islamic banking towards profit-sharing *muḍārabah*, with a view to the changing banking culture and a new phase of disintermediation that is gaining momentum.

WHY DO FR-MODES PREVAIL?

All Islamic modes of finance draw from one and the same origin, which is the Qur'ānic verse: 'Allah hath permitted sale [trade] and prohibited usury.' (Sūrah al Baqarah 2:275). Hence, the difference between FR-modes and profit-sharing *muḍārabah* is nothing more than one of deliberate financial structuring. Forbidden usury aside, it is only trade in goods and services that furnishes the groundwork of the Islamic financial system. Any potential Islamic mode of financing must have some real exchange transaction at its core.[4] The Islamic concept of financial return is identical to the concept of trade profit, which is the difference between the sale and purchase prices of a good or service.

The basic structure that characterises the FR-modes consists of three main elements:

1. A well-tailored single transaction.
2. A fixed return, which stems from fixity of sale price and purchase price for a given good or service.[5]
3. An element of credit facility, where deferred payment of price is provided.

The above three properties have made it possible to restructure the otherwise non-bankable traditional sale contracts, and hence satisfy the two basic requisites of bankable modes, first the financing function, and second the risk-hedging function. *Muḍārabah* automatically satisfies the financing function. But it has not been particularly appealing for bankers since it involves the taking of open positions in all four elements which justify *muḍārabah* profit: (1) the unknown volume of *muḍārabah* goods; (2) the unknown cost of *muḍārabah* goods; (3) unknown market sale prices (and hence, revenue); and (4) unknown potential buyers of the *muḍārabah* goods. In turn, the full exposure of *muḍārabah* capital to market risk has led to the emergence of a daunting 'moral hazard' problem resulting from the fact that the *muḍārib* has a 'hand of trust' on capital (*yadd amānah*). A dishonest *muḍārib* may easily underreport the true profit, and the *rabb al-māl* will have no recourse other than to trust whatever profit or loss is reported.

The question, however, is whether or not such lack of appeal in *muḍārabah* can be attributed to the problems of market risk and moral hazard? The answer is largely negative! In the first place, the low-risk appeal of FR financing modes has not been inherited from received jurisprudence. Had it not been for the deliberate restructuring of the original jurist sale contracts in an effort to yield low-risk FR-modes, these would be no better qualified to the banking function in their original jurist forms than the *muḍārabah* contract. Therefore, a fundamental question of financial choice was addressed at the very beginning of the Islamic banking experience, when restructuring was yet to be considered out of crude traditional modes. All options were open on an equal footing, since nothing in the original jurist modes was better off in terms of financial risk and moral hazards. Naturally, in the absence of an existing viable Islamic example, choice would be governed by an *a priori* vision of what was believed to constitute a 'bank'.[6]

It is no wonder that the conventional vision of fixed rate banking has triggered off the current momentum of FR Islamic banking since the 1970s. The challenge to accommodate appropriately the new banking experience within the prevalent banking culture seems to have been a decisive factor in the structuring of FR-modes. The experience reflects a prior banking vision held by the pioneering architects of Islamic banking, more so than the risk-hedging technical difficulties of *muḍārabah*. Perhaps we could have witnessed a completely different story for Islamic banking had the vision of a profit-sharing bank been the initial trigger! In place of adopting the current culture of credit cost accounting, trade hedging, tools could have been more commonly used to cover the above open positions in *muḍārabah*. Apparently, it was much safer for the new challenging experience to utilise the available conventional banking expertise than to break new but unknown grounds. Yet, as it was argued above, the world is changing at a fast rate and the future horizon of Islamic banking seems to demand a significant change of vision.

A LESSON FROM CURRENT EXPERIENCE

The objective function that appears to govern the current restructuring practice of Islamic risk management is the minimisation of financial risk subject to the jurist contract-specific structure risks (CSSRs). This principle is visible in all FR-modes. To satisfy both the financing function and the risk-hedging function of an Islamic banking mode, every effort was taken to avoid the non-essential risks of traditional trade. For the sake of brevity, we shall give the example of *murābaḥah* financing, although all the FR-modes share the same three properties as mentioned above.

The financing function of *murābaḥah* has been identified with credit sales, thus fitting firmly within the conventional debt-based culture. The hedging function was particularly needed to relieve the bank from the risks of exposure to real goods inventories. Two structures have been introduced to minimise these risks. First, the special provision of 'buying to the order of the client' relieves the bank from taking open positions in goods. Second, the signing of a 'binding promise to buy' by the client resolves the potential moral hazard of clients' failure to honour their promises to buy. In fact, such a moral hazard problem has been radically solved in all FR-modes.

Moreover, risk of goods' delivery is substantially reduced. The bank's representative can simply sign the *murābaḥah* contract with the client at the same time and place where the goods are originally bought to his order. It is unlikely such provisions were common in the traditional *murābaḥah*. As we mentioned before, the idea has been to minimise total banking risks subject to the jurist's CSSR. The CSSR in the case of *murābaḥah* consists of two main sources of risk to be borne by the bank:

1. The bank's obligation to make an effective delivery of the required good to the client. This risk is called *tabi'at al-halāk* in Islamic jurisprudence. This is essentially the 'commodity risk' in modern jargon.
2. The client's default risk, since there is no possibility to charge late payment penalties once the payment schedule has been agreed.

Non-Islamic elements creep into the contract when the last two sources of risk are not borne by the bank. That is, when *tabi'at al-halāk* is passed over to the buyer of the good, or when late payment charges are imposed on the client. The bank is permitted to take all reasonable measures to minimise the risk of exposure to goods' prices provided that this risk is not shifted over to the client. Notably, the banking restructuring process seems to have alienated 'sale contracts' from their traditional trade practices. But in defence of banking *murābaḥah*, it is believed to be a commendable practice so long as banks can realise the ultimate outcome of sale contracts through an efficient set of procedures that eliminate unnecessary risks. Banks may meet their real *murābaḥah* obligations even better than traders, although traders seem to bear *tabi'at al-halāk* through a set of procedures that are irrelevant to the banking practice.

CRUCIAL PROBLEMS WITH FR-MODES

Controversy around the legitimacy of *murābaḥah* is far from coming to an end. The strongest defence of *murābaḥah*, namely that it is a very good substitute for forbidden interest, has been viewed by many as its most vulnerable point. The concern that the economic evils of interest are not far removed from *murābaḥah* is real, notwithstanding its jurist approval. This has been partly reflected in a counter-*murābaḥah* policy by the Bank of Sudan where banks are encouraged to promote the profit-sharing modes of *muḍārabah* and *mushārakah* while observing an upper ceiling on *murābaḥah* financing.

However, *murābaḥah* is not unique in that respect, since all FR-modes share the same property of being cost-of-funds modes. The predominance of *murābaḥah* and other FR-modes promoted a debt-oriented culture within Muslim communities that has raised deep concerns among many Islamic economists. More generally, there are five main limitations of FR-modes which justify the call for reorientating the banking experience towards profit-sharing (Tag El-Din 2002):

1. Confinement to single transaction: being mostly confined to a single pre-specified fixed-price transaction, a FR-mode cannot satisfy the needs of clients who prefer a broader discretion in utilising their funds. Islamic banking clients often complain of too limited scope for pure cash financing.

2. Non-adjustable rates: this restriction places FR-assets at a disadvantage relative to the banking convention of adopting floating interest rates in response to future price changes. Since FR receivables are related to a fixed price of sold good or service, it is juristically impermissible to allow for automatic readjustment of rates within a given contract.

3. Non-competitive pricing: people tend allusively to compare Islamic banking rates with competitive interest rates without allowing for the practice of delayed payment penalties in conventional banking. Because this practice represents *ribā*, the tendency has been to price Islamic FR-assets above conventional rates in anticipation of default risk. However, it renders Islamic FR-assets less attractive than their conventional counterparts.

4. Restricted negotiability: pure debt FR-assets, such as *murābaḥah*, *istiṣnāʿ* and *salam*, are mostly of the receivable debt type, which cannot be traded for liquidity at a discount. The only exception is lease-based assets, since they embody sale of an equity share in a real good.

5. Restricted hedging: Islamic juristic rules in currency exchange prohibit any deferred payment contracts. Hence, most of the newly developed financial derivatives, like currency futures, options and swaps, cannot be utilised for

hedging against currency risks. This may also contribute to the non-competitive pricing of Islamic FR-assets.

As it appears, there is a limited potential for the current FR strategy to keep pace with the growth of conventional interest rate financing, since fixity of financial return is an exception in Islamic jurisprudence rather than the rule. It seems that FR-engineering has already exhausted all the potential juristic support, but with little hope of attaining the efficiency standards of conventional banking. Hence, with the current FR financial order, it may be unfortunate that Islamic banking will continue to trail behind conventional banking in terms of efficiency, leaving the critical search for a genuine Islamic alternative still an open issue.

PROFIT-SHARING AND TRADE-HEDGING

The efficient structuring of Islamic banking modes, it has been shown, is governed by the principle of minimising financial risk subject to the jurist CSSR for any particular mode. The meaning of the CSSR in relation to profit-sharing *muḍārabah* has already been defined. It is argued, however, that a preconceived conventional vision of 'bank' has dedicated much of the structuring effort to the refinement of FR-modes in the current Islamic banking experience, giving little attention to profit-sharing finance. Alternatively, to adopt the vision of a profit-sharing bank, closer intimacy ought to be maintained with real trade practices. The commonly practised trade-hedging tools will then become more relevant to the risk management of Islamic banking than the risk-hedging tools of conventional banking.

It is noteworthy that trade-hedging tools are particularly addressed to the threat of price volatility which dominates modern commodity markets. To protect its market position and meet future demands for its products, a typical firm would have to set its production plan with a forward view to the expected cost and revenue. Recourse to futures and options is justified by the need to secure the supply of needed inputs as well as the sale of final output at future prices which make it possible to lock in reasonable profit margins.

Yet, the traditional jurist position appears to be mostly unfavourable to the idea of forward contracting. The simultaneous deferment of both price and quantity tends to be characterised as a prohibited *bayʿ al-kālī bil kālī* in a reported ḥadīth, which is commonly interpreted as the prohibition of debt for debt sale (*bayʿ al-dayn bil-dayn*). In his characterisation of the Islamic futures market, Khan (1995) identifies the modern forward contract with the prohibited debt for debt sale. However, this traditional viewpoint has become subject to increasing criticism over the last decades (Tag El-Din 2001; Kamali 2000;

Muhiuddin 1986; Hammad 1984). Kamali provided a critical appraisal of this jurist opinion as regards futures and options. At an earlier stage, Muhiuddin showed the non-authenticity of the ḥadīth about *bay' al-kālī bil kālī*. Both Kamali and Muhiuddin demonstrated the relevant sources regarding the jurist evaluation of the modern forward contract, arguing that the prohibition of the forward contract does not rely upon firm jurist grounds. Hammad has also established the non-authenticity of the above ḥadīth. Although he seems to confirm the jurist prohibition of the modern forward contract, he approves of its adoption with reference to the 'special need' criterion of Islamic jurisprudence.

Apparently, the prevalence of such a traditional opinion is attributable to the limited relevance of real commodity markets to the current Islamic banking movement, more so than to a strong jurist prohibition. There has been no pressure from the current Islamic banking experience to place this issue into sharp focus. Yet, if Islamic banking chooses to move towards the profit-sharing vision, the hedging of *muḍārabah* against price volatility should more readily acquire Sharī'ah approval than has been the case for the approved FR-modes. In the first place, forward price hedging has nothing to do with the undisputed evil of *ribā* or its cost-of-credit culture, which nonetheless is embodied in FR-modes. Hammad's approval of forward contracting by reference to the 'special need' criterion provides good testimony that the received juristic positions are sufficiently responsive to the imperatives of modern markets when clear evils are avoided. In particular, the hedging of profit-sharing *muḍārabah* is a special need that justifies genuine consideration from Islamic jurists. Capitalising on the inherent flexibility of the *istiṣnā'* contract as a means for price hedging, Tag El-Din (2001) proposed a special approach to the Islamic futures market.

Admittedly, price volatility was not uncommon in ancient civilisations, but it has taken an unprecedented turn in the post-industrial world. Phenomenal mass production achieved through advanced technology, both quantitatively and qualitatively, has resulted in greater economic dynamism and financial risks. The legally binding forward contract emerged as a protective tool to farmers' incomes against drastic falls in prices when enormous mountains of agricultural output flooded marketplaces at harvest seasons (Edwards and Ma 1992). It is the basic idea that has inspired the development of various institutional structures to support the management of standardised commodity, currency and financial security futures. Alternatively, options are also commonly used as effective price-hedging tools, though they tend to be more costly than the forward contract.

Some writers such as Masood (1984) attributed the principal/agent problem of moral hazard in *muḍārabah* to a declining trend in people's moral commitment, but this is highly questionable! Moral hazard itself is a function of the level of uncertainty. In general, a wider room for moral hazard is expected in a highly volatile economic environment than in a slack and a (more or less) steady state one. The higher the price volatility, the greater will be the scope of moral hazard in profit-sharing. It appears it is the phenomenal price volatility rather than a change in people's moral integrity that has significantly diminished the appeal of profit-sharing systems in modern financial systems. But for practising traders, the remedy exists in specially developed hedging tools.

TWO BASIC TOOLS

Considering the special need to support the risk management of a profit-sharing system in Islamic banking, there are two basic tools that can be safely borrowed from the current menu of trade-hedging tools: the forward contract for financing industrial production; and the put option contract for trade more generally.

Forward contracting

Forward contracting has already been defended in a previous study (Tag El-Din 2001) as a straightforward development to the *istiṣnāʿ* contract. The latter differs from *salam* financing in several respects. First, it is a means of financing non-fungible industrial production rather than naturally fungible output; hence, Islamic jurists' objection against debt for debt sale does not apply to *istiṣnāʿ*. Second, and for this reason, the price of an *istiṣnāʿ* good need not be fully paid at the time of the contract. This provides the means for partially postponing price to a future date without violating the jurist prohibition of debt for debt sale. This flexibility is attributable to the fact that industrial products cannot act as objects of debt like naturally fungible products.

More specifically, the proposal of the modern forward contract as a development of the traditional *istiṣnāʿ* contract has been based on four points. First, there is an inherent recognition of the economic need for hedging in *istiṣnāʿ* as it provides for two distinct services: a partial financing service to the product maker; and a partial quality hedging service to the product demander. The former is satisfied through the partial prepayment of price to the product maker, while the latter is satisfied through the postponement of the remainder price till the time when the final product proves to satisfy the demander's quality specifications. The idea is that people like to hedge themselves against the possibility of bad-quality products; and therefore, not to advance the whole price until they satisfy themselves with the quality of the good produced. Obviously, the extent of the hedging service as opposed to the financing service is a relative matter depending on the special circumstances of any particular contract.

This is in fact the major source of flexibility in the *istiṣnāʿ* contract. Alternatively, if *istiṣnāʿ* was subjected literally to *salam* rules, people would rather purchase ready-made products than engage themselves with otherwise highly risky *istiṣnāʿ* contracts. The end result would be a drastic reduction in *istiṣnāʿ*

contracts and greater dependence on ready-made goods. There would be economic damage to Muslim economies if they depended on the provision of ready-made products from other economies with more flexible *istiṣnāʿ* rules. Ḥanafīte approval of *istiṣnāʿ* on the basis of *istiḥsān* was effectively a far-sighted vision which encouraged Muslims to finance their own industrial activity rather than depend upon the purchase of final products from non-Muslim communities (Tag El-Din 2001).

Second, this flexibility of the *istiṣnāʿ* contract enables it to be utilised purely as a hedging tool, without violating the jurist prohibition of debt for debt sale. This is the case if the partial financing function is no longer needed and *istiṣnāʿ* becomes totally devoted to the hedging function. It is only then that *istiṣnāʿ* boils down to the current forward contract. Yet it will act as a hedging tool against price volatility rather than lower quality. The quality-hedging service of *istiṣnāʿ* has now been replaced by better-quality assurances and standards in the modern industrial environment and, therefore, it is not the targeted service.

The *istiṣnāʿ* contract will, thus, become a price-hedging tool for industrial producers, who may then approach Islamic banks to finance the required output on a profit-sharing basis. In this manner, all three 'open positions' in *muḍārabah* contracts can be locked up: expected output, expected cost and expected revenue. Islamic banks would then find it sufficiently attractive to commit their funds to profit-sharing contracts.

Third, it is true that the current financing function of the *istiṣnāʿ* contract as an FR-mode will be sacrificed if it becomes specialised as a pure price-hedging tool. Yet it has already been argued that FR-modes are better replaced by a profit-sharing system. This is particularly the case for *istiṣnāʿ*, where its current Islamic banking practice suffers from various limitations when the Islamic bank assumes the status of product maker (Tag El-Din 2001). Bank clients would rather have cash financing than an industrial or technical service from the bank. The artificial financial structure of an *istiṣnāʿ* contract with the client and a parallel *istiṣnāʿ* contract with the actual producer creates unnecessary complications. It confuses the client and places undue technical liabilities on the Islamic bank in the running of industrial projects.

Hence, the best service that the *istiṣnāʿ* contract can offer in the modern industrial order is to act as a price-hedging tool for a profit-sharing scheme. This proposition is based upon the jurist postulate that *istiṣnāʿ* is not subject to the debt for debt sale charge. Hence, the resultant forward contract is only relevant for industrial production.

Traded options

The basic limitation of the price-hedging service of the *istiṣnāʿ* contract is that it suits only industrial production. The juristic problem of debt for debt sale relates primarily to naturally produced fungible goods – agricultural output and mining products – where the restrictive conditions of the *salam* contract must apply. *Salam* with its restrictive conditions as regards the spot payment of price is a good hedge for the buyer (capital provider), not for the seller (Tag El-Din 2001). We may refer to the arguments offered by Kamali and Muhiuddin to generalise the forward contract to all lines of production, but in the absence of a current juristic consensus it is advisable to seek alternative solutions.

Although more expensive than futures, traded options can still be utilised as possible hedges against price volatility. It is noteworthy that the call option, where a buyer seeks to protect himself against rising prices, is equivalent to *bay' al-'arbūn* which is approved in the Ḥanbalī School of jurisprudence.[7] As a call option, *bay' al-'arbūn* involves paying a price to a seller of a certain good to acquire the option of buying that good at a specified price. But *bay' al-'arbūn* is a hedging tool for the buyer, not for the producer or seller. Alternatively, it is the put option that protects the seller from the risk of falling prices below a stipulated level. But the problem with the put option is that it is not the *bay' al-'arbūn* which is recognised in the received jurisprudence. Put options represent reverse *bay' al-'arbūn* since it is the seller who buys from a potential buyer the option of selling a particular good.

In this respect, Kamali's defence of traded options is well placed. As a matter of principle, there is no point in approving call options with reference to the received jurisprudence of *bay' al-'arbūn* while disapproving of put options. It can be argued that call options are useful tools within the context of a price-control policy to protect consumers' interests; yet, it is nowhere arguable in Islamic jurisprudence that the protection of sellers against falling prices is less of a priority than the protection of buyers against rising prices. In the Prophet's own tradition (peace be upon him) he deliberately protected the interests of sellers. This is clearly shown in the authentic ḥadīth when the Prophet abstained from lowering goods' prices in response to his companions' request, for fear of injustice.[8]

CONCLUSIONS

The theory of Islamic banking identified profit- and risk-sharing as the main features of Islamic banking. However, in practice, FR-modes have dominated. It is commonly alleged that the risks of profit-sharing make *muḍārabah* financing less appealing than the FR-modes. From a juristic point of view, FR-modes imply similar potential risks as those borne by *muḍārabah*. Thus, the real appeal of FR-modes is attributable to the conventional banking vision that seems to have inspired the practitioners of Islamic banking. The same banking culture of money capital pricing and cost-of-credit accounting has been structured into FR-modes. In the present-day variable and floating rate culture, FR-modes are becoming less appealing. It is high time for Islamic banking to revitalise its core vision of profit-sharing through a shift from seeking conventional banking returns to seeking real trade profits. This would, however, require that appropriate hedging instruments are employed. Many effective hedging tools are already known and commonly practised in real trading as compared to financial transactions. These can be employed by Islamic banks if they go into profit-sharing based on real sector activities. Many more instruments would be developed once such profit-sharing modes were put into practice.

NOTES

1. *Muḍārabah* in the current practice is mostly defined as a contractual umbrella over prestructured transactions or *murābaḥah*, *ijārah* or other FR-modes. In this sense, it boils down to being a credit facility like other FR-modes.
2. Either party is risk-averse, wishing to rid themselves completely of any risk, but fairness makes it imperative that each party must bear its fair share.
3. The term *iḥsān* means perfection of any job that is requested to be done. The Prophet says 'God has demanded *iḥsān* on everything'.
4. Naturally, the concept of trade includes production sectors for goods and services as well as commercial distribution sectors. Services include leasing, given the juristic position that lease is a sale of an asset's service – or usufruct.
5. Prices ought to be unambiguously prespecified from a strict jurist perspective.
6. It is noteworthy that the first FR-mode to be developed was *murābaḥah*. The idea emerged from the pioneering work of an experienced conventional banker, Sami Hamoud, which was then well received by banking practitioners. Hamoud's contribution was to draw attention to the jurist idea of '*murābaḥah* to the order of the buyer', showing how such a traditional sale contract can be appropriately restructured into a banking financing mode (Hamoud 1982). Incidentally, the same principle was adopted in the later development of other FR-modes from traditional sale contracts – notably *ijārah* and *istiṣnā'*.
7. *Bay' al-'arbūn* is admissible in the Ḥanbalī School where a buyer makes some payment (called *'arbūn*) to a seller of a specific commodity on the condition that the seller reserves that commodity for the buyer till he decides to pay the rest of the price and take it away. Otherwise, the buyer forfeits the *'arbūn*. This is the same principle as that covered by 'call options'.
8. He answered his Companions saying: 'Allah alone grants plenty or scarcity. He is the Sustainer and the real price-maker, and I wish to go to Him having done no injustice to anyone in blood or in property.'

PART V

Equity Finance and Venture Capital

12

Stock Market Operation and Equity Price Determination in an Economy with an Interest-Free Banking System: The Case of Iran

Karim Eslamloueyan

This chapter employs an Autoregressive Distributed Lag (ARDL) model to examine the stock price movements on the Tehran Stock Exchange (TSE) after the introduction of Islamic banking in the country. It concludes that domestic and international interest rate differentials are not important determinants of stock prices in the TSE due to restrictions on capital mobility and the implementation of the non-interest banking system in Iran. In the short run, stock prices are positively affected by their lagged value, exchange rates and current prices of foreign goods. Industrial production, the lagged values of domestic and foreign goods and a lagged exchange rate inversely affect stock prices, whereas the current level of domestic goods' prices has no impact. In the long run, the production level of large manufacturing companies and the price levels of domestic and foreign goods are negatively related with stock prices, while the exchange rate has no impact. The results of the error correction model (ECM) show that about 26.0 per cent of deviation of the stock price from its long-run equilibrium path is corrected each period.

INTRODUCTION

Many attempts have been made to show that an economy that relies less on credit and more on equity may be superior in its overall performance to one that relies mainly on credit, particularly on short-term credit.[1] Given this premise, the question is how does the stock market operate in an Islamic country like Iran that has adopted an interest-free banking system? Iran reactivated its stock market in 1989 with the boosting of private sector activity and the privatisation of state-owned companies after the end of the Iran-Iraq War. Since then, the stock market in Iran has expanded constantly, and by the end of January 2003 a total of 326 companies were listed on the TSE.

What role does the TSE play in the Iranian economy? How does the stock market operate in a country like Iran where interest on loans and bonds is forbidden and most banks are nationalised? What can other Muslim countries learn from Iran's experience in this respect? This research addresses some of these issues. More specifically, this chapter contains two main parts. The first part examines the historical changes and evolution of the TSE. The second part investigates the macroeconomic determinants of equity price in Iran. An Autoregressive Distributed Lag (ARDL) model is used to examine the main macroeconomic factors affecting stock prices on the TSE.

A BRIEF HISTORY OF THE TSE

In order to understand the current status of the TSE it is important to have an understanding of how it has evolved. While the idea of establishing a stock market dates back to the 1930s, its establishment was delayed until 1967 when the Stock Exchange Act was ratified. The TSE commenced its operation in April 1968. Initially, the TSE started trading in government bonds and land reform bills. In 1968, only six companies were listed, but by 1970 stocks of 23 companies were traded. During the 1970s the transfer of shares of state-owned companies to the private sector boosted stock market activity, and as a result the number of companies on the TSE had increased to 102 by 1978. Of the listed companies, 24 were banks.

Following the Islamic Revolution in 1979, the control of government over the economy increased and hence the demand for private capital decreased. Indeed, all banks, insurance companies and many large manufacturing companies were nationalised in 1979. As a result, 36 banks were put under government control. Nationalisation ended the trading in shares of private banks and 24 major industrial companies.

In 1983 the law of non-interest banking was implemented and as a result trade in interest-bearing bonds was eliminated from the TSE. One should note that trade in bonds represented a large proportion of total trade in the TSE before 1979. The Iran-Iraq War also intensified the government's control over the economy and hence further weakened the stock market activity in Iran between 1980 and 1988. However, in 1988 the war with Iraq came to an end and the privatisation of state-owned companies started. Despite the absence of trade in interest-bearing bonds, a large increase in trading started in the TSE in 1989. Since then the TSE has been one of the fastest-growing stock markets in the world. It was admitted as a full member of the International Federation of Stock Exchanges in 1992, and joined the Federation of Euro-Asian Exchanges as one of its founders in 1995. Since its revitalisation, in 1989, the number of shares and companies has increased dramatically. By the end of April 2003 a total of 335 companies with a market capitalisation of 127,499 billion rials were listed on the TSE. The share price index displayed a long-term upward trend as depicted in Figure 12.1.[2]

Figure 12.1: The logarithm of the Tehran Stock Price Index, TEPIX

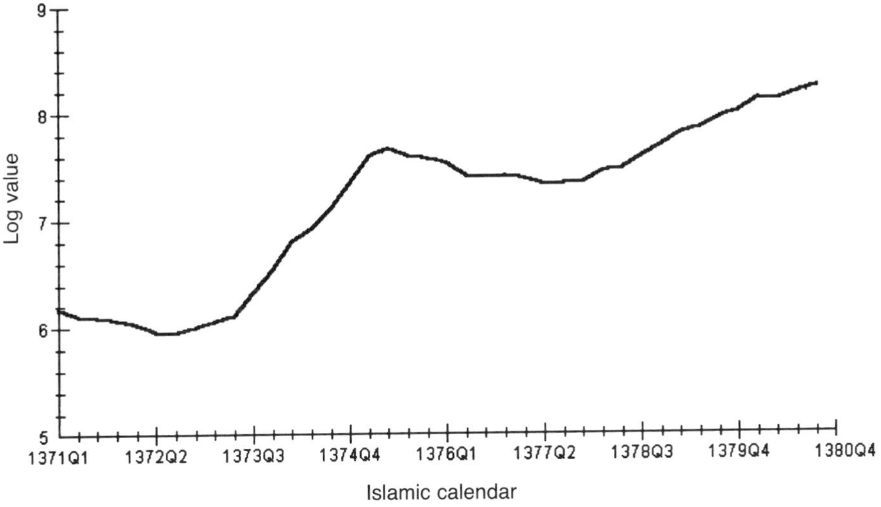

In recent years high stock returns have made the TSE an attractive place for investors. Given the fact that banks are not allowed to pay interest to depositors in Iran and capital mobility is restricted, many people now prefer to invest in the stock market.

From the above historical overview we can conclude that, contrary to other stock markets, some macro factors such as domestic interest rates and international interest rates differential are not among the main variables affecting stock returns in the TSE. The relatively low real profit rate paid by banks to their depositors compared to the high stock returns in the TSE has made this market an attractive place for private investors and even nationalised banks. Since stock prices reflect the present discounted value of expected future earnings, in the next section we develop a simple econometric model to study stock price movements in the TSE after its revitalisation.

THE BASIC MODEL

According to standard theoretical models, stock prices mirror the present discounted value of expected future earnings of stocks. Hence, macroeconomic variables that affect future earnings and the discount rate might have an impact on stock prices. The literature on the relationship between stock price performance and macroeconomic variables is expanding rapidly. For example, there is evidence that indicates that inflation has an adverse impact on the stock market in the short run. Using a cointegration approach, Ely and Robinson (1997) explore international evidence on the relationship between stock prices and goods' prices. They show that for most of the countries under their investigation, stocks maintain their value relative to goods prices. One important exception is the US, where stocks do not persevere their value relative to goods price when the source of inflation is a real shock.

Using a small macroeconomic model, Groenwold et al. (1997) examine the relationship between stock returns and inflation. They conclude that an increase in expected inflation rate might raise real output, which in turn might have an adverse impact on stock returns. Cheung and Lai (1999) examine long-run co-movements of national stock markets in France, Germany and Italy. They study whether these long-run co-movements can be linked to similar co-movements in the money supply, dividends and industrial production. Their results confirm a limited role of these macroeconomic variables in accounting for the stock market co-movement in these European countries.

Binswanger (2000) explores the relationship between stock return variations and real activity in the US. He found that stock returns have ceased to lead real economic activity in the US since the 1980s. This author argues that stock price changes are more independent from variations in real activity due to the existence of bubbles or fads in the US. Using monthly data on Canadian and US markets, Kia (forthcoming) estimates a macro-determinant model of stock prices in a small open economy. He introduces commodity prices, domestic-foreign price differentials and risk premium into standard models used in the literature and shows that these factors are key components of stock price determination. According to this study, bubbles are short-lived. Furthermore, he shows that agents in the stock market are forward-looking.

We follow the above literature on stock price determination and assume that the stock price is a function of exchange rates, the domestic price level, the foreign price level and the production level of manufacturing companies. Our model ignores some other variables used in the literature, such as domestic and foreign interest rates and the foreign industrial production level. Interest-bearing bond trading is not allowed in the TSE as already indicated due to the law of non-interest banking adopted in 1983 in Iran. Banks are also not allowed to pay interest on their investment deposits. Formally there is no interest rate in the banking system. Furthermore, since there are restrictions on international capital mobility, the international interest rates differential is not an important determinant of stock prices. Hence, the following model is used to study stock price determination in Iran:[3]

$$LTEPIX_t = f\,(LYM_t, LOER_t, L(P/P^*)_t),$$

in which $LTEPIX_t$ is the log of the Tehran equity price index, LYM_t is the log of the production level of large manufacturing companies, $LOER_t$ is the log of the official exchange rate, and $L(P/P^*)_t$ is the log of the domestic commodity price level relative to the foreign commodity price level. Since there is a restriction on capital mobility in the Iranian economy, we do not expect that the production of foreign manufacturing companies and international interest rates differentials to be important factors affecting equity prices in Iran. Hence, these variables are omitted from the model.

THE MODEL ESTIMATION

It has been shown that the Ordinary Least Squares (OLS) estimator in a small sample might be biased and inconsistent.[4] To remove this inconsistency, it is suggested that an over-parameterised model be used. In other words, using more lags is preferable to fewer lags. Another reason that makes the use of lagged variables important is the fact that we cannot understand the adjustment process unless we know the short-run dynamics. This allows us to see how a short-run disequilibrium error corrects itself through time. Hence, to study the stock price movement in the TSE we need to estimate the long-run equilibrium and the short-run relations simultaneously. This can be done by using the ARDL model for cointegration analysis.[5] Moreover, the ARDL approach proposed by Pesaran and Shin (1997) allows us to use I(1) and I(0) variables together. Consider the following ARDL(p,q) model:[6]

$$LTEPIX_t = \alpha_0 + \sum_{i=1}^{p} \alpha_i LTEPIX_{t-i} + \sum_{j=0}^{q} \beta_{1j} LYM_{t-j} + \sum_{j=0}^{q} \beta_{2j} LOER_{t-j} + \sum_{j=0}^{q} \beta_{3j} L(P_t/P_t^*) + u_t, \quad (1)$$

in which α's and β's are parameters and u_t is a white noise. The above model is estimated for all possible combinations of p and q ($p=q=0,1,2,\ldots$,m). After determining the maximum lag (namely, choosing m) in the model, a different model, $(m+1)^{k+1}$ is estimated. At this stage, we then use the Akaike Information Criterion (AIC), the Schwarz Bayesian Criterion (SBC) and the Hannan-Quinn Criterion (HQC) to choose the most appropriate estimated short-run model.

Next we use the result of the estimated short-run model to derive the long-run estimated parameters. Given there is a long-run equilibrium relation between variables,[7] the following error correction model (ECM) can be estimated:

$$A(L)\Delta LTEPIX_t = B(L)\Delta X_t + (1+\Pi)\, ECT_{t-1} + \Gamma' W_t + u_t, \quad (2)$$

where L is a polynomial lag operator,

$A(L) = 1 - \alpha_1 L - \alpha_2 L^2 - \ldots - \alpha_p L^p$, and

$B(L) = 1 - \beta_{i1} L - \beta_{i2} L^2 - \ldots - \beta_{iqi} L^{q}_{i}$ $(i=1,\ldots,4)$, $X=(LOER, LP, LP^*, LYM)$,

Δ denotes the first difference,

ECT_{t-1} is error correction term,

$\Pi=(\alpha_1+\alpha_2+\ldots+\alpha_p)$, W_t is a vector of deterministic variables such as the constant term and exogenous variables with fixed lags (if there is any) and Γ is a vector of parameters. The disturbance term, u_t, is assumed to be a white noise. In general the following ECM model is estimated:

$$A(L)\Delta LTEPIX_t = \sum_{i=1}^{k} B_i(L)\Delta X_{it} + \rho\varepsilon_{t-1t} + \Gamma' W_t + u_t, \quad (3)$$

where ρ is a parameter, ε_{t-1} is error correction term (that is, ECT_{t-1}) and other parameters and variables are as defined before. The coefficient of the error correction term shows the speed of adjustment towards long-run equilibrium. Thus, this approach allows us to study the long-run relation among variables and short-run behaviour at the same time. We use quarterly data to estimate the model for the period January 1995–January 2002. The lack of quarterly data for some variables prevented us going beyond this period. However, our sample size is large enough to determine the equity price in the short run and to study the behaviour of the TSE after its revitalisation.

Prior to estimating our model, we examined whether our time series data were stationary. The results of unit root tests are presented in Appendix 7. As the results show, the augmented Dicky-Fuller tests indicated that LYM, LOER and L(P/P*) are integrated of degree one, that is, I(1) and LTEPIX[8] is integrated of degree zero, I(0). Since we have a combination of I(1) and I(0) variables, the ARDL approach proposed by Pesaran and Shin (1997) is an appropriate method to estimate our model.

Using Microfit software, equation (1) is estimated for the Iranian economy. Table 12.1 shows the estimation results of the short-run model. Based on the Schwarz Bayesian Criterion,[9] the selected order of our Autoregressive Distributed Lag (ARDL) is (4,3,2,2).

The ARDL estimation presented in Table 12.1 indicates that the stock price has a positive impact on the current level of stock price with one lag. As the short-run results show, in general the production level of large manufacturing companies positively affect the stock price in Iran. The current level of the exchange rate has a positive impact on the equity price in the TSE. However, the exchange rate inversely affects the equity price with one lag. The short-run results also indicate that an increase in the current level of relative price level will decrease the equity price index. One should note that since the order of our ARDL model is (4,3,2,2) it is not easy to come up with a straightforward explanation. Indeed, the result of the ARDL model is important for us because it will be used to derive the coefficient of our long-run model.

Diagnostic tests of the above estimation presented in Table 12.2 indicated that there are no serial correlation, functional form, normality and heteroscedasticity problems in our model.

Table 12.1: Autoregressive distributed lag estimates

ARDL(4,3,2,2) selected based on the Schwarz Bayesian Criterion
Dependent variable is LTEPIX

Regressor	*Coefficient*	*Standard Error*	*T-Ratio [Prob]*
LTEPIX(-1)	1.2726	.19938	6.3828[.000]
LTEPIX(-2)	−.34595	.36750	−.94138[.369]
LTEPIX(-3)	.27227	.37686	.72248[.487]
LTEPIX(-4)	−.87840	.29870	−2.9407[.015]
LYM	.21008	.28914	.72655[.484]
LYM(-1)	1.4572	.42647	3.4167[.007]
LYM(-2)	1.3365	.44453	3.0066[.013]
LYM(-3)	.59138	.31538	1.8751[.090]
LOER	.15455	.083827	1.8437[.095]
LOER(-1)	−.32482	.14859	−2.1861[.054]
LOER(-2)	.30040	.18855	1.5932[.142]
$L(P/P^*)$	−2.8879	1.1149	−2.5903[.027]
$L(P/P^*)$ (-1)	−1.5822	1.2297	−1.2866[.227]
$L(P/P^*)$ (-2)	2.9284	1.0383	2.8205[.018]
C_0	−12.2780	4.8388	−2.5374[.029]
R-Squared	.99374	R-Bar-Squared	.98497
S.E. of Regression	.039157	F-stat. F(14, 10)	113.3479[.000]
Mean of Dependent Variable	7.6952	S.D. of Dependent Variable	.31940
Residual Sum of Squares	.015332	Equation Log-likelihood	56.9849
Akaike Info. Criterion	41.9849	Schwarz Bayesian Criterion	32.8433

Next we used the CUSUM and CUSUMSQ tests to examine the structural stability of estimated parameters. The first test checked whether there are systematic changes in the estimated coefficients. The second test is useful when there is a sudden and random departure from the constancy of the parameters.[10] The results of these two tests are presented in Figures 12.2 and 12.3. Each figure exhibits a pair of straight lines drawn at the 5.0 per cent significance level. If CUSUM or CUSUMSQ crosses either of these lines, the regression equation is not correctly specified.

As Figure 12.2 shows, the cumulative sum of recursive residuals is inside the critical bounds at the 5.0 per cent significance level and hence the null hypothesis is not rejected.

Figure 12.3 also indicates that the cumulative sum of squares of recursive

Table 12.2: Diagnostic tests of the model

Test Statistics	*LM Version*	*F Version*
A: Serial Correlation CHSQ(4)=	7.0907[.131]	F(4, 6)= .59388[.680]
B: Functional Form CHSQ(1)=	2.2151[.137]	F(1, 9)= .87497[.374]
C: Normality CHSQ(2)=	.064624[.968]	Not applicable
D: Heteroscedasticity CHSQ(1)=	.45906[.498]	F(1, 23)= .43023[.518]

A: Lagrange multiplier test of residual serial correlation.
B: Ramsey's RESET test using the square of the fitted values.
C: Based on a test of the skewness and kurtosis of residuals.
D: Based on the regression of squared residuals on squared fitted values.

residuals is inside the critical bounds at the 5.0 per cent significance level. Hence, according to both tests the estimated coefficients are stable.

Next, we used the result of our estimated ARDL model to derive the long-run coefficients. Table 12.3 presents the estimated long-run coefficients of the model.

As the results of Table 12.3 indicate, the coefficient of logarithms of the production levels of large manufacturing companies (LYM) is positive and significant. This means a 1.0 per cent increase in the level of industrial production leads to about a 5.0 per cent increase in the stock price level. This confirms the results of other researches in the literature. A higher industrial production level means a higher expected profit rate and hence higher stock prices. The coefficient for the official exchange rate is not significant.[11] This means that movement in the official exchange rate is not an important determinant of the equity price in the TSE. The coefficient of $L(P/P^*)$ shows that there is a

Figure 12.2: CUSUM test for the LTEPIX model

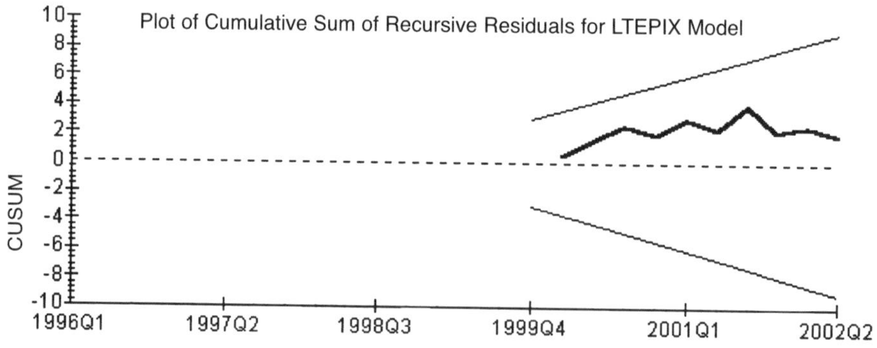

The straight lines represent critical bounds at 5 per cent significance level.

Figure 12.3: CUSUMSQ test for the LTEPIX model

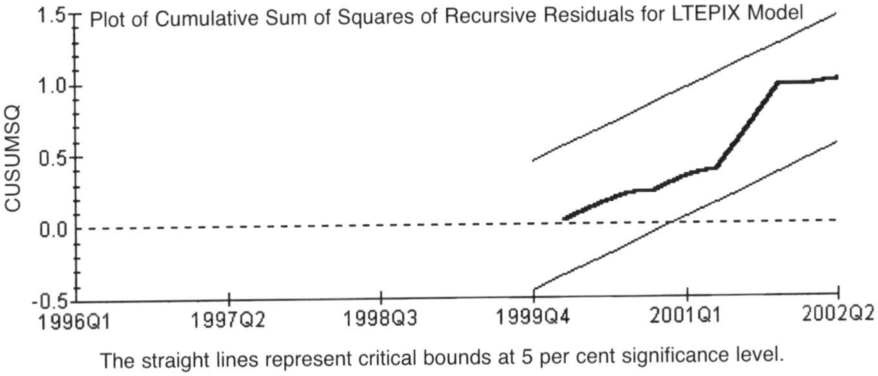

negative relationship between the stock price and the ratio of home to foreign goods price levels. An increase in the relative domestic price level makes Iranian goods relatively more expensive. Hence, the country becomes less competitive in the international market. This in turn might lower the expected rate of profit and hence domestic stock prices.[12] Thus, this result does not conform to the so-called 'puzzle' discussed in the literature. Finally, we estimate the error correction model (equation 3). The estimation results are given in Table 12.4.

As the table indicates, the coefficient of ECM is negative and significant. It shows that about 67.0 per cent of deviation of stock price from its long-run equilibrium path will be corrected each period.

Since the model involves I(0) and I(1) variables, we use the bound testing approach proposed by Pesaran et al. (2001) to find out whether or not there exists a level relationship among variables. According to Pesaran et al., first we have to decide about the presence of trend and intercept in the error correction

Table 12.3: Estimated long-run coefficients using the ARDL approach

ARDL(4,3,2,2) selected based on Schwarz Bayesian Criterion
Dependent variable is LTEPIX

Regressor	*Coefficient*	*Standard Error*	*T-Ratio [Prob]*
LTEPIX(-1)	1.2726	.19938	6.3828[.000]
LYM	5.2911	1.1234	4.7101[.001]
LOER	.19152	.19114	1.0020 [.340]
$L(P/P^*)$	−2.2691	−.58584	−3.8733[.003]
C_0	−18.0701	4.3608	4.1438[.002]

Table 12.4: Error correction estimation of the model

ARDL(4,3,2,2) selected based on Schwarz Bayesian Criterion
Dependent variable is DLTEPIX

Regressor	*Coefficient*	*Standard Error*	*T-Ratio [Prob]*
LTEPIX(-1)	1.2726	.19938	6.3828[.000]
DLTEPIX1	.95208	.22496	4.2322[.001]
DLTEPIX2	.60613	.30726	1.9727[.070]
DLTEPIX3	.87840	.29870	2.9407[.011]
DLYM	.21008	.28914	.72655[.480]
DLYM1	−1.9279	.70713	−2.7264[.017]
DLYM2	−.59138	.31538	−1.8751[.083]
DLOER	.15455	.083827	1.8437[.088]
DLOER1	−.30040	.18855	−1.5932[.135]
$D\,L(P/P^*)$	−2.8879	1.1149	−2.5903[.022]
$D\,L(P/P^*)1$	−2.9284	1.0383	−2.8205[.014]
DC_0	−12.2780	4.8388	−2.5374[.025]
¡ (-1)	−.67947	.15285	−4.4452[.001]

Ecm = LTEPIX -5.2911LYM -.19152LOER + 2.2691 $L(P/P^*)$ + 18.0701C_0

R-Squared	.90282	R-Bar-Squared	.76678
S.E. of Regression	.039157	F-stat. F(11, 13)	8.4459[.000]
Mean of Dependent Variable	.040774	S.D. of Dependent Variable	.081081
Residual Sum of Squares	.015332	Equation Log-likelihood	56.9849
Akaike Info. Criterion	41.9849	Schwarz Bayesian Criterion	32.8433
DW-statistic	2.4158		

model (ECM) and also assess whether their coefficients should be restricted. Hence, we examined different cases to see whether to include trend and/or intercept in the ECM. Finally, case 5 (that is, unrestricted intercept and unrestricted trend) was chosen. The Schwarz Bayesian Criterion was used to select the optimal lags of variables. The result of the bound test is presented in Appendix 8. According to this, statistics from the ECM is 10.09. From Pesaran et al. the critical value bounds for the F statistics at the 0.05 significance level are 3.47 and 4.57 for the unrestricted intercept and unrestricted trend case when k=4. Since the calculated F lies outside the critical value bounds, the hypothesis of no level LTEPIX equation is rejected. In other words, the test indicates that there is a relationship between the dependent variable and the explanatory variables.

In order to reconfirm the existence of a long-run relationship among variables obtained in the bound test, we also carried out an ARDL unit root test of the null hypothesis of no cointegration as proposed by Banerjee, Dolado and Mestre.[13] According to this test, the sum of α_i (i=1,...p) in equation (1) must be less than one for the dynamic model to converge to a long-run solution. Thus, dividing ($\Sigma\alpha_i$-1) by the sum of their associated standard errors provides a t-type test statistic, which can be compared against the critical values given by Banerjee, Dolado and Mestre in order to test the null hypothesis. This test was conducted for our model. From Table 12.1 the computed t* ratio is equal to 7.6, which is above the critical value reported by Banerjee et al. Thus, we reject the null hypothesis of no cointegration. Hence, both tests verify the existence of a long-run relationship among the variables in the model.

CONCLUSION

This chapter examines the main features of TSE. Iran's banking system was nationalised after the Islamic Revolution. Moreover, according to the law of non-interest banking implemented in 1983, interest on loans and bonds is forbidden in Iran. Hence, interest-bearing bond trading on the TSE is not allowed. In addition, capital mobility is restricted. Despite such restrictions the stock exchange market (TSE) not only has survived, but is also growing very rapidly.

The results show that domestic interest rates, international interest rate differentials and foreign industrial production levels are not important determinants of stock prices on the TSE, due to restrictions on capital mobility and the law of non-interest banking. The long-run results indicate that the production level of large manufacturing companies directly affects stock price levels. We also find that the exchange rate has no impact on equity prices. A negative relationship was found between the rise of stock prices on the TSE and the ratio of home to foreign goods' price levels. A higher relative domestic price level makes Iran less competitive in international markets. This, in turn, can lower the expected rate of profit and thus domestic stock prices. The coefficient of ECM shows about 67.0 per cent deviation of the Tehran stock price from its long-run equilibrium path corrects each period.

NOTES

1. Paul S. Mills and John R. Presley (1999), *Islamic Finance: Theory and Practice*, Basingstoke: Macmillan, pp. 58–72; M. Umer Chapra (1985), *Towards a Just Monetary System*, Leicester, UK: The Islamic Foundation, pp. 107–45; M. Umer Chapra (1992), *Islam and the Economic Challenge*, Leicester, UK: The Islamic Foundation, pp. 327–34.
2. This section is mainly based on TSE reports.

3. One should note that (expected) profit rates for investment deposits are determined exogenously by the Council of Money and Credit in Iran and hence were fixed for the period under investigation. This means that the mark-up rate (*murābaḥa* rate) was also fixed. Hence, they are not included in our model.
4. For more details, see for example Harris (1995) and Pesaran and Shine (1997).
5. In order to test whether different I(1) series are cointegrated, Engel and Granger proposed checking the stationarity of the residual obtained from estimation of the long-run model.
6. Moreover, since the supply of money is also another important macro variable, we introduced M2 into our model. But the estimation result (not reported here) showed that it was not a significant explanatory variable and hence was omitted from the model.
7. That is, the null hypothesis of no cointegration is rejected.
8. The Phillips-Peron test also shows that LTEPIX is I(0).
9. According to Pesaran and Shine (1997), SBC economises the use of lags.
10. See Pesaran and Pesaran (1997, pp. 116, 387–8) for more detail.
11. We also incorporated the unofficial exchange rate as another explanatory variable in our model and estimated the equation. However, the estimation results of that model showed that the black market exchange rate had no impact on the stock price. The estimation results of our model with black market exchange rate are not reported here.
12. See for example Groenwold et al. (1997).
13. See Harris (1995) for more details.

13

The Demand for *Mushārakah* in Urban Egypt by Small Business as a Test of the Pecking Order Hypothesis

Mohamed Nasr

For a long time Islamic finance has been tackled from the supply side, and asymmetric information and agency problems have been given as the reasons for lack of use of *mushārakah* by Islamic banks. This chapter attempts to investigate the lack of use of *mushārakah* from the demand side. It argues that if the Pecking Order Hypothesis (POH) holds, then perhaps the notion that Islamic banks are reluctant to use *mushārakah* mainly because of supply factors, such as the high risk embedded in such an instrument, needs to be reconsidered. The study has implications for Islamic financial institutions in so far as they should know their target clients very well.

INTRODUCTION

The objective of this chapter is to provide some empirical evidence on the relationship between *mushārakah* and the degree of preference by end users of such a tool. While the relationship between equity finance and control is well documented in the literature, the relation in terms of Islamic finance is not. Therefore, this chapter attempts to link Islamic finance tools with the mainstream theory of finance.

Islamic finance for a long time has been tackled from the supply side, and asymmetric information and agency problems have been always given as the reasons for the lack of use of *mushārakah* by Islamic banks. The Islamic finance industry views its clients as given. The general attitude among many of the experts and researchers is that the demand is unlimited. They see clients as statistics that are measured in terms of their beliefs in Islamic principles; therefore, they will spontaneously be clients for Islamic banks. This is not always the case. A study conducted by Kamal Naser et al. (1999) in Jordan focusing on the Islamic banking market revealed that respondents showed a good level of awareness of some of the Islamic banks' products and services, but only a limited number indicated that they used them.

During the last two decades the operations of the majority of Islamic banks showed a widespread preference for *murābaḥah* or mark-up financing, fixed return modes, and to a lesser degree *mushārakah* and *muḍārabah* partnership or equity financing and profit and loss financing. According to the International Association of Islamic Banks, *mushārakah* and *muḍārabah* account for less than 20.0 per cent of financing undertaken by Islamic banks world-wide (International Association of Islamic Banks 1996).

Not only do Islamic banks have a negligible proportion of their funds invested in *muḍārabah* or *mushārakah*, but even specialised Islamic firms as well. Almost all Islamic banks, investment companies and investment funds offer trade and project finance on a mark-up basis and equity finance is only marginally used (Dar and Presley 2000). This is often lamented as a relabelling of the non-Islamic financing system (Al-Harran 1993; El-Gamal 2000).

This chapter will therefore mainly focus on *mushārakah*. As pointed out by Choudhury (2001), *mushārakah* is a pre-Islamic financing instrument that came into use in contemporary Islamic financing. It has some common features with conventional equity finance or partnership financing. Partnership financing mainly takes two forms in Islamic finance, namely *muḍārabah* and *mushārakah* contracts. In *muḍārabah*, the financier provides capital and the entrepreneur provides management, whereas for *mushārakah* all partners provide capital and can participate in the management of the business (Usmani 2002). Both forms can be considered as a type of equity finance, where there are some parallels with venture capital. Although they are not really the same as conventional equity financing for quoted companies as understood in the West, for the purpose of this chapter *muḍārabah* and *mushārakah* will be regarded as forms of equity participation or equity finance.

Different explanations have been given for the lack of use of equity finance. Agency problems, asymmetric information and moral hazard were among the major explanations for its unpopularity (El-Din 1991; Ahmed 2002). Also further justification was given, notably that Islamic banks and investment companies have to offer relatively less risky modes of financing because of competition from conventional banks and other financial institutions. Researchers found that equity financing is not feasible for funding short-term projects due to their high degree of risk and the nature of banks as short-term financing institutions (Abalkhail and Presley 2002). Some researchers even try to justify this trend through highlighting the influence of management and control on the internal governance of Islamic finance institutions (Dar and Presley 2000). The common line in all of these justifications for such a trend was mainly focusing on the supply side; that is, Islam's institutions avoiding high-risk instruments.

It is easy to prove that equity finance and profit and loss sharing arrangements are superior to interest in all sorts of situations, but it is one matter proving the theory and another applying it in practice. If equity finance is so superior, why are banks and entrepreneurs not using it? This chapter attempts to answer this question. Most of the research seeking explanations for this avoidance of equity finance has focused on the supply side; from the demand side very few studies, or almost none, have been undertaken. The mainstream theory of finance is of relevance here, notably the Pecking Order Hypothesis (POH), which will be discussed in the next section.

If the POH is valid, then the notion that Islamic banks are reluctant to use *mushārakah* mainly because of supply factors, such as the high risk embedded in such an instrument, needs to be reconsidered. This chapter, first, discusses the existing literature on the POH and the empirical results of similar studies. Second, the hypothesis and research methodology are briefly discussed. Third, empirical results are presented. Finally, an attempt to draw more general lessons from the findings of this study concludes the chapter.

THE PECKING ORDER HYPOTHESIS (POH)

The POH emphasises that enterprises prefer internal to external financing and debt to equity financing. It suggests that there is a hierarchical preference over the sources of financing. Myers (1984) stated that finance theories do not adequately explain financing behaviour. He provided an alternative explanation for capital structure based on information asymmetry in which enterprise managers, or insiders, are assumed to possess private information about the characteristics of an enterprise's expected income stream and investment opportunities. He observed that managers/owners follow a pecking order in choosing the sources of finance, in which internal funds are preferred, followed by debt, and then as a last resort a new issue of ordinary shares. The POH is hardly new; Donaldson mentioned it earlier in a 1961 study of the financing practices of a sample of large corporations (Myers 1984). There are two different ways of explaining the POH. The traditional view argues that the pecking order can be observed under high transaction costs, taxes and agency costs. The other explanation proposed by Myers (1984) assumes that enterprise insiders have more information than outsiders. To avoid paying too much for new financing, managers secure funding in a pecking order.

Despite the fact that the POH was used in relation to listed companies, several researchers such as Cosh and Hughes (1994) managed to make use of the insights of the POH to show that the financial structure of smaller businesses compared with larger ones is consistent with a POH. Small- and medium-sized enterprises represent the majority of Islamic banks' customers. Therefore, the findings of several studies which attempted to identify the capital structure of small business, for example McMahon et al. (1993), Cosh and Hughes (1994), Islam et al. (1994), Baydas and Graham (1995), Hamilton and Fox (1998), Ozer

Figure 13.1: Representation of the POH applied to small business finance

Source of Small Business Finance					
Internal		External			
Personal savings/ Retained profits	Family/ Friends	Bank overdraft	Bank loan	Factoring	Equity
– – – – – – – – – – – – – – – – – – → Decreasing preference					

Source: Adapted from Read (1998), p. 51.

and Yamak (2000) and Romano et al. (2000), show some support for the concept of the POH and found it equally applicable to small unlisted companies which cannot raise additional funding through the issue of stock to the public. Arguably this work has major implications for Islamic financial institutions.

The findings of these studies showed that internal financing is assumed to be preferred to external financing, such as overdrafts, loans, leasing and hire-purchase, as shown in Figure 13.1.

These findings have been explained using Myers' (1984) reasoning, which implies that managers/owners are guided by a pecking order when choosing among financing opportunities. The most popular reason for explaining this behaviour, as mentioned by McMahon et al. (1993), Cosh and Hughes (1994), Baydas and Graham (1995) and Read (1998), is due to control, which is the desire to avoid external interference and maintain independence. The amount of debt or equity sought is determined, to a large extent, by enterprise owners'/managers' goals of protecting their control of the enterprise. This is to be expected, given the fact that in many cases an entrepreneur has established a small business to be self-employed and to avoid the control of outside directors. Ownership and management are almost the same in small business, and usually they have a personal financial stake in the business. They therefore tend not to dilute ownership or control over the assets.

The admission of additional owners would therefore be very low under an owner's pecking order. Furthermore, owner-managers prefer internal funds, as this form of funding ensures the maintenance of control over operations and assets. Where debt funding becomes necessary, finance is sought in a way that does not constrain management. Independence is so important to some small businesses that the owners will choose it at the expense of access to more flexible forms of finance (Myers 1984; Cosh and Hughes 1994).

HYPOTHESIS DEVELOPMENT AND RESEARCH METHODOLOGY

Based on the argument proved by several researchers that the desire to retain control of small and medium enterprises is so strong that enterprise owners will protect it at any cost (Cosh and Hughes 1994; Read 1998; Howorth 1999), and on the POH, this research investigates the following hypothesis:

> The primary reason for small business owners rejecting *mushārakah* financing is their preference to remain independent.

In order to address in a logical way whether such a dislike of *mushārakah* as a financing tool exists among end users, it was necessary to focus on generating relevant detailed primary data on *mushārakah* contracting rather than relying on secondary data. It was decided that primary data would be generated by means of a survey. Therefore, this research relied on a field survey in the form of direct interviews, which were carried out across a sample of small businesses. Ninety-five enterprises were surveyed in Shubra, an urban district of Cairo. Face-to-face interviews were carried out at enterprises' locations, which gave the data more reliability. Fifty enterprises were selected randomly from the database of a small business financing programme operating in this district. The rest of the sample, 45 enterprises, was selected randomly from the same area of the study, but they did not deal with the financing programme. Both groups were asked the same questions. Table 13.1 summarises the main characteristics of the study sample with regard to the business sector and the ownership structure.

Limiting the study to the area of Shubra raises the question of representation, or in other words to what extent this area is representative of the total urban small business population of Egypt. However, as mentioned by Gibb in Read (1998), the search for a representative sample in any small businesses research is

Table 13.1: Characteristics of the study sample

Variables	*Attributes*	*Frequency*	*%*
Business sector/activity	Trading	46	48.4
	Trading & Services	22	23.2
	Manufacturing	20	21.0
	Services	7	7.4
	Total	95	100.0
Ownership structure	Sole proprietorship	45	47.4
	Family partnership	42	44.2
	Non-family partnership	6	6.3
	Limited liability company	2	2.1
	Total	95	100.0

difficult as small businesses are so diverse. There are several factors that may potentially restrict the conclusions to be drawn from the study. The first limitation may be because the initial sample group of 50 small businesses was selected first, it might be probable that the structure of the sample was influenced by their characteristics of applying to deal with a specific financing programme. The second limitation may be the fact that the sample contains a high percentage of Christians, more than 20.0 per cent, which reflects the nature of this area of Egypt. To investigate the effect of this matter, the respondents were regrouped into Muslims and Christians and tested for statistical difference with regard to their replies. A chi square test was used to see if there was any significant difference in responses. The results showed that there was no significant difference between the two groups, except when they were asked about their personal opinions for not dealing with conventional banks; more than 31.0 per cent of the Muslim group mentioned that it was due to religious principles.

Aside from these limitations, the results of the survey are believed to be generally applicable to urban areas throughout the country, based on the fact that Egyptian society is homogenous, and any segment of the population should be a fairly accurate representation of the population as a whole. Nevertheless, this study does not claim that the sample is a representation of all urban areas in Egypt.

RESULTS

To test if small business owners in urban Egypt reveal such a preference ordering in their demand for financing sources, both groups were asked to specify the acceptable percentage that could be owned by a partner, or in other words external equity participation. The majority of the respondents, 65.0 per cent, as shown in Table 13.2, indicated that they did not need a partner. Even among those who might accept external equity, *mushārakah*, they still did not want a partner to have a controlling percentage, which is further illustrated in Table 13.3.

Table 13.2: The acceptable percentage that could be owned by a partner

	Frequency	%
Don't mind having a partner	33	34.7
Less than 25%	11	11.6
From 26% to 49%	19	20.0
From 50% to 75%	2	2.1
More than 75%	1	1.0
Don't need a partner	62	65.3
Total	95	100.0

To investigate this matter further, respondents were asked to identify the main reasons for their not wanting a partner, as shown in Table 13.3. This table reveals that the majority, almost 86.0 per cent, gave as their main reason the wish to retain control of the business, which is in line with the POH.

Table 13.3: Reasons for not wanting a partner

	Frequency	%
Want to keep control of the enterprise	53	85.5
Find difficulty in cooperating with others	9	14.5
Total	62	100.0

By taking the investigation one step further, respondents who said that they did not mind having a partner were asked what kind of work such a partner would be responsible for, as shown in Table 13.4. This reveals that almost 85.0 per cent preferred the partner to supply finance only; in essence, they preferred *muḍārabah*. Less than 10.0 per cent did not mind involving the partner in running day-to-day operations; in other words, involving them in the administration of the business. Table 13.4 reveals the preference of small business owners towards *muḍārabah* financing rather than *mushārakah* for those owners who prefer partnership financing.

Table 13.4: The kind of work a partner should be responsible for

Extent of involvement	*Frequency*	%
Administration (100 per cent involvement)	3	9
Marketing (sales) only	2	6.1
Providing finance only	28	84.9
Total	33	100.0

Furthermore, respondents were given six sources of finance and were asked to rank them according to their preference from one, the most preferred, to six, the least preferred. Table 13.5 gives the results. It is worth mentioning that it was necessary to explain what each type of financing involved to more than 95.0 per cent of total respondents. This high percentage is a reflection of the fact that small business owners are not aware of how Islamic financial instruments operate. It is worth also mentioning that 11 of the total respondents refused to answer this question, as they personally did not believe there was any difference between Islamic and conventional financing (out of those 11 respondents, 7 were Christian).

Table 13.5: Respondents' preferences for Islamic sources

Finance source/method	*Ranking* order
Internal	
Self financing personal savings/retained earnings	4.58
Family/ friends	2.71
External	
Murābaḥah	2.40
Ijārah wa iqtinā'	1.80
Muḍārabah	1.63
Mushārakah	1.10
Total respondents	84

The survey revealed that the religious reason for not dealing with conventional banks, that is, the objection to fixed interest, was cited by only 16.0 per cent of total respondents. Only 4.0 per cent of the sample had an account with an Islamic bank, compared to 50.0 per cent who held accounts with conventional banks. This finding demonstrates that there is little resistance to being involved in interest-based banks among small businesses in urban Egypt – perhaps largely out of ignorance as to the prohibition of interest in Islam.

Although there was no strong statistical evidence, due to the nature and the relatively small number of the sample, to support significantly the hypothesis, the strong preferences revealed in Tables 13.2, 13.3 and 13.5 support the research hypothesis. The overall aversion for using equity finance is revealed by the survey results, especially Table 13.2. Given the fact that the majority of small business owners work alone without partners, and where they do have partners, they are usually relatives or friends, as illustrated by Table 13.1, this aversion to *mushārakah* is not surprising. Most respondents were reluctant to be involved in profit and loss sharing; they preferred to know the cost of financing in advance, hence their preference for *murābaḥah*. This finding is in line with similar studies, as mentioned by Dar and Presley (1999), notably a study carried out in Saudi Arabia by Al Hajjar on small business in 1989, which revealed that only 16.0 per cent of the sample were prepared to accept *mushārakah*.[1] Additionally, a similar study in Oman by Al-Said, in 1995, revealed that only 29.0 per cent of total respondents were prepared to accept *mushārakah*.

Furthermore, this strong preference is supported by several other studies, for example Islam et al. (1994), Baydas and Graham (1995), Baydas et al. (1997), Buckley (1997), Read (1998) and Ozer and Yamak (2000), where they found that small business owners do not welcome any source of finance that may lead to interference that would deny them their independence and control over their businesses. In all these studies, respondents indicated a preference for debt

Figure 13.2: Representation of the POH applied to small business' preference for Islamic sources of finance

Preference of Small Business Finance					
Internal		External			
Personal savings/ Retained profits	Family/ Friends	*Murābaḥah*	*Ijiārah wa iqtinā'*	*Muḍārabah*	*Mushārakah*
→ Decreasing preference					

rather than equity finance. The same results were also mentioned in the Bolton Report in the UK (Cosh and Hughes 1994). Furthermore, in a similar study by Smith (1997) in Scotland, over 50.0 per cent of respondents were unwilling to give up any share at all of their equity holdings in the small business. Furthermore, most enterprises wished to retain at least a controlling share of their businesses; that is, greater than 50.0 per cent. Also in a study by Howorth (1999), the issue of ownership and control was central to the attitude towards introducing new equity. On average, 41.0 per cent of owners would consider a new equity investor, if this did not affect their control of the business, but, if new equity meant some weakening or sharing of control, then only 22.0 per cent of owners would be interested.

Therefore, based on the above discussion, it is evident that Islamic financial institutions should not be blamed for their very limited use of *mushārakah*. By classifying Islamic financing instruments according to the extent of control by the financier, *murābaḥah* would be among the least restricted forms of control. On the other hand, *mushārakah* would be among the most restricted tools of finance in terms of control. It can be concluded that small business owners' demand for Islamic financing takes precedence over supply factors, following a pecking order of internal resources, as illustrated in Figure 13.2.

CONCLUSIONS

The findings of this study have implications at both theoretical and institutional levels. At the theoretical level, this chapter has shown that financing preferences at the outset are constrained towards *mushārakah* financing. It suggests that the primary reason for this is the small business owners' requirements for independence, which is consistent with the pecking order theory proposed by Myers (1984). Furthermore, the relevance of the pecking order theory raises serious questions about the lack of use of *mushārakah* extensively by Islamic financial institutions. If such a preference ordering does exist, then perhaps the notion that Islamic banks are reluctant to use *mushārakah* because of supply factors, such as the high risk embedded in such an instrument, needs to be reconsidered.

Furthermore, this research attempted to draw the attention of academics, practitioners and financial institutions to the other side of the equation which is the demand side, where further research and comprehensive studies across more than one Islamic country are needed, especially to explain why different results are obtained in similar studies in non-Muslim countries that favour equity finance. For example, a study by Jalaludin (2002) conducted in Sydney metropolitan area in late 1998 of 385 small businesses revealed that 59.5 per cent of respondents expressed a readiness to borrow funds on a profit and loss sharing basis.

At the institutional level, for a long time demand for some Islamic financing tools has been taken for granted, without taking into consideration the desire and personal characteristics of clients. Islamic financial institutions have been reluctant to tailor their tools according to their clients' real demand, partly due to the frequently held notion of high risk. Most current Islamic financial institutions forget to listen to their clients, as taking account of the clients' demands is not part of their culture. If they want to have a better future, listening to clients' needs and aspirations should be integrated into their thinking, especially with respect to designing new Islamic financial products. Additionally, Islamic financial institutions should know their target clients very well, and their corporate cultures should be more customer-oriented. Further studies are needed on the extent of acceptability of the financial instruments provided by Islamic financial institutions, and not just theoretical work. Most Islamic financial institutions and researchers have been focusing on the Islamisation of the different financing tools and have lost sight of the end user.

Finally, the survey demonstrates the need to educate the Muslim community on the issue of interest; explain methods compatible with the Sharīʿah; and how they can be put into practice. What was obvious from this study is that some of the respondents have acknowledged the prohibition of interest in Islam but seem to be unaware of any alternative permissible financing tools in Islam to support their business. Unfortunately, no matter how much academics may discuss the issues, the majority of Muslims are still not aware of their financial obligations under Islam and thus do not demand Islamic banking products. Islamic banks and Shariʿah-based profit-sharing will only blossom when demand actually appears.

NOTE

1. J. W. Wright, Bandar Al-Hajjar and John Presley (1996), 'Attitudes, Culture and Capital Distribution in Saudi Arabia', in J. W. Wright (ed.), *Business and Economic Development in Saudi Arabia*, Macmillan, pp. 127–39.

14

Islamic Finance and Venture Capital: A Practical Approach

Saqib Rashid

The literature on Islamic finance has focused on mimicking the traditional banking model while bypassing the interest mechanism through complex contracts. Very little attention has been paid to the potential impact of venture capital. This is a serious omission since venture capital is founded on the same principles that guide Islamic finance and because venture capital has been a key engine of growth in the most successful economy in the world, the US. A properly functioning venture capital industry benefits society at large by directing scarce economic resources to entrepreneurs with the most promising ideas, and the determination to turn these ideas into productive companies. This chapter attempts to increase the awareness of the prevailing US-based VC model as an acceptable Islamic investment vehicle by providing a critical analysis of this mode of financing in the context of Islamic economic principles. This chapter makes a case that establishing a thriving venture capital industry is essential not only for further evolution of the Islamic finance industry, but also for the long-term health of ailing economies in the Muslim World.

INTRODUCTION

A unique challenge facing the Muslim World today is how to improve economic performance while operating within the guidelines of Islamic finance, which differs from the prevailing capitalist financial system in that it forbids interest. A central focus of recent literature on Islamic finance has involved mimicking the traditional banking model while bypassing the interest mechanism through complex contracts. However, very little attention has been paid to the potential impact of venture capital (or VC), which is virtually nonexistent in the Muslim World. Yet VC is founded on the same principles that guide Islamic finance, and it has been a key engine of growth in the US, the most successful economy in the world. In fact, Robert Grady, Managing Partner of Carlyle Venture Partners, a part of The Carlyle Group, recently remarked: 'The availability of risk capital has been one of the most important factors driving the strong performance of the US economy over the past two decades.'[1] Inevitably, a properly functioning VC industry brings benefits to society at large by directing scarce economic resources to entrepreneurs with the most promising ideas, and the determination to turn these ideas into productive companies. At this critical juncture, establishing a thriving VC industry is essential not only for the evolution of the rapidly growing Islamic finance industry, but also for the long-term health of ailing economies of the Muslim World.

The primary goal of this chapter is to increase awareness of the prevailing US-based VC model as an acceptable Islamic investment vehicle by providing a critical analysis of this mode of financing in the context of Islamic economic principles. In doing so, this chapter will scrutinise the underlying legal contract between the investor and entrepreneur, where the distinctions between VC and Islamic finance are more readily apparent. Of major concern is the issue of common versus preferred stock. While the former is accepted in Islamic finance circles, the latter is categorically rejected since it provides one investor with a liquidity preference over another. Just how important is this topic? Based on interviews with several well-known US-based VC funds, which collectively manage over $1 billion in assets, the preferred stock structure is used in more than 90.0 per cent of their investments.[2] Does this mean that the Islamic-oriented investor is left out of the lucrative and burgeoning US VC industry? Is the US VC model viable in Islamic finance? In an effort to address these dilemmas, first the perspectives and ideologies of both VC and Islamic finance must be addressed, since this debate should ultimately focus on the spirit, rather than the letter, of the law.

WHAT IS VENTURE CAPITAL?

Broadly defined, VC is the use of equity, or risk, capital to finance high-growth business. To put it simply, a venture capitalist provides money, along with management expertise and a value-added network of contacts, to start-up companies in return for an ownership stake. VC investments are unique in that they are made at such an early stage. The funding is often used by the recipient company to recruit the initial management team, or to introduce a new product or service to the market. Importantly, these investments are highly illiquid, and therefore a major concern for venture capitalists is ensuring that there is a viable exit strategy. Due to the inherent risk associated with illiquid, early stage investments, venture capitalists expect to receive an above-average portfolio return, somewhere in the range of 40.0 per cent versus 12.0 per cent in the more established Standard & Poor 500 public stock index. Although a sizable industry in itself, VC is a subset of the more general private equity (or PE) sector, which refers to any equity investment in a private business. An important distinction between VC and other PE investments is that the latter tend to focus on companies that are more established and mature; eventually, this difference translates into significantly divergent views on risk and return that are important for the Islamic-oriented investor to understand.

The term 'venture capital' was coined at Harvard University in the 1940s, when VC was less of an industry and more of a small, informal market controlled by a few wealthy families. However, within the span of a decade two major events occurred in the US that fundamentally altered the industry landscape: first, the success of American Research and Development, the prototype of the modern-day VC firm; and second, the Small Business Act of 1958, which channelled subsidised government funds to the VC industry through the establishment of the Small Business Investment Company programme. The former proved that the VC model was viable when its original $70,000 investment in Digital Equipment in 1957 rose to a value of $355 million in a little over a decade.[3] The latter played a major role in the creation of hundreds of private sector VC firms, some of which were fortunate enough to provide early stage financing for Fortune 500 companies such as Intel, Apple Computer, Federal Express and Home Depot.[4] From this humble beginning, the US VC industry has now reached a critical mass and can be considered a unique and viable alternative asset class. From a base of only $3 billion worth of capital raised in 1980, the VC industry grew to over $100 billion by the year 2000, a compound annual growth rate of 19.0 per cent.[5] Driven by the success of the US market, the broader PE asset class has started to emerge on a global scale and the numbers are staggering. In 2000, global PE commitments totalled slightly over $200 billion, with 30.0 per cent of this activity occurring outside the US.[6]

Although VC commitments in the US have slowed from this recent brisk pace of investment, the industry has proven to be a significant engine of growth for the economy. For the first time, a recent study commissioned by the National Venture Capital Association measured the quantitative impact of VC activity on the US economy over the period 1970–2000. The study indicated that VC-backed companies generated approximately twice the sales revenue, twice the level of exports, paid almost three times the federal taxes and invested almost three times as much in R&D as the average non-VC-backed public company, per each $1,000 of assets. Additionally, 11.0 per cent of US GDP and one out of every nine jobs in 2000 were generated by an originally venture-backed enterprise.[7] These findings should come as no surprise since, by definition, VC targets companies with the highest growth potential.

As the VC industry continues to grow and present opportunities for significant wealth creation, determining the suitability of such investment is an important step in the evolution of the Islamic finance industry and for the broader Muslim World. On the surface, it would appear that the two are compatible. To be sure, the concept of an investor and entrepreneur partnering together to share in the risks and rewards of a business is nothing new; in fact, it was a popular means of conducting trade during the early years of Islam. However, the environment has changed considerably since then. The primary purpose of this chapter is to examine whether this new paradigm is consistent with the principles of Islam, which has its own views on how economies and businesses should be managed.

ISLAMIC FINANCE AS RISK CAPITAL

At its core, Islamic finance is based on the concept of optimally allocating scarce resources in a socially acceptable framework. Although numerous definitions exist, almost all incorporate a system that promotes risk-taking and discourages financing based on a fixed, predetermined return. In particular, there are seven basic principles that constitute an Islamic economic system:

1. Justice, equality and solidarity.
2. Avoiding things declared *ḥarām* by the Sharīʿah.
3. Recognition of basic property rights.
4. Property (or wealth) should be used in a rational but fair way.
5. No gain without effort or liability.
6. Leniency in general conditions of distress.
7. Risk- and reward-sharing.

For the purposes of this chapter, focus will be on the last three, from which two basic rules are derived: prohibition of interest, and partnership based on profit and loss sharing contracts.[8] A primary reason for the prohibition of interest, which is expressly forbidden in the Qur'ān and Old Testament, is to ensure that money is not hoarded unnecessarily but rather optimally recycled through an economic system built on risk and reward-sharing.[9] In order for money to increase in value, either effort must be expended or liability must be assumed (principle 5). This reasoning is logical when one analyses the pre-Islamic Makkan period, which was characterised by rampant loan-sharking whereby the wealthy often took advantage of those in need of funds.[10] Today, an individual may argue that if he deposits funds in a bank at a reasonable 4.0 per cent savings rate, and this bank in turn lends money to businesses at a reasonable 10.0 per cent interest rate, and these businesses in turn create additional jobs for society, then he has earned the right to a return on his investment. Yes, neither 4.0 per cent nor 10.0 per cent is necessarily considered loan-sharking, but the fundamental issues remain: the depositor neither put forth any personal effort nor did he accept any liability on his deposit. The first case is obvious since the depositor does not even know to whom his specific funds are allotted. The latter point, at least in the case of the US, is a function of federal deposit insurance, which basically guarantees the depositor a fixed return regardless of the overall performance of the loan portfolio of their bank.

Rather than an instrument used to generate wealth, lending in Islam is viewed as an act of charity and goodwill. Although the debtor is obliged to honour the terms of the original loan agreement, the Islamic view is that such persons should also be granted leniency in hardship cases (principle 6). Leniency in Islam implies not charging fees for late payment, but rather granting the debtor a reasonable delay without penalty. Consequently, the onus is placed on the lender when extending funds to a debtor. Such a system has the effect of decreasing unnecessary debts in society since, without recourse and compensating interest rates, lending would primarily occur on a more philanthropic basis. Contrast this with the prevailing interest-based financial system where loans are extended under the guise that the burden is placed on the debtor, who is granted additional credit or forced to liquidate personal assets if they fail to honour the original loan agreement. Yes, this is a marked improvement from the pre-Islamic Makkan period, where failure to repay a loan may have resulted in slavery, but it nevertheless results in an unforgiving lending environment. Furthermore, an interest-dominated financial system is inherently inefficient since funds are channelled to clients that can predictably service debt rather than to risky ventures that have the potential to create the most value.

In Islam, the primary mode of wealth creation is by way of equity investments in the form of profit and loss sharing contracts. These investments are consistent with Islamic principles when the underlying contracts are structured to ensure that both parties judicially share in the risks and rewards of a business venture and neither can benefit at the expense of the other (principle 7). In Islam, the contract vehicles that have historically been the basis for profit and loss sharing investments are referred to as *muḍārabah* and *mushārakah*. It is important to note that these contracts were prevalent in the pre-Islamic Makkan period and are not a direct product of the Islamic finance system that subsequently evolved. To be more precise, they are accepted instruments today only because they were not rejected as forms for conducting trade.[11] Although they provide a constructive model on how to structure profit and loss sharing contracts, *muḍārabah* and *mushārakah* should not be considered the only acceptable means of accomplishing this task.

In both *muḍārabah* and *mushārakah* contracts, the profit ratio should be predetermined and losses are to be borne in proportion to the amount that each partner originally contributed. Herein is the crux of the problem regarding the adoption of preferred stock in Islamic finance circles, since in the case of preferred stock, losses are not necessarily borne in proportion to the amount invested. Unique to *mushārakah* financing is the view that all parties should be actively involved in the management of the venture. An example of this form of financing would be common stock-based VC investments, where a VC firm invests in a start-up company alongside the founding entrepreneur, and both are equally active in managing the company. Many scholars consider *mushārakah* the closest in form and function to the ideals of an Islamic finance system.

Ironically, true profit and loss sharing contracts are significantly under-represented in the nascent Islamic finance industry, currently accounting for less than 10.0 per cent of Islamic banking assets.[12] Previous research has indicated that a major reason for this discrepancy is the inherent agency problem, whereby entrepreneurs have a disincentive to expend effort since they are likely to be compensated less than their marginal contribution in the production process.[13] This outcome should come as no surprise. After all, why would an entrepreneur contribute 80.0 per cent of the effort to a business venture when he or she only owns 10.0 per cent of the company? On the other hand, how can financial investors who are not involved in the day-to-day operation, resulting in a situation of information asymmetry, adequately protect themselves if they allow the entrepreneur to retain a majority ownership stake? The modern-day US VC model has addressed this dilemma through the use of preferred stock and incentive-based stock options. Although this chapter focuses on the former, it is worth mentioning the multitude of millionaires, many of whom were non-managerial employees, created through the employee stock option plans of once start-up, venture-backed enterprises such as Microsoft, Intel and Dell Computers. Does this modern-day version of VC offer an improved, Islamic-compliant version of the traditional profit and loss sharing contract? So far, any reference to VC has implied that which occurs in the US. Certainly, one could also point out that there are large VC markets in other parts of the world; but to one degree or another, and more so for the successful ones, they have adopted many of the best practices from their more advanced US predecessor.

THE US VENTURE CAPITAL MODEL

The company life cycle

One of the cornerstones of modern corporate finance is the theory of a balanced risk/reward relationship. Therefore, in order to analyse critically the VC industry it is necessary to understand how the life cycle of a company affects investment returns. In a simplified scenario, a company will go through four principal stages: idea/seed, early, expansion and late. The venture capitalist will primarily be involved in the initial stages, while the traditional PE firm will be involved in the final two stages. Importantly, the stage of the company life cycle that a VC fund focuses on will drive its overall investment strategy in key areas such as: expected return; structure of the investment; participation in management; and exit strategy.

After having witnessed the abnormally high success rate of VC firms in the 1990s, one can be tempted to conclude that early stage investments are a one-way bet. However, a recent survey by Venture Economics indicated that the failure rate of start-ups has consistently hovered around 40.0 per cent over the past five years.[14] In order to compensate for this high probability of failure and still generate an acceptable risk-based portfolio return, a venture capitalist typically structures each investment to provide an internal rate of return (or IRR) of 40.0 per cent in the base case, or most likely, scenario. Therefore, 40.0 per cent can be considered the hurdle rate needed to entice investors. VC funds are also unique in that they are reliant on one or two investments to drive the overall performance of the portfolio; in fact, the expectation is that one out of every ten investments will provide a spectacular return, defined here as ten times the original cash investment.[15] This dependency on the success of a few investments makes VC firms vulnerable to market conditions. A recent phenomenon, to the surprise of investors who have become accustomed to seemingly limitless returns, is that many VC funds that started investing in 1999 and 2000 are drastically underperforming. This is because even the 40.0 per cent risk premium has not been able to compensate VC firms in the current liquidity-starved environment. Specifically, the market for initial public offerings (or IPO) and mergers/acquisitions (or M&A), the two lucrative exit scenarios that generate the spectacular ten-times returns, are in a state of flux. The result is that investors have been reluctant to provide additional money to any new VC funds. Yet, even with the 70.0 per cent drop in new capital fundraising in 2002, there remains an estimated $150 billion overhang of uninvested capital in existing VC funds. Note that this figure is more than the cumulative amount of VC invested between 1970 and 1997.[16] The concern that there is an oversupply of money in the market is a major reason that industry analysts expect 50.0 per cent of VC funds to go out of business by 2006.[17] The seemingly invulnerable VC industry has once again become a risky business.

By contrast, traditional PE firms tend to be more risk-averse and focused on investing in established businesses. Keen to protect their investment in a neutral or downside scenario, PE investors seek transactions such as leveraged and management buyouts, as well as expansion financings for established businesses, or a simple balance sheet refinancing. Consequently, these firms are not as reliant on the IPO market or the pending success of a few investments. In fact, far from succumbing to current bear market conditions, many traditional PE firms are taking advantage of the opportunity to invest in low-risk businesses at bargain prices. As opposed to the VC model, these funds expect more predictable performance from their portfolio (see Table 14.1). Consistent with the risk/return relationship, a successful traditional PE fund aims to generate a lower 15.0 to 20.0 per cent IRR over a ten-year time horizon.[18] Not surprisingly,

Table 14.1: Venture and private equity capital compared

	VC	PE
• Projected IRR	40%	20%
• Expected portfolio composition (absolute returns)		
10x original cash investment	1	0
2x–4x original cash investment	2	4
Equal to par value	2	4
Recoup 20%–40% of original cash investment	3	1
Complete write-off	2	1
Total number of investments	*10*	*10*
• Investment Strategy		
Early stage, high-growth	X	
Expansion	X	X
Management/Leveraged buyout		X
• Primary Exit Opportunities		
IPO	X	
M&A or sale to strategic buyer	X	X
Refinancing		X

the majority of funds that were previously earmarked for VC-type deals are now being shifted to late stage investments.

Employee stock options

Independent of the different risk/return profiles, one commonality between VC and traditional PE models is a strong belief in properly aligning the incentives of the management team and investors. Over the past 20 years, the primary tool used to accomplish this objective has been stock options, which, through their appeal, have increasingly made their way down to non-managerial employees as well. By definition, stock options are the right to purchase or sell a share of stock at a specific price within a specific period of time, and are commonly used as long-term incentive compensation for employees and management. The most important and effective feature of stock options is that they are tied to the creation of shareholder value. VC funds in particular dedicate a significant portion of their time to structuring the employee stock option plan (or ESOP) prior to making any investment, since an early stage company is extraordinarily dependent on attracting and retaining key employees. Under the belief that these employees are ultimately responsible for the success or failure of the company, VC firms often insist that they collectively retain a significant equity stake; for this reason, an individual VC firm will almost always be a minority investor.

Fund structure

In most cases a VC fund is set up as a limited partnership, which is composed of two distinct legal entities: first, limited partners (or LPs) who provide the capital to invest; and second, general partners (or GPs) who are responsible for managing the fund. Since the GPs manage the investment process, they are liable for any actions of the limited partnership, whereas passive LP investors are generally protected from legal actions and any losses beyond their original investment. The GP receives a management fee and a percentage of profits, while the LPs receive income, capital gains and tax benefits. From an Islamic perspective, the structure of this relationship is strikingly similar in form and function to the traditional *muḍārabah* contract. Both encourage a system of 'trust' where one party is a passive financier while the other is the fund manager. Both also require the profit ratio to be predetermined, with losses to be borne solely by the financier in proportion to the amount invested. Consistent with the VC model, a major reason this 'silent partnership' arrangement has been successful is due to the focus on properly aligning the incentives of the GPs, who have direct responsibility for making investments, with passive LP investors.

In the vast majority of funds, the distribution of profits are set so that the LPs are repaid their contributed capital on a 1:1 basis before the GPs receive anything. Again, since this distribution refers specifically to profits, it does not provide the LPs with a guaranteed return and is therefore consistent with Islamic principles. After LPs have been compensated, the remaining proceeds are typically split 80.0 per cent LPs and 20.0 per cent GPs. This variable compensation structure, in which the compensation of the GP is heavily dependent on the success of the portfolio, has been extremely effective in creating the proper incentives and trust between passive LP investors and GPs.

Structuring the transaction

The main activities of a VC fund are to source/screen, negotiate/structure and monitor/exit investments over a specified time period. For the purposes of this chapter, the focus is on the negotiation/structuring phase, where the seemingly minute difference between VC and traditional PE manifests into structural and legal changes that are important for the Islamic-oriented investor to understand. In general, traditional PE investments tend to have more debt-like features, while VC investments involve a purer form of equity that is analogous to the concept of an entrepreneur and financier partnering to share in the risks and rewards of a business venture – a primary objective of an Islamic finance system.

To illustrate the different investment structures, assume that VC firm 'ABC Ventures' makes a $5 million investment in company 'XYZ Inc.' in return for a 49.0 per cent ownership stake. In industry terms, this would refer to a post-money or post-investment valuation of $10 million ($5 million ÷ 49%). Note that the equivalent pre-money or pre-investment valuation is $5 million (or the post-investment valuation less the new investment). Assume also that the founding entrepreneur previously made a $1 million common stock investment to start XYZ Inc., and owns the remaining shares.

Common stock

As can be inferred from its name, common stock does not have any special rights outside of the company's organisational documents, and the holders of such stock are the last to be paid in a sale or liquidation of the company, after all contingent liabilities and preferred stock. Although a VC firm will often require the entrepreneur's equity to be structured as common stock, in this example a common stock investment could be mistakenly harmful to ABC Ventures. For instance, assume that after ABC Ventures makes a $5 million common stock investment, an offer is made to purchase XYZ Inc. for $8 million. The entrepreneur, who has retained 51.0 per cent ownership, will most likely approve the sale and earn a handsome $3 million profit, while ABC Ventures will realise a $1 million loss on their investment. Understandably, ABC Ventures would seek to protect their investment against this situation through the issuance of a different class of stock.

Preferred stock

Since VC firms are typically minority shareholders, they choose to protect themselves against the previous scenario by investing in preferred stock. Preferred stock provides the holder with preference over common shareholders in the event of a sale or liquidation of the company, and may have additional rights such as control over management decisions or the ability to receive dividends. Although several variations exist, the two most prevalent types of preferred stock are convertible preferred and participating preferred.

1. Convertible preferred stock: convertible preferred stock offers the holder the option to receive either the face value of their original investment or their share in the common stock proceeds on an 'as if converted basis'. Again, assume that an $8 million offer is made to purchase XYZ Inc. Since the value of their 49.0 per cent common shares on an 'as if converted' basis would only be $4 million, ABC Ventures would elect to redeem the $5 million face value of their original investment and forfeit their equity stake. Subsequently, the entrepreneur's ownership will accrete to 100 per cent and they will receive the remaining proceeds.

2. Participating preferred stock: participating preferred stock entitles the holder to receive the face value of the original investment and their share in the common stock proceeds on an 'as if converted' basis. Refer again to the $8

million offer for XYZ Inc. In this instance, ABC Ventures would receive their original $5 million investment as well as 49.0 per cent of the remaining $3 million proceeds, for a total of $6.5 million. In industry terminology, this ability to receive the face value of the original investment and share in the common stock proceeds is referred to as 'double-dipping'.

As demonstrated, each type of security has a different risk profile. All things being equal, common/convertible preferred stock is significantly more risky than a participating preferred instrument. Based on the previous risk/return discussion, an investor will expect to be compensated accordingly for taking additional risk. Therefore, from the perspective of the investor, common/convertible preferred stock is often priced at a premium versus less risky participating preferred stock, frequently as high as 50.0 per cent. In the case of XYZ Inc., this would imply that ABC Ventures could invest $5 million in a participating preferred instrument for 25.0 per cent ownership, or invest the same amount in a common/convertible instrument for 49.0 per cent ownership. In this section, the important point to note is that PE investments can be structured in unique ways depending on the risk/return profile of the investor.

IS VENTURE CAPITAL SHARĪʿAH-COMPATIBLE?

As stated earlier, there is a common bond between Islamic finance and PE, given that both encourage partnership based on risk- and reward-sharing. However, there are also several debatable practices in the PE industry that have the effect of clouding this relationship. The aim in this section is to provide an opinion on these issues, again with a focus on the spirit rather than the letter of the law. To this end, an important consideration involves invoking the Islamic principle of *ibāḥah* in *muʿāmalāt*, which, simply stated, advises that in commercial dealings 'everything is permitted unless clearly prohibited'; therefore, the approach is to demonstrate whether the underlying characteristics of each unique structure clearly violate Islamic principles.

Simple convertible preferred

On the surface, it would appear that in order for the entrepreneur and financier judicially to share in the risks and rewards of a business, they should both invest in the same security, in this case common stock. However, such a system works best when the parties involved contribute the effort required to run the venture in proportion to the amount of money they each invest. In most VC deals this scenario is rare, since these firms provide the majority of capital yet prefer to be minority investors and only participate in high-level, strategic decisions. The use of convertible preferred stock allows minority investors such as VC firms to allocate a disproportionate equity stake to the management team while ensuring that they are adequately protected. In doing so, it is important to determine whether this instrument remains consistent with Islamic principles.

Some scholars argue that convertible preferred stock is a debt instrument in disguise, allowing investors to preserve the face value of their original investment or predetermine their rate of return. Others argue that the existence of a liquidation preference artificially favours one party at the expense of another. However, a closer examination of the VC model disputes these claims. First, even from the perspective of the company the VC firm is not underwriting a debt instrument, otherwise there would be no equity 'upside' offered in conjunction with the investment. From a portfolio management viewpoint, convertible preferred investments are regularly updated in accordance with any significant company events, either positive or negative. This sharply contrasts with the conventional banking model, where the value of a loan can only decrease depending on whether there is reason to believe that repayment of principal is in jeopardy.

Second, a convertible preferred investment does not present the holder with a guaranteed return. To illustrate, suppose that ABC Ventures invests $5 million in a convertible preferred investment and then XYZ Inc. is only sold for $5 million two years later. In this instance, ABC Ventures will recoup all of their original investment while the entrepreneur receives nothing. Is this fair? Certainly, neither the GP nor the LP gains from simply receiving their original capital back. In fact, a more accurate way to view this outcome is a zero-interest loan to XYZ Inc. With the understanding that the entrepreneur has ultimate control of the company, and that equity is essentially performance-based compensation, the more compelling question becomes whether an entrepreneur should receive a bonus for adding nothing to shareholder wealth? To be sure, if the investment is a success then the entrepreneur will benefit significantly more than the VC firm, and few would argue against the logic of this compensation.

In reality, a convertible preferred instrument is extremely effective in aligning the interest of all parties when the size of the investment is not proportionate to the management of the venture. Furthermore, the convertible preferred structure forces each party to expend effort with the same end goal of creating shareholder value, since neither will benefit in a neutral or negative scenario. This formula is ideal for investors taking a minority stake in a privately held enterprise. By creating a mutually beneficial partnership, convertible preferred stock is consistent with the Islamic principle that both the entrepreneur and financier judicially share in the risks and rewards of a business venture.

But is participating preferred stock fundamentally the same instrument? Recall that such stock provides the holder with the ability to 'double dip'; that is, to receive the face value of their investment and retain their equity ownership in the company. A simple analysis indicates that this instrument more closely resembles deeply subordinated debt rather than 'true' equity. For example, assume that ABC Ventures selects a participating preferred structure in return for 25.0 per cent ownership of XYZ Inc. As opposed to the convertible preferred investor, who will not earn a profit unless the exit value of XYZ Inc. is greater than the $10 million post-investment valuation, the participating preferred instrument generates a positive return at each valuation point above $5 million, which is simply the pre-investment valuation of the company. Therefore, one could argue that ABC Ventures is not accepting any 'true' risk, since they will realise a positive return even if the management team sits idly with the money and the exit value remains $10 million. Essentially, the participating preferred structure is similar in nature to a variable-rate loan, albeit deferred, with the yield a function of the realised exit value of the company. This situation goes against the Islamic principle of 'no gain without effort or liability'.

Table 14.2 summarises the effect of each type of stock based on three different exit values for XYZ Inc. Consistent with the previous examples, assume a $5 million pre-investment valuation and $5 million new investment. The key is to focus on scenario B where the exit value of the company is only between $5 million and $10 million, implying that the entrepreneur and investor were not able to generate any shareholder value in conjunction with the investment. While the convertible preferred instruments act like a loan in this instance, the participating preferred stock will actually generate a profit.

In demonstrating that the convertible preferred structure is consistent with Islamic principles, the assumption has been that there are no synthetic mechanisms used to enhance returns in a non-compliant manner. However, several such 'sweeteners' have become probable as investors have sought to boost their returns during the recent industry downturn. Individually, each is significant because it can alter the underlying characteristics of an otherwise simple convertible preferred investment.

Table 14.2: Common stock, convertible preferred and participating preferred investment compared

Scenario	*Exit Value of XYZ Inc.*	*Common Stock*	*Convertible Preferred**	*Participating Preferred**
A	Greater than $10 million	Equity	Equity	Loan with high yield
B	$5 million < XYZ < $10 million	Equity	Zero-interest rate loan	Loan with medium yield
C	Less than $5 million	Equity	Zero-interest rate loan	Zero-interest rate loan

Note: *Assumes no dividends, ratchets or multiple liquidation preferences.

Preferred dividends

Preferred stock can also be structured to provide the investor with additional compensation in the form of preference-in-kind (or PIK) dividends. Since PIK dividends are rarely structured to fluctuate based on performance, this added compensation significantly changes the risk profile of a convertible preferred instrument. For instance, suppose ABC Ventures invests $5 million in a convertible preferred instrument with a 10.0 per cent annual PIK dividend; their investment would accrue by $500 thousand per year regardless of the performance of XYZ Inc. In the neutral scenario defined above, the convertible preferred investment effectively changes from a zero-interest loan to a deferred-interest loan. Needless to say, this is not an acceptable structure under the guidelines of Islamic finance. However, it is important to note that PIK dividends are equity instruments, and if they are structured to fluctuate based on company performance a case could be made for their legitimacy.

The vulture capitalist

A more pronounced trend is the use of multiple liquidation preferences, which provide the holder with the right to recoup an amount greater than the face value of their original investment prior to any other distributions. To illustrate, assume that ABC Ventures invests $5 million in a convertible preferred instrument at a post-investment valuation of $10 million. If ABC Ventures negotiates a three-times liquidation preference in their contract, then the value of XYZ Inc. at the time of exit will have to surpass $15 million (or 1.5 x $10 million post-investment valuation) before common shareholders receive anything. In effect, the value of the company could increase 50.0 per cent and produce a handsome profit for the VC firm, yet the entrepreneur would receive no monetary reward. The primary purpose of this instrument is to protect investors in a neutral scenario, but one can easily see how it effectively favours one party at the expense of the other. Therefore, multiple liquidation preferences are not consistent with the principle of properly aligning the incentives of the financier and entrepreneur.

Similarly, ratchets are a method whereby the preferred stock holder can fortify their return at the expense of common shareholders. For example, ABC Ventures can create certain contractual hurdles that, if not met, essentially 'ratchet' up their ownership. To illustrate, assume ABC Ventures makes a $5 million convertible preferred investment under the condition that if XYZ Inc. fails to generate $3 million in profit by year two then the equity stake of ABC Ventures will increase from 49.0 per cent to 90.0 per cent. Now suppose that XYZ's profit in year two is only $2 million and ABC Ventures' ownership increases to 90.0 per cent at the expense of the entrepreneur, whose shares are now significantly diluted. Even if the company is sold for only $6 million (or three-times cash flow), ABC Ventures will realise a $400,000 gain. In essence, the VC firm is not 'truly' underwriting the potential of XYZ Inc. to reach $3 million in profit. Although extreme, this example is not rare and illustrates how a ratchet mechanism can limit the risk of the VC firm to the point that it effectively results in a guaranteed return, barring some drastic circumstance. Such an arrangement is not consistent with the Islamic philosophy of ensuring that both parties genuinely share in the risks and rewards of a business.

Company debt

The earlier discussion reiterated that conventional interest-bearing debt is against the tenets of an Islamic economic system. However, it is hardly the norm to find a company today that does not somehow participate in the interest-dominated banking system. This is especially true of more mature companies that generate a predictable stream of revenue or own assets that can be issued as collateral. For this reason, some scholars have ruled that there is an acceptable level of interest-bearing debt that a company can hold and still be considered a legitimate destination for Islamic investment. The most universal threshold is a total debt/total assets ratio of less than 33.0 per cent; the popular Dow Jones Islamic Market Index (or DJIMI) uses this criterion to screen acceptable investments.[19] Although such a rule is a compromise of Islamic principles in the face of reality, it nevertheless serves as a realistic goal of maintaining a limit on interest-based transactions.

Employee stock option plans

It is important to draw a distinction between ESOPs versus exotic options and derivative contracts. In theory the latter utilise leverage to speculate on the directional movement on an underlying security; or simply stated, the option holder bets that an asset's value will either increase or decrease in the future. This situation closely resembles gambling, which is categorically shunned in Islam.[20] By contrast, employees who receive an offer to buy additional shares of their company are directly responsible for increasing the value of such shares through their work efforts. Due to this direct involvement, these options should not be grouped in the same genre as other speculative instruments; not surprisingly, most scholars agree on the legitimacy of ESOPs.[21]

CAPITALISING ON VENTURE CAPITAL

The previous analysis indicates that there are some favourable and unfavourable aspects of PE investments from an Islamic perspective. Unfortunately, the industry is not normally viewed with these issues in mind. Therefore, the pertinent question becomes whether there is a way manually to segment the market effectively to screen acceptable PE funds. Although there are several methodologies to choose from, the most useful way is to cross-reference funds based on their investment strategy and industry focus. The latter can ensure that funds are not allocated to unethical businesses, which in Islam would include companies whose primary source of income involves interest-based finance, insurance products, alcohol or gambling. Since this is rather straightforward, the attention is on screening non-compliant investments by focusing on investment strategy, with an emphasis on early versus late stage investments as the key differentiating factor.

Refer back to the section that segmented companies into two categories based on their stage in the life cycle: seed/early stage versus expansion/later stage. Many of the principles of Islamic finance are not consistent with the latter group. A primary reason is that as companies mature they are able to collateralise their existing assets and finance their growth with cheaper debt, which provides the benefit of a tax shelter and does not dilute existing shareholders. This is exactly the case with many leveraged buyout transactions, wherein a traditional PE firm leverages the assets of an existing business to raise debt and finance the purchase of the target company using as little equity as possible in an effort to maximise their potential return. In many cases the debt/equity ratio of buyout transactions exceeds 60.0 per cent. Clearly, the use of such a high amount of interest-bearing debt is against Islamic principles.

Expansion stage companies provide a more interesting case. Although these companies may appear to raise adequate amounts of equity while maintaining minimal levels of debt, a closer look at the equity reveals that it is frequently structured as participating preferred and often includes multiple liquidation preferences or other 'sweeteners'. As noted earlier, these devices are not consistent with the ideals of Islamic finance. Furthermore, an increasingly popular trend in this category is the use of mezzanine financing, which is a form of subordinated, interest-bearing debt. For these reasons, the recommendation is that the Islamic-oriented investor does not invest in traditional PE funds unless the investment philosophy of the GPs is amenable to these issues.

This brings us to the domain of seed/early stage investments. Due to reluctance of banks to underwrite loans to a company that does not have sufficient collateral or a predictable operating history, early stage companies are forced to rely on equity in order to finance their growth. It is rare, in fact, to find an early stage company in a net debt position. Furthermore, the equity invested at these early stages is more reflective of 'true' equity, since the use of participating preferred stock and multiple liquidation preferences/ratchets is not customary. When asked directly, one partner at a successful billion dollar early stage VC fund confirmed that the use of such tactics is rare, based on the philosophy that they are 'too punitive to management and make it difficult to attract and retain good people'.[22] Rather than use gimmicks to protect their investment, early stage VC firms seek to take more risk and optimise their ownership based on the expectation that the company will be a winner. A recent survey conducted by VC Experts confirmed that convertible preferred stock is the most prevalent structure in early stage financings.[23] As previously discussed, this instrument is compatible with the major principles of Islamic finance since first, the investor is assuming a degree of risk; second, effort is required in order to generate a return; and third, the financial interests are properly aligned such that neither party benefits at the expense of the other.

However, prior to making VC an acceptable investment vehicle for the Islamic-oriented investor, there is a considerable amount of research to be done. First, a comprehensive survey and analysis of the VC industry is needed in order to determine which funds are compliant with Islamic principles. This task will prove difficult since these firms tend to be unwilling to disclose information; but it should not be impossible, especially if it allows early stage VC firms to raise additional money. Similar to the DJIMI methodology, a comprehensive database of compliant VC funds could be created for the benefit of Islamic investors. One issue that is sure to emerge is the non-standardisation of the VC industry. For instance, it would be rare to come across even a very early stage VC fund that only invested in simple convertible preferred stock or would never impose a PIK dividend. In reality, each VC deal is unique and may be structured with some of the devices previously mentioned as non-compliant. To address this concern, perhaps a model similar to the DJIMI can be implemented, whereby a minimal level of such activity is deemed acceptable. Once these and other relatable issues are addressed, the global VC market can become a welcome destination for the increasing number of Islamic-managed investment funds.

WEALTH CREATION IN THE MUSLIM WORLD

Financial institutions serve an important purpose in society by efficiently allocating scarce economic resources. An inevitable by-product of a properly functioning VC industry is the goal of empowering talented individuals by means of opportunity, which has the effect of stemming the 'brain-drain' that plagues most developing countries when they lose their most precious human resources to more advanced countries. Realising the critical impact of risk-capital on long-term economic growth, the governments of Israel, India and China have all singled out the development of a domestic VC market as one of their top priorities. In the case of Israel, the focus has been on encouraging joint-venture partnerships between local and US firms, who are eager to invest in the world-class engineering talent that the country offers. India and China have taken a different approach by encouraging their numerous expatriate citizens, many of whom have been extremely successful in the US VC industry, to reinvest back home. So far these activities can be deemed an early success, with VC activity in these three countries collectively increasing from less than $100 million per year in 1990 to more than $2 billion per year in the late 1990s.[24] To be sure, a VC industry cannot be built overnight, but often it is easier and more advantageous to find a way to benefit from the success of the US model. However, at the same time the industry continues to grow on a global scale, there remains a noticeable dearth of such investment in the Muslim World. The obvious irony here is that the underlying philosophy of risk-taking and partnership, clearly lacking in the Muslim World today, is explicitly encouraged in the widely adopted Islamic faith.

Banking on Islamic banks

A popular saying is: 'Through misfortune comes opportunity.' Indeed, the newly emerging Islamic finance industry is in a unique position to bridge this divide by demonstrating how to create an economic system based on the principles of Islam. Perhaps the most suitable institutions to serve as the catalyst for such change are the rapidly growing Islamic banks, which have amassed over $280 billion in assets and continue to grow at an annual rate in excess of 15.0 per cent. Importantly, these banks have the financial wherewithal and institutional presence to develop key relationships with some of the leading VC firms in the world, in the way that large investment banks such as JP Morgan and CS First Boston have established their multibillion dollar PE portfolios.

So far, one Islamic institution that has made such an effort is Dallah Al-Baraka Group (or DBG), which, in conjunction with MapleWood Partners, recently launched Manar Private Equity Fund Limited, the 'first of its kind' Islamic PE fund targeted at the US market.[25] Specifically, MapleWood Partners will be responsible for making the investments while Al-Tawfeek Company for Investment Funds, a subsidiary of DBG, will actively monitor the fund's compliance with Islamic principles. This is definitely an important milestone but such a model will be difficult to scale, especially since VC funds have been able to raise money with relative ease over the past several years. Such an environment makes it unlikely that these funds will allow an LP actively to monitor their investment criteria; this effect is compounded for investors who want access to the top-tier funds, in which participation is typically by invitation only.

For this reason, the model envisioned is similar to that of the increasingly popular fund-of-funds approach, whereby an Islamic bank would purchase an interest in a range of early stage VC funds focused on specific industries such as life sciences, information technology and telecommunications. In so doing, Islamic banks have the opportunity to train individuals on the dynamics of the VC industry, such as how to monitor and measure performance, with the aim of transferring this knowledge back to the Muslim World and planting the seeds of a domestic VC market. Such investment is not possible now, for reasons ranging from underdeveloped legal systems to political issues, but the learning process cannot begin soon enough.

Islamic banks have much to benefit by including VC in their asset allocation strategy. First, many of these banks are faced with the problem of excess liquidity due to a lack of Islamic-compliant long-term investment alternatives.[26] VC provides the opportunity to channel this excess not only into long-term but also potentially high-yield investments. Furthermore, an encouraging development in the VC industry has been the emergence of a large secondary market for trading LP interests, which has grown from under $500 million in 1997 to over $3 billion in 2001.[27] This new feature provides investors, especially large institutions, with the opportunity to better manage their liquidity and asset allocation strategies. Lastly, the US VC sector continues to outperform other asset classes over the long term. Importantly, these returns are not perfectly correlated to other sectors such as public equities and real estate, which together make up the bulk of long-term Islamic finance assets. Therefore, diversifying into VC presents the opportunity to increase returns without an equivalent increase in risk.

In the end, validating the VC model is a critical step in the evolution of the Islamic finance industry. Eventually, a major goal of the industry must be to improve the ailing economies of the Muslim World. So far, the existing systems have done a poor job of accomplishing this task. A recent report from the UN indicated that the GDP of all Arab countries combined is less than that of a single European country, Spain.[28] The report goes on to note that the Arab countries also have the lowest level of research funding in the world apart from sub-Sahara Africa and, consequently, significant underinvestment in human resource development. When interviewed by *Al-Ahram Weekly*, one Egyptian scientist concurred, 'Why bother working on an idea when the scientist will not benefit personally? He is working for the government and the government will take credit for his work and will implement the idea via a state-run firm.'[29] For Egypt, which is currently in the midst of a large-scale privatisation programme,

Table 14.3: Risk and return profile of venture capital versus other asset classes

Risk/return of asset classes, 1975–2000	*Annual return*	*Standard deviation*	*Correlation*	*Sharpe ratio*
S&P 500	16.1%	15.4%	1.00	1.03
Lehman government/credit index	9.4%	7.4%	0.30	1.25
Venture capital pooled average	21.6%	16.3%	0.19	1.32

Source: Fort Washington Capital Partners.

this is exactly the sort of problem that VC seeks to address. Although VC is virtually nonexistent in the Middle East, one positive development is the recent announcement of a $100 million PE fund based in Dubai. The fund will be managed by HSBC and has been marketed as the 'first of its kind' in the region, not only since it raised the majority of its capital from Arab investors, but also because all of the funds will be destined for companies in the Middle East. Although this particular fund was not structured as an Islamic-oriented investment vehicle, it is worth noting that PE typically appears as a frontrunner to VC. If HSBC can successfully demonstrate there is an untapped market for PE in the Middle East, then it may prove to be a harbinger of things to come. While not a universal remedy, perhaps a thriving VC industry, modelled along the basic principles of Islam, can play a critical role in creating wealth, and more importantly opportunity, in the Muslim World.

CONCLUSIONS

A properly functioning VC industry brings benefits to society at large by directing scarce economic resources to entrepreneurs with the most promising ideas, and the determination to turn these ideas into productive companies. The availability of risk capital has been one of the most important factors in the development experience of advanced countries, especially the US. Unfortunately, very little attention has been paid to the potential impact of venture capital on economic growth in the Muslim World. This is a serious omission since venture capital is founded on the same principles that guide Islamic finance. This chapter has attempted to increase the awareness of the prevailing US-based VC model as an acceptable Islamic investment vehicle by providing a critical analysis of this mode of financing in the context of Islamic economic principles. A case has been made that establishing a thriving venture capital industry is essential not only for further evolution of the Islamic finance industry, but also for the long-term health of ailing economies in the Muslim World.

NOTES

1. DRI-WEFA study (2002) identifies venture capital as a key factor powering US economic growth, The National Venture Capital Association (www.nvca.com).
2. Based on confidential interviews with venture capital funds managing more than $1 billion in early stage investments, Baltimore, MD, 2003.
3. W. D. Bygrave and J. A. Timmons (1992), *Venture Capital at the Crossroads*, Harvard Business School Press.
4. Jeffrey D. Nuechterlein, *International Venture Capital: The Role of Start-Up Financing in the United States, Europe and Asia*, Westview Press or The Global Venture Investors Association (www.gvia.org).

5. Lawrence Penn, The Camelot Group, 'Private Equity Overview and Update', presentation at the International Islamic Finance Forum, Harvard University, 2003.
6. PriceWaterhouseCoopers (2001), Global Private Equity 2000: *A Review of the Global Private Equity and Venture Capital Markets*, New York.
7. The National Venture Capital Association (www.nvca.com).
8. Dierderik Van Schaik, 'Islamic Banking', *The Arab Review*, 2001.
9. Jerry Useem, 'Banking on Allah,' *Fortune Magazine* (www.fortune.com), May 2002.
10. Ibid.
11. A. L. M. Abdul Gafoor, '*Muḍārabah*-based Investment and Finance' (www.islamic-finance.net).
12. Warren Edwards (2001), *Demystification of Islamic Banking and Finance*, Treasury Management International, London.
13. Masudal Alam Choudhury (2001), 'Islamic Venture Capital', *Journal of Economic Studies*, 28 (1):14–33.
14. Venture Economics (www.ventureeconomics.com).
15. Based on confidential interviews with venture capital funds managing more than $1 billion in early stage equity investments, Baltimore, MD, 2003.
16. Lawrence Penn, The Camelot Group, 'Private Equity Overview and Update', see n.5 above.
17. Kelly Swanson, *Seed Money is Drying Up*, The Street.com.2003 (www.thestreet.com).
18. Based on confidential interviews with private equity funds managing more than $200 million in late stage equity investments, Baltimore, MD, 2001.
19. Rushdi Siddiqui (2000), 'Dow Jones Islamic Market Index', presentation at the Islamic Banking and Finance America 2000 Conference, New York, 2000.
20. Dr Muhammad Hamidullah, 'The Economic System of Islam' (www.sharik.org.uk).
21. Yusuf Talal Delorenzo, Central Mosque.com (www.central-mosque.com).
22. Based on confidential interviews with venture capital funds managing more than $1 billion in early stage equity investments, Baltimore, MD, 2003.
23. VC Experts (wwww.vcexperts.com).
24. Sources: *Asian Venture Capital Journal* (wwww.avcj.com) and Israeli Venture Capital Association.
25. Naseeruddin Ahmed Khan (2001), 'Success of Islamic Investment Funds: An Experience of Al-Tawfeek', presentation at Lariba Symposium.
26. Interview with Moshen Khallaf, General Manager Islamic banking division, United Bank of Egypt, 2003.
27. Lawrence Penn, The Camelot Group, 'Private Equity Overview and Update', see n.5 above.
28. United Nations Development Programme, 'Arab Human Development Report', 2002.
29. *Al-Ahram Weekly*, 24–30 September 1998.

References and Bibliography

CHAPTER 1: ISLAMIC BANKING AT THE CROSSROADS: THEORY VERSUS PRACTICE

Ahmad, Ziauddin: (1985), 'The Present State of the Islamic Finance Movement', Conference on the Impact and Role of Islamic Banking in International Finance, New York City.

Al-Imam Al-Tabari (1992), *Jami Al Byan fi Tawil Al Qur'ān (Tafsir Al Tabari)*, Beirut: Dar Al Kutub Al Ilmiyyah.

Al-Misri, R. (1997), *Bay' al Taqsīt: Taḥlīl Fiqhī wa Iqtisādī*, Damascus: Dar Al Qalam.

Bank Islam, Malaysia: *Annual Reports 1984–2000*.

Bank Negara, Malaysia: *Annual Report 2000, 2001* and *2002*.

Chapra, M. U. (1985), *Toward a Just Monetary System*, Leicester, UK: The Islamic Foundation.

El-Gamal, Mahmoud A. (2001), 'An Economic Explanation of Ribā in Classical Islamic Jurisprudence': 1–20, *http://www. ruf.rice.edu/~elgamal*.

Halim, Abdul (2001), 'The Deferred Contracts of Exchange: Al-Qur'ān in Contrast with the Islamic Economists' Theory on Banking and Finance', Malaysia: IKIM.

Hasan, Zubair (1985), 'Determination of Profit and Loss Sharing Ratios in Interest-free Business Finance', *Journal of Research in Islamic Economics*, 3(1): 13–29.

Hasan, Zubair (1989), 'The Financial System and Monetary Policy in an Islamic Economy by Mohsin Khan and Abbas Mirakhor: Comments', *JKAU: Islamic Economics*, 1(1): 85–93.

Hasan, Zubair (2002), '*Muḍārabah* as a Mode of Financing in Islamic Banking: Theory, Practice, and Problems', *The Middle East Business and Economic Review*, 14(2): 41–53.

Hassan, M. Kabir (2003), 'Dividend Signalling Hypothesis and Short-term Asset Concentration of the Islamic Interest-free Banking', *Islamic Economic Studies*, 11(1): 1–30.

Kamali, M. Hashim (1999), *Principles of Islamic Jurisprudence*, Reprint, Petaling Jaya, Malaysia: Ilmiah Publishers.

Khan, M. Fahim (1995) *Essays in Islamic Finance*, Leicester: The Islamic Foundation.

Saadullah, Rida (1994), 'Concept of Time in Islamic Economics', *Islamic Economic Studies*, 4(1): 1–15.

Siddiqi, M. N. (1983), *Issues in Islamic Banking*, Leicester: The Islamic Foundation.

Siddiqi, M. N. (1985), *Partnership and Profit Sharing in Islamic Law*, Leicester: The Islamic Foundation.

Usmani, M. Taqi (1998) *An Introduction to Islamic Finance*, Karachi, Pakistan: Idaratul Ma'arif.

Wilson, Rodney (2002), 'The Evolution of the Islamic Financial System', in Simon Archer and Rifat Ahmad Abdul Karim (eds), *Islamic Finance Innovation and Growth*, Nelson House, Playhouse Yard, London: Euromoney Books.

CHAPTER 2: ISLAMIC BANKING MODES OF FINANCE: PROPOSALS FOR FURTHER EVOLUTION

Al Jassas, *Aḥkām al Qur'ān*.

Al Jaziri, A. Al Rahamn, *Kitāb al Fiqh 'Ala Mazāhib al Arba'*, Dar al Fiqr Publishers.

Ariff, M. and M. A. Mannan (eds) (1990), *Developing a System of Financial Instruments*, Jeddah: Islamic Research and Training Institute, Islamic Development Bank.

Banking Activity from the Legal Point of View in Arab Countries, Beirut: Arab Banks Association Publications (17).

The Council of Islamic Ideology (1980), *The Elimination of Interest from the Economy*, Reports of the Panel of Economists and Bankers, Islamabad, Pakistan: The Council of Islamic Ideology.

Elgari, Mohammed (1990), 'Financial Markets', paper presented to The Financial Markets Symposium, Rabat, Morocco, organised by the Islamic Research and Training Institute and the Islamic Fiqh Academy.

Elgari, Mohammed (1993), 'Towards an Islamic Stock Market', *Islamic Economic* Studies, 1(1): 1–20.

Hammad, Nazih (1990), *Studies in Principles of Debts in Islamic Fiqh*, Taif: Saudi Arabia: Dar Al Farooq.

Hammad, Nazih (1994), *Salam Fiqh and its Contemporary Applications* (Arabic), Jeddah: Islamic Research and Training Institute, Islamic Development Bank.

Hamoud, Sami Hassan (1985), *Islamic Banking*, London: Arabian Information.

Ibn Hazm, *Al Muhalla*.

Ibn Rusd, *Bidāyat al Mujtahid*.

Institute of Islamic Banking and Insurance (1993), *Islamic Banking and its Problems*, London.

Kahf, Monzer (1994), *Ijārah Securities* (Arabic), Jeddah: Islamic Research and Training Institute, Islamic Development Bank.

Kahf, Monzer and T. Khan (1992), *Principles of Islamic Financing*, Jeddah: Islamic Research and Training Institute, Islamic Development Bank.

McKenzie, J. H. and K. Schap (1988), *Hedging Financial Instruments*, Chicago: Probus Publishing.

Rayan, A. (1994), *Unlawful Sales in Sharī'ah and their Contemporary Applications in Islamic Banks*, Eminent Scholars' Lecture Series, Jeddah: Islamic Research and Training Institute, Islamic Development Bank.

Wilson, Rodney (1990), 'Development of Financial Instruments in an Islamic Framework', paper presented at the Seminar on Financial Institutions According to Sharī'ah, Indonesia (September).

CHAPTER 3: WEALTH MOBILISATION BY ISLAMIC BANKS: THE MALAYSIAN CASE

Ali, A. H. (1999), 'Islamic Banking Culture', *New Horizon* (83), January, 11–13.

Al-Harran, S. A. S. (1993), *Islamic Finance: Partnership Financing*, Selangor, Darul Ehsan, Malaysia: Pelanduk Publications.

Al-Harran, S. A. S. (1995), *Leading Issues in Islamic Banking and Finance*, Selangor Darul Ehsan, Malaysia: Penlanduk Publications.

Ariff, M. (1988), *Islamic Banking in South-East Asia*, Singapore: Institute of South East Asian Studies.

Badrul, H. and M. Rohani (2003), 'A Study of Religiosity Influence on the Buying Behavior of Muslim Consumers', Proceedings of an International Conference: *Asia Pacific Business Environment: Innovative Responses to Regional Events*, Selangor Darul Ehsan, Malaysia.

Bank Islam Malaysia Berhad, *Annual Report*, various issues, Kuala Lumpur, Malaysia.

Bank Kerjasama Rakyat Malaysia Berhad, *Annual Report*, various issues, Kuala Lumpur, Malaysia.

Bank Negara Malaysia (1999), *The Central Bank and the Financial System in Malaysia*, Kuala Lumpur, Malaysia.

Bank Negara Malaysia, *Monthly Statistical Bulletin*, various issues, Kuala Lumpur, Malaysia.

Chapra, M. U. (1985), *Towards a Just Monetary System*, Leicester: The Islamic Foundation.

Haron, S. (1996), *Principles and Operations of Islamic Banking*, Selangor, Darul Ehsan, Malaysia: Berita Publishing.

Haron, S. (2000), 'Islamic Financial System in Malaysia: Issues Reexamined', Seminar on Islamic Banking System Strategy: Towards 20 Percent Market Share by 2010, Kuala Lumpur, Malaysia.
Haron, S. and B. Shanmugam (2001), *Islamic Banking System: Concepts and Applications*, Malaysia: Pelanduk Publications.
Haron, S., N. Ahmad and S. L. Planisek (1994), 'Bank Patronage Factors of Muslims and Non-Muslim Consumers', *International Journal of Bank Marketing*, 12(1): 32–40.
Kuran, Timur (1986), 'The Economic System in Contemporary Islamic Thought: Interpretation and Assessment', *Journal of Middle Eastern Studies*, 2: 135.
Lewis, Mervyn and Latifa M. Algaoud (2001), *Islamic Banking*, UK: Edward Elgar Publishing Limited.
Mannan, Muhammad Abdul (1986), *Islamic Economics: Theories and Practice*, London, UK: Hodder and Stoughton.
Mirakhor, A. (1987), 'Short-term Asset Concentration and Islamic Banking', in Mohsin S. Khan and Abbas Mirakhor (eds), *Theoretical Studies in Islamic Banking and Finance*, Houston: The Institute for Research in Islamic Studies.
Razali, N. (1995), 'Challenges to the Islamization of Finance: Overview of the Contemporary Issues', Seminar on Contemporary Dimensions in Islamic Financial Systems, Kuala Lumpur, Malaysia.
Rosly, S. A. (1995), 'New Challenges in Islamic Banking and Finance in Malaysia', Seminar on Contemporary Dimensions in Islamic Financial Systems, Kuala Lumpur, Malaysia.
Zakariya, Man (1987), 'The Prospects for *Muḍārabah* and *Mushārakah* Financing', International Seminar on Islamic Economics, Kuala Lumpur, Malaysia.

CHAPTER 4: MANAGING AND MEASURING CUSTOMER SERVICE QUALITY IN ISLAMIC BANKS: A STUDY OF THE KUWAIT FINANCE HOUSE

Abdul Hameed, A. (2001), 'Forty Ḥadith on the Islamic Personality', cited on the internet in March: *http://www.islaam.net/ilm/hadeeth/islaamicpersonality.html*.
Avkiran, N. (1994), 'Developing an Instrument to Measure Customer Service Quality in Branch Banking', *International Journal of Bank Marketing*, 12(6): 10–18.
Berry, L. A. Parasuraman and V. Zeithaml (1990), 'Five Imperatives for Improving SQ', *Sloan Management Review*, 29: 29–38.
Bitran, G. and H. Lojo (1993), 'A Framework for Analysing Service Operations', *European Management Journal*, 11(3): 271–82.

Bolton, R. and J. Drew (1991), 'A Multistage Model of Customers' Assessment of SQ and value', *Journal of Consumer Research*, 17: 375–84.

Boulding, W., A. Kalra, R. Staelin and V. Zeithaml (1993), 'A Dynamic Process Model of SQ: from Expectations to Behavioural Intentions', *Journal of Marketing Research*, 30: 7–27.

BS 7850 (1992), Part 1, *Total Quality Management: Guide to Management Principles*, London: British Standards Institution.

Buttle, F. (1996), 'SERVQUAL: Review, Critique, Research Agenda', *European Journal of Marketing*, 30(1): 8–32.

Buzzell, R. and B. Gale (1987), *The PIMS Principles*, New York: Free Press.

Cronin, J. and S. Taylor (1992), 'Measuring SQ: A Re-examination and Extension', *Journal of Marketing*, 56: 55–68.

Cronin, J. and S. Taylor (1994), 'SERVPERF versus SERVQUAL: Reconciling Performance-based and Perceptions-minus-expectations Measurement of SQ', *Journal of Marketing*, 58: 125–31.

Crosby, P. (1979), *Quality Is Free*, New York: McGraw-Hill.

Gronroos, C. (1984), 'A SQ model and its Marketing Implications', *European Journal of Marketing*, 18: 36–44.

Gronroos, C. (1988), 'SQ: the Six Criteria of Good Perceived SQ', *Review of Business*, 9(3): 10–13.

Kotler, P. (1997), *Marketing Management: Analysis, Planning, Implementation and Control*, 9th edn, Englewood Cliffs, NJ: Prentice Hall, Inc.

Kwon, W. and T. Lee (1994), 'Measuring SQ in Singapore Retail Banking', *Singapore Management Review*, 6(2): 1–24.

Le Blanc, G. and N. Nguyen (1988), 'Customers' Perceptions of Service Quality in Financial Institutions', *International Journal of Bank Marketing*, 6(4): 7–18.

Oliver, R. L. (1993), 'A Conceptual Model of SQ and Service Satisfaction: Compatible Goals, Different Concepts', *Advances in Services Marketing and Management*, 2: 65–85, Greenwich, CT: JAI Press.

Parasuraman, A., L. Berry and V. Zeithaml (1985), 'A Conceptual Model of SQ and its Implications for Future Research,' *Journal of Marketing*, 49: 41–50.

Parasuraman, A., L. Berry and V. Zeithaml (1988), 'SERVQUAL: a Multi-item Scale for Measuring Consumer Perceptions of SQ', *Journal of Retailing*, 64: 12–40.

Parasuraman, A., L. Berry and V. Zeithaml (1991), 'Perceived Service Quality as a Customer-based Performance Measure: an Empirical Examination of Organizational Barriers Using an Extended Service Quality Model', *Human Resource Management*, 30(3): 335–64.

Parasuraman, A., L. Berry and V. Zeithaml (1993), 'Research Note: More on Improving SQ Measurement', *Journal of Retailing*, 69: 140–7.

Parasuraman, A., L. Berry and V. Zeithaml (1994), 'Reassessment of Expectations as a Comparison Standard in Measuring SQ: Implications for Further Research', *Journal of Marketing*, 58: 111–24.

Peter, J. (1979), 'Reliability: A Review of Psychometric Basics and Recent Marketing Practices', *Journal of Marketing Research*, 16: 6–17.

Peters, J. (1999), 'Total SQ Management', *Managing SQ*, 29(1): 6–12.

Reicheld, F. and W. Sasser (1990), 'Zero Defections: Quality Comes to Service', *Harvard Business Review*, September–October, 105–11.

Robinson, S. (1999), 'Measuring SQ: Current Thinking and Future Requirements', *Marketing Intelligence & Planning*, 17(1): 21–32.

Rust, R. and A. Zahorik (1993), 'Customer Satisfaction, Customer Retention and Market Share', *Journal of Retailing*, 69(2): 193–215.

Rust, R. T. and R. Oliver (1994), *Service Quality*: London: Sage Publications.

Sabeq, S. (1988), *Fiqh Al-Sunah*, Cairo: At-Turath Publications.

Samuel, K. (1999), 'Change for the Better via ISO 9000 and TQM', *Management Decisions*, 37(4): 381–5.

Urban, G. and J. Hauser (1993), *Design and Marketing of New Products*, 2nd edn, Englewood Cliffs, NJ: Prentice Hall, Inc.

Wong, S. and C. Perry (1991), 'Customer Service Strategies in Financial Retailing', *International Journal of Bank Marketing*, 9(3): 11–16.

Zahorik, A. and R. Rust (1992), 'Modeling the Impact of SQ of Profitability: A Review', *Advances in Services Marketing and Management*, 49–64, Greenwich, CT: JAI Press.

Zeithaml, V. and M. Bitner (1996), *Services Management*, New York: McGraw-Hill.

CHAPTER 5: THE LENDING POLICIES OF ISLAMIC BANKS IN IRAN

Baillie, R. T. and T. Bollerslev (1994), 'Co-integration, Fractional Co-integration and Exchange Rate Dynamics', *Journal of Finance*, 49: 737–45.

Carter, H. and I. Partington (1979), *Applied Economics in Banking and Finance*, Oxford: Oxford University Press.

Crowder, W. J. and D. L. Hoffman (1996), 'The Long-run Relationship Between Nominal Interest Rates and Inflation: the Fisher Equation Revisited', *Journal of Money, Credit and Banking*, 28(1): 103–18.

Enders, Walter (1995), *Applied Econometric Time Series*, New York: John Wiley and Sons.

Gonzalo, J. (1994), 'Five Alternative Methods of Estimating Long-run Equilibrium Relationships', *Journal of Econometrics*, 60: 203–33.

Hendry, David F. (1995), *Dynamic Econometrics*, Oxford: Oxford University Press.

Johansen, S. (1988), 'Statistical Analysis of Co-integrating Vectors', *Journal of Economic Dynamics*, 12: 231–54.

Maddalla, G. S. (1992), *Introduction to Econometrics* (2nd edn), London: Prentice Hall International.

Murinde, V., K. Naser and R. S. O. Wallace (1995), 'Is it Prudent for Islamic Banks to Make Investment Decisions Without the Interest Rate Instrument?', *Research in Accounting in Emerging Economies*, 3: 123–48.

Phillips, P. C. B. and P. Perron (1988), 'Testing for a Unit Root in Time Series Regression', *Biometrika*, 75: 335–46.

Shirazi, Habib (ed.) (1990), *Islamic Banking*, London: Butterworths.

CHAPTER 6: EFFICIENCY IN ARABIAN BANKING

Aigner, D., C. Lovell and P. Schmidt (1977), 'Formulation and Estimation of Stochastic Frontier Production Function Models', *Journal of Econometrics*, (6) (May): 21–37.

Allen, R. and A. Rai (1996), 'Operational Efficiency in Banking: An International Comparison', *Journal of Banking & Finance*, 21: 655–72.

Altunbas, Y., E. Gardener and P. Molyneux (1996), 'Cost Economies and Efficiency in EU Banking Systems', *Journal of Economics and Business*, 48(2): 17–230.

Altunbas, Y., M. Liu, P. Molyneux and R. Seth (1999), 'Efficiency and Risk in Japanese banking', *Journal of Banking & Finance*, 24: 605–1628.

Altunbas, Y., L. Evans and P. Molyneux (2001a), 'Ownership and Efficiency in Banking', *Journal of Money, Credit and Banking*, 33(4): 926–54.

Altunbas, Y., E. P. M. Gardener, P. Molyneux and B. Moore (2001b), 'Efficiency in European Banking', *European Economic Review*, 45: 1931–55.

Aly, H., R. Grabowski, C. Pasurka and N. Rangan (1990), 'Technical, Scale, and Allocative Efficiencies in U.S. Banking: An Empirical Investigation', *The Review of Economics and Statistics*, 72: 211–18.

Barr, R., Seiford, L. and Siems, T. (1994), 'Forecasting bank failure: A Non-parametric Approach', *Recherches Economiques de Louvain*, 60: 411–29.

Battese, G. and T. Coelli (1992), 'Frontier Production Functions, Technical Efficiency and Panel Data: With Application to Paddy Farmers in India', *The Journal of Productivity Analysis*, 3: 153–69.

Battese, G. and T. Coelli (1995), 'A Model for Technical Inefficiency Effects in a Stochastic Frontier Production Function for Panel Data', *Empirical Economies*, 20: 325–32.

Bauer, P. and D. Hancock (1993), 'The Efficiency of the Federal Reserve in Providing Check Processing Services', *Journal of Banking & Finance*, 17: 287–311.

Berg, S., F. Forsund and N. Bukh (1995), 'Banking Efficiency in the Nordic Countries: a Few-country Malmquist Index Analysis', *mimeo*.

Berg, S., F. Forsund and E. Jansen (1992), 'Malmquist Indices of Productivity

Growth during the Deregulation of Norwegian Banking, 1980–89', *Scandinavian Journal of Economics*, 94 (Supplement): 211–28.

Bergendahl, G. (1998), 'DEA and Benchmarks – An Application to Nordic Banks', *Annals of Operations Research*, 82: 233–49.

Berger, A. (1995), 'The Profit-Structure Relationship in Banking-Tests of Market Power and Efficient-structure Hypothesis', *Journal of Money, Credit and Banking*, 27(2): 404–31.

Berger, A. and D. Humphrey (1992), 'Measurement and Efficiency Issues in Commercial Banking', in Zvi Griliches (ed.), *Output Measurement in the Services Sectors*, Chicago: National Bureau of Economic Research Studies in Income and Wealth, University of Chicago, 56: 245–79.

Berger, A. and D. Humphrey (1997), 'Efficiency of Financial Institutions: International Survey and Directions for Future Research', *European Journal of Operational Research*, 98: 175–212.

Berger, A. and L. Mester (1997), 'Inside the Black Box: What Explains Differences in the Efficiencies of Financial Institutions?' *Journal of Banking & Finance*, 21: 895–947.

Berger, A. and L. Mester (1999), 'What Explains the Dramatic Changes in Cost and Profit Performance of the U.S. Banking Industry?', Federal Reserve Board, Washington, DC: (*WP 13/1999*).

Berger, A. and R. DeYoung (1997), 'Problem Loans and Cost Efficiency in Commercial Banks', Federal Reserve Board, Washington, DC: (*WP 8/1997*).

Berger, A. and T. Hannan (1995), 'The Efficiency Cost of Market Power in the Banking Industry: A Test of the Quiet Life and Related Hypotheses', *The Review of Economics and Statistics*, 77: 454–65.

Berger, A., G. Hanweck and D. Humphrey (1993a), 'Bank Efficiency Derived from the Profit Function', *Journal of Banking & Finance*, 17: 317–47.

Berger, A., Leusner, J. and J. Mingo (1997b), 'The Efficiency of Bank Branches', *Journal of Monetary Economics*, 40: 141–62.

Berger, A., W. Hunter and S. Timme (1993b), 'The Efficiency of Financial Institutions: A Review and Preview of Research Past, Present, and Future', *Journal of Banking & Finance*, 17: 221–49.

Bhattacharya, A., C. Lovell and P. Sahay (1997), 'The Impact of Liberalisation on the Productive Efficiency of Indian Banks', *European Journal of Operational Research*, 98: 332–45.

Carbo, S., E. Gardener and J. William (1999), 'A Note on Technical Change in Banking: The Case of European Savings Banks', (Un-published), Institute of European Finance, University of Wales, Bangor.

Cebenoyan, A., E. Cooperman and C. Register (1993), 'Firm Inefficiency and the Regulatory Closure of S&Ls: An Empirical Investigation', *Review of Economics and Statistics*, 75: 540–5.

Chaffai, M. and M. Dietsch (1995), 'Should Banks be "Universal"? The Relationship Between Economies of Scope and Efficiency in the French Banking Industry', (*Working Paper*), University of Robert Schuman of Strasbourg, France.

Chalfant, J. and A. Gallant (1985), 'Estimating Substitution Elasticities with the Fourier Cost Function', *Journal of Econometrics*, 28: 205–22.

Chang, C., I. Hasan and W. Hunter (1998), 'Efficiency of Multinational Banks: An Empirical Investigation', Applied Financial Economics, 8: 1–8.

Clark, J. (1996), 'Economic Cost, Scale Efficiency, and Competitive Viability in Banking', *Journal of Money, Credit and Banking*, 28 (3): 342–64.

Coelli, T. (1996b), 'A Guide to Frontier Version 4.1: A Computer Program for Stochastic Frontier Production and Cost Function Estimation', Centre for Efficiency and Productivity Analysis (CEPA), Armidale, Australia: Department of Econometrics, University of New England (*WP 7/96*).

Coelli, T. (1996c), 'Measurement and Source of Technical Efficiency in Australian Coal-fired Electricity Generation', Centre for Efficiency and Productivity Analysis (CEPA), Armidale, Australia: Department of Econometrics, University of New England (*WP 1/96*).

Dietsch, M., and A. Lozano-Vivas (2000), 'How the Environment Determines Banking Efficiency: A Comparison Between French and Spanish Industries', *Journal of Banking and Finance*, 24: 985–1004.

Eastwood, B. and A. Gallant (1991), 'Adaptive Rules for Semi-nonparametric Estimators that Achieve Asymptotic Normality', *Economic Theory*, 7: 307–40.

Elbadawi, I., A. Gallant and G. Souza (1983), 'An Elasticity Can be Estimated Consistently Without *a Priori* Knowledge of Functional Form', *Econometrica*, 51: 1731–53.

Elyasiani, E. and S. Mehdian (1990a), 'Efficiency in Commercial Banking Industry, a Production Frontier Approach', *Applied Economics*, 22: 539–51.

Elyasiani, E. and S. Mehdian (1990b), 'A Non-parametric Approach to Measurement of Efficiency and Technological Change: the Case of Large US Banks', *Journal of Financial Services Research*, 4: 157–68.

Elyasiani, E. and S. Mehdian (1995), 'The Comparative Efficiency Performance of Small and Large US Commercial Banks in the Pre- and Post-deregulation Eras', *Applied Economics*, 27: 1069–79.

European Commission (1997), 'The Single Market Review', *Credit Institutions and Banking, Sub-series II: Impact on Services*, London: Kogan.

Evanoff, D. and R. Israilevich (1991), 'Productive Efficiency in Banking', *Economic Perspective, Federal Reserve of Chicago*, 15 (July/August): 11–32.

Ferrier, G., S. Grosskopf, K. Hayes and S. Yaisawarng (1993), 'Economies of Diversification in Banking Industry: A Frontier Approach', *Journal of Monetary Economics*, 31: 229–49.

Gallant, A. (1981), 'On the Bias in Flexible Functional Forms and Essentially Unbiased Form: The Fourier Flexible Form', *Journal of Econometrics*, 15: 211–45.

Gallant, A. (1982), 'Unbiased Determination of Production Technologies', *Journal of Econometrics*, 20: 285–324.

Gallant, A. and G. Souza (1991), 'On the Asymptotic Normality of Fourier Flexible Form Estimates', *Journal of Econometrics*, 50: 329–53.

Greene, W. (1990), 'A Gamma-distributed Stochastic Frontier Model', *Journal of Econometrics*, 46: 141–64.

Griffell-Tatjī, E. and C. Lovell (1997), 'Profits and Productivity', The Wharton School, University of Pennsylvania (*WP 18/97*).

Hermalin, B. and N. Wallace (1994), 'The Determinants of Efficiency and Solvency in Savings and Loans', *Rand Journal of Economics*, 25: 361–81.

Hughes, J., W. Lang, L. Mester and C. Moon (1995), 'Recovering Banking Technologies when Managers are not Risk-neutral', Conference on Bank Structure and Competition, Federal Reserve Board of Chicago (May): 349–68.

Hughes, J., L. Mester and C. Moon (1996a), 'Efficient Banking under Interstate Branching', *Journal of Money, Credit and Banking*, 28: 1045–71.

Hughes, J., L. Mester and C. Moon (1996b), 'Safety in Numbers? Geographic Diversification and Bank Insolvency Risk', (*Working Paper 96–14*), Federal Reserve Bank of Philadelphia.

Hughes, J., L. Mester and C. Moon (1997), 'Recovering Risky Technologies Using the Almost Ideal Demand System: An Application to U.S. Banking', (*Working Paper 97–8*), Federal Reserve Bank of Philadelphia.

Humphrey, D. and L. Pulley (1997), 'Banks' Responses to Deregulation: Profits, Technology, and Efficiency', *Journal of Money, Credit and Banking*, 29(1): 73–93.

Ivaldi, M., N. Ladoux, H. Ossard and M. Simioni (1996), 'Comparing Fourier and Translog Specification of Multiproduct Technology: Evidence from an Incomplete Panel of French Farmers', *Journal of Applied Economics*, 11: 649–67.

Jagtiani, J. and A. Khanthavit (1996), 'Scale and Scope Economies at Large Banks: Including Off-balance Sheet Products and Regulatory Effects (1984–1991)', *Journal of Banking & Finance*, 20: 1271–87.

Kaparakis, E., S. Miller and A. Noulas (1994), 'Short-run Cost Inefficiency of Commercial Banks: A Flexible Stochastic Frontier Approach', *Journal of Money, Credit and Banking*, 26: 875–93.

Kumbhakar, S., S. Ghosh and J. McGukin (1991), 'A Generalized Production Frontier Approach for Estimating Determinants of Inefficiency in U.S. Dairy Farms', *Journal of Business and Economic Statistics*, 9: 279–86.

Kwan, S. and R. Eisenbeis (1994), 'An Analysis of Inefficiencies in Banking: A Stochastic Cost Frontier Approach', Federal Reserve Bank of San Francisco, *Working Paper*, (December).

Leightner, E. and C. Lovell (1998), 'The Impact of Financial Liberalisation on the Performance of Thai Banks', *Journal of Economics and Business*, 50: 115–31.

Levine, R. (1997), 'Financial Development and Economic Growth: Views and Agenda', *Journal of Economic Literature*, 35(2): 688–726.

Levine, R. and S. Zervos (1998), 'Stock Markets, Banks, and Economic Growth', *American Economic Review*, 88(3): 537–58.

Levine, R., A. Demirguc-Kunt and T. Beck (1999), 'A New Database in Financial Development and Structure', *IMF Working Paper* (*WP/99/46*).

Levine, R. and N. Loyaza (2000), 'Financial Intermediation and Growth: Causality and Causes', *IMF Working Paper* (*WP/2000/118*).

Levine, R. and A. Demirguc-Kunt (2000), 'Bank-Based and Market-Based Financial Systems: Cross-Country Comparisons' *IMF Working Paper* (*WP/2000/212*).

McAllister, R. and D. McManus (1993), 'Resolving the Scale Efficiency Puzzle in Banking', *Journal of Banking & Finance*, 17: 389–405.

McKinnon, R. (1973), *Money and Capital in Economic Development*, Washington, DC: Brookings Institution.

Meeusen, W. and J. van den Broeck (1977), 'Efficiency Estimation from Cobb-Douglas Production Functions with Composed Error', *International Economic Review*, 18: 435–44.

Mester, L. (1993), 'Efficiency in the Savings and Loan Industry', *Journal of Banking & Finance*, 17: 267–86.

Mester, L. (1996a), 'A Study of Bank Efficiency Taking into Account Risk-Preferences', *Journal of Banking & Finance*, 20: 389–405.

Mester, L. (1996b), 'Measuring Efficiency at U.S. Banks: Accounting for Heterogeneity is Important', *European Journal of Operational Research*, 98: 230–43.

Mitchell, K. and N. Onvural (1996), 'Economies of Scale and Scope at Large Commercial Banks: Evidence from the Fourier-Flexible Functional Form', *Journal of Money, Credit and Banking*, 28(2): 178–99.

Pastor, J. (1995), 'How to Account for Environmental Effects in DEA: an Application to Bank Branches', *Working Paper*, University of Alicante, Spain.

Pi, L. and S. Timme (1993), 'Corporate Control and Bank Efficiency', *Journal of Banking & Finance*, 17: 515–30.

Pitt, M. and L. Lee (1981), 'Measurement and Sources of Technical Inefficiency in the Indonesian Weaving Industry', *Journal of Development Economics*, 9: 43–64.

Rajan, R. G. and L. Zingales (1998), 'Financial Dependence and Growth', *American Economic Review*, 88(3): 559–86.

Shaw, E. (1973), *Financial Deepening in Economic Development*, New York: Oxford University Press.

Sinkey, J. (1992), *Commercial Bank Financial Management in the Financial-Services Industry* (4th edn), New York: Macmillan Publishing Company.

Spong, K., R. Sullivan and R. De Young (1995), 'What Makes a Bank Efficient? A Look at Financial Characteristics and Bank Management and Ownership Structure', *Financial Industry Perspective*, Federal Reserve Bank of Kansas City.

Tolstov, G. (1962), *Fourier Series*, London: Prentice-Hall International.

Whalen, G. (1991), 'A Proportional Hazards Model of Bank Failure: An Examination of Its Usefulness as an Early Warning Tool', *Economic Review*, Federal Reserve Bank of Cleveland Quarter 1, 20–9.

Wheelock, D. and P. Wilson (1995), 'Explaining Bank Failures: Deposit Insurance, Regulation, and Efficiency', *Review of Economics and Statistics*, 77: 689–700.

White, H. (1980), 'A Heteroscedasticity Consistent Covariance Matrix Estimator and a Direct Test of Heteroscedasticity', *Econometrica*, 48: 817–18.

William, J. and E. Gardener (2000), 'Efficiency and European Regional Banking', Unpublished, Bangor: University of Wales.

Zaim, O. (1995), 'The Effect of Financial Liberalisation on the Efficiency of Turkish Commercial Banks', *Applied Financial Economics*, 5: 257–64.

CHAPTER 7: DETERMINANTS OF ISLAMIC BANKING PROFITABILITY

Aggarwal, R. and T. Yousef (2000), 'Islamic Banks and Investment Financing,' *Journal of Money, Credit and Banking*, 32(1): 93–120.

Ahmed, Khurshid (1981), *Studies in Islamic Economics*, Leicester: The Islamic Foundation.

Ahmed, Ziauddin, Munawar Iqbal and M. Fahim Khan (1983), *Fiscal Policy and Resource Allocation in Islam*, Islamabad: Institute of Policy Studies.

Bartholdy, J., G. Boyle and R. Stover (1997), 'Deposit Insurance, Bank Regulation and Interest Rates: Some International Evidence.' *Memo*, University of Otago, New Zealand.

Bashir, A. (1999), 'Risk and Profitability Measures in Islamic Banks: The Case of Two Sudanese Banks', *Islamic Economic Studies*, 6(2): 1–24.

Bashir, A. (2000), 'Determinants of Profitability and Rates of Return Margins in Islamic Banks: Some Evidence From the Middle East', *Mimeo*, Grambling State University.

Bashir, A., A. Darrat and O. Suliman (1993), 'Equity Capital, Profit Sharing Contracts And Investment: Theory and Evidence', *Journal of Business Finance and Accounting*, 20(5): 639–51.

Berger, A. (1995), 'The Relationship Between Capital and Earnings in Banking', *Journal of Money, Credit and Banking*, 27: 432–56.

Bourke, P. (1989), 'Concentration and Other Determinants of Bank Profitability in Europe, North America and Australia', *Journal of Banking & Finance*, 13: 65–79.

Boyd, J. and D. Runkle (1993), 'Size and Performance of Banking Firms: Testing the Prediction of the Theory', *Journal of Monetary Economics*, 31: 47–67.

Demirguc-Kunt, A. and E. Detragiache (1998), 'The Determinants of Banking Crises in Developing and Developed Countries', *IMF Staff Papers*, 45(1): 81–109.

Demirguc-Kunt, A., R. Levine and H. G. Min (1998), 'Opening to Foreign Banks: Issues of Stability, Efficiency, and Growth', in The Implications of Globalization of World Financial Markets (Conference Proceedings: The Bank of Korea, Seoul).

Demirguc-Kunt, A. and H. Huizinga (1997), 'Determinants of Commercial Bank Interest Margins and Profitability: Some International Evidence', *Working Paper*, Development Research Group, Washington, DC: World Bank.

Demirguc-Kunt, A. and V. Maksimovic (1996), 'Stock Market Development and Financing Choices of Firms', *The World Bank Economic Review*, 10(2): 341–69.

Goldberg, L. and A. Rai (1996), 'The Structure-Performance Relationship for European Banking', *Journal of Banking & Finance*, 20: 745–71.

Hassan, M. Kabir (1999), 'Islamic Banking in Theory and Practice: The Experience of Bangladesh', *Managerial Finance* (published in the UK), 25(5): 60–113.

IBCA (2002), BankScope Database, New York: CD-ROM Bureau, Van Dyck.

IFC (2002), Emerging Market Database, Washington, DC: CD-ROM.

IMF (2000), 'Macroprodential Indicators of Financial System Soundness.' *Occasional Paper No.192.*

IMF (2001), 'Macroprodential Analysis: Selected Aspects', *Background Paper*.

IMF (2002), *International Financial Statistics Yearbook*, Washington, DC: CD-ROM.

Karsen, I. (1982), 'Islam and Financial Intermediation', *IMF Staff Papers*.

Karsen, I. and A. Mirakhor (1987), *Theoretical Studies in Islamic Banking and Finance*: Houston: IRIS Books.

Khan, M. (1986), 'Islamic Interest Free Banking: A Theoretical Analysis', *IMF Staff Papers*.

Kim, S. B. and R. Moreno (1994), 'Stock Prices and Bank Lending Behavior in Japan', *Economic Review* (Federal Reserve Bank of San Francisco), 1: 31–42.

Levine, Ross (1996), 'Foreign Banks, Financial Development, and Economic Growth', in Claude Barfield (ed.), *International Financial Markets*, Washington, DC: The American Enterprise Institute.

Molyneux, P. and J. Thornton (1992), 'Determinants of European Bank Profitability: A Note', *Journal of Banking and Finance*, 16: 1173–8.

Schranz, M. (1993), 'Takeovers Improve Firm Performance: Evidence from the Banking Industry', *Journal of Political Economy*, 101(2): 299–326.

Wilson, R. (1990), *Islamic Financial Markets*, London: Routledge.

Zaher, Tarek and M. Kabir Hassan (2001), 'A Comparative Literature Survey of Islamic Finance and Banking', *Financial Markets, Institutions and Instruments*, 10(4): 155–99.

CHAPTER 8: ALLOCATIVE AND TECHNICAL INEFFICIENCY IN SUDANESE ISLAMIC BANKS: AN EMPIRICAL INVESTIGATION

Abdullah, N. and A. Elzahi (2003), 'A Decompositional Analysis of the Sudanese Islamic Banks TFP Growth into Its Source Components', *Tafakur, Aljazeera* University of Sudan, 5(2): 1–28.

Bashir, Abdel-Hameed M. (1999), 'Risk and Profitability Measures in Islamic Banks: The case of Two Sudanese Banks', *Islamic Economic Studies*, 6(2): 1–15.

Berger, A. N. and D. B. Humphrey (1991), 'The Dominance of Inefficiencies over Scale and Product Mix Economies in Banking', *Journal of Monetary Economics*, 28: 117–48.

Berger, A. N. and D. B. Humphrey (1993), 'Bank Scale Economies, Mergers, Concentration, and Efficiency: The U.S. Experience', *Revue Economique Financière*, 27: 123–54. This paper was translated into English at the Wharton School, University of Pennsylvania.

Berger, A. N. and D. B. Humphrey (1997), 'Efficiency of Financial Institutions: International Survey and Directions for Future Research', *European Journal of Operational Research*, 98: 175–212.

Berger, A. N., W. C. Hunter and S. G. Timme (1993), 'The Efficiency of Financial Institutions: A Review and Preview of Past, Present, and Future', *Journal of Banking and Finance*, 17: 221–49.

Ebrahim, M. Shahid and Tan Kai Joo (2001), 'Islamic Banking in Brunei Darussalam', *International Journal of Social Economics*, 28(4): 314–37.

Elzahi, A. (2002), 'The X-efficiency of the Sudanese Islamic Banks', Unpublished Ph.D thesis, International Islamic University Malaysia.

Jondrow, J., C. A. Knox Lovell, I. S. Materov and J. Schmidt (1982), 'On the Estimation of Technical Inefficiency in the Stochastic Frontier Production Function Mode', *Journal of Econometrics*, 19: 233–38.

Mitchell, Karlyn and Nur M. Onvural (1996), 'Economies of Scale and Scope at Large Commercial Banks: Evidence from the Fourier Flexible Functional Form', *Journal of Money, Credit and Banking*, 28(2): 178–99.

Samad, Abdus (1999), 'Comparative Efficiency of Islamic Bank vs. Conventional Banks in Malaysia', *IIUM Journal of Economics & Management*, 7(1): 1–12.

Sengupta, J. (2000), 'Efficiency Analysis by Stochastic Data Envelopment Analysis', *Applied Economics Letters*, 7: 379–83.

CHAPTER 9: ISLAMIC MORTAGES IN THE UNITED KINGDOM

Dar, H. A. (2004), 'Islamic House Financing in the United Kingdom: Problems, Challenges and Prospects', *Review of Islamic Economics*, 12: 47–71.

Datamonitor (2002), *Islamic Mortgages*, Datamonitor, London.

ONS (2004), *UK2004 – The Official Yearbook of the United Kingdom of Great Britain and Northern Ireland*, Office of National Statistics, London.

CHAPTER 10: WEALTH CREATION THROUGH *TAKĀFUL* (ISLAMIC INSURANCE)

ACLI (2001), *Life Insurance Fact Book*, Washington, DC: American Council of Life Insurance.

Aglietta, M. (2000), 'Shareholder Value and Corporate Governance: Some Tricky Questions', *Economy and Society*, 29(1): 146–59.

Anwar, Muhammad (1994), 'Comparative Study of Insurance and *Takāful* (Islamic Insurance)', *The Pakistan Development Review*, 33(4), Part II, Winter: 1315–30.

Bhatty, M. A. (2000), 'Insurance and *Takāful*', *New Horizon*, 102: 10–11.

Bhatty, M. A. (2001), 'Takāful Industry: Global Profile and Trends', *New Horizon*, 108: 10–12.

Billah, M. M. (2001), *Principles & Practices of Takāful and Insurance Compared*, Malaysia: GECD Printing Sdn. Bhd.

BIRT (1996), *Takāful (Islamic Insurance) Concept & Operational System from The Practitioner's Perspective*, Malaysia: BIMB Institute of Research and Training Sdn. Bhd.

Covick, O. E. and M. K. Lewis (1997), 'Insurance, Superannuation and Managed Funds', in M. K. Lewis and R. H. Wallace (eds), *The Australian Financial System: Evolution, Policy and Practice*, Melbourne: Addison, Wesley, Longman, pp. 221–93.

Dhareer, Al Siddiq Mohammad Al-Ameen (1997), *Al-gharar in Contracts and its effects on Contemporary Transactions*, Jeddah: Islamic Development Bank, Islamic Research and Training Institute.

El-Gamal, Mahmoud Amin (2000), *A Basic Guide to Contemporary Islamic Banking and Finance*, Indiana: ISNA.

Fisher, O. C. (2002), 'The Missing Link: *Takāful* and Its Importance for Islamic Finance', *New Horizon*, 123: 3–7.

Hassan, M. K. (2001), 'Nuances of Islamic Mutual Funds', *Islamic Horizons*, 30(3): 16–18.

Institute of Islamic Banking and Insurance (1999), *Directory of Islamic Insurance (Takāful)*, London: Institute of Islamic Banking & Insurance.

Ismail, Azman (1998), 'Insurance & Sharī'ah (2/2) Takāful: A Practical Alternative', *Nida'ul Islam (http://www.islam.org.au)*, April–May, 1–4.

Lewis, M. K. (1992), 'Balance Sheets of Financial Intermediaries', in P. Newman, M. Milgate and J. Eatwell (eds), *New Palgrave Dictionary of Money and Finance* (1), London: Macmillan, pp. 120–2.

Lewis, M. K. and L. M. Algaoud (2001), *Islamic Banking*, Cheltenham: Edward Elgar.

Murvat, S. K. (1992), 'The Legal Framework for Islamic Banking: Pakistan's Experience', in R. C. Effros (ed.), *Current Legal Issues Affecting Central Banking* (1), Washington: International Monetary Fund.

Muslehuddin, M. (1982), *Insurance and Islamic Law*, Delhi: Markazi Maktaba Islāmī.

OECD (1992), *Insurance and other Financial Services Structural Trends*, Paris: Organization for Economic Cooperation and Development.

OECD (1998), *Institutional Investors in the New Financial Landscape*, Paris: Organization for Economic Cooperation and Development.

Sharif, Kamarudin (2000), '*Muḍarabah* and *Tabarru'* in *Takāful* Contracts', International Conference on takāful/Islamic Insurance, 22–23 June, Kuala Lumpur.

Siddiqi, M. N. (1985), *Insurance in an Islamic Economy*, Leicester: The Islamic Foundation.

Taylor, D. (2002), '*Takāful Ta'āwuni*', *New Horizon*, 123: 11–13.

Wahib, Rusil Bin (1999), 'Islamic Takāful Insurance', *New Horizon*, Part 1 (86): 10–12; Part 2 (87): 16–17; Part 3 (88): 10–12.

Yaquby, Nizam (2000), 'Between Sharī'ah Scholars and *Takāful* Practitioners: Bridging the Gap', International Conference on *Takāful*/Islamic Insurance, 22–23 June, Kuala Lumpur.

Yusof, D. M. F. (2001), 'An Overview of the *Takāful* Industry', *New Horizon*, March: 9–11.

CHAPTER 11: TOWARDS OPTIMAL RISK MANAGEMENT FOR PROFIT-SHARING FINANCE

Al-Dharir, Siddique (1976), *Al-gharar wa Athruhu 'ala al-'Uqud, (gharar and its Effect on Contracts)* , Dar Al-Nashr Al-Thaqafiya, Cairo (Arabic).

Chapra, M. Umer (1985), *Towards a Just Monetary System*, Leicester: The Islamic Foundation.

Chapra, M. Umer (2002), *The Future of Economics: an Islamic Perspective*, Leicester: The Islamic Foundation.

Duniya, M. Shawqi (1990), *Al-Ju'ālah wa al-istiṣnā'*, Jeddah: Islamic Development Bank, IRTI.

Edwards, R. and Cindy Ma (1992), *Futures & Options*, New York: McGraw-Hill International Editions.

Faydhuallh, F. Moahammed (1986), *Nadhariyyat al-Dhaman fil fiqh il Islāmī (Theory of ḍamān in Islamic Jurisprudence)*, Kuwait: Dar Al-Turath Library.

Fiqh Encyclopedia (*Al-Mawsū'ah Al-fiqhiyyah*) (1993), 28, Kuwait: Ministry of Aawqāf.

Hammad, Nazih (1984), *Bay' al- kālī' bi al- kālī'*, King Abdulaziz University, Jeddah: Centre for Research in Islamic Economics.

Hamoud, Sami Hasan (1982), *Tatwir Al-'amal Al-Masrafiyyah lima Yattafiq wa Al-Sharī'ah Al-Islamiyyah (Developing Banking Services in Conformity with Islamic Sharī'ah)*, 2nd edn, Amman.

Hassan, Hussain Hamid (1992), 'The Jurisprudence of Financial Transactions', in *Lectures in Islamic Economics*, Jeddah: IDB/IRTI.

Haugen, Robert A. (1986), *Modern Investment Theory*, New Jersey: Prentice-Hall.

Ibn Rushd al-Qurtubi (undated), *Bidāyat al-Mujtahid wa Nihāyat al-Muqtaṣid*, Abu Abdelrahman Abdelkarim ibn 'Aju (ed), al-Matabah al-Tawfiqiyyah, 2.

Ibn Taimiyyah, *Mujmu'āt fatāwā ibn Taimiyyah*, (undated) collected by Abdulrahman ibn Mohammad ibn al-Qasim, Saudi Arabia: Ministry of Islamic Affairs.

Iqbal, Munawar (ed.) (2001), *Islamic Banking and Finance: Current Developments in Theory and Practice*, Leicester: The Islamic Foundation.

Iqbal, Munawar and David Llewellyn (eds) (2002), *Islamic Banking and Finance: New Perspectives on Profit Sharing and Risk*, Cheltenham: Edward Elgar.

Kamali, M. Hashim (2000), *Islamic Commercial Law*, Cambridge: Islamic Texts Society.

Khan, Mohsin S. and Abbas Mirakhor (eds) (1987), *Theoretical Studies in Islamic Banking and Finance* Houston, TX: The Institute for Research and Islamic Studies.

Khan, Tariqullah (1995), 'Demand and Supply of Mark-up and PLS Funds in Islamic Banking: Some Alternative Explanations', *Islamic Economic Studies*, 3(1): 39–78.

Kola, Robert W., and Ricardo J. Rodriguez (1992), *Financial Management*, Baltimore DC: Heath and Company.

Masood, Waqar (1984), *Towards an Interest-Free Islamic Economic System*, Leicester: The Islamic Foundation.

Muhiuddin, Ahmed (1986): *"Amal Sharikāt Al-Iṣtithmār Al-Islamiyyah fil Sūq Al-'Ālamiyyah (The Working of Islamic Investment Companies in International Markets)*, Bahrain: Al-Baraka Bank.

Presley, John R. and John G. Sessions (1994), 'Islamic Economics: The Emergence of a New Paradigm', *Economic Journal* (May).

Siddiqi, M. N. (1983), *Banking Without Interest*, Leicester: The Islamic Foundation.
Siddiqi, M. N. (1996) *Issues in Islamic Banking*, Leicester: The Islamic Foundation.
Siddiqi, M. N. (2000), 'Islamic Banks: Concepts, Precepts, and Prospects', *Review of Islamic Economics* 9: 21–36.
Tag El-Din, Seif I. (1990), 'Risk-aversion Moral Hazard, and the Financial Islamization Policy', *Review of Islamic Economics* 1: 49–66.
Tag El-Din, Seif I. (1992), 'Debt and Equity in a Primary Financial Market: A Theory with Islamic Implications', *Journal of King Abdulaziz University, Islamic Economics*, 4: 3–33.
Tag El-Din, Seif I. (1996), 'Characterising the Stock Exchange from an Islamic Perspective', *Journal of King Abdulaziz University, Islamic Economics* 8: 31–52.
Tag El-Din, Seif I. (2001), 'Islamic Futures Market and the Modern Forward Contract', a working paper presented at the Intensive Orientation Course on Islamic Economics Banking and Finance, held at The Islamic Foundation, Leicester, 26–30 September.
Tag El-Din, Seif I. (2002),'Variable Versus Fixed Return Modes: An analysis of choice under financial risk', *Review of Islamic Economics*, 11: 5.
The International Association of Islamic Banks (1997), *Directory Of Islamic Banks and Financial Institutions*, Jeddah: IAIB.
Uzair, Ahmed (1955), *An Outline of Interest Less Banking*, Karachi and Dhaka: Raihan Publications.
Warde, Ibrahim (2000), *Islamic Finance in the Global Economy*, Edinburgh, Edinburgh University Press.
Weitzman, M. L. (1984), *The Share Economy*, Harvard: Harvard University Press.
Wilson, Rodney (1990), *Islamic Financial Markets*, London and New York: Routledge.

CHAPTER 12: STOCK MARKET OPERATION AND EQUITY PRICE DETERMINATION IN AN ECONOMY WITH AN INTEREST-FREE BANKING SYSTEM: THE CASE OF IRAN

Binswanger, M. (2000), 'Stock Returns and Real Activity: Is There Still a Connection?', *Applied Financial Economics*, 10: 379–87.
Chapra, M. U. (1985), *Towards a Just Monetary System*, Leicester: The Islamic Foundation.
Chapra, M. U. (1992), *Islam and the Economic Challenge*, Leicester: The Islamic Foundation.
Chapra, M. U. (2000), 'Is It Necessary to have Islamic Economics?', *Journal of Socio-Economics*, 29(1): 17–21.
Cheung, Y. W. and K. S. Lai (1999), 'Macroeconomic Determinants of Long-

term Stock Market Comovements among Major EMS Countries', *Applied Financial Economics*, 9: 73–85.

Ely, D. P. and K. J. Robinson (1997), 'Are Stocks a Hedge Against Inflation? International Evidence Using a Long-run Approach', *Journal of International Money and Finance*, 16(1): 141–67.

Eslamloueyan, Karim (2002), 'Globalization, Exchange Rate Regime, and Capital Movement in other countries in comparison with Iran', in (Farsi), *Collection of Papers*, the Twelfth Annual Conference on Monetary and Exchange Policies, Central Bank of Islamic Republic of Iran, Tehran, Iran.

Groenwold, N., G. O'Rourke and S. Thomas (1997), 'Stock Returns and Inflation: A Macro Analysis', *Applied Financial Economics*, 7: 127–36.

Harris, R. I. D. (1995), *Using Cointegration Analysis in Econometric Modeling*, Harvester Wheatsheaf: Padstow Press.

Kia, Amir (forthcoming), 'Forward-Looking Agents and Macroeconomic Determinants of the Equity Price in a Small Open Economy', (*Applied Financial Economics*).

Marone, Heloisa (2003), 'Small African Stock Markets – The Case of the Lusaka Stock Exchange', *IMF Working Paper, WP/03/6*, Washington, DC: International Monetary Fund.

Mills, P. S. and J. R. Presley (1999), *Islamic Finance: Theory and Practice*, Basingstoke: Macmillan Press.

Pesaran, M. Hashem and Bahram Pesaran (1997), *Working With Microfit 4.0: Interactive Econometric Analysis*, Windows Version, Cambridge, London.

Pesaran, M. Hashem and Yongcheol Shin (1999), 'An Autoregressive Distributed Lag Modeling Approach to Cointegration Analysis', in S. Strom (ed.), *Econometrics and Economic Theory in the 20th Century: The Ragnar Frisch Centennial Symposium*, Chapter 11. Cambridge: Cambridge University Press.

Pesaran, M. Hashem, Yongcheol Shin and Richard J. Smith (2001), 'Bound Testing Approaches to the Analysis of Level Relationships', *Journal of Applied Econometrics*, 16: 289–326.

CHAPTER 13: THE DEMAND FOR *MUSHĀRAKAH* IN URBAN EGYPT BY SMALL BUSINESS AS A TEST OF THE PECKING ORDER HYPOTHESIS

Al-Harran, S. (1993), *Islamic Finance, Partnership Financing*, Petaling Jaya: Pelaunduk Publications.

Baydas, M. M. and D. H. Graham (1995), 'Capital Structure Determinants Among Manufacturing Enterprises: The Case of Developing Financial Markets in Ghana and the Gambia. Economics and Sociology', Occasional Paper 2205, Columbus, Ohio: The Ohio State University.

Baydas, M. M., J. M. Porges, S. P. Wade and J. L. Walker (1997), 'Financial Reform for Small Business Development in Egypt', *Development Economic Policy Reform Analysis (DEPRA) Project*, Cairo.

Buckley, G. (1997), 'Microfinance in Africa: Is It Either the Problem or the Solution?' *World Development*, 25(7): 1081–93.

Chapra, M. U. (2000), 'Is it Necessary to Have Islamic Economics?', *The Journal of Socio-Economics*, 29(1): 21–37.

Choudhury, M. A. (2001), 'Islamic Venture Capital a Critical Examination', *Journal of Economic Studies*, 28(1): 14–33.

Cosh, A. and A. Hughes (1994), 'Size, Financial Structure and Profitability: UK Companies in the 1980s', in A. Hughes and D. J. Storey (eds), *Finance and the Small Firm*, London: Routledge, pp. 18–63.

Dar, H. A. and J. R. Presley (1999), 'Attitudes Towards Islamic Finance: an Update of Empirical Evidence', A paper prepared for the Seventh International Orientation Seminar on Islamic Economics, Banking and Finance, Leicester, UK: The Islamic Foundation.

Dar, H. A. and J. R. Presley (2000), 'Lack of Profit and Loss Sharing in Islamic Banking: Management and Control Imbalances', *International Journal of Islamic Financial Services*, 2(2): 3–18.

El-Din, S. I. T. (1991), 'Risk Aversion, Moral Hazard and Financial Islamization Policy', *Review of Islamic Economics*, 1(1): 49–66.

El-Gamal, M. A. (2000), 'A Basic Guide to Contemporary Islamic Banking and Finance', available from: *http://www.ruf.rice.edu/~elgamal/files/primer.pdf*.

Hamilton, R. T. and M. A. Fox (1998), 'The Financing Preferences of Small Firm Owners', *International Journal of Entrepreneurial Behaviour and Research*, 4(3): 239–49.

Howorth, C. (1999), 'The Demand for Finance: Exploring the Pecking Order Hypothesis within Small Firm Case Studies', in *Proceedings of International Conference on Funding Gaps Controversies*, UK: University of Warwick.

International Association of Islamic Banks (1996), Cairo, Egypt: IAIB.

Iqbal, M. and David T. Llewellyn (eds), *Islamic Banking and Finance: New Perspective on Profit-Sharing and Risk*, Cheltenham: Edward Elgar, pp. 40–56.

Islam, R., J. D. V. Pischke and J. M. D. Waard (eds) (1994), 'Small Firms Informally Financed: Studies from Bangladesh', Washington, DC: The World Bank.

Jalaludin, A. (2002), 'Attitudes Towards and Probability of Applying Profit/loss Sharing Method of Finance by Western Small Business Firms: an Analysis of Survey Results', in *Proceedings of the Fourth International Conference on Islamic Economics and Banking: Islamic Finance: Challenges and Opportunities in the Twenty-First Century*, UK: Loughborough University, pp. 315–28.

Kamal, Naser, A. Jamal and K. Al-Khatib (1999), 'Islamic Banking: a Study of

Customer Satisfaction and Preferences in Jordan', *International Journal of Bank Marketing*, 17(3): 135–50.

McMahon, R. G. P., S. Holmes, P. J. Hutchinson and D. M. Forsaith (1993), 'Small Business Financial Management: Theory and Practice', Australia: Harcourt Brace & Company.

Myers, S. C. (1984), 'The Capital Structure Puzzle', *The Journal of Finance*, 29(3): 575–92.

Ozer, B. and S. Yamak (2000), 'Self-Sustaining Pattern of Finance in Small Businesses: Evidence from Turkey', *International Journal of Hospitality Management*, 19: 261–73.

Read, L. (1998), *The Financing of Small Business: A Comparative Study of Male and Female Business Owner*, London: Routledge.

Romano, C. A., G. A. Tanewski and K. X. Smyrnios (2000), 'Capital Structure Decision Making: a Model for Family Business', *Journal of Business Venturing*, 16: 285–310.

Smith, J. A. (1997), 'The Behaviour and Performance of Young Micro Firms: Evidence from New Businesses in Scotland', *Report No. 9711*, St Andrews, Scotland: Centre for Research into Industry, Enterprise, Finance and the Firm (CRIEFF).

Wright, J.W., Bandar Al-Hajjar and John Presley (1996), 'Attitudes, Culture and Capital Distribution in Saudi Arabia', in J. W. Wright (ed.), *Business and Economic Development in Saudi Arabia*, Macmillan, pp. 127–39.

Usmani, M. T. (2002), *An Introduction to Islamic Finance*. The Hague: Kluwer Law International.

Appendices

APPENDIX I: FIVE DIMENSIONS OF SQ

Tangibles	The appearance of physical facilities, equipment, personnel and communication materials. • Physical facilities and appearance of personnel; • Tools or equipment used to provide the service; • Physical representations of the service, such as a plastic credit card.
Reliability	The ability to perform service dependably and accurately. It includes: • Accuracy in billing • Performing the service at the designated time.
Responsiveness	The willingness to help customers and provide prompt service. It may involve: • Mailing a transaction slip immediately; • Calling the customer back quickly; • Giving prompt service (for example, setting up appointments quickly).
Assurance	The knowledge and courtesy of employees and their ability to convey trust and confidence. *Courtesy* (politeness, respect, consideration and friendliness; also clean and neat appearance of public contact personnel). *Competence* (knowledge and skill of the contact personnel, knowledge and skill of operational support personnel and research capability of the organisation). *Communication* (explaining the service itself and how much the service will cost, explaining the trade-offs between service and cost, and assuring the consumer that a problem will be handled).
Empathy	The caring, individualised attention the institution provides its customers. *Security* may involve: • Physical safety; • Financial security and confidentiality. *Credibility* involves: • Company name and reputation; • Personal characteristics of the contact personnel; • The degree of hard sell involved in interactions with the customer. *Access* may include: • The service is easily accessible by telephone. • Waiting time to receive service is not extensive. • Convenient hours of operation and convenient location of service facility.

Source: Adapted from Parasuraman et al. (1985, 1988, 1990, 1991, 1993, 1994).

APPENDIX 2: SERVQUAL 22-ITEMS

1. Modern-looking equipment.
2. Visually appealing physical facilities.
3. Neat appearance by employees.
4. Visually appealing materials associated with the service.
5. Keeping a promise to do something by a certain time.
6. Showing sincere interest in solving customers' problems.
7. Performing the service correctly the first time.
8. Providing the service at the time the service was promised.
9. Insisting on error-free records.
10. Employees telling customers exactly what services will be performed.
11. Employees giving prompt service to customers.
12. Employees always willing to help customers.
13. Employees are never too busy to ignore customers' requests.
14. The behaviour of employees instilling confidence in their customers.
15. Customers feeling safe in their transactions.
16. Employees being consistently courteous with their customers.
17. Employees having the knowledge to answer customers' questions.
18. Giving customers individual attention.
19. Providing operating hours convenient to all customers.
20. Employees giving customers personal attention.
21. Having the customers' best interest at heart.
22. Employees understanding the specific needs of their customers.

APPENDIX 3: SURVEY RESULTS

Dimensions	*Items*	*Average importance*	*Percent-age*	*Items rank*	*Dim. rank*
Compliance	1. Run on Islamic law and principles	4.60	93%	1	α=0.70
	2. No interest paid nor taken on savings and loans	3.99	73%	3	M=3.95 ra=1
	3. Provision of Islamic products and services	4.62	91%	2	
	4. Provision of interest-free loans	2.71	28%	34	
	5. Provision of profit-sharing investment products	3.83	68%	7	
Assurance	6. Polite and friendly staff	3.40	54%	23	α=0.81
	7. Provider of financial advice	3.04	36%	30	M=3.51
	8. Interior comfort of KFH	3.64	63%	11	ra=2
	9. Ease of access to account information	3.47	61%	17	
	10. Knowledgeable and experienced management team	3.83	72%	6	
Reliability	11. Convenience (short time for service anywhere)	3.41	53%	22	α=0.79 M=3.41
	12. Integrated value-added services	2.96	33%	32	ra=5
	13. Wide range of products and services provided	3.78	68%	8	
	14. Security of transactions	3.45	54%	19	
	15. More tills open at peak times	3.33	50%	27	
Tangible	16. External appearance	3.67	60%	12	α=0.89
	17. Speed and efficiency of transactions	3.37	52%	26	M=3.38
	18. Opening hours of operations	3.53	54%	15	ra=6
	19. Counter partitions in bank and its branches	3.66	59%	13	
	20. Overdraft privileges on current accounts	2.65	29%	33	
Empathy	21. Bank location (easy to get to the bank	3.72	62%	10	α=0.77 M=3.47
	22. Bank's familiarity, reputation and image	3.76	66%	9	ra=4
	23. Bank size in assets and capital	3.08	39%	28	
	24. Parking available	3.39	48%	25	
	25. Confidentiality of bank	3.53	47%	16	
	26. Confidence in bank's management	3.84	72%	5	
	27. Product and service profitability	3.44	54%	20	
	28. Lower service charge	2.96	39%	31	

Dimensions	*Items*	*Average importance*	*Percent-age*	*Items rank*	*Dim. rank*
Responsiveness	29. Knowledge of customer's business or willing to help	3.03	33%	29	α=0.79 M=3.49 ra=3
	30. Able to fulfil individual/personal needs	3.44	55%	21	
	31. Way staff treat customers	3.64	59%	14	
	32. Availability of credit on favourable terms	3.40	54%	24	
	33. Branching	3.94	74%	4	
	34. Fast and efficient counter services	3.49	53%	18	

α=alpha, M=the average dimension mean, ra=dimension rank based on importance percentage.

APPENDIX 4: CARTER ITEMS' WEIGHTS

Items	*Dimension*	*Weight*	*Process/ Outcome*
1. Run on Islamic law and principles	Comp.	92	P
2. Provision of Islamic products and services	Comp.	92	P/O
3. No interest paid nor taken on savings and loans	Comp.	80	P
4. Branching	Respon.	79	P/O
5. Confidence in bank's management	Empathy	77	O
6. Provision of profit-sharing investment products	Comp.	77	P/O
7. Knowledgeable and experienced management team	Assurance	76	O
8. Wide range of products and services provided	Reliability	75.6	O
9. Bank's familiarity, reputation and image	Empathy	75.2	O
10. Ease of access to account information	Assurance	75	P
11. Bank location (easy to get to the bank)	Empathy	74.4	P/O
12. External appearance	Tangible	73.4	O
13. Interior comfort of KFH	Assurance	73	P/O
14. Counter partitions in bank and its branches	Tangible	73	O
15. Way staff treat customers	Respon.	72.8	P
16. Opening hours of operations	Tangible	71	P
17. Confidentiality of bank	Empathy	70.6	O
18. Fast and efficient counter services	Respon.	69.8	P
19. Security of transactions	Reliability	69	P
20. Able to fulfil individual/personal needs	Respon.	68.8	P
21. Product and service profitability	Empathy	68.8	P/O
22. Polite and friendly staff	Assurance	68	P
23. Convenience (short time for service anywhere)	Reliability	68	P
24. Availability of credit on favourable terms	Respon.	68	P
25. Parking available	Empathy	67.8	P/O
26. Speed and efficiency of transactions	Tangible	67.4	P
27. More tills open at peak times	Reliability	66.6	P
28. Bank size in assets and capital	Empathy	61.6	O
29. Provider of financial advice	Assurance	61	P
30. Knowledge of customer's business or willing to help	Respon.	60.6	O
31. Integrated value-added services	Reliability	59	P
32. Lower service charge	Empathy	59	P/O
33. Provision of interest-free loans	Comp.	54	P
34. Overdraft privileges on current accounts	Tangible	53	P

APPENDIX 5: RANKING OF SQ DIMENSIONS BY KFH'S CUSTOMERS

SQ Dimension	*Relative weight based on Compliance av. 3.95*	*Relative weight based on the highest scale point (5)*
Compliance	100	79
Assurance	89	70
Responsiveness	88	69.8
Empathy	87	69.4
Reliability	86	68.2
Tangible	85	67.6

APPENDIX 6: MAXIMUM LIKELIHOOD ESTIMATES OF THE PREFERRED COST FUNCTION

	The variables (all are logged)	*Coefficient*	*Standard-error*	*t-ratio*
α		115.71	0.97	118.76
γ1	lny1	0.54	0.54	1.00
γ2	lny2	0.78	0.90	0.87
γ3	lny3	0.17	0.38	0.44
β1	Lnw1/w3	-14.15	0.65	-21.92
β2	lnw2/w3	28.76	0.45	63.58
γ11	lny1lny1	0.08	0.08	1.05
γ12	lny1lny2	–0.15	0.08	–1.77
γ13	lny1lny3	–0.05	0.08	–0.65
η11	lny1lnw1/w3	0.07	0.19	0.38
η12	lny1lnw2/w3	0.18	0.27	0.65
γ22	lny2lny2	0.01	0.13	0.09
γ23	lny2lny3	0.07	0.07	0.97
η21	lny2lnw1/w3	0.02	0.24	0.08
η22	lny2lnw2/w3	0.03	0.05	0.57
γ33	lny3lny3	–0.02	0.03	–0.59
η31	lny3lnw1/w3	–0.01	0.14	–0.09
η32	lny3lnw2/w3	–0.08	0.30	–0.27
β11	lnw1/3lnw1/w3	3.16	0.40	7.97
β12	lnw1/w3lnw2/w3	–1.69	0.36	–4.65
β22	lnw2/w3lnw2/w3	–16.62	0.38	–43.26
ϕ1	Cos(y1)	–0.19	0.27	–0.70
ω1	Sin(y1)	0.03	0.38	0.08
ϕ2	Cos(y2)	0.02	0.28	0.08
ω2	Sin(y2)	0.03	0.22	0.13
ϕ3	Cos(y3)	0.03	0.30	0.10
ω3	Sin(y3)	0.00	0.17	0.00
ϕ4	Cos(w1/w3)	–4.00	0.56	–7.10
ω4	Sin(w1/w3)	3.87	0.51	7.56
ϕ5	Cos(w2/w3)	–15.04	0.78	–19.18
ω5	Sin(w2/w3)	–14.05	0.76	–18.46
ϕ11	Cos(y1+y1)	0.00	0.02	–0.13
ω11	Sin(y1+y1)	–0.03	0.04	–0.68
ϕ12	Cos(y1+y2)	0.04	0.08	0.55
ω12	Sin(y1+y2)	–0.05	0.09	–0.54
ϕ13	Cos(y1+y3)	0.00	0.06	0.02
ω13	Sin(y1+y3)	0.00	0.04	0.11
ϕ14	Cos(y1+w1/w3)	–0.03	0.26	–0.12
ω14	Sin(y1+w1/w3)	0.08	0.12	0.63
ϕ15	Cos(y1+w2/w3)	0.05	0.21	0.24

	The variables (all are logged)	*Coefficient*	*Standard-error*	*t-ratio*
ω15	Sin(y1+w2/w3)	–0.03	0.27	–0.10
ϕ22	Cos(y2+y2)	–0.01	0.07	–0.13
ω22	Sin(y2+y2)	0.04	0.01	5.96
ϕ23	Cos(y2+y3)	0.00	0.03	0.03
ω23	Sin(y2+y3)	0.00	0.04	–0.07
ϕ24	Cos(y2+w1/w3)	–0.01	0.20	–0.03
ω24	Sin(y2+w1/w3)	–0.10	0.16	–0.61
ϕ25	Cos(y2+w2/w3)	0.03	0.09	0.36
ω25	Sin(y2+w2/w3)	0.03	0.34	0.10
ϕ33	Cos(y3+y3)	0.01	0.00	1.67
ω33	Sin(y3+y3)	0.00	0.04	–0.02
ϕ34	Cos(y3+w1/w3)	–0.01	0.10	–0.13
ω34	Sin(y3+w1/w3)	0.01	0.33	0.03
ϕ35	Cos(y3+w2/w3)	–0.02	0.20	–0.08
ω35	Sin(y3+w2/w3)	–0.02	0.14	–0.17
ϕ44	Cos(w1/w3+w1/w3)	0.09	0.33	0.29
ω44	Sin(w1/w3+w1/w3)	1.14	0.42	2.70
ϕ45	Cos(w1/w3+w2/w3)	0.96	0.51	1.89
ω45	Sin(w1/w3+w2/w3)	0.14	0.24	0.57
ϕ55	Cos(w2/w3+w2/w3)	0.24	0.50	0.49
ω55	Sin(w2/w3+w2/w3)	3.81	0.42	9.05
ϕ111	Cos(y1+y1+y1)	–0.01	0.05	–0.25
ω111	Sin(y1+y1+y1)	0.02	0.02	0.65
ϕ222	Cos(y2+y2+y2)	0.00	0.02	–0.21
ω222	Sin(y2+y2+y2)	0.00	0.03	–0.10
ϕ333	Cos(y3+y3+y3)	0.01	0.02	0.36
ω333	Sin(y3+y3+y3)	0.00	0.03	–0.06
ϕ444	Cos(w1/w3+w1/w3+w1/w3)	0.33	0.17	1.90
ω444	Sin(w1/w3+w1/w3+w1/w3)	0.23	0.22	1.01
ϕ555	Cos(w2/w3+w2/w3+w2/w3)	0.32	0.28	1.11
ω555	Sin(w2/w3+w2/w3+w2/w3)	–0.58	0.19	–2.99
δ0		–0.05	0.57	–0.08
δ1	L	0.13	0.56	0.23
δ2	TA	0.00	0.00	0.34
δ3	B	–0.09	0.23	–0.40
δ4	J	0.13	0.69	0.18
δ5	E	0.11	0.25	0.43
δ6	Com	0.01	0.61	0.01
δ7	Inv.	0.05	0.47	0.10
δ8	Isl.	–0.06	0.39	–0.16
δ9	3–FCR	–0.02	0.16	–0.12
δ10	MS	–0.17	1.26	–0.14
Sigma-squared (S)		0.08	0.01	9.42

The variables (all are logged)	*Coefficient*	*Standard-error*	*t-ratio*
Gamma	0.008	0.006	1.263
Sigma-squared	0.001		
Sigma-squared (v)	0.082		
Lambda	0.089		
The relative contribution of the inefficiency effect to the total variance term	0.003		
Log likelihood function	69.06		
LR test of the one-sided error	90.72		
[note that this statistic has a mixed chi-squared distribution]			

Source: Adapted from Al-Jarrah and Molyneux (2003).

APPENDIX 7: UNIT ROOT TEST RESULTS

Table A.1: ADF unit root test for variables at level

Variables	*ADF Test Statistic without trend*	*95% Critical Value*	*ADF Test Statistic with intercept and trend*	*95% Critical Value*
LTEPIX	–1.3900	–2.9400	–4.2370*	–3.5313
LYM	–.57870	–2.9850	–2.5023	–3.6027
LOER	–2.6625	–2.9303	–2.9983	–3.5162
LM2	–.52886	–2.9303	–2.2688	–3.5162
L(P/P*)	.51954	–2.8855	–2.4202	–3.4475
LP	–1.5036	–2.9320	–2.0229	–3.5189
LP*	–1.2560	–2.9320	–2.9539	–3.5189

MacKinnon critical values for rejection of hypothesis of a unit root.
* Rejection of the unit root at 5.0 per cent .

Table A.2: ADF for first difference of variables

Variables	*ADF Test Statistic without trend*	*95% Critical Value*	*ADF Test Statistic with intercept and trend*	*95% Critical Value*
DLYM	–2.9184**	–2.9850	–5.9915*	–3.6027
DLOER	–4.0113*	–2.9591	–4.5803*	–3.5615
DL(P/P*)	–3.2561*	–2.8857	–3.6213*	–3.4478
DLP	–3.7594*	–2.9627	–4.6539*	–3.5671
DLP*	–3.2024**	–2.9627	–3.2414**	–3.5671

MacKinnon critical values for rejection of hypothesis of a unit root.
* Rejection of the unit root at 5.0 per cent.
** Rejection of the unit root at 10.0 per cent.

APPENDIX 8: BOUND TEST RESULT FOR LTEPIX MODEL

Variable Addition Test (OLS Case)
Dependent Variable is DLTEPIX
List of the Variables added to the Regression:
LTEPIX(–1) LYM(–1) LOER(–1) LPPUSA(–1)
Estimation from 1996Q1 to 2002Q2

Regressor	*Coefficient*	*Standard Error*	*T-Ratio[Prob]*
INPT	–4.5327	12.9265	–.35065[.733]
TREND	.051400	.017348	2.9630[.014]
DLTEPIX(–1)	.59377	.16374	3.6263[.005]
DLTEPIX(–2)	.33063	.23464	1.4091[.189]
DLTEPIX(–3)	.56840	.16092	3.5322[.005]
DLYM	–2.0012	.78062	–2.5636[.028]
DLYM(–1)	–2.2065	18.6568	–.11827[.908]
DLYM(–2)	3.6463	1.3316	2.7383[.021]
DLOER	.14584	.072114	2.0223[.071]
DLOER(–1)	–.21726	.16636	–1.3060[.221]
DLPPUSA	–2.8789	.93196	–3.0891[.011]
DLPPUSA(–1)	–2.7383	.85606	–3.1987[.010]
LTEPIX(–1)	–.65320	.10656	–6.1301[.000]
LYM(–1)	1.1185	3.5748	.31290[.761]
LOER(–1)	.16855	.11545	1.4600[.175]
LPPUSA(–1)	–1.6461	.46257	–3.5586[.005]

Joint test of zero restrictions on the coefficients of additional variables:
Lagrange Multiplier Statistic CHSQ(4) = 20.8382[.000]
Likelihood Ratio Statistic CHSQ(4) = 42.0371[.000]
F Statistic F(4, 10) = 10.0925[.002]

Glossary of Arabic Terms

'Adl Justice, fairness, balance.

Al-Qur'ān (also written as Qur'ān only) The Holy Book of Muslims, consisting of the revelations made by God to the Prophet Muhammad (peace be upon him). The Qur'ān lays down the fundamentals of the Islamic faith, including beliefs and all aspects of the Islamic way of life.

Amānah Trust.

Ar-rahnu (also written as *Al-rahn*) Mortgage, pawn, pledge, lien.

Awqāf (also *waqfs*) Plural of *waqf*. For meaning, see below.

Āyah A verse of al-Qur'ān.

Bait al-māl Public treasury. Also used for a charitable institution meant to help the poor and needy.

Bay' Stands for sale. It is often used as a prefix in referring to different sales-based modes of Islamic finance, like *murābaḥah*, *istiṣnā'*, and *salam*.

Bay' al-ājil or *Bay' bi thaman al-ājil* Same as *bay'al-mu'ajjal*. See below.

Bay' al-'arbūn Sale based on an advance deposit. In case the borrower does not complete the sale, the advance deposit is forfeited by the seller.

Bay' al-kālī bil kālī Sale where both payment of price and delivery of good is postponed (cf. futures sale). According to the dominant Islamic view, it is not permissible.

Bay' al-'inah Sale of a commodity with an agreement from the seller to buy back. According to most schools of thought, this is not permissible.

Bay'al-istiṣnā' Refers to a contract whereby a manufacturer (contractor) agrees to produce (build) and deliver a well-described good (or premises) at a given price on a given date in the future. In contrast to *salam*, in *istiṣnā'* the price need not be paid in advance. It may be paid in instalments in line with the preferences of the parties or partly at the front end and the balance later on as agreed.

Bay' al-mu'ajjal Sale on credit, that is, a sale in which goods are delivered immediately but payment is deferred.

Bay' al-salam A sale in which payment is made in advance by the buyer and the delivery of the goods is deferred by the seller.

Ḍamān Guarantee, security.

Farḍ kifāyah An obligatory duty, the fulfilment of which is a joint responsibility of all members of the community. If someone performs it, it is considered to have been fulfilled, otherwise all members of the community are considered defaulters.

Fatāwa Plural of *fatwa*. Religious verdicts by *fuqahā'*.

Fiqh Refers to the whole corpus of Islamic jurisprudence. In contrast with conventional law, *fiqh* covers all aspects of life, religious, political, social, commercial or economic. The whole corpus of *fiqh* is based primarily on interpretations of the Qur'ān and the Sunnah, and secondarily on *ijmā'* (consensus) and *ijtihād* (individual judgement). While the Qur'ān and the Sunnah are immutable, *fiqhī* verdicts may change due to changing circumstances.

Fiqhī Relating to *fiqh*.

Fuqahā' Plural of *faqīh* meaning jurist, who gives rulings on various juristic issues in the light of the Qur'ān and the Sunnah.

Gharar Literally, it means deception, danger, risk and uncertainty. Technically it means exposing oneself to excessive risk and danger in a business transaction as a result of uncertainty about the price, the quality and the quantity of the counter-value, the date of delivery, the ability of either the buyer or the seller to fulfil his commitment, or ambiguity in the terms of the deal; thereby, exposing either of the two parties to unnecessary risks. *Gharar* has two sub-categories: *gharar yasīr* or a little bit of *gharar*. This is tolerable because it may be unavoidable; and *gharar fāḥish* or considerable amount of *gharar*, which is prohibited.

Ḥadīth Sayings, deeds and endorsements of the Prophet Muhammad (peace be upon him) narrated by his Companions.

Ḥajj Pilgrimage to Makkah (Mecca). It is obligatory on every Muslim once in a lifetime if one can afford it, physically as well as financially.

Ḥalāl Objects or activities permitted by the Sharī'ah.

Ḥanafī A school of Islamic jurisprudence named after Imam Abu Ḥanīfa.

Ḥanbalī A school of Islamic jurisprudence named after Imam Ahmed bin Ḥanbal.

Ḥarām Objects or activities prohibited by the Sharī'ah.

Ibāḥah Permissibility from a Sharī'ah point of view.

Iḥsān Beneficence, kindness, virtue.

Ijārah Leasing. Sale of usufruct of an asset. The lessor retains the ownership of the asset with all the rights and the responsibilities that go with ownership.

Ijārah bi sharṭ al tamlīk or *Ijārah muntahiya bil tamlīk* A variant of *ijārah* whereby the lessee buys the right to own the asset after a specified period.

Ijārah wa iqtinā' Same as *ijārah bi sharṭ al tamlīk*.

Ijtihād In technical terms, it refers to the endeavour of a jurist to derive a rule or reach a judgement based on evidence found in the Islamic sources of law, predominantly the Qur'ān and the Sunnah.

Infāq Spending. In the literature of Islamic economics, it usually refers to spending in the way of Allah.

Istiḥsān It refers to departure from a ruling in a particular situation in favour of another ruling, which brings about ease. This is done by taking a lenient view of an act which would be considered a 'violation' on a stricter interpretation of the action based on earlier *qiyās*.

Istiṣnā' Short form for *bay'al-istiṣnā'*. For meaning, see above.

Itqān Perfection, that is, doing something in the best possible manner. It is a highly recommended Islamic value.

Ju'ālah Performing a given task against a prescribed fee in a given period.

Kafālah A contract whereby a person accepts to guarantee or take responsibility for a liability or duty of another person.

Kafil Guarantor.

Māl Asset. Property.

Mālikī A school of Islamic jurisprudence named after Imam Mālik

Maqāṣid al-Sharī'ah Basic objectives of the Sharī'ah. These are protection of faith, life, progeny, property and reason.

Maysir or *Maisir* Literally, it refers to an ancient Arabian game of chance with arrows used for stakes of slaughtered animals. Technically, gambling or any game of chance.

Mu'āmalāt Relationships/contracts among human beings as against *ibādāt* which define the relationship between God and His creatures.

Mu'āwaḍāt As against charity, it refers to those contracts which carry quid pro quo, that is, exchange contacts.

Muḍārabah A contract between two parties, capital owner(s) or financiers (called *rabb al-māl*) and an investment manager (called *muḍārib*). Profit is distributed between the two parties in accordance with the ratio upon which they agree at the time of the contract. Financial loss is borne only by the financier(s). The entrepreneur's loss lies in not getting any reward for his services.

Muḍārib An investment manager in a *muḍārabah* contract.

Murābaḥah Sale at a specified profit margin. The term, however, is now used to refer to a sale agreement whereby the seller purchases the goods desired by the buyer and sells them at an agreed marked-up price, the payment being settled within an agreed time frame, either in instalments or in a lump sum. The seller bears the risk for the goods until they have been delivered to the buyer. *Murābaḥah* is also referred to as *bay' mu'ajjal*.

Musāqah A contract in which the owner of a garden agrees to share its produce with someone in an agreed proportion in return for the latter's services in irrigating and looking after the garden.

Mushārakah Partnership. A *mushārakah* contract is similar to a *muḍārabah* contract, the difference being that in the former both the partners participate in the management and the provision of capital, and share in the profit and loss. Profits are distributed between the partners in accordance with the ratios initially set, whereas loss is distributed in proportion to each one's share in the capital.

Muzāra'ah A contract whereby one party agrees to till the land owned by the other party in consideration for an agreed share in the produce of the land.

Najsh In reference to sales contract, it means contriving with the seller and bidding a higher price, not with an intention to buy but simply to fetch a higher price from other potential buyers.

Niṣāb In reference to *zakāh*, the limit of wealth that marks the beginning of the imposition of *zakāh* liability. Wealth below this limit is exempt.

Qaḍā' wal Qadr Belief in destiny.

Qarḍ al-ḥasan or *Qarḍ ḥasanah* A loan extended without interest or any other compensation from the borrower. The lender expects a reward only from God.

Qurūḍ ḥasanah Plural of *qarḍ al-ḥasan*.

Rabb al-māl Capital owner (financier) in a *muḍārabah* contract.

Ribā Literally, it means increase or addition or growth. Technically it refers to the 'premium' that must be paid by the borrower to the lender along with the principal amount as a condition for the loan or an extension in its maturity. Interest as commonly known today is regarded by a predominant majority of *fuqahā'* to be equivalent to *ribā*.

Ribā al-faḍl *Ribā* pertaining to trade contracts. It refers to exchange of different quantities (but different qualities) of the same commodity. Such exchange in particular commodities defined in Sharī'ah is not allowed. Different schools of *fiqh* apply this prohibition to different commodities.

Ribā al-nasa', or *ribā al-nasi'ah*, or *ribā al-duyūn* *Ribā* pertaining to loan contracts.

Rizq Bounties of God.

Ṣadaqah An act of charity.

Salaf The short form of *bay' al-salaf*. It has the same meaning as *salam*. See below.

Salam The short form of *bay' al-salam*.

Shāfi'ī A school of Islamic jurisprudence named after Imam Shāfī'ī

Sharī'ah Refers to the corpus of Islamic law based on Divine guidance as given by the Qur'ān and the Sunnah, and embodies all aspects of the Islamic faith, including beliefs and practices.

Shirākah Partnership. Technically, it is equivalent to *mushārakah*.

Shuf'ah Right of someone to purchase something before it can be offered for public sale.

Ṣukūk Plural of *ṣakk*, which refers to a financial paper showing entitlement of the holder to the amount of money shown on it. The English word 'cheque' has been derived from it. Technically, *ṣukūk* are financial instruments entitling their holders to some financial claims.

Sunnah The Sunnah is the second most important source of the Islamic faith after the Qur'ān and refers to the Prophet's (peace be upon him) example as indicated by his practice of the faith. The only way to know the Sunnah is through the collection of *aḥādīth*, which consist of reports about the sayings, deeds and endorsements of the Prophet (peace be upon him).

Sūrah A chapter of Al-Qur'ān.

Ta'āwun Cooperation.

Tabarru' Charity.

Takāful An alternative for the contemporary insurance contract. A group of persons agree to share certain risk (for example, damage by fire) by collecting a specified sum from each. In case of loss to any one of the group, the loss is met from the collected funds.

Tawakkul Literally means to entrust, to deputise. In Islamic writings it refers to entrusting things/results to God. More specifically, after having made one's efforts to the best of one's abilities, being satisfied with whatever results they bear.

Ummah The nation of Muslims.

'Uqūd Plural of *'aqd*, meaning contract.

Wadī'ah Deposit for safekeeping.

Wakālah Contract of agency. In this contract, one person appoints someone else to perform a certain task on his behalf, usually against a fixed fee.

Waqf Appropriation or tying up a property in perpetuity for specific purposes. No property rights can be exercised over the corpus. Only the usufruct is applied towards the objectives (usually charitable) of the *waqf*.

Zakāh The amount payable by a Muslim on his net worth as a part of his religious obligations, mainly for the benefit of the poor and the needy.

Index